*Third Edition*

# Multicultural Education of Children and Adolescents

## M. Lee Manning
*Old Dominion University*

## Leroy G. Baruth
*Appalachian State University*

**Allyn and Bacon**
*Boston • London • Toronto • Sydney • Tokyo • Singapore*

*Editor-in-Chief, Education:* Paul Smith
*Series Editorial Assistant:* Bridget Keane
*Marketing Manager:* Brad Parkins
*Sr. Editorial Production Administrator:* Susan McIntyre
*Editorial Production Service:* Nesbitt Graphics, Inc.
*Composition Buyer:* Linda Cox
*Manufacturing Buyer:* Suzanne Lareau
*Cover Administrator:* Jenny Hart
*Electronic Composition:* Omegatype Typography, Inc.

Copyright © 2000, 1996, 1992 by Allyn & Bacon
A Pearson Education Company
160 Gould Street
Needham Heights, MA 02494
Internet: www.abacon.com

*Library of Congress Cataloging-in-Publication Data*
Manning, M. Lee.
    Multicultural education of children and adolescents / M. Lee
Manning, Leroy G. Baruth.—3rd ed.
        p.  cm.
    Includes bibliographical references (p. ) and indexes.
    ISBN 0-205-29760-9
    1. Multicultural education—United States. 2. Indians of North
America—Education. 3. Afro-American children—Education. 4. Asian
American children—Education. 5. Hispanic American children—
Education.   I. Baruth, Leroy G.   II. Title.
LC1099.3.M36   2000
370.117—dc21                                                    99-29162
                                                                   CIP

Printed in the United States of America
10  9  8  7  6  5  4  3  2  1     04  03  02  01  00  99

*To my family: My wife, Marianne, my children, Jennifer and
Michael, and the children's grandmother, Margaret
MLM*

*To daughters Katey, Kelly, and Seana, and my wife, Carmella, for
their continuing example of the benefits of living in a diverse society
LGB*

# Contents

## PART IV    *The Future of Multicultural Education*    337

# *P r e f a c e*

## *Our Nation's Increasing Cultural Diversity*

*Multicultural Education of Children and Adolescents* is based on the premise that people from culturally different backgrounds enrich the United States and that a better understanding of people and their differences leads to higher levels of acceptance and respect for all people. This third edition is being published at a time when all demographic projections indicate that the number of people of differing cultures in the United States will increase.

Predictions suggest that the Hispanic American population will soon outnumber the African American population and that people of European ancestry will soon be in the minority. At this time, the Asian American population is increasing dramatically. Without doubt, the high birthrates among some cultural groups, increasing numbers of Spanish-speaking people, and the recent influxes of immigrants from Southeast Asia will increase the cultural diversity of the United States and challenge its citizens to accept and respect all people whatever their cultural background, ethnicity, race, sexual orientation, socioeconomic status, gender, or religion.

At one time during the nation's history, the "melting pot" theory proposed to erase differences and to acculturate or "melt" cultural differences. In essence, the person of a different cultural background was supposed to forsake cherished and traditional cultural values and adopt "American values," probably those of the middle-class European American population. This concept viewed differences as wrong or inferior and promoted wholesale abandonment of cultural heritage.

Realistically, for any number of reasons, the melting pot is not an accurate model—people have difficulty giving up cultural characteristics or they live in enclaves in which assimilation with the mainstream society is unnecessary. Likewise, some people chose to maintain their culture as well as to adopt American values. Regardless of the reasons, the melting pot did not account for all the citizenry as some proposed; the nation is a heterogenous mixture of different peoples.

Serious questions continue to plague educators and other concerned people: Why is there an increase in racism? After almost fifty years since the landmark *Brown* decision, why are schools still segregated? Why do elementary and secondary schools address primarily the needs of some learners and allow others to fall behind? Why do people fear diversity? Why are victims often blamed for their problems? These questions defy easy answers and evince many people's belief that differences are negative manifestations in need of eradication.

Rather than provoking anger or causing fear, differences in values, customs, and traditions should be celebrated and considered a means of enriching the United States. We do not claim that the people who perceive differences as enriching will eliminate racism and acts of violence. Celebrating differences, though, is a first step, especially if efforts focus on today's children and adolescents, who will lead the nation during the twenty-first century. Considering differences to be positive and enriching, however, is only a beginning. Significant change will require more comprehensive and deliberate efforts.

Elementary and secondary schools can play a major role in teaching acceptance and respect for all forms of diversity. The schools, in fact, are logical places to begin instilling feelings of acceptance for all people. Schools, however, must do more than pay lip service; effective curriculum reflects diversity, and appropriate learning materials represent all people in positive and meaningful roles. We believe wholeheartedly that multicultural education should be a total-school approach, rather than simply a unit or Multicultural Education Week approach. Although teaching about multiculturalism is an admirable concept, schools should also model acceptance and respect for cultural diversity. Schools that teach about cultural differences and celebrate diversity, but whose actions indicate racism or a lack of respect, fail in their multicultural efforts.

## Our Reasons for Writing This Book

We wrote this third edition of *Multicultural Education of Children and Adolescents* to provide preservice and in-service educators with a knowledge of the five prevalent cultural groups and to show the components of responsive multicultural education programs. The text staunchly maintains that multicultural education programs should be a total-school effort—that is, that administrators, teachers, library media specialists, special-education teachers, counselors, and communications disorder specialists have vital roles in the multicultural education program. Similarly, we believe that multicultural efforts should be comprehensive. The curriculum, instructional strategies, materials, environment, and school practices should reflect multiculturalism and should show a genuine respect for all forms of diversity.

### Our Selection of Cultural Groups

After careful consideration of and reflection on the increasing cultural diversity of the United States, we decided to focus on five broad groups of people (listed alphabetically): African, Asian, European, Hispanic, and Native American. These groups are, and in all likelihood will continue to be, the most populous groups in elementary and secondary schools. Choosing only these groups does not negate the importance of other cultures. We hope and expect that learning about diversity in these cultures will motivate readers to explore the values, customs, and traditions of other cultures.

## A Word of Caution

Any discussion focusing on characteristics of children and adolescents and their cultural backgrounds risks stereotyping and an overdependence on generalizations. The many differences resulting from cultural, intracultural, socioeconomic, geographic, generational, gender, sexual orientation, and individuality factors among people contribute to their diversity and to the difficulty of describing individuals of various cultures. Although we based this text on current and objective information, it remains crucial for educators to understand individual children and adolescents within a culture through conscientious study and firsthand contact. Failing to understand individuals and failing to consider crucial differences may result in assuming too much cultural homogeneity—for example, that all Hispanic cultural groups share identical values, problems, and cultural expectations or that all Asian Americans fit the "model minority" label.

## The Organization of the Book

*Multicultural Education of Children and Adolescents* is divided into four parts and thirteen chapters. Part I introduces multicultural education as a concept and documents the increasing cultural diversity of the United States. Part II provides a cultural portrait of children and adolescents in the African, Asian, European, Hispanic, and Native American cultures. Part III focuses on aspects that educators should consider when planning and implementing programs that teach acceptance and respect for cultural diversity. Part IV examines issues that will continue to challenge educators in the twenty-first century.

## Pedagogical Features

Pedagogical features of *Multicultural Education of Children and Adolescents* include:

- The *Culture Quiz* at the beginning of each chapter is an interesting way to show readers how much they already know and provides an indication of the chapter's content.
- *Case Studies* throughout the text show how educators have addressed the chapters' topics.
- *Implementing Research* boxes throughout the text provide readers with research studies that focus on children and adolescents of culturally different backgrounds and give practical suggestions for implementing the research. In an attempt to provide readers with a wide range of information and sources, we define research in its broadest sense.
- *Expanding Your Horizons: Additional Journal Readings and Books*, located at the end of each chapter, provides readers with resources for further study and consideration.

- *Expanding Your Students' Horizons: Appropriate Books for Children and Adolescents* is located at the end of Chapters 3, 4, 5, 6, and 7.
- *Using Children's Literature,* located in Chapters 3, 4, 5, 6, and 7, provides titles and a brief annotation of developmentally appropriate children's and adolescents' literature that can help learners better understand their cultural heritages.
- *For Additional Information,* located in Chapters 3, 4, 5, 6, and 7, provides names and addresses of organizations and groups that promote cultural diversity and that act as disseminators of information about the respective cultures.
- *Suggestions for Collaborative Efforts,* at the end of each chapter, provides readers with opportunities to work cooperatively and collaboratively toward group goals.
- *Gender Perspectives,* located in selected chapters throughout the text, highlights current research and scholarly opinion on females and underscores the importance of understanding gender as well as cultural and other diversities.

## New to the Third Edition

In addition to updating these pedagogical features and the book as a whole, this third edition also includes new foci that help readers better understand our nation's diversity:

- *Follow Through* boxes, located throughout the text, are activities designed either to assist educators in understanding cultural diversity or to help educators as they plan activities for multicultural education programs.
- An emphasis on sexual orientation as a form of diversity to be included in a definition of multicultural education and the inclusion of research and scholarly opinion that adds credence to our belief that gays and lesbians have a "culture of their own."
- *For Additional Information: Internet Addresses,* also located in selected chapters, provides additional sources for readers interested in learning more about particular aspects of multicultural education.

## Our Appreciation to Others

An author's only chance and hope for making a valuable contribution lies in the willingness of others to offer advice and to share their expertise. We would like to thank reviewer Leslie Irwin, Arizona State University West, for her helpful comments. Our appreciation is also extended to people of all cultures who have contributed to the richness of our lives and the nation.

MLM
LGB

# Multicultural Education and Its Response to Our Nation's Increasing Diversity

Part I introduces multicultural education as a concept and documents the increasing cultural diversity of the United States. Chapter 1 examines the multicultural education movement and its role in elementary and secondary schools. Chapter 2 looks at our nation's increasing cultural diversity and the ways that people's differences enrich our schools. These chapters reflect a belief that educators have a professional responsibility to teach respect for diversity as well as to teach all students the concepts of justice, equality, and democracy.

# Chapter *1*

# *Multicultural Education*

Understanding the material and activities in this chapter will help the reader to:

- Define multicultural education and explain its fundamental purposes.
- List several goals, assumptions, concepts, and principles of multicultural education.
- List several myths and misconceptions about multicultural education.
- Explain briefly the historical milestones and legal precedents of multicultural education.
- List several characteristics of effective multicultural educators.
- List several controversial issues in multicultural education.

## *Overview*

The tremendous cultural, ethnic, religious, and socioeconomic diversity in schools today calls for multicultural education programs that reflect understanding and respect for children's and adolescents' differences. The multicultural education movement has particular relevance for the new century because of the continuing influx of people into the United States and because of the enlightened and more humane perspective that diversity enriches, rather than weakens, a nation. This chapter examines the fundamentals and principles of multicultural education and considers the various aspects that make programs successful.

## *Multicultural Education for Culturally Pluralistic Schools*

In this section we describe our (the authors') preferred definition of multicultural education and examine principles, concepts, goals, and assumptions that form the basis for responsive multicultural education programs. We then look at several

---

**THE CULTURE QUIZ   Multicultural Education**

*Directions:* Mark the following True or False.

_____ 1. Multicultural education should be an integral part of the elementary but not the secondary curriculum and should focus on academic matters.

_____ 2. Multicultural education programs are necessary only in schools that have considerable cultural diversity among learners.

_____ 3. Multicultural education programs should emphasize to all learners the importance of meeting and assimilating majority culture expectations.

_____ 4. Multicultural education programs should use a unit or thematic teaching approach, rather than be incorporated into all areas of the curriculum.

_____ 5. Multicultural education programs should address as many cultural groups as possible.

_____ 6. Multicultural education programs are a political tool that forces cultural diversity on European Americans.

_____ 7. Multicultural education programs do not interfere with academic areas of learning.

_____ 8. Multicultural education is a popular trend in education and will likely lose its impetus as its popularity wanes.

_____ 9. Multicultural education should focus on cultural and ethnic diversity as well as on racism, sexism, classism, and the acceptance of disabling conditions.

_____ 10. Multicultural education can have a significant and positive impact on the education reform currently occurring in the United States.

(Answers to the Culture Quiz are located at the end of the chapter.)

---

myths and provide an overview of historical events and court decisions that have contributed to multicultural education.

## Definition

Various groups and individuals define multicultural education in numerous ways. Some definitions address the perspectives of specific disciplines, such as educa-

---

**FOLLOW THROUGH 1-1   Determining Differences to Include in Multicultural Education**

Consider the differences and characteristics we included in our definition. Some might disagree with nontraditional views on sexual orientation, ability/disability, and gender. What do you think? Do people whose views are nontraditional have a culture of their own? For example, each person has his or her own cultural background, but wouldn't he or she also have a "culture" of sexual orientation, a "culture" associated with a disabling condition, or a culture associated with being either male or female? How inclusive do you think multicultural education should be?

tion, anthropology, sociology, and psychology. Other definitions represent the views of accrediting agencies and professional organizations that are concerned with what teachers need to teach and what students need to learn.

We think the following definition most effectively meets the goals and purposes of multicultural education for children and adolescents. Multicultural education is both a concept and deliberate process designed to:

- teach learners to recognize, accept, and appreciate differences in culture, ethnicity, social class, sexual orientation, religion, ability/disability, and gender.
- instill in learners during their crucial developmental years a sense of responsibility and a commitment to work toward the democratic ideals of justice, equality, and democracy.

Case Study 1-1 examines the importance of having a multicultural education program that considers diversity in its broadest forms.

Gender Perspectives 1-1 on page 6 shows the need to address gender bias and emphasizes the importance of including gender in multicultural education programs.

## Principles

Appropriate multicultural education requires more than simply providing cultural information about ethnic groups. Several "fundamentals" necessary to the promotion of effective multicultural education allow learners and teachers of various cultures to maintain integrity and dignity. First, students need curricular

---

**CASE STUDY 1-1     Toward an All-Encompassing Definition
of Multicultural Education**

The administration, faculty, and staff at PS 105 decided on a broad approach to their multicultural education program. This group agreed that rather than address only "cultural backgrounds," their program should direct attention to a broad range of differences, including ethnicity, race, gender, social class, and individual.

Children and adolescents of respective cultures are vastly different. Consider, for example, the many different cultures that make up the Hispanic American population, the vast differences among Asian Americans, and the diversity among African Americans.

The question for PS 105 was how to address so many differences. The committee decided first to examine each difference and its influence on learning and other school-related activities and then to look at the curriculum, instructional approaches, print and nonprint media, school policies, extracurricular activities, and cultural composition of the administration, faculty, and staff. Although this constituted a task of some magnitude, the group recognized the advantages of having a multicultural education program that genuinely addressed diversity in its broadest definition.

### GENDER PERSPECTIVES 1-1    Gender Equity

Beverly Hardcastle Stanford (1996) wrote that two major patterns have emerged in student–teacher interactions and gender discrimination: (1) teachers give boys more attention, both positive and negative, and (2) boys demand more teacher attention. In her discussion, Stanford examined such issues as progress in mathematics and science achievement, Title IX, girls' decline in self-esteem, sexual harassment, boys' and girls' learning styles, single-sex schools, and principles to guide practice.

Specific practices that lead to gender-fair teaching include:

1. equalization of teacher–student interactions by teachers' becoming conscious of the degree and type of attention they give to each gender in classroom interactions;

2. resistance to the dominance of several "star" students, usually boys;

3. using a variety of teaching strategies to include cooperative learning, team learning, and leaderless student discussions that downplay the teacher's role;

4. the modeling by teachers of gender equity;

5. provision of an equitable environment through measures such as evenly distributing boys and girls in classrooms, displaying on bulletin boards accomplishments of both genders, and avoiding gender-stereotypical images;

6. selection of nondiscriminatory curricular materials that actively contribute to a sense of gender equity in the classroom.

*Source:* Stanford, B. H. (1996). Gender equity in the classroom. In D. A. Byrnes, & G. Kiger (Eds.), *Common bonds: Anti-Bias teaching in a diverse society* (2nd ed.) (pp. 79–94). Olney, MD: Association for Childhood Education International.

materials appropriate to their cultural backgrounds. These materials should enhance students' self-concept, engage student interest in classroom learning, and provide examples, vocabulary, and models that relate to students' cultural backgrounds. Second, major curricular focuses should include skills in analysis and critical thinking. Third, materials, activities, and experiences should be authentic and multidimensional to help students understand ethnic differences and cultural diversity. They should include both cognitive and affective skills (Grant & Sleeter, 1986).

### FOLLOW THROUGH 1-2    Surveying for Gender Bias

Visit several elementary or secondary schools to determine gender bias. Prepare a survey that examines (but is not limited to) such items as teacher–student interactions, instructional methods, grouping strategies, questioning strategies, and classroom environment. What evidence do you see that teachers recognize and address gender differences? Are boys and girls being treated equally and equitably? How might multicultural education address the bias in treatment of boys and girls (if, in fact you find evidence of bias)?

## Concepts

It is especially important for teachers to understand three concepts of multicultural education, because it is the educator's concept of the term that determines his or her program's direction and issues.

First, multicultural education is a product in which there is emphasis on the study of ethnicity—for example, the contributions or characteristics of a group of people. This concept, which addresses teaching about different ethnic and cultural groups, may be best described as *ethnic studies.*

Second, multicultural education emphasizes the role of oppression of one group by another and the oppressors' atonement or compensation for past injustices. Dealing primarily with targeted oppressed groups (and possible solutions to their problems), this concept considers multicultural education a concern only of minorities.

The third concept views multicultural education as a teaching process and includes aspects such as product and entitlement. It extends even further than product and entitlement, because teachers focus on the concept of culture as an entity separate from ethnicity. It emphasizes the intrinsic aspects of culture and its influence on teaching and learning processes. Such a concept of multicultural education recognizes the entitlement aspect in the belief that to obtain what one is entitled to requires a fair system and an equal chance to acquire social and academic skills. It incorporates the product view in that (1) certain historical facts and events must be taught and (2) an adequate understanding of present conditions, as well as general human behavior, comes about with knowledge of historical facts. This idea of multicultural education as a process includes all educational variables, such as methodology, curriculum, and instructional techniques (Payne, 1984).

---

**FOR ADDITIONAL INFORMATION**   **Internet Addresses**

**Multicultural Pavilion**
http://curry.edschool.Virginia.edu/go/multicultural/   Provides conceptualizations and goals of multicultural education as well as resources for teachers.

**National Association for Multicultural Education**
http://www.inform.umd.edu/NAME/   Provides information on the purposes, design, and implementation of effective multicultural education programs.

*STANDARDS: The International Journal of Multicultural Studies*
http://stripe.colorado.edu/~standard/   Focuses on multiculturalism in education; includes on-line syllabi, lesson plans, and book reviews.

**ED334 320**
http://www.msue.msu.edu/msue/imp/moddp/1118016.html   Provides a paradigm for examining multicultural education.

**ED 240 224**
http://eric-web.tc.columbia.edu/abstracts/ed240224.html   Describes how educators can move multicultural education to higher levels of effectiveness and sophistication.

**Infoseek: Multicultural Education**
http://guide-p.infoseek.com/Education/K_12/Resources_for-educators/Multicultural_education   Provides multicultural educational resources for grades K–12.

## Goals

An integral aspect of all multicultural education focuses on the development of skills and attitudes necessary for people to function in a culturally diverse society. Not only should educators learn about other cultures, they should also develop the attitudes and skills to function in multicultural situations, including an awareness, understanding, and acceptance of cultural differences. Additionally, educators may need to develop empathy with members of other cultures and modify their own cultural values.

One goal of multicultural education is to change the total educational environment so that it promotes a respect for a wide range of cultural groups and enables all cultural groups to experience equal educational opportunities (Banks, 1987, p. 29). Developing cross-cultural competency is another goal and includes an awareness of the skills, attitudes, and knowledge necessary to live within the individual's own ethnic culture and the universal American culture, as well as within and across ethnic cultures (Banks, 1987, pp. 35–36).

Educators need to be enlightened on the social, political, and economic realities they will encounter in a culturally diverse and complex society. Other goals of multicultural education include recognizing and respecting the nature of cultural differences and similarities; understanding intracultural differences as well as individuals' many differences; developing a better understanding of the nature and impact of racism and of the implications for positive or negative influence; and developing a positive attitude toward one's own cultural background.

Ramsey (1987) offers several goals that differ slightly from those of Banks and the professional organization. First, in her goals for teaching from multicultural perspectives, Ramsey feels it necessary "to help children develop positive gender, racial, cultural, class, and individual identities, and to recognize and accept their membership in many different groups" (p. 3). Another goal is to encourage social relationships in which there is "an openness and interest with others, a willingness to include others, and a desire to cooperate" (p. 4). A third, different goal is to "empower children to become autonomous and critical analysts and activists in their social environment" (p. 4). Another difference, a major focus of this text, is the inclusion of immediate and extended families, as Ramsey wrote, "to promote effective and reciprocal relationships between schools and families" (p. 5).

## Assumptions

Several assumptions underlie multicultural education and are, in fact, the philosophy on which this book, *Multicultural Education of Children and Adolescents*, is based.

*Assumption 1.* Cultural diversity is a positive, enriching element in a society because it provides individuals increased opportunities to experience other cultures and thus to become more fulfilled as human beings (Banks, 1988). Rather than perceiving it as a weakness to be remediated, educators should view cultural diversity as a strength with the potential for helping individuals better understand their own cultures. Similarly, as people reach higher levels of understanding and acceptance of other cultures, we hope that they will achieve similar heights of understanding and sensitivity in areas such as racism, sexism, and classism.

*Assumption 2.* Multicultural education is for all students (Hernandez, 1989). Some people believe that multicultural education is only for minority children and adolescents. For example, some states require multicultural education only in districts having at least one school with a 25 percent minority student population (Hernandez, 1989). This and similar policies are based on the odd notion that only minority youngsters need multicultural education. This notion completely fails to recognize that majority cultures can benefit from a better understanding of cultural differences and, eventually, of their own cultural backgrounds.

*Assumption 3.* Teaching is a cross-cultural encounter (Hernandez, 1989). All teachers and students have their own cultural baggage—their backgrounds, values, customs, perceptions, and, perhaps, prejudices. These cultural aspects play a significant role in teaching and learning situations and can have a substantial effect on behavior and learning. Socioeconomic status, ethnicity, gender, and language have a powerful and dynamic effect on one's outlook and attitude toward school and on one's actual school achievement (Hernandez, 1989).

*Assumption 4.* Multicultural education should permeate the total school curriculum rather than be doled out in a "one-course" or a teaching-unit approach. Responsive multicultural education programs cannot accomplish lasting and worthwhile goals through "one-shot" approaches. The school must be genuinely multicultural. Multiculturalism must embrace the curriculum, as defined in the broadest sense (every aspect of the school with which learners come in contact); the composition of the administration, faculty, and staff; expectations that reflect an understanding of different cultural groups, their attitudes toward school success, and their learning styles; and the recognition of all other aspects that may affect both minority- and majority-culture learners. A school that appears to address only majority needs and expectations will cause learners from culturally different backgrounds to feel like "intruders" or "outsiders."

*Assumption 5.* The education system has not served all students equally well (Hernandez, 1989). Generally speaking, members of minority groups, students from low-income families, and students who are culturally different or speak a language other than English have not fared well in U.S. school systems. Any number of reasons may account for such students' lack of achievement: differing achievement orientations; problems resulting from language barriers; differing learning styles; curricula and school policies that are unresponsive to minority student needs; testing and assessment procedures that may be designed for middle-class white students; and a lack of understanding or acceptance of cultural differences. In any event, the high dropout rate among Native Americans (Sanders, 1987), African Americans (Wilson, 1989), and Hispanic Americans (Closing the Educational Gap for Hispanics, 1987) substantiates the position that learners from culturally different backgrounds often do not succeed in U.S. schools.

*Assumption 6.* Schools will continue to experience and reflect increasing cultural diversity because of influxes of immigrants and refugees and the high birthrates of some cultural groups. To say that American society continues to grow

---

**FOLLOW THROUGH 1-3   Accommodating the Needs of Diverse Student Populations**

Most people agree that the population of the United States will continue to grow more and more diverse. Schools will be challenged to address the needs of students from many backgrounds. What mindsets must educators change to accommodate the needs of a diverse student population? Name several specific recommendations that might improve the educational experience, such as making the curriculum more culturally relevant and responsive.

---

more diverse is an understatement. The arrival in this country of increasing numbers of people from culturally different backgrounds is one example. Increasing recognition of differences in gender, religion, socioeconomic group, sexual orientation, and geography are others. Multicultural education programs have the responsibility to reflect the rich diversity that characterizes U.S. society.

*Assumption 7.* Elementary and secondary schools have a responsibility to implement appropriate multicultural education programs. These programs must contribute to a better understanding of cultural differences, show the dangers of stereotyping, and reduce racism, sexism, and classism. Families are unquestionably children's first teachers of values, opinions, and attitudes. Ideally, families teach acceptance and respect for all people and their differences. Realistically speaking, however, children may learn that their culture, race, or ethnic backgrounds are "right" but that those of others are "wrong" or "inferior." Because considerable cultural diversity characterizes the U.S. educational system, the transmission of understanding and respect for cultural diversity is most feasible in elementary and secondary schools. Responsive programs must teach genuine respect and must work toward reducing racism, sexism, and classism. Admittedly, this is an undertaking of considerable magnitude; the teaching and modeling of respect for all people, however, may have the most dramatic impact during children's formative years.

## Myths and Misconceptions

At one time or another, most people have probably heard someone voice concerns about the dire consequences of multicultural education. Banks (1993), an acknowledged leader in the multicultural education movement, identifies and debunks several misconceptions about multicultural education.

*Misconception 1:* Multicultural education is for others. Some people argue that multicultural education is an entitlement program and a curriculum movement for African Americans, Hispanics, the poor, women, and other victimized groups. Banks debunks this misconception. In fact, multicultural education as designed during the 1980s called for a restructuring of educational institutions so that all learners will acquire the knowledge, skills, and attitudes necessary to function effectively in a culturally diverse nation. Rather than focus only on specific gender and ethnic movements, multicultural education tries to empower all students to become knowledgeable, caring, active citizens (Banks, 1993).

*Misconception 2:* Multicultural education is opposed to the Western tradition. Banks (1993) maintains that multicultural education is not anti-West, because many writers from culturally diverse backgrounds such as Rudolfo Anaya, Paula Gunn Allen, Maxine Hong Kingston, Maya Angelou, and Toni Morrison are Western writers. In fact, multicultural education is a thoroughly Western movement, which grew out of the civil rights movement and is grounded in such democratic ideals as freedom, justice, and equality (Banks, 1993).

*Misconception 3:* Multicultural education will divide the nation and undercut its unity. This misconception is based partly on questionable assumptions about the nature of U.S. society and partly on a mistaken understanding of multicultural education. The claim that multicultural education will divide the nation assumes an already united nation. Without doubt, the United States is one nation politically; sociologically, however, our nation is deeply divided along lines of race, gender, and class. Multicultural education seeks to unify a deeply divided nation rather than to divide a highly cohesive one.

Traditionally, U.S. society and the schools tried to create unity by "assimilating" students from diverse racial and ethnic groups into a mythical Anglo-American culture. Assimilation would require a process of self-alienation. But, even when students from different backgrounds became culturally "assimilated," they continued to experience exclusion from mainstream society (Banks, 1993).

## A Brief Historical Overview

Before 1978 the Education Index did not include multicultural education in its listings; few pedagogical journals addressed the topic. During the 1970s and 1980s, however, increasing numbers of articles and books have focused on multicultural education (Tiedt & Tiedt, 1995). Three forces contributed to the emergence of the multicultural education movement: (1) the civil rights movement came of age, (2) school textbooks came under critical analysis, and (3) assumptions underlying the deficiency orientation were changed to a more positive perspective.

The civil rights movement began as a passive, nonviolent means of changing laws that oppressed specific racial groups. By the late 1960s, the movement had matured into an energetic coalition uniting all Americans of color and directed toward self-determination and power. The movement severely criticized the U.S. school system because of its segregation and curricula that focused attention only on Western culture. Similarly, few teachers knew about minority groups, their rich cultural diversity, their individual strengths and weaknesses, and their learning styles. In fact, schools considered cultural and ethnic differences primarily weaknesses in need of remediation (Sleeter & Grant, 1988).

The 1970s saw the development of multicultural education into a more comprehensive approach. With cultural diversity and equal opportunity serving as an impetus, the multicultural education movement encouraged educators to examine and consider the relationships among culture, ethnicity, language, gender, disabling conditions, and social class in developing educational programs. Multicultural education that takes a social reconstructionist tack is a recent and controversial approach that represents an extension of multicultural education toward more definitive social action. This approach incorporates a curricular emphasis on (1) active student involvement in social issues such as sexism, racism, and classism; (2) the development of problem-solving ability and political action skills; and (3) the implementation of curricular adaptations, cooperative learning, and decision-making skills (Hernandez, 1989).

Banks (1988) described phases that place multicultural education in its proper historical perspective. During Phase I (monoethnic studies), the black civil rights movement began and African Americans demanded more African American teachers, more control of community schools, and the rewriting of textbooks to provide a more accurate portrayal of African Americans, their culture, and their contributions. Phase II (multiethnic studies) provided courses that focused on several minority groups and viewed experiences of ethnic groups from comparative perspectives. During Phase III (multiethnic education), an increasing number of educators recognized that the mere reforming of courses was insufficient to result in genuine educational reform.

In Phase IV (multicultural education), some educators became interested in an even broader development of pluralistic education that focused on reform of the total school environment. *Multicultural education* emerged as the preferred concept because it enabled educators to broaden their perspective to include a wider range of groups rather than maintain a limited focus on racial and ethnic minorities. Phase V is a slowly occurring process that includes strategies designed to increase the pace and scope of the institutionalization of multiethnic and multicultural education within schools (Banks, 1988).

The two world wars, mass immigrations to the United States, the intercultural movements, and racial disturbances all contributed to the emergence and development of multicultural education.

## The Influence of Court Decisions

Ruling in favor of equal opportunity and human rights, several court decisions and laws also contributed to the present multicultural education movement. The Supreme Court in *Brown v. Topeka Board of Education* (1954) ruled unconstitutional the segregation of black and white learners. In 1957, the U.S. Commission on Civil Rights was established to investigate complaints that alleged the denial of civil rights. In 1968, the Bilingual Education Act (BEA) was passed as part of Title VII of the Elementary and Secondary Education Act.

The U.S. Commission on Civil Rights issued a report in 1975 called A Better Chance to Learn: Bilingual–Bicultural Education, designed for educators as a means of providing equal opportunity for language-minority students. This report provides only a brief listing of a few representative events that recognized cultural diversity and equal rights. These and other events, however, were the forerunners of the movement to recognize and teach respect for people from culturally differ-

---

**CASE STUDY 1-2** **"We Don't Need a Multicultural Education Program."**

After the faculty meeting in which the principal has just formed a committee to plan a multicultural education program, you hear Mr. Brown say, "But we don't need a multicultural program in our school. We do not have any racial problems." School professionals and parents sometimes feel that multicultural education is not necessary unless racial problems exist. But Mr. Brown is missing an important goal of multicultural education. First, students in his school need a better understanding of each others' cultural backgrounds. Second, if the school waits to form a multicultural education program after racial disturbances emerge, it may be too late. The school may hurriedly implement the program without giving it sufficient thought.

---

ent backgrounds. Schools continue to have a major responsibility in breaking down stereotypes, promoting multicultural understandings, and making a difference in the lives of individual learners (Tiedt & Tiedt, 1995).

Some educators believe that if racial problems are not visible, then multicultural education programs are not necessary. Case Study 1-2 examines just such a situation.

## Interdisciplinary Approaches

Multicultural education should be an integral aspect of all curricular areas, rather than just be administered through the social studies course. Likewise, a once-a-year Multicultural Week or unit focusing on African American history, tacos, and Oriental dress and customs will not suffice. Such approaches have not worked and will not work, because diversity awareness does not necessarily result in acceptance of and respect for individuals within a cultural group. The curriculum, learning environments, and mindset of learners, faculty, and staff should become genuinely multicultural in nature and should reflect the cultural diversity of the school. Second, well-meaning multicultural education programs may serve only cosmetic purposes if students and school personnel harbor long-held cultural biases and stereotypes. In essence, to be effective, responsive multicultural education programs must recognize the need both to inform and to change negative attitudes and long-held prejudices.

---

**FOLLOW THROUGH 1-4** **Planning Interdisciplinary Approaches**

Talk with several teachers who are experienced with interdisciplinary curricular approaches (in fact, several might be students in your class). Ask them to offer suggestions for integrating multiculturalism into the curriculum. Your specific questions should focus on culturally appropriate topics, for example, and on materials that offer diverse perspectives and show respect for diversity, instructional methods that cater to diverse learning styles, and culturally appropriate assessment techniques.

**CASE STUDY 1-3   Interdisciplinary Approaches**

The administrators, faculty, and staff at Browning High School worked conscientiously toward developing their multicultural education program. The committee had decided to fully support an interdisciplinary program. They had decided the goals, curriculum content, instructional practices, school policies, and how best to evaluate both print and nonprint media. Although the committee recognized the legitimacy of approaches and that regard multicultural education as a single subject, it also recognized that an interdisciplinary approach would be most effective for several reasons. Specifically, the interdisciplinary approach could:

1. Function as a means of including multicultural education experiences in all subject areas—showing, for example, the contributions of all cultural groups in the various disciplines.

2. Ensure broad involvement of all educators responsible for the various discipline areas.
3. Show students from culturally different backgrounds as well as majority-culture learners that the school is committed to serious multicultural education efforts.
4. Provide a wide variety of instructional approaches and learning experiences.
5. Empower all school personnel to be a part of the multicultural education program and responsible for its success.

The educators at Browning felt good about their multicultural education efforts: Everybody was involved. Teachers and administrators examined curricular and instructional practices, they reconsidered school policies, and efforts crossed discipline lines.

Case Study 1-3 shows the advantages of an interdisciplinary approach to multicultural education.

## The Effective Multicultural Educator

Competencies for effective multicultural educators fall into three categories—knowledge, skills, and attitudes—each necessary to the existence of the other. We briefly examine several examples here. Chapter 9 takes a more in-depth look at knowledge, attitudes, and skills and more specific teaching behaviors.

*Knowledge* includes an understanding of individual learners' cultures. Native Americans for example, place great importance on the concept of sharing. African Americans value the extended family and have a unique language usage. Asian Americans have a unique concept of generational and family relationships. Machismo is an integral part of Hispanic American culture, as is commitment to the Spanish language.

*Skills* include recognizing and responding appropriately to learners' strengths and weaknesses and responding to the relationship between learning styles and culture. Skills-based teaching provides school experiences that embrace learners' orientations toward school and academic success. It requires teachers to select standardized tests and evaluation instruments with the least cultural bias and use

---

**FOLLOW THROUGH 1-5   Acquiring Knowledge, Skills, and Attitudes**

Most teachers trained in the past ten to fifteen years have had experience with multicultural education because state and national accrediting associations have required such training. Other teachers, however, probably graduated before the required training, and some may have graduated from programs that provided only the minimum. How might a teacher develop the knowledge, skills, and attitudes necessary to become an effective educator in multicultural situations? Specifically, how might the teacher acquire such knowledge, skills, and attitudes?

---

teaching methods that have proven especially appropriate for children and adolescents from culturally different backgrounds.

*Attitudes* include developing positive outlooks and values, creating culturally appropriate learning environments, and modeling for children respect and concern for all people. See Chapter 9 for a more detailed analysis of effective teaching behaviors in multicultural settings.

## Challenges of Designing Multicultural Education Programs

History constantly reminds us how many people have been on the receiving end of cruel and inhumane treatment primarily because of cultural differences. Just a few examples include the injustices Native Americans and their land suffered at the hands of colonists and other immigrants; the racism and discrimination in education, employment, and housing that have affected the progress of African and Hispanic Americans for centuries; and the cruel treatment of Asian Americans on their arrival in the United States. Twenty-first-century educators face the challenge of molding a more humane and equitable society by providing multicultural education programs that teach respect for cultural differences. They have the opportunity to address the need for positive cultural identities and respond with decisive action to the often disastrous effects of racism and stereotyping.

---

**FOLLOW THROUGH 1-6   Changing Attitudes through Multicultural Education**

Several areas that multicultural education programs need to address include: (1) teaching respect for cultural differences, (2) addressing the need for positive cultural identities, and (3) responding appropriately to racism, stereotyping, and all forms of injustice and discrimination. These are indeed lofty goals and will be more difficult to implement than to espouse. Choose at least one of the three topics and list four or five ways to achieve effective implementation. Name several other areas that you think should be included with these three.

Although considerable racism and discrimination continue to exist and to restrain minority entrance into mainstream America, the turn of the century can be a time for recognition and acceptance of cultural diversity. Factors and events that may contribute to such recognition include the increasing numbers of people from culturally diverse backgrounds, the efforts directed at children and adolescents in elementary and secondary schools (e.g., multicultural education courses); the multicultural emphasis of the National Council for Accreditation of Teacher Education; the increasing recognition that the nation actually benefits from cultural diversity; and increasing numbers of organizations working to instill cultural pride.

## *Ethnocentrism*

Ethnocentrism is the belief that one's own cultural ways are not only valid and superior to those of others but also universally applicable in evaluating human behavior (Hernandez, 1989, p. 25). People with strong ethnocentric attitudes and beliefs—especially unconscious ones—may have difficulty appreciating and accepting the range of cultural differences that exist in societies (Hernandez, 1989).

Because culture influences the way we think, feel, and act, it is our means of judging the world (Gollnick & Chinn, 1998). Culture becomes the only natural way to function in the world. It gives us the notion that our own common sense is the norm for common sense in other cultures of the world. As a result, we evaluate other cultures by our cultural standards and beliefs and find it virtually impossible to view another culture as separate from our own.

In essence, ethnocentrism is a universal characteristic in which one views one's own cultural traits as natural, correct, and superior and perceives those of others' cultures as odd or inferior (Gollnick & Chinn, 1998).

Case Study 1-4 examines the problem of ethnocentrism and suggests several ways to address it.

The challenge for educators in multicultural situations is to understand ethnocentrism, to recognize its dangers, and to respond appropriately. Textbooks and other instructional materials can perpetuate ethnocentrism in subtle ways that educators may find difficult to recognize. Because we are likely to accept without question a perspective consistent with our own vantage point, attitudes, and values, we may not even be aware that another cultural perspective exists (Gollnick & Chinn, 1998).

---

**FOLLOW THROUGH 1-7   Addressing Ethnocentrism**

Belief in the superiority of and universal applicability of one's culture is the direct cause of considerable injustice and discrimination. In all cultures are people who believe their culture is the "best" or the standard by which to evaluate others. List several ways to convince people to consider their enthnocentric beliefs. What could you do to get them to engage in an objective examination of their cultural beliefs?

---

**CASE STUDY 1-4    Reducing Ethnocentrism**

People all too often believe that their culture and cultural traditions are "correct" and that those of all others are "wrong." Dr. Farnsworth (let's call him) was one of these people. He either misunderstood or was unwilling to accept that people from culturally diverse backgrounds have different opinions of what is important, different perceptions of immediate and extended families, and different degrees of allegiance to the elderly. Such opinions and perceptions may have become ingrained early in Dr. Farnsworth. He never considered his ethnocentrism objectively.

Educators like Dr. Farnsworth and those who teach ethnocentric children and adolescents should take action. First, educators must address their own ethnocentrism and that of their colleagues. Second, they must seek ways to reduce their own ethnocentrism and that of their colleagues and students. Although reducing ethnocentrism is difficult, educators can use several approaches to further this goal with children and adolescents.

1. Instill in children and adolescents the idea that one should not consider cultural differences right or wrong, superior or inferior.
2. Arrange teaching and learning situations (e.g., cooperative learning and cross-age tutoring) in which learners of varying cultures can have firsthand experiences with each other.
3. Model acceptance of and respect for all people.
4. Respond appropriately to statements indicating a lack of understanding or acceptance of cultural differences.
5. Encourage respect for all differences—cultural and ethnic, socioeconomic, differences in ability/disability, gender, and other characteristics that contribute to diversity.

---

## *Developing Positive Cultural Identities*

Identity is a person's sense of place in the world; it is the meaning we attach to ourselves in the broader context of life (Vander Zanden, 1989). Identity answers questions such as "Who am I?" and "Who am I to be?"

It is important for educators to show children and adolescents that people may have several identities at once; that is, an individual might be Hispanic American, a member of any of the Spanish-speaking cultures, someone's brother, a Catholic, and an inhabitant of a specific geographic region in the United States.

The educator's first challenge is to view students as unique individuals rather than as a homogeneous group. Educators who assume too much homogeneity among students often fail to address individual and cultural differences and then fail to provide experiences that lead to positive cultural identities.

Second, educators must understand that all individuals need to clarify personal attitudes toward their cultural and ethnic backgrounds. Educators' goals can be to teach self-acceptance, to instill in learners an acceptance and understanding of both the positive and negative attributes of their cultural groups, and to teach learners the importance of acquiring genuine pride. Individuals who have positive ethnic, national, and global identifications value their ethnic, national, and global communities highly and are proud of these identifications. They desire and are able to take actions that support and reinforce the values and norms of these communities (Banks, 1988).

---

**FOLLOW THROUGH 1-8    Clarifying Multiple Identities**

Ask children and adolescents to consider their identities. For example, a child or an adolescent may have a number of different and changing identities. He or she might be

- African, Asian, European, Hispanic, or Native American (just to mention a few in a world full of national origins)
- a person of the specific cultural background
- a member of a minority group
- male or female
- gay or lesbian; bisexual or heterosexual
- a member of a particular school and grade
- a son or daughter, a grandchild, and a nephew or niece
- someone's best friend
- a person with a disability

---

In some situations, people of differing cultural backgrounds might feel they have to give up their identities in order to be accepted and successful in the majority society. Nevertheless, people of differing cultural backgrounds might not view the attitudes and behaviors of the dominant group appropriate for them. People who adopt attitudes and behaviors of the dominant group might experience an identity crisis or an internal opposition to giving up their cultural beliefs. The relationship between identity and school success can result in students believing that "for a minority person to succeed, academically, he or she must learn to think and act white" (Ogbu, 1988, p. 177).

To avoid situations in which students feel they must "act white," educators need to redesign teaching–learning experiences. Students must be able to feel that they can maintain their cultural identities and still experience school success. Educators need to demonstrate their respect for students' cultural identities, understand that students' perceptions of motivation may vary with culture, and allow students to learn in culturally relevant ways (i.e., working collaboratively rather than competitively). Educators must also provide curricular content and learning materials that show the contributions of various cultural groups, and help students to feel they are accepted in the majority-culture school system.

## *Racism*

Often defined as the domination of one social or ethnic group by another, racism is an ideological system used to justify discrimination by some racial groups against others. Although we continue to hope that the twenty-first century will bring greater acceptance and recognition of cultural diversity, we must acknowledge that discrimination, racism, and bigotry continue in the United States. As victims of overt racism and discrimination as well as the more covert forms that often deny them employment and housing opportunities, African Americans and other minorities continue to experience inequities and inequalities. Racial injustices perhaps not as visible as they were several decades ago nonetheless continue to affect people's progress and well-being. Educators of all cultures may have to deal with problems resulting from these realities in the United States and may have to sort through their own personal biases and long-held cultural beliefs.

Racism and its negative effects have been with us for centuries, and unfortunately little evidence suggests this evil will ever be eliminated. Implementing Research 1-1 discusses Bernard Lewis's view of the historical roots of racism, an evil that all Americans must act deliberately to reduce.

How can multicultural education programs respond to the racism that has affected people for centuries? Multicultural education should not focus only on past events, it must provide an impetus for changing the future. Educators are challenged to reduce the ignorance that breeds racism and to develop and support

---

**IMPLEMENTING RESEARCH 1-1    The Historical Roots of Racism**

In an excellent essay on racism, Bernard Lewis (1998) examines people's contempt for and suspicion of others who are different. Maintaining that barriers exist between insiders and outsiders, some people feel that "those who do not share our culture are barbarians; those who do not share our religion are unbelievers; those who are not citizens of our city are aliens" (Lewis, 1998, p. 17). Dealing with individuals who are different is a comparatively simple matter. Far more difficult is the case of the outsider who becomes part of our community (historically by conquest, contemporarily by immigration) yet wishes to retain his or her otherness. Racism, suspicion, and hostility sometimes result when people who are different join a community and refuse to give up their beliefs and adopt majority beliefs. Some people cannot tolerate those who accept citizenship but do not fully share the common identity and loyalties. Some societies have categorically refused them and tried to terminate their presence by expelling them, forcefully converting them, or physically destroying them. All three methods have precedents in history and have found practitioners in more modern times.

**Implementing the Research**

Educators as well as other members of society need to understand the evils of racism and how it has affected and still affects people. Lewis's essay is particularly relevant today as more and more immigrants enter the United States.

Anyone who reads newspapers can attest to the racism that plagues the United States. Educators need to focus attention on teaching children and adolescents what racism is as well as how to develop more accepting attitudes toward others and how to take a deliberate stance against racism. Many children, adolescents, and other members of our society understand neither racism nor its effects on people. Racism's many forms must be addressed and eventually reduced, but unfortunately they probably will never be eliminated.

---

*Source:* Lewis, B. (1998). The historical roots of racism. *The American Scholar, 67*(1), 17–25.

antiracist understanding and behavior in their students. The goal of multicultural education is founded on these tenets:

1. It is worthwhile for educators to focus on the reduction of racial and ethnic prejudice and discrimination.
2. It is appropriate for schools to teach certain humanistic values, such as the negative effects of racism, prejudice, and discrimination.
3. It is possible to reduce racial and ethnic prejudice and discrimination through appropriate educational experiences (Bennett, 1986).

Implementing Research 1-2 focuses on three myths about racism in America.

---

**IMPLEMENTING RESEARCH 1-2    Three Myths about Racism in America**

From a distance, there appear to be reasons to be optimistic about U.S. racism: Racial stereotypes and attitudes appear to have decreased and media depictions of racial minorities seem more favorable. In absolute terms, indicators for minorities have improved and race relations seem to be less strained. Waller (1997) argues that this rosy picture is misleading and supported by three myths: (1) Life is good for racial minorities, (2) racism is declining, and (3) U.S. society can be color-blind. Waller maintains that in fact these myths have been embraced not only by uneducated, narrow-minded bigots but also by well-educated and open-minded people.

Waller believes that something can be done to address racism, but that the problem of racism and the necessity for teaching racial tolerance will be perpetual. Educational programs and other efforts aimed at teaching tolerance are vital to the effort to combat racism. Only by critically addressing the myths Waller identifies can we begin to offer sensible hope for the future of race relations in America.

**Implementing the Research**

1. Educators need to recognize that racism continues (and will continue) in the United States as well as in U.S. schools. Although not as blatant as it was in the past, it continues as a human plague that must be addressed.
2. Educators need to look for both overt and subtle forms of racism. Racism includes more than graffiti and name-calling—it also can manifest itself in grouping practices, in the composition of athletic teams, and in evaluation of student abilities and motivational levels.
3. Educators can provide students with written and oral exercises (perhaps in a small group setting) to provide a better understanding of racism: what constitutes it, how it affects all people, and how people can address it.
4. Educators also need to understand prejudices based on differences other than race, including gender, age, social class, sexual orientation, and religion.

---

*Source:* Waller, J. (1997). The foundations of teaching racial tolerance: Three myths about racism in America. *The High School Magazine, 5*(2), 38–43.

## Stereotypes, Prejudices, and Generalizations

Stereotyping can be defined as holding attitudes toward a person or group that supposedly characterize or describe an entire age group, gender, race, or religion. It is discussed in more detail in Chapter 2. Stereotypes produce a generalized mental picture that usually results in a judgment (negative or positive) of a person or an entire culture.

It is imperative that educators approach all stereotypes with skepticism and acknowledge that most are based on prejudice—like or dislike, approval or disapproval of a culture or even an age group. Recognizing that stereotypes all too often contribute to people's benefiting from or being victims of discrimination, effective multicultural educators seek to understand and respond appropriately to others' and their own beliefs about people.

How can educators counter biases and stereotypes? How can teachers design multicultural education programs to encourage understanding and reduce stereotypical beliefs?

1. Educators should be aware of their own biases and stereotypes.
2. Educators should have equal, high expectations of all students, whatever their cultural background.
3. Educators should examine and confront the biases and stereotypes their students hold.
4. Educators should ensure that library materials and other instructional materials portray characters in a realistic, nonsexist, nonracist, nonstereotypical manner.
5. Educators should arrange heterogeneous class mixes that allow students an opportunity to build long-term, sustained interethnic and interracial relationships.
6. Educators should provide role-playing situations and simulation activities that allow students a better understanding of their own stereotypes (Garcia, 1984).

Cultural stereotypes and generalizations have the potential to severely damage interpersonal counseling and the outcome of educational efforts. Whatever one's prejudice—that all learners from different cultural backgrounds are underachievers or that all adolescents are involved in drugs and sex—stereotypes and generalizations can be detrimental to learners, educators, and the student–teacher relationship. Too often, cultural stereotypes and generalizations are considered "facts" and become the basis for professional decisions that affect people's lives.

---

**FOLLOW THROUGH 1-9   Clarifying Stereotypes**

List several stereotypes that people might harbor about people. How do you think these stereotypes originated? Is there any objective basis for them? How might such stereotypes affect educational decisions? List several ways educators can gain a better understanding of people rather than rely on stereotypical generalizations.

## Myths and Realities

We must eliminate myths and misconceptions that influence attitudes and actions toward those who are culturally different. Examples of current myths and misconceptions include both negative and positive stereotypes:

All children of the same ethnic background have the same needs and intellectual abilities.

All children who speak broken English or a dialect are intellectually deficient.

All minorities are disadvantaged, lazy, and on welfare.

All Oriental children are academically gifted.

All minorities are inferior.

Other myths and misconceptions exist about people from different cultural and socioeconomic backgrounds. Clearly, cultural stereotyping tends to encourage negative attitudes about oneself and others and diminishes perception and appreciation of individual cultures.

## Understanding Learners from Culturally Different Backgrounds

Recognizing the diversity in cultural backgrounds challenges all educators, especially those with a powerful sense of ethnocentrism and a steadfast belief that their culture is superior to others. Prejudiced educators may assume that learners should surrender their unique cultural values and beliefs.

All educators must understand individual learners and cultural diversity. Professionals who have a genuine caring attitude are on the right track, but they must also understand learners' families, language, religion, and other significant aspects of their lives. Educators are continually challenged to learn what it is like to be a child or adolescent in a specific culture, how it feels to attend a school that often appears to have strange rules and expectations, and how it feels to experience communication problems. Educators can meet the challenge by

1. Reading textbooks, journal articles, internet articles, and other material on cultural diversity and teaching and learning in multicultural settings.
2. Requesting information from organizations that disseminate objective information and promote various cultures.
3. Meeting on a firsthand basis learners and their families (perhaps in their homes) to gain a better understanding of what it means to be a learner from a different cultural background.
4. Attending conferences that focus on cultural diversity and working with children and adolescents from various cultures.
5. Reading about cultural diversity in books and magazines written primarily for children and adolescents.

## *Controversial Issues in Multicultural Education*

We examine multicultural education as a concept in more detail in Chapter 13, but we must explain several issues at this point. Although the last several decades have seen multicultural education emerging as a means of promoting under-standing, acceptance, and good will among people, it is somewhat ironic that some circles have not wholeheartedly accepted multicultural programs. In some cases, multicultural education has evoked criticism and controversy. It is important for educators to recognize several controversial areas and the claims of the critics of multicultural education.

Bennett (1986) reported that serious limitations plague the various approaches to multicultural education. Education for the culturally different is basically a con-descending approach; it assumes that a student's failure in school results from cul-tural differences. Education about cultural differences is designed to teach their value, an understanding of the concept of culture, and acceptance of others' dif-ferences. It also leads, ironically, to a kind of stereotyping that ignores similarities among all groups and neglects differences within any one group. Also, multi-cultural education has underestimated the impact of racism; one cannot assume that developing ethnic literacy and cultural appreciation will end racism, preju-dice, and discrimination (Bennett, 1986).

A second criticism of multicultural education is based on the belief that in the United States, "society does not promote sufficient love and interpersonal caring for a fulfilling existence" (Sleeter & Grant, 1988, p. 165). This criticism holds that by emphasizing cognitive knowledge about cultural groups over the exploration of interpersonal feelings multicultural education becomes misdirected. Although multicultural education might provide students a broad knowledge base, educa-tors must also stress and experience interpersonal relationships in order to effect change in attitudes and prejudices (Sleeter & Grant, 1988).

A third criticism arises because the words *culture, race,* and *class* have multi-ple interpretations. Some people perceive these words as accusatory, connoting prejudice, fears of job or housing discrimination, and isolation and alienation from the larger society. Ramsey (1987) wrote:

> *One Head Start teacher talked about the resistance of her low-income white par-ents whenever she said the word* multicultural. *It appeared from the parents' comments that the term meant glorifying "those people who get all the jobs and services." Because the teacher knew the community and was aware of the contro-versies and cutbacks related to jobs and welfare, she understood that, before the parents could hear anything positive about other groups of people, they had to ex-plore and share their own feelings of economic and social threat. After some of their anger was dissipated, she tried to help them feel more personally powerful and optimistic, through activities designed to foster their feelings of self-appreci-ation and confidence. After several sessions, the parents were more receptive to the idea of multicultural education. (p. 176)*

Ramsey also (1987) pointed out that some parents who identify with mainstream society feel threatened by the arrival of different people and may resent schools' efforts to have their children think positively about these groups. Responsive educators recognize that these problematic situations have the potential to limit the success of multicultural programs. They also realize the crucial need for planning appropriate ways to help change parental and community attitudes.

As John Gallagher reported, critics as well as advocates of multicultural education make vocal statements about multiculturalism. See Implementing Research 1-3.

---

**IMPLEMENTING RESEARCH 1-3    Multiculturalism at the Crossroads**

John Gallagher (1998b) maintains, "Few issues spark as much controversy nationally as multicultural education. The term has become a regular salvo in political skirmishes, shorthand for the anxiety various groups feel about affirmative action, political correctness, and homosexuality" (p. 11).

Critics often contend that multiculturalism violates basic social principles, such as the vision of the United States as a melting pot for generations of immigrants. They argue that multiculturalism stresses differences at the expense of our common bonds, driving us apart rather than bringing us together. Other critics argue that multicultural education is a cover for indoctrinating students in liberal political ideologies. Advocates of multicultural education feel that the movement addresses inequities and various conflicts in the United States; it has the potential to contribute to equal access and equal opportunities.

Gallagher also cites an article Michael Dirda wrote in the *Washington Post Magazine.* Dirda thinks multiculturalism links different peoples. For example, most multicultural curricula are based on simple justice and common sense. By teaching material related to Hispanic, Asian, and African Americans, teachers can capture the attention and enthusiasm of these frequently disadvantaged students as well as convey information to students of other backgrounds.

**Implementing the Research**

1. As an educator, you can explain the merits of multiculturalism to parents and the general public—what it is and what it is not, myths about the movement, and what children and adolescents actually learn.
2. Implement comprehensive multicultural education programs that extend beyond "Tacos on Tuesday" (Gallagher, 1998, p. 13) and other such superficial programs.
3. Secure the assistance and support of school administrators who are in a position to coordinate and oversee school programs.

---

*Source:* Gallagher, J. (1998). Multiculturalism at a crossroads: Can the push for pluralism in education survive the pull of America's melting pot? *Middle Ground, 1*(3), 10–14, 42.

---

**FOLLOW THROUGH 1-10   Determining Controversial Issues**

What other controversial issues surround multicultural education? Do you think the definition should embrace sexual orientation and disabling conditions? Should it include European Americans? Is it discriminatory to unrepresented groups? How might the issues you have selected be resolved? How do unresolved issues affect the progress of multicultural education?

---

## Summing Up

Educators planning and implementing multicultural education programs should remember to:

**1.** Address the wrongs of the past, such as racism, prejudice, and discrimination, but maintain the primary focus on the present understanding, respect, and acceptance of people of differing cultural backgrounds.

**2.** Consider multicultural education as an emerging concept that will continue to evolve as necessary to meet the needs of a society that is becoming increasingly diverse culturally.

**3.** Transmit facts and knowledge (including an awareness of cultural diversity) to help learners develop the skills necessary to interrelate positively with people of culturally diverse backgrounds.

**4.** Consider a total school curricular approach that integrates multicultural education in all teaching and learning situations.

**5.** Recognize multicultural education as an endeavor that has received considerable recognition and respect. Several areas of controversy and criticism continue to exist, however, and deserve attention.

**6.** Direct attention to issues such as sexism, agism, and classism, create more positive attitudes toward the disabled, and eliminate the racism, prejudice, and discrimination that plague U.S. society.

**7.** Address the ethnocentrism of learners and educators both.

**8.** Insist on multicultural education programs in all schools, rather than just in schools that have a culturally diverse student population.

## Suggested Learning Activities

**1.** Outline a multicultural education program for a school that has a population 50 percent European American, 25 percent African American, 20 percent Hispanic American, and approximately 5 percent other culturally diverse groups. Respond specifically to such areas as the extent of emphasis on each culture; a determination of the content of the program and examination of attitudes; appropriate in-service sessions for administration, faculty, and staff; appropriate curriculum and instruction methods and materials; and methods of assessing the program.

2. Read several definitions of multicultural education and then, on the basis of these definitions and your opinions, write your own definition of multicultural education. Should multicultural education include more than just "culture," for example, and should the definition include diversity in religion, gender, social class, and sexual orientation?

3. As a potential or practicing educator in our increasingly multicultural society, how should you attempt to address racism? Do you think you have ever been a victim of racism? Do you address racism when you see or hear it, or do you just ignore it? Name three or four ways you could help reduce racism in your school.

## Suggestions for Collaborative Efforts

Form groups of three or four people that, if possible, represent our nation's cultural and gender diversity. Working collaboratively, focus your group's attention toward the following efforts:

1. In your group, discuss the following statement: "There are more differences in social class than there are differences in culture. For example, middle- or upper-class people of various cultures may be more alike (e.g., in terms of preferences in food, clothing, customs, traditions, and religion) than people of a given culture or race. In essence, social class may be the distinguishing factor among people." Have several members of your group interview people from different social classes and several people from different cultural backgrounds to compare and contrast differences and similarities.

2. Have one or two of your group members visit a school to examine and compare the multicultural education programs. How do schools differ in philosophy, commitment, approaches (unit or total curriculum integration), goals and objectives, treatment of holidays, and overall attempts to have a truly "multicultural" school.

3. Select a school known for its diverse student population. Have your group formulate an instrument (survey or checklist) to assess the school's efforts in multicultural education. Make sure it examines the cultural, racial, and ethnic composition of faculty, staff, and other professional personnel; whether organization and grouping methods segregate learners by race; and whether the curriculum and instruction materials reflect cultural diversity.

## Expanding Your Horizons: Additional Journal Readings and Books

Banks, C. A., & Banks, J. A. (1997). Reforming schools in a democratic pluralistic society. *Educational Policy, 11*(2), 183–193.

*These noted authorities on multicultural education maintain that to meet national and global* *needs, reform efforts must incorporate diversity issues, promote democratic ideals, and help students gain the knowledge, attitudes, and skills to construct moral and just communities.*

Boyd, B. F. (1998). Issues in education: A guide to multicultural education. *Childhood Education, 75*(1), 33.

*Boyd describes a book,* Beyond heroes and holidays: A practical guide to K–12 anti-racist, multicultural education and staff development *(Lee, Menkart, & Okazawa-Rey, 1998) and its many practical strategies.*

Byrnes, D. A., & Kiger, G. (Eds.). (1996). *Common bonds: Anti-bias teaching in a diverse society.* Olney, MD: Association for Childhood Education International.

*Byrnes and Kiger examine the growing diversity in our schools, identify various forms of diversity, and suggest ways teachers can build inclusive classroom environments.*

Gollnick, D. M., & Chinn, P. C. (1998). *Multicultural education in a pluralistic society* (5th ed.). Columbus, OH: Merrill.

*Gollnick and Chinn provide an excellent look at differences such as race, class, ethnicity and race, gender, and exceptionality.*

Kang, H., & Dutton, B. (1997). Becoming multicultural: Focusing on the process. *Multicultural Education, 4*(4), 19–22.

*Kang and Dutton suggest that students need to develop intercultural competence and teachers need to provide learning experiences that teach this competence.*

Manning, M. L. (1994). *Celebrating diversity: Multicultural education in middle level schools.* Columbus, OH: National Middle School Association.

*In this monograph Manning examines multicultural education as it relates to young adolescents and middle-level schools.*

Marinoble, R. M. (1998). Counseling and supporting our gay students. *The Education Digest, 64*(3), 54–59.

*Marinoble examines identity conflict and feelings of isolation and stigmatization as she offers recommendations for curricular and support services for gay students.*

Silva, C., & Patton, M. M. (1997). Multicultural education: Theory to practice. *Teacher Education and Practice, 13*(1), 22–38.

*Silva and Patton examine multicultural educational practices (i.e., content integration, instructional and grouping practices, and parent-community involvement) in two elementary schools.*

Vogl, B. D., & Jaros, G. G. (1998). Can we achieve a celebration of diversity? *The Educational Forum, 62,* 334–340.

*These authors maintain that when most educators speak of celebrating diversity, they refer only to ethnic and racial groups; however, people need to think beyond traditional beliefs and take their thinking to higher levels.*

## *Answers to the Culture Quiz: Multicultural Education*

| | | | | |
|---|---|---|---|---|
| **1.** F | **3.** F | **5.** T | **7.** T | **9.** T |
| **2.** F | **4.** F | **6.** F | **8.** F | **10.** T |

*Chapter* 2

# An Increasingly Multicultural Society

Understanding the material and activities in this chapter will help the reader to:

- Grasp the historical and contemporary perspectives toward cultural diversity—that is, the melting pot and salad bowl ideologies, respectively.
- Provide a cultural classification of populations presently living in the United States.
- Explain concepts such as culture, ethnicity, race, socioeconomic status, and gender; and explain why understanding these concepts is important when working with children and adolescents from various cultures.
- Explicate perspectives toward cultural diversity such as cultural deficit and cultural mismatch and provide a rationale for adopting a positive and enriching perspective that appreciates cultural difference or cultural diversity.
- Explain how racism, discrimination, and stereotypes can hurt children and adolescents who are culturally different; and how elementary and secondary schools can provide appropriate responses.
- Provide concrete evidence that the United States is becoming increasingly culturally diverse, and explain the roles of elementary and secondary schools in addressing the needs of learners from differing cultural backgrounds.

## Overview

The increasing cultural diversity of the United States challenges elementary- and secondary-school educators to understand differing values, customs, and traditions and to provide responsive multicultural experiences for all learners. The melting pot theory, once thought to be a model of the assimilation of immigrants

**THE CULTURE QUIZ**   **Knowledge of Cultures**

*Directions:* Match the culture with the characteristic by placing the appropriate letter or letters before each numbered characteristic.

a. Native American
b. African American
c. Asian American
d. Hispanic American
e. European American

_____ 1. The culture is often stereotyped as the "model minority."

_____ 2. A member of this culture delivered the "I Have a Dream" speech in a Washington, D.C., protest march.

_____ 3. This culture is experiencing rapid population growth and may be the most populous cultural group during the first several decades of the twenty-first century.

_____ 4. The immigration proportion of this cultural group declined from 85 percent in 1900 to 22 percent in 1990.

_____ 5. A member of this culture pioneered processes for storing blood plasma, thus saving thousands of lives during World War II.

_____ 6. This culture's deep respect and reverence for the earth and all living things requires that the earth not be harmed.

_____ 7. A member of this culture was a computer executive and built a multimillion-dollar company.

_____ 8. Population numbers of this culture include Aleuts and Eskimos.

_____ 9. A member of this culture traveled through towns in the South documenting lynchings.

_____ 10. Population numbers of this culture include Pacific Islanders—more specifically, Hawaiians, Samoans, and Guamanians.

_____ 11. Racism, discrimination, and injustice have hampered this culture's economic, social, and educational progress.

_____ 12. Immigration records, started in 1820, show that until 1970, most immigrants were from this cultural group.

_____ 13. Educators and other professionals take extra care to avoid stereotyping this culture because considerable diversity exists among its children and adolescents.

_____ 14. This culture currently outnumbers African Americans in such cities as New York, Los Angeles, San Diego, and San Francisco.

(Answers to the Culture Quiz are located at the end of the chapter.)

into the United States, obviously is not valid. People do not lose their differences when they immigrate to the United States. In fact, the diversity of their cultural backgrounds deeply enriches the nation.

The melting pot theory is no longer considered a model, much less a means of achieving a just, equal, and accepting society. Educators need a sound understanding of cultural, ethnic, racial, socioeconomic, gender, and individual differences, especially in light of the wealth of cultural diversity of the nation that increases daily. This chapter examines cultural diversity in the United States and suggests that responsive multicultural education programs can address many challenges.

## Historical and Contemporary Perspectives

The melting pot metaphor used to describe the cultural composition of the United States, does not, in reality, describe it accurately. People who immigrate to the United States are increasingly reluctant to forsake their cultural traditions and values to become like mainstream society. Asians and Hispanics are often reluctant to give up ethnic customs and traditions in favor of middle-class European American habits that might appear to contradict beliefs they were taught early in life. The United States is hardly a melting pot resulting in a homogeneous group of people; Many people continue to hold onto old-world traditions and cherished values.

African Americans have fought to overcome oppression and discrimination and, through efforts such as the civil rights movement, have sought to understand and maintain their cultural heritage. This need to recognize and respect individual differences and similarities within cultures becomes clear when one considers the geographic, generational, and social class differences among African, Asian, Hispanic, European, and Native American learners.

Some cultural assimilation has undoubtedly taken place as people have adopted majority culture customs and standards. Generally speaking, however, the melting pot concept has given way to a perspective in which each group holds onto its unique identity and culture. This latter perspective is more realistic and by far more humane. Whether they arrive from Southeast Asia, one of the Spanish-speaking countries, or Europe people should not have to forsake their cultural heritages and traditions. Although some degree of assimilation might be necessary to survive economically and to cope with the challenges of everyday life, people can nevertheless hold fast to time-honored cultural traditions and customs. The more contemporary perspective views differences not as elements to be "melted away," but as personal characteristics that enrich U.S. society.

A survey in *Newsweek* revealed that attitudes toward immigration are changing. For example, 59 percent of people in the past thought immigration was a

---

**FOLLOW THROUGH 2-1   Examining Your Feelings**

Clearly, as Morganthau's *Newsweek* survey showed, attitudes toward immigration are changing. People do not feel as positive about immigration as they did in the past. Do you think these changes of attitudes are justified? How do you perceive immigration? Do you think it should be tougher for people to immigrate to America? Offer several possible reasons that attitudes might be growing more negative toward immigration. How might the change in attitudes toward immigration affect attitudes toward children and adolescents (e.g., the push to end or limit affirmative action or to end bilingual programs)?

**TABLE 2-1    Selected Cultural Groups in the United States**

| Group | Population Numbers | Percentage Increase (1990 to 1996) |
|---|---|---|
| Native Americans (Various tribes, Aleuts, and Eskimos) | 2,288,000 | 10.8% |
| African Americans | 33,503,000 | 9.9% |
| Asian Americans and Pacific Islanders | 9,743,000 | 30.6% |
| Hispanic Americans | 27,787,000 | 25.6% |
| European Americans | | Not available |

*Source:* U.S. Bureau of the Census. (1997a). *Statistical abstracts of the United States* (117th ed.). Washington, D.C.

good thing, and 31 percent considered it a bad thing. However, 60 percent of people today think immigration is a bad thing, compared with 29 percent who consider it good. Sixty-six percent of respondents felt that immigrants seek to maintain their identity, while only 20 percent still felt that the nation is a melting pot. Also, 62 percent think immigrants take jobs from U.S. workers; 78 percent felt immigrants work hard and accept jobs that Americans do not want; and 59 percent felt that immigrants end up on welfare, thus raising taxes for Americans (Morganthau, 1993).

Cultural pluralism can pose problems for educators who, on the one hand, are to infuse multiculturalism into their subject matter and, on the other hand, are to produce graduates who are culturally literate in the traditional sense. Teachers also face difficult choices among many topics and curriculum materials, which may take either assimilationist or pluralistic perspectives (Janzen, 1994).

Table 2-1 shows a breakdown of cultural groups and documents in an increasingly multicultural society. We will give more detailed information with the discussion of each cultural group.

Figure 2-1 shows the foreign-born population of the United States from 1900 to 1990. Table 2-2 shows selected immigrants by country of birth, citizenship status, and year of entry. Table 2-3 shows states where immigrants have selected to assume residence. Implementing Research 2-1 shows how U.S. society is growing increasingly diverse.

Case Study 2-1 shows how Mrs. Rowe helped the teachers in her school better understand the advantages of adopting a "salad bowl" perspective toward cultural diversity.

## The Culturally Different: Demographics

Present trends and projections for the United States indicate that the influx and growth of diverse cultural groups will continue. While many different cultural

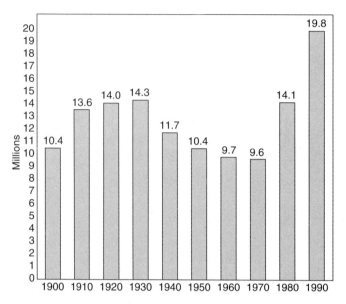

**FIGURE 2-1    Foreign-Born Population in the United States, 1900–1990**

*Source:* From *We the American . . . Foreign Born* by U.S. Bureau of the Census, 1993d, September. Washington, D.C.

**TABLE 2-2    Country of Birth, Citizenship Status, and Year of Entry (in thousands)**

| Country of Birth | Total Foreign Born | Naturalized Citizens | 1980–1990 | 1990–1996 |
|---|---|---|---|---|
| All countries | 24,557 | 7,904 | 8,416 | 6,579 |
| Mexico | 6,679 | 852 | 2,428 | 1,900 |
| Philippines | 1,164 | 610 | 451 | 260 |
| China | 801 | 276 | 313 | 274 |
| Cuba | 772 | 361 | 201 | 106 |
| India | 757 | 285 | 299 | 224 |
| Vietnam | 740 | 308 | 323 | 302 |
| El Salvador | 701 | 113 | 373 | 154 |
| Canada | 660 | 315 | 119 | 105 |
| Great Britain | 579 | 273 | 112 | 88 |
| Korea | 550 | 167 | 278 | 155 |
| Germany | 523 | 371 | 19 | 53 |
| Dominican Republic | 515 | 126 | 195 | 166 |
| Jamaica | 506 | 158 | 191 | 128 |

*Source:* U. S. Bureau of the Census. (1997b). More recent immigrants are generally younger. *Census and You, 32*(6), 1. Washington, D.C.
*Note:* Countries with totals under 500,000 are not shown.

**TABLE 2-3   Countries of Origin of the Immigrant Population of Six States**

| California | | Illinois | | Texas | |
|---|---|---|---|---|---|
| Mexico | 69% | Mexico | 54% | Mexico | 80% |
| Philippines | 4% | Poland | 9% | El Salvador | 4% |
| El Salvador | 3% | India | 5% | Vietnam | 2% |
| Vietnam | 3% | Philippines | 4% | Others | 14% |
| China | 2% | Former Soviet Union | 4% | | |
| Others | 19% | Others | 24% | | |

| Arizona | | New York | | Florida | |
|---|---|---|---|---|---|
| Mexico | 86% | Dominican Republic | 12% | Mexico | 30% |
| Vietnam | 2% | Former Soviet Union | 10% | Haiti | 21% |
| Others | 12% | Jamaica | 6% | Cuba | 6% |
| | | China | 5% | Jamaica | 4% |
| | | India | 5% | Colombia | 4% |
| | | Others | 62% | Others | 35% |

*Source:* Morganthau, T. (1993, August 9). America: Still a melting pot? *Newsweek* 16–25.

---

### CASE STUDY 2-1   Toward a Salad Bowl Perspective

Mrs. Rowe, a fourth grade teacher, realized early that her school expected learners to assimilate middle-class European American values and customs. Textbooks emphasized middle-class white characters, while downplaying other cultural groups; teaching styles and instructional strategies addressed the needs of white learners. School rules and policies, however, applied to all learners; school environments did little to celebrate cultural or gender diversity; and the ethnic composition of the administration, faculty, and staff indicated that the school system had not sought to employ professionals from a variety of cultures. Learners from culturally different backgrounds who were unable or unwilling to adopt middle-class white values suffered the consequences of low achievement, poor self-esteem, and a feeling of nonacceptance in the school.

Mrs. Rowe thought of ways to move the school toward a more "salad bowl" perspective in which learners from all cultures could retain cultural values and traditions and in which the school could address the needs of all learners. Mrs. Rowe sought the administration's advice and support. The administration then formed a committee consisting of Mrs. Rowe, a speech correctionist, a special educator, a guidance counselor, several classroom teachers, and several parents representing different cultural groups.

The committee decided to take deliberate action to make the entire school more responsive to learners from differing cultural backgrounds. They made plans to examine all phases of the school: textbooks and other curricular materials, the overall curriculum, instructional strategies, the efforts of special school personnel, the school environment, and efforts designed to celebrate diversity. Mrs. Rowe and the committee realized the need to be realistic—changing the school would take time, commitment, and the efforts of all educators. They had, however, taken two crucial steps: The school had realized the need for change and decided to take planned and deliberate action.

**IMPLEMENTING RESEARCH 2-1   Our Increasingly Diverse Society**

Harold Hodgkinson (1998) cited some startling statistics:

- By 2010, whites will account for only 9 percent of the world's population—compared with 17 percent in 1997—making them the world's smallest ethnic minority.
- The youngest children in America are the most diverse: Whereas 26 percent of all Americans are nonwhite, among school children, 37 percent are nonwhite. The percentage of nonwhite preschool children is 38 percent.
- There are 215 nations in the world, and people from every one of them live in the United States, some of whom marry people of different ethnic origins. For example, a quarter of Hispanics marry non-Hispanics. Among Asian Americans, a quarter of marriages are to non-Asians. All these statistics indicate that the white population will decline across the board.
- Poverty continues to hurt people—there is emerging suburban growth around declining core areas of major cities. While poverty is not decreasing in the cities, it is increasing in the suburbs.
- In the South, there are two black populations. One is the new middle class, many of them college graduates who are migrating to the South to accept management jobs in major corporations. The other group is the black population in the rural Mississippi Delta.
- By the first few decades of 2000, there will be more Hispanic children than African American children for the first time in America's history. This situation will not change because there is very little black immigration and there are very many Hispanic immigrants, the largest group coming from Mexico.

**Implementing the Research**

1. Educators need to understand the changes our nation's increasing diversity will bring in such areas as curriculum, organizational patterns, behavior management expectations, and parent and family involvement in schools.
2. Educators should recognize that some students will not fit neatly into specific categories of ethnic origin. Rather than being considered only Hispanic or Asian, for example, they might have a more diverse origin and might prefer to be considered to be of diverse ethnic heritage.
3. Educators need to recognize and whenever possible address poverty and its ill effects. No longer merely an urban plague, it has now spread to the suburbs.

*Source:* Hodgkinson, H. (1998). The demographics of diversity. *Principal 78*(1), 26–32.

groups enter the United States each year, space allows us to mention only representative groups. Interested readers are referred to the many readily available census documents that provide a more comprehensive examination of many cultural groups.

FOLLOW THROUGH 2-2 Determining Preferred Designations

To show respect for cultural backgrounds and to promote cultural identities, educators need to call African Americans (who have been called black, black American, Afro-American, Negro, and colored) by the term that best describes their cultural heritage. Some do not like *African American* because they feel a stronger allegiance to the United States than to Africa; others respect *African American* because it reflects their cultural heritage. It is essential for educators (indeed all people) to show genuine respect by referring to people by the term they prefer. Survey a number of African Americans to determine their preferred term.

## African Americans

As Table 2-1 indicates, the African American population totaled approximately 33,503,000 in 1997. Although most of the population growth (percentage increase shown in the righthand column of Table 2-1) resulted from a natural increase, immigration from Caribbean and African countries also contributed to the growth.

The African American birthrate is slightly above replacement levels (the death rate) and will bring the total African American population from 11.5 percent of the total U.S. population in 1980 to thirteen percent in 2020. (The Hispanic Policy Development Project, 1997).

When the government took the first census in 1790 , African Americans in the United States numbered about 760,000. By 1860, as the Civil War began, the African American population had increased to 4.4 million. By 1900, population numbers had doubled and reached 8.8 million. By 1950 population numbers of African Americans reached the 15 million mark and were close to 27 million in 1980.

Table 2-4 categorizes the African American school-age population by age and gender.

African Americans for the most part live in metropolitan areas—nationally, 84 percent. At least 95 percent of all African Americans in the Northeast, Midwest, and West regions live in metropolitan areas. The ten cities with the largest African

### TABLE 2-4 African American Children and Adolescents

| Age | Population | |
|---|---|---|
| | Male | Female |
| Under 5 years | 1,494,000 | 1,454,000 |
| 5–9 years | 1,569,000 | 1,524,000 |
| 10–14 years | 1,475,000 | 1,430,000 |
| 15–19 years | 1,475,000 | 1,429,000 |

*Source:* U.S. Bureau of the Census. (1997a). *Statistical abstracts of the United States* (117th ed.). Washington, D.C.

American population in 1990 included New York, Chicago, Detroit, Philadelphia, Los Angeles, Houston, Baltimore, Washington, Memphis, and New Orleans. The 1990 census indicated that African Americans live in every state of the Union, from about 2,000 in Vermont to 2.9 million in New York. Sixteen states in that census had an African American population of one million or more. California and New York each have African American populations exceeding two million (U.S. Bureau of the Census, 1993b).

## Asian Americans

The Asian American population includes a wide array of people from Asia and the Pacific Islands. Census documents include Chinese, Filipinos, Koreans, Asian Indians, Japanese, Vietnamese, Cambodians, Laotians, Hmong, and Thai people in the Asian populations (U.S. Bureau of the Census, 1993a). They also include people of Polynesian (Hawaiians, Samoans, Tongans, and Tahitians), Micronesian (primarily Guamanians or Chamorros but also Mariana Islanders, Marshall Islanders, Palauans and several other groups), and Melanesian (primarily the Fijian people) descent (U.S. Bureau of the Census, 1993f).

Asians constitute the most rapidly growing minority group percentage in the United States. It is estimated that by 2020, Asians will account for 6.5 percent of the total U.S. population (The Hispanic Policy Development Project, 1997).

In three decades, the numbers of Asians and Pacific Islanders in the United States nearly quintupled—growing from 1.5 million in 1970 to 3.7 million in 1980 to 7.3 million in 1990. The percentage of Asians and Pacific Islanders in the total population also nearly doubled during the 1980s, from 1.5 percent to 2.9 percent (U.S. Bureau of the Census, 1993f).

The 1990 census counted nearly 7 million Asians living in the United States, a 99 percent increase over the 1980 count. The largest proportion of Asian Americans were Chinese (24 percent) and Filipino (20 percent) followed by Japanese (12 percent). New immigration groups, including Laotian, Cambodian, Thai, and Hmong, each accounted for 2 percent or less of the Asians in the United States.

Immigration contributed significantly to the growth of the Asian population in the 1970s and 1980s, but the percentages who are foreign born differ considerably from group to group. Sixty-six percent of Asians were born in foreign countries. Among Asian groups, Vietnamese, Laotian, and Cambodian groups had the

---

**FOLLOW THROUGH 2-3   Developing Objective Understandings**

The fact that many Asian Americans have been very successful in American schools and society has stereotyped them as the "model minority." Not all Asian Americans have fared equally well, however. Some experience culture-related problems, socioeconomic difficulties, and language problems. How can educators gain an accurate and objective understanding of Asian Americans (such as getting to know individual Asian groups as well as individual Asian Americans)?

highest proportion of foreign born and Japanese had the lowest proportion. Most of the Asian populations live in the West. Approximately 66 percent of Asians live in just five states: California, New York, Hawaii, Texas, and Illinois. The population is highly concentrated in California, New York, and Hawaii.

Asians had a median age of thirty years in 1990, younger than the national median of thirty-three years. Only 6 percent of the Asian population were sixty-five years old or older compared with 13 percent of the total population. The Japanese were the eldest of the Asian populations with a median age of thirty-six years, in part because fewer Japanese were foreign born. The Hmong and Cambodian, with their large numbers of recent immigrants were the youngest Asians, with a median age of thirteen years and nineteen years, respectively. In 1990, Asian males were younger than Asian females with median ages of twenty-nine years and thirty-one years, respectively (U.S. Bureau of the Census, 1993a). Table 2-5 categorizes the Asian American school-age population by age group and gender.

The Pacific Islander population of the United States shares many similarities with the other Asian populations. Hawaiians, of course, native to the United States, represent 58 percent of the total Pacific Islander population. Samoans and Guamanians were the next largest groups in the 1990 census, representing 17 percent and 14 percent, respectively, followed by Tongans and Fijians who were 5 percent and 2 percent, respectively, of all Pacific Islanders. Other Pacific Islanders such as the Palauans, Northern Mariana Islanders, and Tahitians each constituted less than one-half of 1 percent of Pacific Islander Americans (U.S. Bureau of the Census, 1993d; U.S. Bureau of the Census, 1993f).

Eighty-six percent of all Pacific Islanders live in the West. Approximately 75 percent of Pacific Islanders live in just two states, California and Hawaii. These two states had more than 100,000 Pacific Islanders each. Other states with significant populations of Pacific Islanders include Washington, Oregon, Texas, and Utah. Also, like the other Asian populations, Pacific Islanders are relatively young. They had a median age of twenty-five years in 1990. Only about 4 percent were sixty-five years old and over compared with 6 percent of all Asians and Pacific Islanders and 13 percent of the entire population. Hawaiians have the oldest median age among Pacific Islanders, twenty-six years, followed by Guamanians with a

**TABLE 2-5   Asian American Children and Adolescents**

| Age | Population | |
|---|---|---|
| | Male | Female |
| Under 5 years | 432,000 | 414,000 |
| 5–9 years | 391,000 | 370,000 |
| 10–14 years | 388,000 | 373,000 |
| 15–19 years | 360,000 | 349,000 |

*Source:* U.S. Bureau of the Census. (1997a). *Statistical abstracts of the United States* (117th ed.). Washington, D.C.

median age of twenty-five. Samoans, at twenty-two years, had the youngest median age among Pacific Islanders (U.S. Bureau of the Census, 1993d; U.S. Bureau of the Census, 1993f).

### European Americans and Other Cultural Groups

European and Australian peoples also inhabit the United States, adding to its diversity. Table 2-6 provides population numbers from different parts of Europe.

As the earlier discussions of cultural groups illustrated, most immigrants today come from Asia and Latin America. This pattern contrasts significantly with that of previous decades. Of the nearly 42 million people who immigrated between 1820 and 1960, for example, 34 million were European. In the forty years since then, only 2.7 percent of the 15 million immigrants entering the United States have been from Europe. In 1900, 85 percent of the immigrants were from Europe; in 1990, only 22 percent came from Europe (U.S. Bureau of the Census, 1993d). By 2050 at the latest, the majority of U.S. citizens will no longer be white. The white population is not replacing itself and the numbers of nonwhite groups are growing at higher-than-replacement rates through both natural increase and immigration (The Hispanic Policy Development Project, 1997).

It is interesting to note that some cultural groups actually lost population between 1980 and 1990. Of the forty groups with more than 100,000 foreign-born people in 1990, fourteen declined in size. With the exception of Canadians, all of these groups were European. Italians, followed by Scottish, Hungarians, Germans, and Greeks had the largest declines.

Implementing Research 2-2 looks at psychosocial problems of immigrant youth.

### TABLE 2-6    European Immigrants to the United States, by Country of Birth, 1995

| Country of Birth | Population Numbers (thousands) |
| --- | --- |
| Europe | 128.2 |
| France | 2.5 |
| Germany | 6.2 |
| Greece | 1.3 |
| Ireland | 5.3 |
| Italy | 2.2 |
| Poland | 13.8 |
| Portugal | 2.6 |
| Romania | 4.9 |
| Former Soviet Union | 54.4 |

*Source:* U.S. Bureau of the Census. (1997a). *Statistical abstracts of the United States* (117th ed.).Washington, D.C.

**IMPLEMENTING RESEARCH 2-2**   **Psychosocial Problems of Immigrant Youth**

Immigrant youth experience a number of problems resulting from their immigration status. When they immigrate to the United States, they leave behind their familiar language, culture, community, and social system. Likewise, they experience a variety of emotional and cognitive adjustments to the realities of life in the United States. Many of these conflicts and adjustments place immigrant youth at increased risk for psychosocial problems, school failure, drug use, and other risk-taking behaviors.

Delores James (1997) discussed several problems that immigrant youth face and suggested silence was the most universal response. Silence—the universal characteristic of the uprooting experience—is the way most immigrant children deal with their problems, irrespective of nationality, economic status, and family stability. It might be the one response that elementary and secondary educators can best examine.

**Implementing the Research**

1.  Educators need to realize that immigrant youth often have limited support systems and also that immigrants often do not take advantage of available support services (because of language barriers or assessment procedures). In some cases they have a cultural prohibition against sharing emotional problems with strangers.
2.  Educators can claim the responsibility to nurture children who have been left to fend for themselves. Comprehensive school programs can provide more than traditional health education programs.
3.  Educators and counselors need to understand that interventions must be culturally responsive. They must include accurate assessment of students' problems and in-service training of all school personnel in the cultural adjustment of immigrant children.
4.  Educators can implement a peer-counseling program in which peers (both immigrants and others) offer guidance and nurturing from the elementary or secondary students' perspective.

*Source:* James, C. S. D. (1997). Coping with a new society: The unique psychosocial problems of immigrant youth. *Journal of School Health, 67*(3), 98–102.

## Hispanic Americans

Hispanic people trace their origins to Spain, Mexico, Puerto Rico, Cuba, and many other Spanish-speaking countries of Latin America (U.S. Bureau of the Census, 1993e). Hispanic people share many similarities such as history, customs, the Spanish language, and sometimes country of origin; but the wide diversity within Hispanic culture requires educators to consider, whenever possible, people as individuals.

Hispanic populations have not always appeared in the census as a separate ethnic group. In 1930, the government counted the number of Mexicans who had immigrated to the United States and in 1940, the census included "persons of Spanish mother tongue." The 1950 and 1960 censuses enumerated "persons of Spanish surname." The 1970 census asked people about their "origins," and listed several Hispanic cultures. In the 1980 and 1990 censuses, the categories constituting people of "Spanish/Hispanic" origin included Mexican, Puerto Rican, Cuban, and "other Hispanic." The 1990 census accounted for about thirty additional groups of Hispanic origin (U.S. Bureau of the Census, 1993e).

Hispanics—the most rapidly growing U.S. immigrant group in terms of absolute numbers—increased by 53 percent between 1980 and 1990. By 2015, the number of Hispanics in the United States will equal or slightly exceed the number of African Americans. It is estimated that by 2020, Asians, African Americans, and Hispanics will account for 16 percent of the total U.S. population. Today, there are 27 million Hispanics in 7.6 million households concentrated predominantly in five states—California, Texas, Florida, New York, and Illinois. By 2050, Hispanics will represent the second largest racial and ethnic group in the U.S. population—their numbers will have risen to 84 million (The Hispanic Policy Development Project, 1997).

Several factors have contributed to the tremendous increase in Hispanic population in the United States. Among them are birthrates higher than those of the rest of the population and a substantial immigration from Mexico, Central America, the Caribbean, and South America. In fact, in 1990, there were 22.4 million Hispanics in the United States, almost 9 percent of the nation's 250 million people. The Hispanic population in 1990 numbered slightly less than the entire U.S. population in 1850. Also, the Census Bureau's 1992 middle series projections suggest that rapid population growth may continue into the twenty-first century. The population could rise from 24 million in 1992 to 31 million by the year 2000, and 59 million by 2030, and 81 million by 2050.

People of Hispanic heritage come from many different origins. Although Hispanic people have much in common, between groups many differences exist that deserve understanding. Interesting for educators is the number of Hispanic children and adolescents attending schools today. Table 2-7 categorizes the Hispanic American school-age population by age and gender.

Implementing Research 2-3 examines interracial marriages in the United States and how U.S. demographics might reflect beige and black rather than white and black.

**TABLE 2-7  Hispanic American Children and Adolescents**

| | Population | |
|---|---|---|
| Age | Male | Female |
| Under 5 | 1,677,000 | 1,596,000 |
| 5–9 years | 1,403,000 | 1,340,000 |
| 10–14 years | 1,255,000 | 1,194,000 |
| 15–19 years | 1,316,000 | 1,168,000 |

*Source:* U.S. Bureau of the Census. (1997a). *Statistical abstracts of the United States* (117th ed.). Washington, D.C.

**IMPLEMENTING RESEARCH 2-3    The Beige and the Black**

Michael Lind (1998) questions predictions that whites will eventually become a minority in the twenty-first century. Instead, demographic trends suggest that the historic white-black dichotomy in America will be replaced by a new division, one between beige and black. Writing in the *New York Times Magazine,* Lind noted shifting patterns of racial intermarriage which suggest that, during the twenty-first century, the U.S. population is not likely to be sharply divided into whites, blacks, Hispanics, Asians, and Native Americans. Nor is it likely to be split in two ways, between whites and nonwhites. The overall picture might be something more complicated: a white-Asian-Hispanic majority, a group of beige Americans, and a group of blacks.

The U.S. Supreme Court in *Loving v. Virginia* (1967) struck down the last antimiscegenation laws of the states. Marriage across racial lines is growing at a remarkable rate. Between 1960 and 1990, interracial marriages in this country increased by more than 800 percent. Roughly 1 in 25 American married couples today are interracial. At least three million children of mixed-raced parentage live in the United States. In the 25–34 age group, 31.6 percent of native-born Hispanic husbands and 31.4 percent of native-born Hispanic wives had white spouses. The figures were even higher for Asians: 36 percent for native-born Asian husbands and 45.2 percent for native-born Asian wives.

Intermarriage varies significantly by region. White men in California in 1990 were more than six times as likely as Midwestern white men to marry outside their race. Overall, interracial marriages are more than twice as common in California (1 in 10 new couples) than in the rest of the country (1 in 25).

As Lind (1998) put it, "For what seems to be emerging in the United States is a new dichotomy between blacks and nonblacks. Increasingly, whites, Asians, and Hispanics are creating a broad community from which black Americans may be excluded" (p. 38). Some blacks, he noted, frown on blacks who marry out of their race and consider such relationships disloyal. Prejudice against blacks may also be a reason that they marry people of other cultures less than do Hispanics, Asians, and Native Americans.

## Implementing the Research

As the number of interracial marriages continues to increase, elementary and secondary school educators in the United States will face several challenges. First, they will need to understand interracial children and adolescents and problems such as cultural identity that might need to be addressed. They will need to show genuine acceptance of interracial students and be prepared to deal with any prejudices and stereotypes they might harbor toward these students. Second, elementary and secondary school educators will need to recognize that interracial parents and families face challenges of their own. They might, for example, feel accepted or rejected on account of their choice of a marriage partner. Third, curricular and instructional materials need to show interracial couples as well as interracial children and adolescents. Fourth, they need to rethink traditional mindsets toward whites constituting the majority. Fifth, elementary and secondary school educators need to work to reduce all forms of prejudice—prejudice toward blacks, interracial couples and children, and whites who choose to as well as those who choose not to marry interracially.

*Source:* Lind, M. (1998, August 16). The beige and the black. *The New York Times Magazine,* 38–39.

## Native Americans

A number of different names have been used to identify the first Americans: "Original Americans," "Native People," "American Indians," and "Native Americans." We use *Native Americans* in this text. This term is currently the preferred one.

The most reliable population numbers, which the U.S. Bureau of the Census supplies, include Eskimos and Aleuts in the Native American population. There have been estimates of Native American population numbers since the founding of the nation, but it was not until 1860 that the federal government actually counted Native Americans, including them in the census only if they had left the reservations and were living among other Americans. The 1890 census was the first to obtain a complete count of Native Americans throughout the country.

Data from the U.S. Bureau of the Census report the Native American population at approximately 1.95 million in 1997. Projections suggest the Native American population will reach 4.6 million by 2050. As Table 2-8 shows, the approximately 500 tribes vary in size.

Nearly one-half of the Native American population lived west of the Mississippi River in the 1990 census. Two of every three Native Americans (including Eskimos and Aleuts) live in ten states. Of these states, only North Carolina, Michigan, and New York are east of the Mississippi River. As of 1990, more than half of the Native American population lived in just six states: Oklahoma, California, Arizona, New Mexico, Alaska, and Washington.

Table 2-9 on page 43 categorizes the Native American school-age population by age and gender.

The Native American population is a relatively young group. Thirty-nine percent of the Native American population (including Eskimos and Aleuts) was under twenty years old in 1990. Only about 8 percent of all Native Americans were sixty years old. The median age was twenty-six years, considerably younger than the U.S. median age of thirty-three years (U.S. Bureau of the Census, 1993c).

**TABLE 2-8    Ten Largest Native American Tribes**

| Tribe | Population |
|---|---|
| Cherokee | 308,132 |
| Navajo | 219,198 |
| Chippewa | 103,826 |
| Sioux | 103,255 |
| Choctaw | 82,299 |
| Pueblo | 52,939 |
| Apache | 50,051 |
| Iroquois | 49,038 |
| Lumbee | 48,444 |
| Creek | 43,550 |

*Source:* U.S. Bureau of the Census. (1997a). *Statistical abstracts of the United States* (117th ed.). Washington, D.C.

TABLE 2-9    **Native American Children and Adolescents**

|  | Population | |
|---|---|---|
| Age | Male | Female |
| Under 5 | 102,000 | 100,000 |
| 5–9 years | 115,000 | 111,000 |
| 10–14 years | 120,000 | 117,000 |
| 15–19 years | 107,000 | 105,000 |

*Source:* U.S. Bureau of the Census. (1997a). *Statistical abstracts of the United States* (117th ed.). Washington, D.C.

---

**FOLLOW THROUGH  2-4    Determining a School's Diversity**

Survey an elementary or secondary school in your area to determine its cultural composition. To what extent has each culture increased or decreased over the last ten years? Give several examples of how the school has responded to cultural differences. Also, give several examples of other ways the school can better address cultural diversity.

---

**FOR ADDITIONAL INFORMATION    Internet Addresses**

**Main**
http://funnelweb.utcc.utk.edu/~csma/ main.html   Provides learning opportunities for people interested in the study of multicultural societies.

**ANU—Centre for Immigration & Multicultural Studies**
http://coombs.anu.edu.au/SpecialProj/CIMS/ CIMSHomePage.html   Provides information and research on social sciences and Pacific and Asian Studies.

**IUME: The Institute for Urban and Minority Education**
http://iume.tc.columbia.edu/   Provides research to better understand the experiences of diverse urban and minority-group populations.

**Asian Americans—Tables, Figures, Boxes**
http://www.prb.org./pubs/bulletin/bu53-2/ tfb.htm   Provides a summary of Asian Americans' diversity and increasing numbers.

**USDLC 1995–96 Program Series**
http://www.esc20.tenet.edu/star/prog.html   Provides information on how educators in today's classrooms of changing demographics can address cultural diversity.

## Understanding Diversity

### Culture

Culture can be defined in a number of ways; but recent definitions, while worded differently, basically connote similar meanings. We define *culture* as people's values, language, religion, ideals, artistic expressions, patterns of social and interpersonal relationships, and ways of perceiving, behaving, and thinking. People's basis for perceptions as well as their actual perceptions differ culturally. How we feel, think, respond, and behave reflects our cultural background.

It is important to say that all people have culture. While such a statement might appear strange, a century or so ago *culture* was thought to be the province of only some people. Educated people, well-read, literate, and knowledgeable in areas such as music, the arts, and drama had culture; those who did not were thought to lack culture. Today, we recognize that all people have culture.

People referred to as bicultural have competencies and can function effectively in two cultures. These people have mastered the knowledge of and are able to function effectively in two cultures. They feel comfortable in two cultures and have a strong desire to function effectively in them.

The reasons for and levels of biculturalism vary. Some African Americans, for example, learn to function effectively in the European American culture in an attempt to attain social and economic mobility during the formal working day. In their private lives, however, these same individuals may be highly African American and monocultural (Gollnick & Chinn, 1998).

### Race

Although the term *race* refers to biological differences among people, it has long been used to differentiate groups of people. Determining racial categories often proves difficult because of the wide variety of traits and characteristics people and groups share. Society has generally recognized differences between races (e.g., physical differences), but these differences satisfy only biological aspects and do not explain differences in social behavior (Pedersen, 1988).

There are several important points concerning race. First, despite the movements of large numbers of people from one geographic region to another and the influence of intermarriage across racial groups, the concept of race today still has a significant social meaning. Second, race contributes few insights to cultural

---

**FOLLOW THROUGH 2-5   Determining "Cultures"**

Consider your culture—how many do you have? You have a "cultural background," but you also have a culture of region, sexual orientation, socioeconomic status, and professional status: Are you a preservice or an in-service teacher?

understanding. There is seldom cultural correspondence between a person's nationality, geography, language, and religion and his or her racial category. Therefore, knowledge of a person's racial identity does not reveal much about his or her nationality, religion, and language.

Difficulties the U.S. Bureau of the Census experienced in its documents show the confusion regarding race and ethnicity. For example, the census may ask people to define themselves in categories that are not mutually exclusive, that is, a person can have more than one racial or ethnic designation.

## Ethnicity

The definition of ethnicity takes into consideration people's national origin, religion, race, and any combination thereof. Attributes associated with ethnicity include group image and sense of identity derived from contemporary cultural patterns; shared political and economic interests; and involuntary membership, although individual identification with the group may be optional. The extent to which individuals identify with a particular ethnic group varies considerably, and some may identify with more than one. Strong ethnic identification suggests a sharing and acceptance of ethnic group values, beliefs, behaviors, language, and ways of thinking.

The definition of ethnicity also includes a community of people within a larger society who are set apart by others or who set themselves apart primarily on the basis of racial identity and cultural characteristics such as religion, language, or tradition. The central factor is the notion of being set apart because of physical or cultural attributes or both.

## Gender

The term *gender* describes masculinity and femininity—the thoughts, feelings, and behavior that identify one as either male or female (Butler & Manning, 1998). A multicultural education text would be remiss if it failed to address gender differences. Although many similarities exist between males and females, differences also exist, which educators should recognize and for which they should plan gender-appropriate educational experiences. Likewise, educators have a responsibility to clarify stereotypical beliefs about males and females.

Recent reports such as *How Schools Shortchange Girls* (American Association of University Women, 1992) provide evidence to support our contention that the acceptance, appreciation, and addressing of gender differences should be an integral component of multicultural education programs. As Gender Perspectives 2-1 on page 46 suggests, *gender* issues involve females *and* males.

As Gender Perspectives 2-1 shows, educators need to take a deliberate stand to balance their treatment of girls and boys and to address the unequal treatment that girls have often received. Chapman's work substantiates our opinion that gender diversity needs to be addressed in multicultural education.

---

### GENDER PERSPECTIVES 2-1    Gender Equity: The Great Balancing Act

Anne Chapman (1997) in *A Great Balancing Act* argues that (1) schools need to address the needs of boys as well as girls, and (2) schools (and society as a whole) sometimes give girls second-class treatment. She reports disturbing findings:

- Nearly one girl in three and nearly one boy in five reported being "often" sexually harassed (p. 20).
- The media, especially television, have real effects on students' behavior and attitudes (p. 8) as gender stereotypes are reinforced.
- The curriculum to a large extent focuses on political events and issues and historical chronology from a gender-biased perspective. The focus on inventions, politics, and military actions tends to highlight men's roles in society. Women's roles in history or women's issues are rarely noted, except perhaps during Women's History Week.

- Parents, particularly fathers, initiate boys into the traditions of sports, whereas parental and societal expectations for girls' participation are more neutral. Also, as the differences in physical abilities between girls and boys become more marked around the middle school years, physiological attributes that give girls the advantage as strong swimmers, runners, or walkers are less valued than boys' attributes of weight and muscle mass, which are deemed more important in sports. To address this problem, Chapman calls for, as much as possible, mixed-gender teams and outdoor sports that require boys and girls to work together. Such scenarios place less pressure on boys and encourage girls more, help coaches examine the language they use in coaching, and encourage more women to coach.

*Source:* Chapman, A. (1997). *A great balancing act: Equitable education for girls and boys.* Washington, D.C.: National Association of Independent Schools.

---

How might females differ from males? Research on gender and its effects have focused mainly on health concerns, social networks, self-esteem, achievement, self-image, and sex role attitudes and behaviors.

**1.** Females and males report the same number of best friends; attributes they considered important in themselves and their same-sex friends differed according to sex. Males had larger social networks than females (Benenson, 1990).

**2.** Females feel less positive about their bodies than males feel about theirs, and assign more different values than males do to different aspects of their bodies. Changes affecting the female body may make girls disappointed in their bodies. Boys, by contrast, may be less concerned with physical appearance and more interested in task mastery and effectiveness (Koff, Rierdan, & Stubbs, 1990).

**3.** Females who have curricular choices often choose fewer mathematics courses than do males. The reason for this difference, however, is attributed to educators and counselors who steer females away from mathematics and science and not to actual weaknesses in females' native ability (Butler & Sperry, 1991).

**4.** Females prove significantly more nontraditional in their sex-role behaviors. Both genders demonstrate more nontraditionalism in sex-role attitudes than in actual sex-role behaviors (Nelson & Keith, 1990).

**5.** Females benefit more from group-oriented collaborative learning projects (e.g., cooperative learning) rather than individualistic and competitive projects, which many males prefer (Grossman & Grossman, 1994).

Schmuck and Schmuck (1994) consider the treatment of girls in high schools today. They cite the American Association of University Women (AAUW) study, *How Schools Shortchange Girls*, which reviews more than 450 studies and concludes that girls are "invisible in our nation's schools" (p. 23). Schmuck and Schmuck provide a detailed list of resources on gender equity in schools. They maintain that exclusionary high schools promote the status quo and, in fact, exclude the experiences of girls and other minorities. Girls are shortchanged, often without being aware that they are. Principals who want to be nondiscriminatory try to comply with legal mandates of nondiscrimination by examining curricular and extracurricular offerings, reviewing policies that may unintentionally discriminate, and actively seeking changes in school policy and practice to reduce discriminatory policy. In essence, principals and other educators should attempt to include all members in a democratic society (Schmuck & Schmuck, 1994).

### Sexual Orientation

One debate among multiculturalists concerns the inclusiveness of the definition of multiculturalism. One side favors an inclusive definition of multiculturalism (including race, ethnicity, and sexual orientation); the other side supports an exclusive definition, or one favoring only ethnic and racial minorities (Pope, 1995).

Some people think the definition of multiculturalism should be restricted to cultural and ethnic differences. While W. M. L. Lee (1996) directs attention solely toward multicultural counseling, she maintains that in defining multiculturalism, some oppose a more inclusive definition, especially when dealing with differences involving males and females, gays and lesbians, elderly people, and people with physical disabilities. Others contend that unequal treatment and discrimination are not limited to racial and ethnic differences (Lee, 1996).

We believe multicultural education should include people of differing sexual orientation. We believe gays and lesbians share specific cultural characteristics, experience injustices and discrimination the way racial and ethnic minorities do, and deserve educators capable of providing effective educational experiences. We also believe those with physical disabilities should be included in the definition because they have a "culture" of their own and often experience injustices in U.S.

---

**FOLLOW THROUGH 2-6   School Practices and Gender**

Make a list of school practices or education-related issues that might fail to address gender differences. Why do you think educators sometimes use school practices and harbor expectations that fail to address gender differences?

society. Such a position does not imply that these people do not share many similarities with others. It simply implies that, because of their differences and potential as targets of injustice, they should be included in the definition of multiculturalism and in multicultural education programs.

Gays, lesbians, and bisexuals have their own culture and experience many of the same problems as minorities. Educators teaching gay and lesbian students need to understand the special challenges (e.g., loneliness, isolation, ridicule) that gays and lesbians experience. We feel that sexual orientation should be perceived as a cultural difference, just as gender, race, ethnicity, and social class are considered differences. Teaching gay and lesbian students requires trying to understand these students' worldviews and perspectives on life.

Researchers have generally accepted consistently that 10 percent of the population is gay or lesbian and that this portion represents every race, creed, social class, and degree of disability. In fact, estimates suggest there are 2.9 million gay or lesbian adolescents in the United States. These students are from all cultural groups and from rural as well as urban schools. They have for the most part sat passively through the years of schooling where their identities as gay and lesbian people have been ignored or denied. They have done so because of their own fears and isolation and because of the failure of society, full of taboos and fear of controversy, to take up their cause (Bailey & Phariss, 1996).

Educators and others in the helping profession are beginning to realize that these "invisible" (Bailey & Phariss, 1996, p. 39) students are becoming more visible each day through increased numbers of referrals to school counselors, school social workers, substance-abuse personnel, and various other support staff. Individual reasons for these referrals are diverse, but among the most common are efforts to clarify sexual orientation, anxiety, suicide attempts, substance abuse, low self-esteem, family conflict, and emotional isolation.

Baily and Phariss recommend (1) providing factual information about youth sexuality, (2) abandoning the myth that discussing homosexuality will cause young people to grow up to be gay or lesbian, (3) promoting and protecting the human and civil rights of all people in the classroom, and (4) encouraging the hiring of and supporting gay and lesbian educators who can provide healthy role models (Bailey & Phariss, 1996).

## Individual

Children's and adolescents' individual differences are yet another form of diversity that educators need to understand so that they may plan appropriate educational experiences. It is an equally serious mistake to assume too much cultural homogeneity among learners; one should not, for example, assume that all Hispanic learners are alike simply because they all speak Spanish. Likewise, there is great variety among African American learners according to socioeconomic background and geographic location.

For an objective and clear understanding of learners, educators should consider individual differences when they plan teaching and learning experiences: overall

---

**FOLLOW THROUGH 2-7     Determining Other Individual Differences**

We have looked at culture, race, ethnicity, gender, sexual orientation, and socioeconomic status—what might other "individual" differences be? What other forms of diversity might an elementary or secondary student bring to educational situations? Divide a sheet of paper into halves—on the left side list differences, and on the right, ways you might address these individual differences.

---

abilities, interests, intelligence, problem-solving abilities, critical-thinking skills, motivation, previous academic backgrounds, and the ability to use English or the language in which educators provide instruction. Likewise, it is important to consider intelligence and motivation from a cultural perspective—that is, perceptions of intelligence and motivation may vary from culture to culture. Educators should not view intelligence and motivation from only a middle-class white perspective.

Teachers may address individual differences in several ways: individualized instruction, cooperative learning, use of materials of varying levels of difficulty, the timed and untimed pacing of study, and changing the levels of learning, that is, mastery, understanding, and application.

## Socioeconomic Factors

Socioeconomic differences play a significant role in determining how a person acts, thinks, lives, and relates to others. Differences in values between students and educators basically represent social-class differences, because many minority group learners come from the lower socioeconomic classes. Educators coming from middle- or upper-class backgrounds may have difficulty understanding the social and economic problems facing children and adolescents from lower socioeconomic homes. Many educators are far removed from poor people's experience of poverty, low wages, lack of property, and indeed of the most basic needs. The accompanying differences in values, attitudes, behaviors, and beliefs among the various socioeconomic groups warrant the professional's consideration (Atkinson, Morten, & Sue, 1993).

Remember that a person's social class is sometimes thought to indicate his or her ambitions or motivation to achieve. It is a serious mistake, however, to stereotype people by social class—to assume, for example, that the lower classes lack ambition and do not want to work or improve their education status. It is not unreasonable to suggest that lower-class families, regardless of cultural background, want to improve their social status in life but meet with considerable frustration when faced with poverty and its accompanying conditions.

Social class differences in some cases may be more pronounced than differences resulting from cultural diversity. For example, lower-class African Americans may have more cultural commonalities with lower-class European Americans than they do with middle- or upper-class African Americans.

**TABLE 2-10   Percentages of People Entering and Exiting Poverty in the United States 1992–1993**

| Nonpoor persons in 1992 who *entered* poverty in 1993 | | Poor persons in 1992 who *exited* poverty in 1993 | |
|---|---|---|---|
| All persons | 3.0% | All persons | 21.6% |
| White | 2.6% | White | 25.7% |
| Black | 6.7% | Black | 13.2% |
| Hispanic | 8.6% | Hispanic | 18.4% |
| Under 18 | 4.0% | Under 18 | 17.7% |
| Married-couple families | 1.6% | Married-couple families | 28.6% |
| Other family types | 6.2% | Other family types | 12.2% |

*Source:* U.S. Bureau of the Census (1996, September). Almost half of the nation's chronic poor are children. *Census and You, 31*(9), 7. Washington, D.C.

Children made up almost half of the chronic poor in 1993. In fact, children were more likely than adults to remain poor in each month of a two-year period (U.S. Bureau of the Census, 1996, September). "Chronic" or long-term poverty means living consistently below the poverty line for two years. Table 2-10 shows the numbers of people *entering* and *exiting* poverty between 1992 and 1993.

## Challenges in a Culturally Diverse Society

Educators and other professionals need to examine their perspectives toward diversity and to determine if diversity appears as a "cultural deficit" (implying the need for change), a "cultural mismatch" (implying that learners from different cultural backgrounds fail because their traits are incompatible with schools' teaching practices), or as "culturally different" (implying that differences enrich the classroom and make individuals unique). This is more important than just an academic question; educators' perception of diversity determines their philosophical beliefs toward learners and toward their own instructional practices.

### The Cultural Deficit Model

In the cultural deficit model, students who are culturally different are thought of as "deprived," "disadvantaged," and "socially deprived" only because their behavior, language, and customs are different from those the middle class values. The notion that some cultures do not seek to advance themselves because of a cultural deficit results in "blaming the victim." The individual is at fault for not being more successful (educationally, socially, and so on). The cultural deficit model has failed to address the implicit cultural biases that shape negative perceptions and inhibit the understanding of the roles of sociopolitical forces (Draguns, 1989).

## *The Cultural Mismatch Model*

In contrast to the cultural deficit model, the cultural mismatch perspective assumes that cultures are inherently different but not necessarily superior or inferior to one another. It assumes that people from culturally different backgrounds fail to achieve academically because their cultural traits do not match those of the dominant culture reflected in schools. Thus, in the mismatch model, the educational performance of diverse groups is related to the degree of incongruence between group values and traits and those of the educational system: The better the match, the greater the likelihood of academic success. Efforts to improve the performance of students from culturally different backgrounds aim at increasing the congruence between the schools and the various cultures (Hernandez, 1989).

Case Study 2-2 examines one teacher's opinions about diversity and another teacher's attempts to provide a more positive perspective.

## *The Culturally Different Model*

The "culturally different" model recognizes differences as strengths that are valuable and enriching to schools and to society as a whole. Its proponents believe nonetheless that all children and adolescents need to learn mainstream cultural values and knowledge. Researchers have begun to establish a research base documenting that differences in learning styles and language are not deficiencies. The differences can be a foundation to facilitate learning.

---

**CASE STUDY 2-2   The Importance of Perspective**

Mrs. Williams overheard a conversation in the teacher's lounge: "Those minorities—I don't know what to do—are different and so difficult to change, so far behind, can't do so many things; they are just not suited for my classes." Mrs. Williams considered what she had heard and thought about what she had learned in a recent multicultural education course. This teacher is expressing the cultural deficit, or cultural mismatch model, she thought. Realizing such an attitude could hurt students' chances of learning, she decided to speak with this teacher about his attitudes about diversity.

Mrs. Williams met with the teacher and tried to make him aware of the dangers of harboring such perspectives. Believing that people must eliminate or change their differences reveals negative attitudes toward diversity—atti-tudes that undoubtedly affect feelings toward learners of differing cultural backgrounds. Likewise, expecting learners to change to meet the teacher's instructional strategies is in opposition to what is known about effective education. A student's achievement and behavior can also be affected by a teacher's expectations of poor performance and behavior. In reality, Mrs. Williams knew how hard it is to change such thinking toward diversity.

Mrs. Williams wondered how many other teachers in the school harbored such feelings toward cultural differences. She decided to design an informal assessment device to determine other teachers' perspectives and to ask the principal if it would be possible to arrange in-service activities designed to help teachers adopt appropriate perspectives toward diversity.

---

**FOLLOW THROUGH 2-8    Determining School Opinions toward Differences**

Visit an elementary or secondary school to learn about its educational philosophy, grouping practices, curricular and library materials, and extracurricular activities. Do you think the school's practices and policies indicate an acceptance of a cultural deficit, mismatch, or difference model? What are the implications of the model the school chooses?

---

A certain degree of cultural compatibility is necessary as teachers and students become increasingly aware of each others' cultural differences, whether differences relate to school or home expectations. The situation for children and adolescents might be even more acute than for teachers, especially because learners must switch from home to school cultures and vice versa. In any event, educators should not condemn learners for their language or culture, and they should encourage the students to retain and build on these differences, whenever possible (Sleeter & Grant, 1988).

## *Understanding and Reducing Racism*

Incidents of racism continue to plague U.S. society and, in some cases, appear to be increasing in number and severity. Evidence of racism fills the popular press and the news media: hate groups spread their opinions and literature, people are attacked solely because of cultural and racial heritage, and people are denied opportunities simply because their culture is different from the prevailing culture.

Eight common patterns of racism in schools include: hostile and insensitive acts toward others; bias in the use of punishment; bias in giving attention to students; bias in curriculum materials; inequality in the amount of instruction; bias in attitudes toward students; failure to employ educational professionals from various cultural backgrounds; and denial of racist acts (Murray & Clark, 1990).

Evidence (Duncan, 1993) suggests that other forms of racism occur during a typical school day. For example, if a student seeks a teacher's assistance, the request is usually a sign of motivation, an indication that the student wants to learn and perhaps even excel. If African American students seek help from a teacher, however, the teacher may perceive the request as an indication of African Americans' inability to learn or to cope with academic tasks. Hence, when such perceptions reinforce a general perception of African American children's low achievement, the teacher's expectations begin to limit the learning opportunities of these students. Equally damaging are perceptions of African and Latin American students that cause some educators to dilute curriculum and institute austere classroom management procedures (Duncan, 1993).

Racism also has the potential to attack children's developing sense of group membership as well as their individual and cultural identities. In fact, children are often more susceptible to racism's harm than are adults (Derman-Sparks, 1993/1994).

---

**FOLLOW THROUGH 2-9   Addressing Racism**

There is a serious need to address racism in all its forms: hostile and insensitive acts, bias in use of punishment, bias in giving attention, bias in curricular materials, and inequality in quality of instruction. Unfortunately, racism is a societal ill that will never be totally eliminated. It can, however, be reduced. List several forms of racism teachers might encounter and suggest ways to reduce this evil.

---

A Chinese American girl, for example, enrolled in a kindergarten. Her teacher, deciding her name was too difficult to pronounce, renamed her "Mary." Now that the child had an "American" name, it would be easier for the teacher to deal with her. But the teacher did not consider the effects on the child. The young girl asked, "What is wrong with my name? What was wrong with my parents to give me such a name?"

## *Understanding and Dispelling Stereotypes*

*Stereotyping* can be defined as holding attitudes toward a person or group that supposedly characterize or describe an entire group, gender, race, or religion. Stereotypes usually tend to emphasize differences between ourselves and other individuals or groups. They tend to be negative. Unfortunately, many people base their first impressions of others on stereotypes, which can result, conscious or unconscious, in negative attitudes and a lack of overall interpersonal understanding and communication.

Stereotyping can have at least two negative results. First, an over general perception of people usually results in a judgmental negative or positive image of people or their entire culture. Second, stereotypes have the potential to influence educators' professional decisions about students. When teachers use stereotypes to group students, to prescribe their course of study, and to help them plan their extracurricular activities, they do individuals a disservice. For example, when educators or counselors use culture or gender as the basis to advise students—some to join the chess club and others to a study block, some to play on the basketball team and others on the tennis team, and some to take literature instead of mathematics and science subjects—educators might be basing educational decisions on stereotypes. Students need careful and thoughtful guidance; decisions about them need to be based on accurate and objective information, not stereotypical generalizations about their culture and gender.

The dangers of stereotyping learners are all too clear: educators do students a terrible misservice when they use stereotypes to conclude that African American learners misbehave and are slow learners; that Asian Americans are all high-ability learners and that all are "bright and motivated"; that Hispanic Americans have reading and behavior problems. Although we mention stereotyping here only briefly, Chapters 3, 4, 5, 6, and 7 on children and adolescents have sections on the respective cultures.

---

**FOLLOW THROUGH 2-10  Promoting Cultural Identities**

All people, whatever their cultural background, need to have a positive cultural identity—they need to understand and appreciate their cultural heritages. List six to eight
ways you can help children and adolescents have a positive cultural identity.

---

## Helping Learners Develop Positive Cultural Identities

Among the significant challenges educators face daily is the fact that children and
adolescents are constantly developing perceptions of their individual and cultural
identities. Learners' perceptions of cultural differences and their opinions of others' perceptions play significant roles in their degree of self-worth and self-image.
For example, a student who comes from a different culture and a lower socioeconomic level than the teacher may, indeed, understandably consider "differences"
as inferior or wrong. Perceptive educators recognize the disastrous consequences
such feelings can have on learners' sense of personal worth.

Educators can help learners from majority and from culturally different backgrounds as well to understand "culture," recognize how culture affects peoples'
lives, and understand that one cannot readily place values on culture. Likewise,
educators can work toward providing all children and adolescents with accurate
and objective materials and lead discussions of culture and cultural differences
that lay to rest as many myths, distortions, and stereotypes as possible.

## Summing Up

Educators who wish to plan an appropriate response to our nation's cultural diversity and to provide effective multicultural education programs should:

**1.** Understand the melting pot ideology and the more realistic contemporary perspectives toward cultural diversity.

**2.** Understand that cultural differences have value and are enriching to the
United States.

**3.** Understand terms such as *culture, ethnicity, race, social class,* and *gender.*

**4.** Address and stand against racism in all forms, regardless of the victim's cultural and racial backgrounds.

**5.** Form a perspective on culture and cultural diversity that perceives differences
as "positives" rather than disadvantages that must be eliminated.

## Suggested Learning Activities

**1.** Suggest several methods of helping children and adolescents develop positive individual and cultural identities. What would be your response to an educator who stated,
"My work is teaching content—improving cultural identities is not my job!"

2. Give at least four examples of racist acts and offer a solution (a difficult task indeed) to each racist act. To what extent should reducing racism be a role of the school?

3. Name four or five stereotypical images of Native, African, Asian, Hispanic, or European American children or adolescents. Suggest how such images may have originated and how schools can provide appropriate responses.

## Suggestions for Collaborative Efforts

Form groups of three or four that, if possible, represent our nation's cultural and gender diversity. Working collaboratively, focus your group's attention toward the following efforts:

1. Survey a number of elementary, middle, or secondary schools to determine the cultural composition of the student body. What has been the school's response to meeting the needs of students' cultural differences? What efforts has the school made to teach majority cultures about minority cultures and vice versa?

2. Increasingly, gender and gender differences are important topics in multicultural education programs. Does your group feel gender should be a minor or major emphasis in multicultural education programs? Does your group feel that there is a "culture of gender" or that there is an overemphasis of gender differences? What role should educators play (or not play) in making gender an integral component of multicultural education programs?

3. How inclusive should multicultural education be? Originally, the idea prevailed that the term *multicultural education* included only culture, ethnicity, and race. Now, it has been expanded to include cultures of gender, sexual orientation, and ability/disability. How inclusive does your group think multiculturalism should be? Have scholars taken the "inclusiveness" idea too far? Or do we need to make "multiculturalism" even more inclusive?

## Expanding Your Horizons: Additional Journal Readings and Books

Banks, J. A. (1998). The lives and values of researchers: Implications for educating citizens in a multicultural society. *Educational Researcher, 27*(7), 4–17.

*Banks, a noted expert in multicultural education, describes a number of cross-cultural researchers and focuses on the lives of social scientists whose work has helped marginalized communities and whose ideas embrace democratic values.*

Evans, K. M. (1997). Multicultural training needs for counselors of gifted African American children. *Multicultural Education 5*(1), 16–19.

*Evans looks at counselors' lack of training and proposes steps toward effective training.*

Lawrence, V. J. (1997). Multiculturalism, diversity, cultural pluralism . . . "Tell the whole truth, and nothing but the truth." *Journal of Black Studies, 27*(3), 318–333.

*Lawrence argues that a multicultural curriculum will result in diversity flowing from knowledge.*

Lewis, B. (1998). The historical roots of racism. *The American Scholar, 67*(1), 17–25.

*In this excellent article, Lewis traces the roots of racism and explains its effects on people of all races.*

Lind, M. (1998, August 16). The beige and the black. *The New York Times Magazine,* 38–39.

*In this interesting article, Lind questions whether whites will eventually become a minority in the twenty-first century and theorizes about the replacement of the historical white–black dichotomy in America with a new one between beige and black.*

Manning, M. L. (1996). Addressing the fears of diversity. *Kappa Delta Pi Record 33,* 4–7.

*As the title implies, this article examines our nation's diversity and offers ways to lessen fears associated with others' differences.*

## Answers to the Culture Quiz: Knowledge of Cultures

**1.** c

**2.** b (Dr. Martin Luther King)

**3.** d

**4.** e

**5.** b (Dr. Charles Drew)

**6.** a

**7.** c (Dr. An Wang)

**8.** a

**9.** b (Ida B. Wells-Barnett)

**10.** c

**11.** a, b, c, d, e

**12.** e

**13.** a, b, c, d, e

**14.** d

*P a r t*  *II*

# *Understanding Learners and Their Cultural Backgrounds*

Part II includes Chapters 3, 4, 5, 6, and 7 and provides a portrait of children and adolescents in the African, Asian, European, Hispanic, and Native American cultures. To understand, accept, and respect learners from all cultural backgrounds is of primary importance, as is to provide them with culturally relevant educational experiences.

# Understanding African American Children and Adolescents

Understanding the material and activities in this chapter will help the reader to:

- Describe the cultural, gender, socioeconomic, familial, and language characteristics of African American children and adolescents.

- List several stereotypes of African American children and adolescents, and explain how these beliefs affect curriculum and school practices.

- Describe the educational achievement of African American children and adolescents and be able to explain the importance of self-esteem to learning achievement.

- Understand African American English dialect as a valued cultural trait, and be able to explain its importance to achievement in school and development of self-esteem.

- Explain the importance of understanding learning styles and the uniqueness of African American learning styles.

- List several points educators should remember when planning educational experiences for African American children and adolescents.

- Incorporate practical activities, suggest appropriate children's literature, implement research findings, and respond appropriately in school situations involving African American learners.

## Overview

A responsive multicultural curriculum recognizes the cultural diversity of African American children and adolescents and provides appropriate educational experiences based on an understanding of both the individual and the culture. The culture of African American children and adolescents as well as socioeconomic class, family, and language play significant roles and interact in a complex fashion to create unique learners with individual strengths and needs. Providing appropriate teaching and learning experiences for African American learners requires an understanding of the individual's development, learning styles, achievement levels, and self-esteem. This chapter examines African American children and adolescents and explores educational issues germane to these learners.

## Origins

African American people have lived in United States for many centuries. Arriving in North America either as explorers or slaves, African American people have experienced a long history of struggle. The first Africans in the Americas were explorers: Columbus's last voyage to the Americas included an African man, Balboa's crew brought an African man, and an African explored the territory that is now Kansas with Coronado. Africans were among the first nonnative settlers. African people were part of the ill-fated South Carolina colony, San Miguel de Guadalupe, in 1526; and African people helped to establish Saint Augustine, Florida, in 1665.

Slave traders brought other Africans to this continent on slave ships in which they endured degrading and dehumanizing conditions. On completing the long and arduous trip, Africans were put to work as slaves on large plantations, which specialized in growing tobacco and cotton (Banks, 1987). One important distinction deserves understanding: Many multicultural groups elected to immigrate to the United States in hopes of improving their lives, to seek religious freedom, or

---

**USING CHILDREN'S LITERATURE    Understanding Slavery and Racism**

These Newbery Award–winners offer an excellent representation of slavery and racism.

Armstrong, William. *Sounder.* Delacorte, 1983. This story describes the racism and prejudice a black sharecropper and his family experience. (Reading Level: 6; Interest Level: Ages 10 and above.)

Fox, Paula. *The Slave Dancer.* Bradbury, 1973. A young boy plays the fife on a slave ship. (Reading Level: 7; Interest Level: 12 and above.)

Taylor, Mildred D. *Roll of Thunder, Hear My Cry.* Dial, 1976. A black family in 1933 Mississippi experiences humiliating experiences yet retains its pride. (Reading Level: 6; Interest Level: 10 and above.)

**THE CULTURE QUIZ**   **African Americans**

*Directions:* Match the individuals with their contributions or achievements by placing the appropriate letter before each name.

| | |
|---|---|
| _____ **1.** Rosa Parks | **a.** Determined woman who drove a stagecoach and delivered the mail in the Old West |
| _____ **2.** Thomas Bradley | **b.** Confirmed as the first African American to hold nation's top military post |
| _____ **3.** Martin Luther King, Jr. | |
| _____ **4.** Thurgood Marshall | **c.** First African American mayor of Los Angeles |
| _____ **5.** Matthew Henson | **d.** Congresswoman from Texas, first African American woman from a southern state to serve in Congress |
| _____ **6.** Guion S. Bluefield | |
| _____ **7.** Alice Walker | **e.** Author of Pulitzer Prize–winning book *The Color Purple* |
| _____ **8.** Barbara Jordan | **f.** Syndicated columnist |
| _____ **9.** Colin Powell | **g.** Former president of Morehouse College; civil rights leader, minister, and educator |
| _____ **10.** Mary Fields | |
| _____ **11.** Benjamin Mays | **h.** First African American astronaut to travel in space |
| _____ **12.** Carl Rowan | **i.** First man to stand atop the world in 1909 when he reached the North Pole |
| | **j.** Woman who refused to move to the back of the bus in Montgomery, Alabama |
| | **k.** First African American associate justice of the Supreme Court of the United States |
| | **l.** Speaker who addressed 200,000 civil rights demonstrators in Washington, D.C. in 1963 |

(Answers to the Culture Quiz are located at the end of the chapter.)

to get away from oppressive conditions or war-torn areas. Most Africans, on the other hand, were transported against their will to a foreign land and forced to work and live in cruel and inhumane conditions.

## African Americans Today

African Americans presently constitute the largest U.S. ethnic minority group. The latest annual population estimates (1993) indicate that African Americans total nearly 30 million or 13 percent of the nation's population. The African American population has been growing at a faster rate than the total population. About one-third of the African American population in 1990 was under eighteen years old. Most African Americans live in metropolitan areas, but the number of suburban African Americans grew by 29 percent between 1980 and 1990, and today stands at about 7 percent of the U.S. suburban population. Educators in city schools work

---

**USING CHILDREN'S LITERATURE    Nonfiction Books about the African American Experience**

Patterson, Lillie. *Frederick Douglass: Freedom Fighter.* Garrand, 1965. The story of Douglass's life in slavery, protest against slavery, escape from slave owners and slave hunters, and his championing of the rights of all people. (Reading Level: Grade 3; Interest Level: Age 8 and above.)

Dekay, James T. *Meet Martin Luther King.* Random House, 1969. Dekay stresses King's tremendous work and his reasons for fighting against injustice and prejudice. (Reading Level: Grade 4; Interest Level: Ages 7–12.)

---

with significant numbers of African Americans, but educators in suburban schools will increasingly work with African Americans as more and more move away from the inner city.

The African American population in 1990 exceeded one million in each of sixteen states and two million in each of three states—New York, California, and Texas. Other states with significant African American populations (one million or more) include Florida, Georgia, Illinois, North Carolina, Louisiana, Michigan, and Maryland (U.S. Bureau of the Census, September 1993b).

Decades after the civil rights movement forced the United States to confront racial inequities, disturbing disparities remain on one of the most basic human levels: Blacks get sick more easily, stay sick longer, and die sooner than whites. From birth, a black baby's life expectancy is six and one-half years shorter than a white baby's. Blacks are more likely to be born weighing too little and less likely to survive their first year. Blacks face a higher risk of asthma, hypertension, cancer. They are nearly twice as likely as whites to die of a stroke, 40 percent more likely to die of heart disease, and they face a 35 percent higher cancer rate than whites.

Blacks are more than twice as likely to be without health insurance. People cite many reasons for blacks' health predicament: Blacks face extra stresses living in a racist society, blacks have an unhealthy diet (it can be difficult to find fresh vegetables and produce in many inner-city grocery stores), and blacks often mistrust doctors and other health care providers; only 63 percent of blacks say they trust the medical profession (Blacks are slipping through the health gap, 1998).

African Americans have not shared equally in the nation's prosperity. They earn less than whites, and they possess far less wealth. The black-to-white median income ratio has hovered in the mid-50 to mid-60 percentage range for the past 20 years. Fluctuations have been minor. In some respects, the United States has grown accustomed to this benchmark of inequality. In fact, for every dollar whites earn, African American households earn 62 cents (Oliver & Shapiro, 1998).

The loss of community has hit poor and African American people hard. The decline of manufacturing has dried up the pool of well-paid jobs for the unskilled. Racial discrimination prevails in both hiring and housing, and the value of income supports is decreasing. The often inferior and overwhelmed schools and public services, the flight of the middle class to the suburbs, the easy availability of drugs: All have contributed to inner-city problems and unhealthy human development (Schorr, 1998).

## *Stereotyping of African American Children and Adolescents*

To be a child or adolescent as well as an African American in a predominantly European American society is to bear a double stigma. Stereotyping has produced negative images of the African American culture and its young people. Youth is the time of identity formation, for this reason it is especially important that everyone objectively accept social, cultural, and age differences among young people. Young African Americans need fair opportunities to develop identities appropriate for their culture and age. Categorizing African American young people as language-deficient because they speak dialectical English or as low achievers and behavior problems negates diversity and individual differences. Educators must take a closer and more objective look at the child and the adolescent in the African American culture to improve their understanding of the learner and the world in which she or he lives. Such knowledge and understanding gives educators an objective and sound foundation for a multicultural curriculum.

Case Study 3-1 shows the detrimental effects of stereotypical statements.

---

**CASE STUDY 3-1   Dealing with Stereotypical Situations**

Mrs. Lewis overhears someone at the grocery store say, "African American students have ruined that school. Their achievement is low. They speak a language nobody can understand. They are always misbehaving. That school has gone to the dogs. It used to be such a nice school, too."

If Mrs. Lewis directly confronts the person in the grocery store, she will probably be unsuccessful. She can, however, politely tell the person of the school's many accomplishments.

What can you do? Perhaps you could launch a communitywide campaign to change the school's image. Make public the school's accomplishments, encourage the school's young people to take an active role in the community, and encourage business leaders to take a greater role in schools and to publicize successful efforts.

Even though such efforts may improve the school's image, stereotypical statements are nonetheless a serious problem. These problems require people to have more objectivity toward and acceptance of differing cultures, as well as to make a larger-scale effort and change of attitude.

---

**FOLLOW THROUGH 3-1   Appreciating African American Contributions**

Make a list of historical and contemporary African Americans who have contributed to their culture and to the United States. Include such leaders of the past as George Washington Carver and Frederick Douglass and contemporary African Americans such as Jesse Jackson and Colin Powell. List their achievements and the ways their actions have contributed to the betterment of all cultures.

**TABLE 3-1**   **Selected Characteristics of African American Children and Adolescents**

| Category | Characteristics |
| --- | --- |
| Behavioral/emotional expressiveness | High-context, rely on nonverbals |
| Verbal | Affective, emotional, interpersonal |
| Nonverbal | Preference for closer space; importance placed on nonverbal behavior |
| Concept of time | Oriented more to situation than to concrete, tangible, and immediate goals |
| Social orientation | Sense of "peoplehood" and collective concern |

*Developed from:* Rivera, B. D. & Rogers-Adkinson, D. (1997). Culturally sensitive interventions: Social skills training with children and parents from culturally and linguistically diverse backgrounds. *Intervention in School and Clinic, 33*(2), 75–80.

## *Cultural Characteristics*

African American children and adolescents are considerably diverse (Table 3-1). Differences exist between lower, middle, and higher socioeconomic groups, between younger and older generations, between African Americans residing in the various geographic locations of the United States, and between urban and rural African Americans.

An educator who understands this diversity among African American children and adolescents can make a valuable contribution to the multicultural curriculum, and base choices on objective and factual information.

African American children daily face two cultures: The African American culture of the home and neighborhood and the European American culture of schools and other social institutions. African American children and children from other cultures need opportunities to learn about one another's cultures and to understand that "different" does not imply "wrong."

Education has focused for many years solely on historical and contemporary whites. Educators sometimes justifiably complain that their education did not pro-

---

**FOLLOW THROUGH 3-2**   **Identifying Cultural Differences**

Make a list of cultural differences between African and European Americans. Then, keeping in mind the characteristics you listed, make another list of social class differences. How are the cultures alike and different? Are the social-class differences more alike or different between the two groups? Are African and European American members of the same social class more alike than African American members of differing social classes?

vide them with examples of the contributions of African Americans. During the past several decades, attempts to instill pride and a better understanding of the African American culture have given rise to learning materials that emphasize the many positive aspects and leaders of the culture.

Although educators should make cultural generalizations cautiously, African Americans *tend* to have large families and respect for immediate and extended families. They also *tend* to have a nonverbal communication style that differs from that of the European American culture (for example, an African American feels comfortable interrupting a speaker to show support and does not find it necessary to look the speaker in the eye). African American children are generally highly expressive emotionally, assertive, and verbal in dealings with peers and adults (Rotheram-Borus & Phinney, 1990). African American children and adolescents are taught respect for the elderly, kinship and extended family bonds, and authoritarian childrearing practices. Once again, we remind readers that individuals within a culture differ and that cultural characteristics vary with socioeconomic class and geographic region.

Urban life for African American males can be difficult as Implementing Research 3-1 on page 66 shows.

A difficult situation exists when African Americans want to retain their cultural heritage, the culture of their ancestors, and the culture with which they can relate and feel comfortable. Some African Americans, however, may also feel that some acculturation with the European Americans is necessary for economic and

---

**USING CHILDREN'S LITERATURE   The African American Experience in Children's Books**

Keats, Ezra Jack. *The Snowy Day.* Viking, 1962. Keats captures the mood of the African American experience in this book. Illustrated with collage. (Reading Level: Grade 2; Interest Level: Ages 2–7.)

Steptoe, John. *Stevie.* Harper & Row, 1969. Robert is unhappy when Stevie wants to play with his toys. (Reading Level: Grades 3–7; Interest Level: Ages 2–8.)

Hamilton, Virginia. *Zeely.* Macmillan, 1967. Geeder is convinced that her neighbor is a Watusi queen. (Reading Level: Grade 4; Interest Level: Ages 7–12.)

---

**USING CHILDREN'S LITERATURE   Contributions of African Americans to the Fine Arts**

Byran, Ashley. *I'm Going to Sing: Black American Spirituals,* vol. 2. Atheneum, 1982. This book includes words and music that help African American children understand their heritage. (Interest Level: All ages.)

Haskins, James. *Black Theater in America.* Crowell, 1982. This text traces the contributions of African Americans from minstrel shows through contemporary protest plays. (Reading Level: 7; Interest Level: Age 9 and above.)

psychological survival. It is important to attain a middle ground on which African American adolescents can not only retain their African heritage but also feel successful in contemporary society.

---

**IMPLEMENTING RESEARCH 3-1   African American Urban Males**

An article by Jackie Boddie spells out the dilemma of the African American urban male. From a young age, many African American males learn attitudes of low self-appraisal and low expectations and sometime by the third grade, perceive themselves as having only a marginal relationship to U.S. mainstream culture. To make matters worse, their families often are unable to provide for them materially and give them the emotional sustenance they need to develop self-esteem and to achieve academically.

African American urban adolescents face barriers to learning and achievement; they often stop trying to relate to teachers, and many lack a positive vision of their future. Failure reaches epidemic proportions and then adolescents are perceived as alienated and uneducable.

Boddie tells of a Washington, D.C., school that designed a ninth-grade program to address the needs of African American urban males and to help them respond positively in classrooms. The school's directions included establishing an environment of interpersonal care that responded to adolescents' psychosocial needs; providing a reward system that dignified students' efforts and incremental successes; and making a conscientious effort to replace the "acting white" (p. 53) dynamic in student thinking with an identity affirming them as successful black learners. The program introduced role models in the community, in public office, in literature, and in history; involved parents and families in the adolescents' education (such as holding them accountable for participation as advocates of their children's school success); and eliminated the school culture of intimidating messages and barriers.

**Implementing the Research**

1. Educators working with African American urban males should be carefully selected to determine their motivation and academic preparation, as well as their understanding of diversity, especially among African American male adolescents in urban settings.
2. Educators need to understand how African American urban males' "acting white" can invite ridicule by peers and result in loss of peer relationships. Perspectives other than traditional white middle-class ones need to be employed with African American males.
3. Educators need to involve parents and families (and whenever possible, various community members) in educative efforts, so urban males will not see efforts as being exclusively "in-school." They need support outside the school walls as well.
4. Elementary and middle-school educators should try to identify urban males headed for trouble. They should undertake preventative efforts in an attempt to avoid serious problems during the secondary school years.

---

*Source:* Boddie, J. L. (1997). Making the grade in high school: African American urban males. *The High School Magazine, 5*(2), 50–55.

**FOLLOW THROUGH 3-3   Helping African American Urban Males**

Design a strategy to help African American urban boys in either elementary or secondary schools. First, decide on a method of determining their needs (either a case study, some diagnostic device, interviews, or observation); second, select instructional methods that reflect their learning styles; third, select curricular materials to which they can relate; fourth, select culturally appropriate assessment devices; and fifth, decide what other guidance or advising topics might address their needs. In addition to these five approaches, what else might you suggest to help African American urban boys?

## Gender

The recent emphasis on gender differences and gender-appropriate education suggests educators should consider African American females and males from different perspectives. Undoubtedly, educators need to consider females' different learning styles, perceptions of motivation, and ways of responding to educators' efforts. Females, however, may need to give special attention to socially acceptable behaviors such as modulating their voices, proper grooming, and developing assertive demeanors (Young, 1994). Such a proposal does not suggest African American males (as well as males from other cultures) do not need educational experiences in similar areas; when addressing these points, however, educators need to consider the female perspective.

Gender Perspectives 3-1 looks at African American high school students' strategies of success.

Teachers also should consider gender differences when planning actual educational experiences for African American females. For example, African American

**GENDER PERSPECTIVES 3-1   Gender and African American High School Students' Success Strategies**

Hubbard analyzed the academic success of female and male African American high school students in the Advancement via Determination (AVID) program, a high school program that places low-achieving, low-income minority students in a special class that offers academic and social support. The study concluded that most of the students went on to college but found that the strategies they used and the attitudes they developed toward going to college differed across gender lines. Hubbard's research also reported the importance of considering academic success as a product of race, class, and gender. The social relationships in the homes and communities of these young people transmit a specific set of messages that are unique to their gender and in response to anticipated roles they will face in the African American home.

*Source:* Hubbard, L. (1997). A gendered look at the academic achievement of low-income African American high school students: Strategies of success. (ERIC Document Reproduction Service No: ED 414 287).

---

**FOR ADDITIONAL INFORMATION**

National Black Child Development Institute, 1463 Rhode Island Ave. NW, Washington, D.C. 20005. This organization is dedicated to improving the quality of life for African American children and youth, and focuses on issues such as health, child welfare, education, and child care.

Minority Caucus of Family Services America, 34 Beacon Street, Boston, MA 02108. This organization participates in policy-making groups and works toward the needs of minority families.

National Black Youth Leadership Council, 250 W. 54th Street, Suite 800, New York, NY 10019. This council provides training and motivation workshops, resources, information, skills, and strategies for fostering leadership development.

---

females might learn better through cooperative efforts rather than in competitive atmospheres. Also, they might benefit more from behavior management systems promoting positive consequences rather than negative ones. Positive environments also contribute to African American females' academic achievement and social development.

## Socioeconomic Status

Within a complex society, social class and ethnicity are two major sociologic structures that produce diversity in human lifestyle and development (Hale-Benson, 1986). Six determinants provide indications of socioeconomic status: income, wealth, occupation, education, prestige, and power (Gollnick & Chinn, 1998). The discrimination African American people experience has resulted in a lack of educational and employment opportunities and has prohibited significant social mobility.

---

**USING CHILDREN'S LITERATURE    Families in African American Children's Books**

Flournoy, Valerie. *The Patchwork Quilt*. Dial, 1985. This is the story of a grandmother's and a granddaughter's developing relationship while constructing a quilt. (Reading Level: Grade 4; Interest Level: Ages 5–10.)

Greenfield, Eloise. *She Come Bringing Me That Little Baby Girl*. Lippincott, 1974. Kevin dislikes all the attention his new baby sister receives. The book shows changing emotions in a warm, loving story. (Reading Level: Grade 3; Interest Level: Ages 6–9.)

Mathias, Sharon Bell. *The Hundred Penny Box*. Viking, 1975. This story focuses on the life and love of great-great-Aunt Dew, an aged African American woman, and Michael, a young boy. (Reading Level: Grade 3; Interest Level: Ages 6–10.)

Yarbrough, Camille. *Cornrows*. Putnam, 1979. An African American great-grandmother braids a young girl's hair and relates the history of her people. (Reading Level: Grade 3; Interest Level: Ages 6–10.)

Because they have long been deprived of equal opportunities and the chance to improve themselves educationally and economically, African American people find themselves disproportionately represented in the lower socioeconomic classes.

Socioeconomic class continues to be a powerful indicator of academic success for American children. Children from higher socioeconomic status (SES) backgrounds score higher on standardized achievement tests, are more likely to finish high school, and are more likely to attend college and do postgraduate work than their less advantaged peers. Because poor children are less likely to pursue higher education, it is difficult to break them out of the cycle of poverty. The relationship between poverty and academic achievement is complicated by ethnicity; a disproportionate number of the poor are members of ethnic minority groups whose long history as victims of discrimination has impeded their chances of academic and material success (Halle, Kurtz-Costes, & Mahoney, 1997).

The odds that African Americans will encounter obstacles to academic success are high. African American children are three times more likely to live in poverty than are white children in the United States. Significant numbers of low-income African American children get off to a bad start, lag behind in the early elementary years, and are twice as likely to drop out of school than their more advantaged white peers. These distressing disparities exist despite a long-standing commitment among African Americans to the belief that education can eliminate poverty and eventually end racial discrimination.

Not that many African American success stories don't exist; many disadvantaged parents—of minority as well as majority cultural groups—are successful in translating their high academic aspirations for their children into reality. Along this line of thinking, it should be noted although some economic hardships and social discrimination provide difficult obstacles to overcome, parents' behaviors, beliefs, attitudes, and goals may circumvent the detrimental effects of poverty (Halle, Kurtz-Costes, & Mahoney, 1997).

When working with African American learners, elementary and secondary educators should:

1. Understand the effects of being a member of a lower socioeconomic group.
2. Understand that children from lower socioeconomic groups might not understand words like *physician, lavatory, wraps,* and *pens* (pens for writing versus pens for confining animals).
3. Understand that language differences are "differences"—not "deficits."
4. Understand the need to work first on concrete learning and then move on to abstract learning.
5. Understand the need to provide positive reinforcement during the learning process, rather than expecting learners to stay motivated by focusing on some faraway goal.
6. Understand the need to involve parents and extended families in the learning process.
7. Understand each learner's individual strengths and needs, and plan teaching and learning experiences that always challenge and instruct.

---

**FOLLOW THROUGH 3-4    Addressing Poverty's Effects**

Although educators can do little to alleviate the poverty and poor socioeconomic conditions of students, what might schools do to address the needs of these students? How might educators better understand the effects of poverty? How can they understand these students and their mindsets toward long-term goals and success?

---

Many African American children today live in a desolate world where physical survival is a daily struggle, where fear and hopelessness frame everyday occurrences, and where the future seems to hold little hope. African American children need to be at the front of the line for attention, where they can receive adequate nutrition, health care, and education. (Edelman, 1989).

The future, however, looks brighter for African American children. Today African Americans have more equality of opportunity, better access to education, and more equitable salaries than they did in the 1960s. Through civil rights legislation, affirmative action programs, and equal employment opportunity, African Americans are able to obtain an education and seek employment. Such gains will result in improved conditions for children. The problem of poverty, however, continues for many people and requires the attention of government, school, and other organizations concerned with the welfare of children.

## *Families*

Educators who work with African American learners need a historical understanding of and perspective on the African American family. To gain such knowledge might prove difficult, because U.S. scholarship has mistreated, ignored, and distorted the African American family. Often, the misconceptions of majority-culture educators may cause them to question African American cultural traditions. Throughout centuries of cultural oppression and repression, for example, African Americans have developed, perhaps as much through necessity as choice, a network of "significant others" who have close ties to and are willing to assist the individual family. Understanding and accepting this African American family tradition continues to be a prerequisite for educators to help students make effective educational decisions.

America had 8.1 million African American families in 1996. Of these, 3.7 million (46 percent) were married-couple families; 3.8 million (47 percent) were families maintained by women (no spouse present). Forty-two percent of African American families had two or more wage earners; about 57 percent had children under 18. Heads of household in African American families were younger than householders of other ethnic backgrounds. Almost 60 percent were younger than 45 years old; only 22 percent were 55 or over. African American families had a real median income of $25,970 in 1995. Married-couple families had a real median of $41,750. Women who maintained households without a spouse present had a real median income of $15,500. Fifty-six percent of all African American families lived

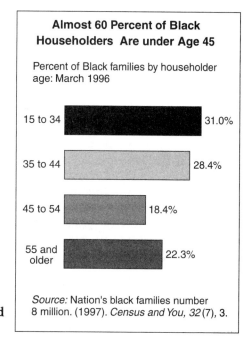

**Almost 60 Percent of Black Householders Are under Age 45**

Percent of Black families by householder age: March 1996

| | |
|---|---|
| 15 to 34 | 31.0% |
| 35 to 44 | 28.4% |
| 45 to 54 | 18.4% |
| 55 and older | 22.3% |

*Source:* Nation's black families number 8 million. (1997). *Census and You, 32*(7), 3.

**FIGURE 3-1    African American Families Categorized by the Age of the Head of Household**

in the South. Figure 3-1 shows the percentage of African American families by householder by age in 1996 (*Nation's black families number 8 million,* 1997).

African American children grow up in homes that are very different from the homes of European American children and adolescents. Minority extended families function on the principles of interdependence and an extensive reliance on networks of people including blood relatives and close friends called kinsmen. A young African American child might be taken into the household of elderly grandparents. In such arrangements children have a sense they belong to an extended family clan, not merely to their parents. Uncles, aunts, cousins, and grandparents have considerable power within the family unit and may take responsibility for the care and rearing of children and for teaching appropriate skills and values.

These strong kinship bonds probably originated from two guiding principles of the African ethos: the survival of the tribe and the oneness of being. Children see early that their families develop a kinship in the African American community

---

**FOLLOW THROUGH 3-5    Interviewing African American Families**

Interview several African American families (maybe you can include extended-family members, too) to determine their expectations of the schools. What do they want for their children? What questions do they have? What do they feel good about? What are their frustrations? On the basis of this information, suggest ways the schools can become more responsive to the educational needs and expectations of African American families?

and that African Americans refer to each other as "sister," "brother," "cousin," "blood brother," or "homeboy" to imply a family closeness even where actual kinship does not exist (Hale-Benson, 1986, p. 49).

Implementing Research 3-2 looks at African American families from a historical perspective and urges readers to consider African Americans' heterogeneity.

## Religion

Religion is a powerful aspect of the African American family orientation that has almost never had empirical documentation. Rather than study the church and religion in relation to children, writers usually focus attention on the role of religion in the civil rights movement, economic leadership, and the quest for equal op-

---

**IMPLEMENTING RESEARCH 3-2    African American Families**

Vivian J. Carroll McCollum (1997) maintains that both internal and such external factors as cultural history, values, sociopolitical conditions, the social environment, and economic conditions help to determine the personality of the African American family. She examines the African American family from a historical perspective: Before slavery the father was the head of the family and a strong provider. The family faced problems, but they maintained their own language, culture, traditions, and values, all of which made them better prepared to deal with those problems.

African American families today should be understood in terms of their heterogeneity, communication styles (including gestures and nonverbal clues), and gender roles. Just as in other cultures, family types include single-parent, two-parent, and extended. Several general themes underlie the diversity of African Americans such as strong kinship bonds; strong work, education, and achievement orientation; high levels of flexibility in family roles; and strong commitment to religious values and church participation. African Americans are found in every socioeconomic group and geographic area of the United States.

**Implementing the Research**

1.  It is essential that educators of children and adolescents recognize the heterogeneity of African American families. Educators cannot assume that all African American families are poor and headed by single mothers.
2.  Educators should know what it means historically and presently to be African American in the United States.
3.  Educators, especially during parent–teacher conferences, as well as in other forms of communication, need to understand the dangers of ineffective communication. Educators must have a good enough understanding of how African Americans communicate that they can communicate effectively with children and parents.

---

*Source:* McCollum, V. J. C. (1997) Evolution of African American family personality: Considerations for family therapy. *Journal of Multicultural Counseling and Development 25*, 219–229.

portunity. Children, however, undoubtedly perceive the African American church as a socializing and peer-group institution, a hub of social life, and a means to aspire to community leadership. Rather than simply a Sunday-morning experience, church membership for children is an integral aspect of African American family life (Hale-Benson, 1986).

The most rapidly growing religion in the United States is Islam. In 1960, there were no mosques in this country; in 1998, there were over 1,000. Muslims are a rapidly increasing part of the American religious scene. The United States needs to appreciate the gifts—their culture, their music, their food, and their philosophy—they bring to U.S. society. It is in the schools that people first start adapting to Muslim cultures and Muslims begin adapting to other U.S. cultures (Hodgkinson, 1998).

## Language

African Americans have a rich oral tradition. Verbal skill is highly valued in the African American community and brings recognition to those who have it. Its roots are in African verbal art.

Aspects of African American oral tradition are observable in African American student behavior. In telling stories, African Americans render abstract observations about life, love, and people in the form of concrete narrative sequences that may seem to meander from the point and to take on an episodic framework. In African American communication styles, we often find overt demonstration of sympathetic involvement through movement and sounds; a prescribed method for how performer and audience react; total involvement of the participants, the tendency to personalize by incorporating personal pronouns and references to self (African American students tend to use first-person singular pronouns to focus attention on themselves); and use of active verbs coupled with adjectives and adverbs with potential for intensification (called features of elongation and variable stress). Prosodic structure of speech often reflects the way information is organized for presentation. All of those observable aspects of the African American communication style provide leads for teaching innovations (Anokye, 1997).

Educators can benefit from objective and reliable information about African American language. Although the child may not experience difficulty at home or in the neighborhood, language differences may cause problems when the child gets to school. The dilemma for African American children is that their language, which is "worthy" at home, may be "different" and unworthy in school.

Considerable diversity exists in the degree to which children speak an English dialect. Dialect use varies with socioeconomic class, geographic location, and the acculturation of the child and the parents. Children of educated and socially mobile urban African American parents may not speak the dialect of rural and less fortunate parents. African American English is used in varying degrees depending on the individual and the situation.

African Americans have developed effective nonverbal communication that other cultures may question. For example, African American children may learn

---

**FOR ADDITIONAL INFORMATION    Internet Addresses**

**MEL: Multicultural & ESL Resources**
http://mel.lib.mi.us/education/edu-mc.esl.
html    Provides information and resources for
teaching African Americans (and about African Americans).

**The Faces of Science: African Americans in
the Sciences**
http://www.lib.lsu.edu/lib/chem/display/
faces.html    Provides information on African
Americans who have made significant contributions in the field of science.

**Black Americans of Achievement Inside**
http://www.baoa.com/index.html    Provides
a look at one of the few traded companies that
is owned and operated by African Americans.

**The Black People of America's First Official
National Flag**
http://www.blacknationalflag.com/    Provides information on African American struggles across the world and that the U.S. flag deals
only with the colonial experience.

**Black Americans for Life**
http://www.nrcl.org/outreach/bal.html    Provides information on the problems African
Americans face and ways this organization tries
to help.

---

early that active listening does not always require looking the speaker in the eye.
Neither is it necessary to nod one's head or make little noises to show that one is
listening.

The language of African American children, albeit an excellent means of communication in the African American culture, may result in communication difficulties and other problems generally associated with not being understood outside
one's social community. Furthermore, children who hear negative statements about
their language and who are urged to change to a more "standard" form of English
undoubtedly have a lower self-esteem and opinion of cultural backgrounds.

## Achievement Levels

Objectivity is fundamental in considering the African American child's achievement (which is closely related to self-esteem). There is no room for stereotypes of
achievement expectations. Nationally, the school dropout rate for African American youth is almost 28 percent and approaches 50 percent in some areas. African
American pupils lag behind European American pupils on standardized tests,
and the debate rages over where the responsibility for low academic performance
lies. School officials too often blame the child's "disadvantaged" or "culturally
deprived" home, although many African American educators point out that generations of European American and Oriental immigrants have performed successfully in schools and have achieved social mobility. These African American
educators call for effective schools in which teachers have an objective under-

standing of African American children and have similar expectations for both African American and European American children (Clark-Johnson, 1988).

African American children's lower performance in the academic areas may be evidence of "blaming the victims" instead of examining the underlying causes of the problem. On national assessments in reading, writing, mathematics, and science, African American students' performance continues to lag behind that of white students, with uneven progress in closing the gap. Several possible reasons exist for this gap, ranging from increased family and community stresses (e.g., poverty, poor health, family difficulties, and community violence) to lower rates of in-school and out-of-school reading among learners, and the declining quality of urban areas where most African American students attend school. Another possibility is that the curriculum in inner-city schools is outdated, inadequate to meet the demands of new curricula experiences and assessment. Many urban systems have focused their curricula more on rote learning of basic skills than on thoughtful examination of serious literature or assignments requiring frequent and extended writing (Darling-Hammond, 1998).

Despite the rhetoric of equality and efforts of many involved in school desegregation and finance reform, problems continue to plague schools attended by many African Americans. African Americans have school experiences substantially separate from and unequal to those of other groups; the physical condition of many schools is poorer; and shortages of funds make it more difficult for rural and urban schools to employ qualified teachers and to provide the equipment that students need (Darling-Hammond, 1998).

Implementing Research 3-3 on page 76 examines why so many African American students experience difficulties in school.

Many African American parents have stressed to their children the importance of exceeding European American children's achievement and behavior, because falling short reflects unfavorably on the whole group. In fact, evidence indicates that achievement orientation is a strength of African American families: Most African American college youths came from families whose members were not college educated. One poll indicated that over 75 percent of African American children said that their mothers wanted them to be one of the best students in the class; interestingly, there appears to be a correlation between maternal warmth (i.e., use

---

**FOLLOW THROUGH 3-6　Increasing African Americans' Achievement**

Brainstorm in groups of three or four *specific* ways to increase African Americans' achievement levels. Consider the academic backgrounds of the students, school practices (such as the curriculum, instructional practices, and school environment), and educators' mindsets toward African American learners.

Remember, you are looking for ways to improve *African Americans' achievement* rather than achievement in general. You will need, therefore, to consider African Americans' cultural background and the characteristics described in Table 3-1.

IMPLEMENTING RESEARCH 3-3    African American Students and the Classroom

Believing that teachers' attitudes and expectations play a major role in academic achievement, Susan Graybill questions why so many African American students have a hard time in school. She argues that a cultural discontinuity affects attitudes and expectations of student behavior and achievement. African American students, because of their language, behavior, and learning styles, often experience conflicts in school.

Because teachers bring their own cultures and values into the classroom, they often expect students of other cultural backgrounds to conform to culture-specific standards. Graybill calls for educators to attain better understanding of African American students' cultural perspectives and learning styles; same-sex schools for males, in which they will have male role models who can be positive yet impose authority and discipline; and more African American teachers to meet the diverse needs of African American students.

### Implementing the Research

1. We agree that majority-culture teachers do not always understand African American students or students of other cultural backgrounds. We also believe that *all* teachers should understand cultural differences (including Asian or Hispanic American teachers who work with African or European American students).

2. Educators should have a solid understanding of the influential role "expectations" play in academic achievement and behavior. Educators (whatever their cultural backgrounds) should have high expectations of all their students whatever *their* cultural backgrounds).

3. Educators need in-service training to understand cultural diversity, students' cultural backgrounds (including gender), and the effects of culture on learning and behavior.

*Source:* Graybill, S. W. (1997). Questions of race and culture: How they relate to the classroom for African American students. *The Clearing House, 70*(6), 311–318.

of reinforcement, consultation with the child, and sensitivity to the child's feelings) and intellectual achievement (Hale-Benson, 1986).

Although statistics reveal lower academic achievement among African Americans, it is important to understand the situation in its historical perspective. For years, many African Americans attended segregated schools in which instruction and materials were often substandard. Substantial progress has been made toward the provision of educational resources to African Americans, but educational opportunities are still not generally equal. Standards of academic performance in schools that serve predominantly African American learners are not equivalent to those that serve predominantly European American learners. Likewise, the amount of encouragement and support the schools provide for educational achievement and attainment are not equal (Jaynes & Williams, 1989).

African American learners face a brighter and more optimistic future. First, African Americans now attend the same schools as their European American counterparts and are receiving more equitable educational opportunities. Second, more opportunities in employment, education, and housing will allow their families an improved standard of living. Third, educators are better trained in diagnostic and remediation approaches and individualized education. Fourth, educators are translating the research on effective teaching, which has grown considerably during the past twenty years, into practical application.

Case Study 3-2 looks at improving academic achievement among African American Learners.

Suggestions for working with elementary and secondary learners include:

**1.** Get to know individual children and their strengths and weaknesses. Hold high expectations for *all* your students.

**2.** Administer interest inventories to determine needs and areas in which instruction might be most effective.

**3.** Administer culturally appropriate diagnostic tests to determine which areas require remediation.

**4.** Work to improve self-esteem and convince learners that they can learn and achieve.

**5.** Work to improve the learner's attitude about the African American culture.

**6.** Teach, evaluate, and reteach basic skills.

## Language Problems

The language of African American children is a function of their culture and plays a significant role in their self-esteem, school achievement, and social and

---

### CASE STUDY 3-2    Improving Academic Achievement among African American Learners

Miss Carter, a new teacher in your school, comments, "I just graduated from the teacher ed. program, and they didn't teach me about all this! I taught students in a nearly all-white school in the suburbs. Now, I have all these African American students. I looked at their achievement test scores and I am floored. What can I do?"

Here are several suggestions for Miss Carter.

**1.** First and foremost, Miss Carter should understand the dangers of believing generalizations and making blanket statements that downplay the academic performance of an entire cultural group in the school.

**2.** She needs to understand African American students, their culture, and the dangers of labeling a whole culture's students academically slow.

**3.** She needs to consider individual students to determine those who are behind academically, and she should make lists of individual strengths and weaknesses.

**4.** She needs to plan diagnostic–remediation efforts for individuals who have documented learning problems.

**5.** She needs to plan developmentally and academically appropriate instruction for average and above-average learners, and to seek assistance from administrators, remedial and resource personnel, and special district personnel as she plans instruction for students who are behind academically.

psychological development. Although the child may not experience communication difficulties at home or in the neighborhood, language differences may cause problems when significant variations exist between home and neighborhood and school languages. Children's language skills are crucial in their education, and much of what educators measure as "intelligence" and "achievement" is actually language and communication skills (Hale-Benson, 1986).

The grammatical structure of African American speech patterns frequently leads listeners to conclude that a genuine structural pattern does not exist. Linguists acquainted with the various vernaculars of African American English realize the fallacy of such thinking. African American speakers who say "Carl hat" and "she book" might have knowledge of possessives in grammar like the speaker who says "Mary's hat" and "his book."

Case Study 3-3 illustrates how Mrs. Johnson becomes annoyed with dialectal differences and how she should consider such differences.

A. Duku Anokye (1997) in Implementing Research 3-4 maintains that African Americans are often on the receiving end of negative attitudes about their language.

---

**FOLLOW THROUGH 3-7    Understanding African Americans'
Language "Problems"**

Are African Americans' language "problems" actually problems or is the real problem the schools' reluctance to accept their grammatical structures? In other words, do the problems result from African Americans' lack of standard English or others' reluctance to accept African American English and dialects? What will happen if African American students are expected to speak one language at school and another at home?

---

**CASE STUDY 3-3    Dialectal Differences and Standard English**

"I ain't got no pencil!" "That Paul pencil—I seen him with it!" Mrs. Johnson, a teacher for many years, gets irritated when learners do not speak the standard English that she and the textbooks try to present. Although these language dialects annoy Mrs. Johnson, she really does not know what to do. She has tried to "change" the students' language to a more acceptable dialect, but nothing seems to work.

First, Mrs. Johnson should avoid a perspective that promotes a "blame the victim" attitude. Second, her attempts to "change" the students' language (which has resulted only in frustration for her and her students) shows a lack of understanding of the students and their cultural heritages. Rather than trying to change language habits, or considering "differences" as "deficits," Mrs. Johnson needs to understand that the students' language dialects and communication patterns work perfectly well in their homes and neighborhoods. It is only in schools and outside the African American community that "others" have difficulty understanding.

**IMPLEMENTING RESEARCH 3-4   Recipients of Negative Language Attitudes**

A. Duku Anokye (1997) argues that African Americans traditionally have been the recipients of negative language attitudes in education and society. Over the years, they have been mislabeled as culturally deprived and culturally disadvantaged, on the basis of their language use. However, African American Vernacular English (AAVE) is a valid language that is not the result of deprivation or disadvantage but instead is simply linguistically different, like other dialects. That fact is yet to be widely accepted by educators.

Anokye maintains that we need to understand that AAVE runs much deeper than the grammatical, syntactic, and morphological differences. In fact, it personifies different cultural expectations and norms for performance as well. Teachers of African American students have an obligation to familiarize themselves with some of the important differences in their students' language and culture that affect their learning in the classroom.

**Implementing the Research**

1. Educators can promote achievement among African American students by using a group-centered approach to learning that allows cooperation and collaboration.
2. Educators need to better understand AAVE, its history, African Americans' communication styles, and how attitudes toward students' language affect academic achievement as well as socialization.
3. Educators, while respecting AAVE, need to emphasize that economic and social success often depends on demonstrable skill in the standard use of the language. Martin Luther King and Jesse Jackson are two such exemplary speakers.

*Source:* Anokye, A. D. (1997). A case for orality in the classroom. *The Clearing House, 70*(5), 229–231.

## Learning Styles: Cultural Considerations

Educators have long recognized that learners respond differently to instruction. While some students learn most efficiently reading alone in a quiet atmosphere, others learn best in a group or cooperative learning project that discusses issues. The "means or conditions" under which a student learns most effectively and efficiently can be termed his or her *learning style*. In essence, learning styles are a complex blend of personal, social, cultural, and behavioral elements that varies from individual to individual and culture to culture.

Although the relationship between culture and learning style is not fully understood, it is an important one: "Culture shapes the way we think (cognition), the way we interact (behavior), and the way we transmit knowledge to the next generation (education)" (Collier & Hoover, 1987, p. 7). Hernandez (1989) explains that cultural and cognitive development are closely intertwined, that social and environmental factors that influence cognitive development are closely intertwined, and that social and environmental factors influence cognitive and affective preferences. These, in turn, reflect themselves in incentives, motivation, interpersonal relationships, and patterns of intellectual abilities (Hernandez, 1989).

Janice Hale-Benson (1986) lists several factors to consider when determining how African American students learn most effectively.

**1.** African American people tend to respond to things in terms of the whole picture rather than its parts.

**2.** African American people tend to prefer inferential reasoning to deductive or inductive reasoning.

**3.** African American people tend to approximate space, numbers, and time rather than be sticklers for accuracy.

**4.** African American people tend to prefer focusing on people and their activities rather than on things.

**5.** African American people tend in general not to be "word" dependents and tend to be proficient in nonverbal communication.

Knowing African American learners' cultural characteristics and their learning styles represents an essential first step when planning and implementing a multicultural curriculum that meets the needs of African American learners.

## School Practices Impeding African Americans' Progress

Educators sometimes develop and implement curricula that either overlook or ignore cultural diversity. African American learners may find themselves in a world of European American rules, expectations, and orientations. Rather than recognize cultural diversity and teach learners as individuals, educators treat learners as groups with homogeneous characteristics. School practices that may impede learning achievement and appropriate behavior include the following.

**1.** Failing to understand African American learners and expecting all learners to conform to European American standards and expectations.

**2.** Grouping by homogeneous ability, which may result in the segregation of learners by culture and by social class.

**3.** Providing insufficient or inappropriate positive reinforcement.

**4.** Downgrading or even punishing learners for using English dialects.

**5.** Providing for African American learners too many worksheets and drill times without a meaningful purpose.

**6.** Using European American–oriented textbooks and curricular materials.

**7.** Basing academic and behavior standards and expectations on stereotypical expectations.

**IMPLEMENTING RESEARCH 3-5    Cultural Perspectives of Rewards and Punishments**

Clifton Casteel (1997) maintains that teachers should become expert managers in the classroom so learning will be the best it can be. To do so, they will need to identify what children regard as rewards or punishments and adapt the educational environment accordingly. Casteel examined 1689 eighth-grade students (African American and Caucasian, ages 12–14) to determine attitudes toward praise, rewards, and punishments. His findings are interesting.

1. Most students of both cultural backgrounds thought they should be rewarded for academic work "sometimes" in preference to "always" or "never."
2. Most students considered "a letter to your parents" the most effective punishment for bad behavior.
3. Most students felt the amount of reward or punishment to be "about right."
4. Both race and gender are sometimes significant factors in student attitudes about reward and punishment.
5. African American students (71%) thought that pleasing the teacher was the greatest priority, while Caucasians (52%) chose pleasing the parent.
6. Girls as a group (54 percent) chose the teacher as the person they would most like to please with their classwork; African American girls (81 percent) chose this response more than any other group of participants.

**Implementing the Research**

1. Educators should consider their own individual students' cultural perspectives, including gender, to find out how they think about praise and punishments.
2. Parents and families should be involved as much as possible, in determining rewards and punishments as well as following the child's overall school progress.
3. Educators should understand intracultural differences as well as individual differences within a culture.

*Source:* Casteel, C. A. (1997). Attitudes of African American and Caucasian eighth grade students about praises, rewards, and punishments. *Elementary School Guidance and Counseling, 31,* 262–272.

Implementing Research 3-5 explains cultural perspectives of rewards and punishments and the need for educators to consider appropriate rewards and punishments.

School practices related to the assessment of children and adolescents is another area that can impede African American learners' progress. Assessment devices designed primarily for middle-class white learners do not always provide an accurate assessment of African American learners.

Isen (1983) recommends four tests for African American learners. See Table 3-2.

Case Study 3-4 shows that educators should listen to and offer a response to parents' concerns.

**TABLE 3-2    Assessing African American Children**

*The Black Intelligence Test of Cultural Homogeneity* (BITCH) is a test whose major objectives are to identify early indicators of intelligence in black children. Test items include black American folklore, history, life experiences, and dialect, which Isen feels are more relevant and fairer to the black culture than other standardized tests.

*Themes of Black Awareness* (TOBA) is a forty-item sentence-completion instrument that elicits thematic material relating to an individual's level of black awareness.

*Themes Concerning Black* (TCB) is a personality inventory for blacks.

*Multicultural Pluralistic Assessment* (SOMPA) is a battery of tests to be used with culturally diverse five- to eleven-year-olds. It is based on the fundamental assumption that U.S. society is pluralistic, both culturally and structurally. The battery includes an interview with parents, a medical examination, and a Wechsler IQ test.

---

**CASE STUDY 3-4    Responding to Parents' Demands**

A vocal and militant group of parents presents a list of demands for improving the school system. They feel that the education their children are receiving does not meet the needs of African Americans. One of their demands is to create all-male classes and to have African American male teachers for kindergarten through grade three.

It is clear that some action is necessary to change the attitudes of these parents toward their school and to have a school that better meets the needs of African American learners. Failing to listen and respond appropriately to the parents' concerns whenever possible can only result in frustration for both parents and school officials and for the children attending the school. The school's response should include these steps.

1. Assess how well the school is meeting African American students' needs in the areas in which the parents perceive it to be failing. Encourage educators to listen to the parents' demands in an atmosphere free of hostility and defensiveness.

2. Complete a multicultural assessment of the overall school curriculum and environment to determine how effectively educators are addressing the needs of African American learners.

3. Form an advisory committee consisting of parents, an administrator, teachers from the school, and several community members to discuss the concerns of the African American parents.

4. Explain that having black male teachers in kindergarten through third grade has not been conclusively proven beneficial and that there aren't enough black male teachers willing to teach the lower grades.

## Promoting Positive Self-Esteem and Cultural Identities

Several studies have sought to ascertain the effects of minority group status on personality development during identity formation. These studies provide concrete evidence for long-held opinions that the society and the culture in which African Americans live adversely affects their personality development, self-esteem, and educational achievements. Lee and Lindsey (1985) maintained that racism and oppression hinders the positive development of the African American child's self-esteem.

Self-esteem may be the most influential factor in a learner's development. The African American child or adolescent's self-perception influences not only his or her academic achievement but also many other social and psychological aspects of development. Distinctive aspects affecting self-esteem include children's perception of themselves, how others perceive them to be, and how the children perceive others. The negative feelings and discrimination African American children and adolescents perceive are devastating to their self-esteem. Historically, African Americans have experienced much to lower their self-esteem, but civil rights efforts and recent decades of progress have helped raise it.

African American parents can help foster self-esteem development in their children. The phrase "You're just as good as anybody else" may help sooth anxieties that arise when their children engage in a social comparison with European American children (Hale-Benson, 1986, p. 64).

Suggestions for educators working with African American children and adolescents include the following.

1. Be open and honest in relationships with African American children.
2. Learn as much as possible about your own culture.
3. Seek to respect and appreciate culturally different attitudes and behaviors.
4. Take advantage of all available opportunities to participate in activities in the African American community.
5. Keep in mind that African American children are members of their unique cultural group and are unique individuals as well.
6. Eliminate all behaviors that suggest prejudice or racism.
7. Implement practices that acknowledge the African American culture.
8. Hold high expectations of African American children, and encourage all who work with African American children to do likewise.
9. Ask questions about the African American culture.
10. Develop culture-specific strategies, mechanisms, techniques, and programs to foster the psychological development of African American children (Locke, 1989).

The identity formation of the African American adolescent has been a source of considerable concern, especially in poverty-ridden households and single-parent homes. New evidence, however, indicates that this concern may be ill-founded, that the African American adolescent might not be as detrimentally affected as once believed. Specifically, single mothers do not usually perceive their families as "broken," because fathers and the extended family and kinship network continue to play a role in their lives. The physical presence or absence of adult males in the home says little about the availability of other male models. Adolescent males living in single-parent households often identify male role models in their neighborhoods and classrooms, and even in instruction from their mothers (Bell-Scott & McKenry, 1986).

Gay African American and Hispanic youths (ages 14–19 years) have a unique set of stressful life events, low self-esteem, emotional distress, and multiple problem behaviors (alcohol use, drug use, and risky sexual behavior). Admitting their sexual

---

**FOLLOW THROUGH 3-8   Comparing and Contrasting Learners**

Using the case study method, compare and contrast two learners, one with self-esteem and one without. What are the differences in such areas as attitudes toward self, school, and the teacher; academic achievement; and overall mental health and psychosocial development? What might you do to help learners with low self-esteem? What might you suggest to parents and extended family members?

---

orientation or having it discovered by others can expose a gay or lesbian to ridicule. Gay and lesbian youth cannot anticipate how others may respond to knowledge of their sexual identity. Stressful events related to being gay or lesbian have been shown to cause significant emotional distress, multiple problem behavior, and low self-esteem. In fact, even good self-esteem does not buffer the relationship between gay-related stressful life events and emotional stress or between these life events and multiple problem behaviors (Rosario, Rotheram-Borus & Reid, 1996).

---

**CULTURAL PORTRAIT   Paul—An African American Learner**

Paul J., a ten-year-old African American learner, attends a large urban elementary school that is approximately half African and half European American. Paul is a low achiever, speaks an English dialect, and has low self-esteem. When speaking of Paul's lack of academic achievement, Mrs. Smith, Paul's teacher, feels he does not listen. "He looks away when I talk to him. I have tried to get him to look at me," Mrs. Smith states. Paul claims he is listening, even though he does not look directly at Mrs. Smith as she speaks. Paul knows Mrs. Smith does not approve of his English dialect, but his language works fine at home and in the playground, so he doesn't see any need to change.

Paul feels he is in a bind: He tries to make higher grades but just cannot seem to do so. He sees himself in the "middle." Some African American students make better grades than he does, and others make worse. Paul feels the frustration of coping in a school that appears to cater to white students and appears to expect African Americans to conform to European American expectations.

*How Paul's Teacher Can Respond*

Mrs. Smith's response can take several directions.

1. First and foremost, she needs to understand that the people of the African American culture do not feel it is necessary to look someone in the eye when listening to him or her.
2. Mrs. Smith also needs to recognize that Paul's English dialect works well for him at home, in the playground, and in the neighborhood.
3. As for Paul's seeing himself in the "middle," Mrs. Smith's response should be to administer the proper diagnostic tests to determine Paul's achievement and to identify any special strengths and weaknesses.
4. The fourth response extends further into the school itself. Mrs. Smith can focus the administration's attention on the school's European American orientation and try to change it. Rather than the school's being genuinely multicultural in nature (and celebrating cultural diversity), it might be continuing an orientation toward European American perspectives and dealing with Paul (and other African American learners) as just another of those liabilities one can expect in urban schools.

## Summing Up

Educators planning a culturally responsive curriculum and school environment for African American learners should:

**1.** Understand the African American culture and its people from a historical and contemporary perspective.

**2.** Understand the close correlation between socioeconomic class and academic achievement among African American learners (and learners of other cultures).

**3.** Address the dilemma of African American English, which needs understanding and appropriate action: African Americans understand one another in home and community situations, and yet they sometimes experience difficulty in school and teaching and learning situations. Remember that "different" does not equate with "wrong" or "inferior."

**4.** Promote the self-esteem and cultural identities that are crucial to African American learners' academic achievement, psychosocial development, and general outlook on life.

**5.** Consider and address African American students' learning styles when planning teaching and learning experiences.

**6.** Consider intracultural, geographic, socioeconomic, urban and rural, and other differences that result in "individuality," rather than categorizing all African American learners as a homogeneous group.

**7.** Understand several factors (appropriate diagnostic and remediation procedures, improving self-esteem, basic skills instruction) that have the potential for improving African American academic achievement.

**8.** Adhere to the commitment that educators should not stereotype African American learners or label them as slow learners. Educators also must not group learners in organization patterns that result in segregation by either culture or social class.

## Suggested Learning Activities

**1.** Complete a case study of two African American learners, each from a different social class—for example, one from a lower class and one from a higher social class. Compare and contrast differences in culture, language, familial traditions, food, and life expectations.

**2.** Using an actual student achievement permanent record (with academic grades, standardized test scores, and anecdotal comments), outline what appear to be the learner's strengths and weaknesses. Administer two different diagnostic instruments designed to determine strengths and weaknesses. With this information, outline a teaching and learning plan designed to improve academic achievement and self-esteem.

**3.** The family, both immediate and extended, is a valued aspect of the African American culture. How can educators use this resource? What can educators do to involve African American families? What special concerns should educators keep in mind during parent conferences?

## Suggestions for Collaborative Efforts

Form groups of three or four that, if possible, represent our nation's cultural and gender diversity. Working collaboratively, focus your group's attention toward the following efforts.

1. Conduct an in-depth study of English dialects. Divide learning assignments in such a manner that each group member has an individual task such as providing specific examples of dialectical differences, providing names of textbooks and other curricular materials that positively reflect dialects, and reviewing the literature on dialects. Working collaboratively, discuss how children and adolescents who are able to communicate in home and community situations may experience difficulties communicating in school.

2. Design a study (case studies, interviews, anecdotal records) to learn more about several African American families. Determine cultural, intracultural, and social class differences. How do these families differ in dress and food preferences, customs, and family behaviors? What other evidence can you find of tremendous diversity among African American families? How can the school provide a curriculum that responds to the African American family?

3. African Americans sometimes want segregated all-black schools for their children and adolescents. They believe that African Americans receive better treatment in such schools and learn more about the African culture. They also believe that educators in such schools address their cultural characteristics and learning styles. Have a discussion in your group as to the advantages and disadvantages of "separate culture" schools. Also, how do these schools differ from the segregated schools that fueled the civil rights movement? Will "separate culture" schools prepare African Americans to live and work with people from other cultures? How can schools address the concerns of parents who want to send their children to all-black schools?

## Expanding Your Horizons: Additional Journal Readings and Books

Halle, T. G., Kurtz-Costes, B., & Mahoney, J. L. (1997). Family influences on school achievement in low-income, African American children. *Journal of Educational Psychology, 89*(3), 527–537.

*These authors examine the achievement-related beliefs and behaviors of parents of economically disadvantaged African American youth, parental factors, and children's self-esteem and achievement.*

Hudley, C. A. (1997). Teacher practices and student motivation in a middle school program for African American males. *Urban Education, 32*(2), 304–319.

*Hudley examines an instructional program emphasizing African American history and culture to determine classroom experiences and the program's impact on academic motivation.*

Mahiri, J. (1998). Streets to schools: African American youth culture and the classroom. *The Clearing House, 71*(6), 335–338.

*Mahiri maintains that 90 percent of all teachers in the United States are white and therefore challenged to understand African American youth. He suggests how teachers can become ethnographers to gain needed cultural competencies.*

National Urban League. (1998). *The state of black America 1988.* New York.

This comprehensive and critical look at black America provides excellent essays on topics such as political economies, black philanthropy, jobless ghettos, student academic performance, and the state of African American politics.

Struchen, W., & Porta, M. (1997). From role-modeling to mentoring for African American youth: Ingredients for successful relationships. *Preventing School Failure, 41*(3), 119–123.

Struchen and Porta examine the mentoring process, specifically the problem of distance between the mentor and African American youth, characteristics of ideal mentors, program structure, roadblocks to success, and African American programming issues.

## Expanding Your Students' Horizons: Appropriate African American Books for Children and Adolescents

Barboza, Steven. *Door of No Return: The Legend of Goree Island*. Cobblehill, 1994.

Belton, Sandra. *May'naise Sandwiches & Sunshine Tea*. Four Winds, 1994.

Belton, Sandra. *From Miss Ida's Porch*. Four Winds, 1993.

Berry, James. *Celebration Song*. Simon & Schuster, 1994.

Bogart, Jo Ellen. *Daniel's Dog*. Scholastic, 1990.

Bray, Rosemary L. *Martin Luther King*. Four Winds, 1994.

Coleman, Evelyn. *The Foot Warmer and the Crow*. Macmillan, 1994.

Coles, Robert. *The Story of Ruby Bridges*. Scholastic, 1994.

Cummings, Pat. *Clean Your Room, Harvey Moon*. Bradbury, 1991.

Gilchrist, Jan Spivey. *Lift Ev'ry Voice and Sing*. Scholastic, 1994.

Hamilton, Virginia. *Jagurundi*. Blue Sky, 1994.

Howard, Elizabeth Fitzgerald. *Aunt Flossie's Hats (Crab Cakes Later)*. Clarion, 1991.

Hudson, Wade. *Five Brave Explorers*. Scholastic, 1994.

Johnson, Angela. *Toning the Sweep*. Orchard, 1993.

Johnson, Delores. *Seminole Diary*. Macmillan, 1994.

Katz, William Loren. *Breaking the Chain: African American Slave Resistance*. Atheneum, 1990.

Kurtz, Jane. *Fire on the Mountain*. Simon & Schuster, 1994.

Lester, Julius. *The Man Who Knew Too Much*. Clarion, 1994.

Lyons, Mary E. *Raw Head, Bloody Bones: African American Tales of the Supernatural*. Atheneum, 1995.

Meltzer, Milton. *Frederick Douglass: In His Own Words*. Harcourt, Brace, 1994.

Miller, William. *Zora Hurston and the Chinaberry Tree*. Lee and Low, 1994.

Myers, Walter Dean. *The Dragon Takes a Wife*. Scholastic, 1994.

Pinkney, Andrea Davis. *Hold Fast to Dreams*, Morrow, 1995.

Pinkwater, Jill. *Tales of the Bronx*. Macmillan, 1991.

Pitts, Mildred. *Mississippi Challenge*. Aladdin, 1995.

Quackenbush, Robert. *Arthur Ashe and His Match With History*. Simon & Schuster, 1994.

Rinaldi, Ann. *Wolf by the Ears*. Scholastic, 1991.

Ritter, Larence. *Leagues Apart: The Men and Times of the Negro Baseball Leagues*. Morrow, 1995.

Rochelle, Belinda. *When Joe Louis Won the Title*. Houghton-Mifflin, 1994.

Woodson, Jacqueline. *I Hadn't Meant to Tell You*. Delacorte, 1994.

## Answers to the Culture Quiz: African Americans

| | | | | | |
|---|---|---|---|---|---|
| **1.** j | **3.** l | **5.** i | **7.** e | **9.** b | **11.** g |
| **2.** c | **4.** k | **6.** h | **8.** d | **10.** a | **12.** f |

$$Chapter \quad 4$$

# Understanding Asian American Children and Adolescents

Understanding the material and activities in this chapter will help the reader to:

- Describe the cultural, gender, socioeconomic, familial, and language characteristics of Asian American children and adolescents.
- Explain the "model minority" stereotype and its effects on Asian American children and adolescents.
- Describe Asian American learners and their development, achievement levels, language problems, and learning styles.
- List several practices that impede Asian American learners' educational progress.
- Offer several concrete suggestions for improving Asian American learners' self-esteem and cultural identities.
- List several points that educators of Asian Americans should remember.
- Suggest appropriate children's literature, implement research findings, and provide culturally appropriate experiences for Asian American learners.

## Overview

Planning teaching and learning experiences for Asian American learners requires an understanding of their developmental characteristics, achievement levels, language problems, learning styles, and cultural characteristics. The diversity among Asian American learners also requires a consideration of their geographic, generational, and socioeconomic differences, as well as intracultural and individual characteristics.

Stereotyping, which plagues learners from all cultures, is a particular problem for Asian Americans. The notable successes of the Asian American people have resulted in a "model minority" stereotype that sometimes leads educators to expect exemplary achievement and behavior of all Asian American learners. This chapter examines the cultural characteristics of Asian American children and adolescents, and then focuses attention on these learners in teaching and learning situations.

## *Origins*

The term *Asian American* includes a number of national, cultural, and religious heritages and includes more than twenty-nine distinct subgroups, each with unique language, religion, and customs. The four major groups of Asian Americans include East Asian, such as Chinese, Japanese, and Korean; Pacific Islander; Southeast Asian, such as Thai and Vietnamese; and South Asian, such as Indian and Pakistani. Undoubtedly, similarities exist among these cultures but educators working with Asian Americans need to remember Asians' different origins, ecological adaptations, and histories (Feng, 1994).

Individual differences also exist in reasons for immigration and related hopes and expectations. Some immigrants are refugees from war-torn countries, and others are from the middle class of stable countries. Some came with nothing, and others came with skills and affluence.

---

**THE CULTURE QUIZ    Asian Americans**

*Directions:* Match the individuals with their contributions or achievements by placing the appropriate letter before each name.

_____ **1.** Akio Morita

_____ **2.** Paul Chu

_____ **3.** Laurence Yep

_____ **4.** I. M. Pei

_____ **5.** Connie Chung

_____ **6.** Thuy Thu Lee

_____ **7.** An Wang

_____ **8.** Chin Yang

**a.** Probably the best known superconductivity scientist in the world; director of Texas Center for superconductivity

**b.** Chairman of the SONY Corporation

**c.** Chinese American CBS News correspondent

**d.** Vietnamese actress who starred in *Casualities of War*

**e.** Chinese American architect; known for such creative urban buildings as the J.F.K. Library in Boston

**f.** Chinese American writer of children's books about Asian Americans, including *The Rainbow People* (1989)

**g.** Shot in the foot at seven in Laos he is now a leading apprentice jockey in the United States

**h.** Engineer from Shanghai who built a six-hundred-dollar investment into a multibillion-dollar company

(Answers to the Culture Quiz are located at the end of the chapter.)

Still other differences exist: Many Asian Americans were not born in the United States; others are fourth- or fifth-generation U.S. citizens. Considerable differences often exist between foreign-born Asians living in this country and American-born Asians, who are often quite acculturated (Feng, 1994).

Asian Americans constitute a rapidly growing, diverse population of the United States. Between 1980 and 1990, the number of Asians living in the United States increased by 99 percent. In 1990, the largest proportions of Asian Americans were Chinese (24 percent) and Filipino (20 percent) followed by Japanese (12 percent). Newer immigrant groups such as Laotian, Cambodian, Thai, and Hmong each accounted for 2 percent or less of the Asians in the United States. Sixty-six percent of Asians were born in foreign countries. Among Asian groups, Vietnamese, Laotian, and Cambodian groups constituted the highest proportion of foreign born, Japanese the lowest (U.S. Bureau of the Census, 1993a).

## Asian Americans Today

Several indicators provide a portrait of Asian Americans today: 54 percent lived in the West in 1990 as compared to 21 percent of the total population; their median age was thirty years, younger than the national median of thirty-three years; their educational attainment varied widely by group; 67 percent of the Asian populations, compared with 65 percent of all Americans, were in the work force; and many work in higher-paying occupations, partly because of higher educational attainment (U.S. Bureau of the Census, 1993a).

There are several characteristics of the cultures of Southeast Asian countries, differences that professionals working with children can misunderstand. Many people refer to any Southeast Asian child as "Vietnamese" without realizing that they may be insulting him or her because of a different cultural heritage. Such labeling fails to realize the bitter feelings among various nationalities and ethnic groups (West, 1983):

> *Children may not know one another's language. They may not be of the same religion; their parents may have been opposing enemies; or they may harbor feelings of superiority, inferiority, or resentment toward one another (pp. 85–86).*

Although Asian Americans are a small group compared with other minority groups, such as African American and Latinos, their potential for growth is enormous for the next decade, given that Asian Americans currently represent approximately 38 percent of all immigrants (Kim, Rendon, & Valadez, 1998).

## Stereotyping of Asian American Children and Adolescents

Asian Americans are often called the "model minority" because of their remarkable educational, occupational, and economic successes. Yao (1988), reflecting on the model minority stereotype, describes Asian American children thus:

> *Not all of them are superior students who have no problems in school. Some have learning problems; some lack motivation, proficiency in English, or financial resources; and some have parents who do not understand the American school system, because of cultural differences, language barriers, or their own single-minded quest for survival (p. 223).*

The media like to portray the contemporary image of Asian Americans as a minority that has achieved great success in the European American society. For example, some reports applaud the educational achievements of Asian Americans and generally stereotype them as successful, law-abiding, and high-achieving minorities. The success of many Asian students has created the "model minority" stereotype. The popular and professional literature often labels them as "whiz kids," and as "problem free." Some claim that Asians are smarter than other groups; others believe there is something in Asian culture that breeds success, perhaps the Confucian ideas that stress family values and education (Feng, 1994).

Other stereotypes include viewing Asian Americans as proficient in mathematics and not competent with verbal tasks. Such stereotypes might lead educators to hold high expectations in some areas and low expectations in others of their Asian American students. Both kinds of expectations can produce bored, frustrated students who are afforded few opportunities to learn at their ability and motivational levels. Educators must remember to view each child as an individual with unique strengths and weaknesses.

The academic successes of some Asian Americans have led to a perception that all Asian Americans are exceptional in all pursuits. To assume, however, such scholarly expertise on the basis of culture alone does not have any greater validity

---

**FOR ADDITIONAL INFORMATION**

Chinese Cultural Center, 159 Lexington Ave., New York, NY 10016. The Cultural Center provides classes and library and information services to promote better understanding of the Chinese culture.

Chinese Cultural Association, P.O. Box 1272, Palo Alto, CA 94302. This worldwide organization promotes communication and better un-

derstanding between the Chinese and people of other cultures.

Southeast Asian Center, 1124–1128 W. Ainslie, Chicago, IL 60640. The Southeast Asian Center promotes the independence and well-being of Lao, Hmong, Cambodian, Vietnamese, and Chinese people.

---

**FOLLOW THROUGH 4-1    Addressing Asian American Diversity**

Visit an elementary or secondary school that has a significant number of Asian American student subgroups. What are the educators in the school doing to address the diversity among the Asian groups? What else might they do?

---

**USING CHILDREN'S LITERATURE    The Asian American Experience**

Children of all cultures can read developmentally appropriate books about the Asian American culture for more enhanced knowledge and better understanding.

Yep, Laurence. *The Rainbow People.* Harper & Row, 1989. This book of folktales presents a lively and enjoyable picture of Chinese culture.

Clark, Ann Noland. *To Stand Against the Wind.* Viking, 1978. An eleven-year-old Vietnamese boy's memories return to the beautiful land before war destroyed it.

Yagawa, Sumiko. *The Crane Wife.* Morrow, 1981. In this traditional Japanese tale, greed and its consequences become clear.

---

than does saying that all African Americans are incapable of high academic achievement or that all Native Americans live on reservations. Cultural misconceptions of oneself can have a detrimental effect on the forming identity and can result in undue and unrealistic pressures and demands. Case Study 4-1 shows steps that one can take to learn about Asian Americans as individuals, rather than assuming the model minority stereotype.

## Cultural Characteristics

Teachers often think of Asian American children as studious, high-achieving, and well-behaved students (Yee, 1988), whom educators expect to excel in the Ameri-

---

**CASE STUDY 4-1    The Model Minority Stereotype**

Ms. Carter, a European American and a first-year teacher, has a large percentage of Asian American learners in the class. She has heard about the excellent reputation of some Asian American learners and wants to challenge them to excel in as many areas as possible. She is also realistic, however, in the sense that she knows not all Asian Americans are "model students," "problem free," and "whiz kids," She wonders how she can have high expectations for learners capable of excelling yet not be too demanding of students unable to excel.

It is good that Ms. Carter recognizes possible discrepancies between stereotypes and realities, but now she has to determine a means of discovering which students can excel and which need assistance. What can she do?

1. Check permanent records to determine previous achievement and areas of strengths and weaknesses.
2. Request a diagnostic or achievement test (as free from cultural bias as possible) from the district assessment personnel.
3. Meet with each student to discuss achievements and areas in which the student needs help.
4. Request that the school language specialist meet with each student for an individual language assessment.
5. Seek any assistance the guidance counselor can offer regarding tests, inventories, and scales to determine capabilities.

can culture and yet retain the Asian American cultures, values, and traditions. Conforming to both Asian American and European American cultures results in high expectations and considerable problems for developing personalities and identities. Emphasizing the need to recognize and understand cultural differences, Divoky (1988) writes:

> *Too often we forget that those whose roots are in Asia are not necessarily alike; a recently arrived Hmong refugee has virtually nothing in common with an affluent Japanese American student whose parents were born and raised in the Midwest. (p. 220)*

Differences between the European American culture of the United States and the many long-accepted traditions, customs, and values of Asian American families (both immediate and extended) contribute to the developing child's sense of confusion regarding role expectations. Children growing up in such a multicultural setting may develop an ethnic identity problem as two major role expectations confront them. Developing children can, indeed, become confused as their identities form. Educators who work with Asian Americans should remember the personality differences between these children and European American children. These differences deserve recognition as cultural variations and should be in proper perspective. For example, people have described Japanese Americans as quiet, reticent, or aloof in interethnic situations and as more dependent, conforming, and obedient to authority and more willing to place family welfare over individual wishes (Feng, 1994).

Table 4-1 looks at selected cultural characteristics of Asian American children and adolescents.

Distinct differences also exist in respect to education and to teachers. West (1983) tells the story of a teacher who felt that she was not "reaching" a Vietnamese

**TABLE 4-1   Selected Characteristics of Asian American Children and Adolescents**

| Category | Characteristics |
| --- | --- |
| Behavioral/emotional expressiveness | Control of emotions and feelings, self-effacement, modest |
| Verbal | Formal, one-way communication from authority figure to individual |
| Nonverbal | Preference for distance between speaker and listener |
| Concept of time | Traditional, living with the past |
| Social orientation | Mutual interdependence; collective responsibility; cooperative rather than competitive |

*Developed from:* Rivera, B. D. & Rogers-Adkinson, D. (1997). Culturally sensitive interventions: Social skills training with children and parents from culturally and linguistically diverse backgrounds. *Intervention in School and Clinic, 33*(2), 75–80.

---

**FOLLOW THROUGH 4-2    Understanding Asian American Families**

Meet with a group of Asian American parents and extended family members to discuss their perceptions and expectations of educators and schools. Allow sufficient time for questions and discussions. Do not be dismayed if parents do not express themselves, because they sometimes perceive teachers as authority figures or place teachers on a pedestal.

---

student. Although he was not disruptive, he was not participating fully in class. When she requested a parent–teacher conference, the father came to school feeling disgraced and sure that his son had done something terrible. The teacher repeatedly explained that she liked the student and that she was only trying to improve communication. The father ordered the boy to apologize, which he did. However, the father struck the child and ordered him to kneel during the apology. The boy immediately obeyed, only to be joined by the teacher, who informed him and his parents that no one in America had to kneel to anyone.

Other cultural differences that warrant educators' attention (West, 1983) include: (1) Physical contact between members of the same sex is permissible but is not acceptable between members of the opposite sex, and (2) Vietnamese rarely touch their heads (either because of a religious belief or the fear of damaging their heads).

Recently arrived Asian children and adolescents may experience particularly acute conflicts. They are caught between their parents' culture and the school and have little power to influence either. These young people often serve as translators, and adults may call on them to complete forms, applications, and licenses (Chen, 1987; Kitano, 1989).

Implementing Research 4-1 looks at cultural values in Asian Americans.

## *Gender*

As in all cultures, particular differences distinguish females from males in the Asian cultures. First, in Asian families, females do not receive the respect that males receive; they are valued less than males. Similarly, they do not receive the opportunities afforded to males. Although these differences are only in cultural *expectations,* they can have far-reaching effects on Asian females' worldviews, motivation, and perception of their "place" in the world and their ability to perform in the home, community, and society.

Second and related, Asian females might show less motivation to succeed in ventures outside the home; they might be more reluctant to participate in class discussions and less willing to excel academically when the opportunity arises. In summary, just as we cannot classify all Asians in a single cultural group, it is equally dangerous to label all males and females as one homogeneous group.

**IMPLEMENTING RESEARCH 4-1    Asian Americans and Cultural Values**

Asakawa and Csikszentmihalyi compared the quality of experiences of Asian and Caucasian American adolescents. They wondered why Asian Americans perform so well academically even though they experience prejudice and discrimination the way other minority groups do.

In their discussion, they urge caution (to avoid stereotyping) because Asian Americans, like all people, differ significantly from each other. With this in mind, they reported several findings:

1.  Asian Americans adolescents reported relatively positive experiences when engaged in activities highly valued in their cultures. For example, when engaged in activities perceived to be like work, they were significantly happier, reported enjoying themselves more, and felt better about themselves than their Caucasian counterparts.
2.  Asian American students had more positive experiences than their Caucasian counterparts in situations where the importance of future goals was high. They were happier, enjoyed themselves, and were more active and less self-conscious.

The researchers concluded that Asian American adolescents seem to have internalized cultural values that contribute to their high academic achievement; that is, they value hard work and high achievement more strongly than Caucasians do. It seems that Caucasian students and parents collaborate more to build children's future.

## Implementing the Research

Educators of children and adolescents should:

1.  Understand the possible relationship between cultural values and academic achievement—some cultures might place a high priority on school achievement. Teachers must not, however, assume that students and parents from other cultures who do not demonstrate similar overt behaviors "do not care."
2.  Recognize the dangers of making too many assumptions or generalizations about reasons for Asian Americans' academic successes—the Asian culture consists of many different people.
3.  Provide parent education classes for parents and families of all cultures, especially Asian Americans, who might not understand the purposes of American education and how they can contribute to students' academic achievement.
4.  Understand cultural differences in parenting such as Asians' practices, which reflect a combination of "authoritarian" and "permissive" (p. 160) styles, as well as Caucasian parents' tendencies toward collaboration with children and adolescents to mold future possibilities.

*Source:* Asakawa, K., & Csikszentmihalyi, M. (1998). The quality of experiences of Asian American adolescents related to future goals. *Journal of Youth and Adolescence, 27*(2), 141–163.

---

**FOLLOW THROUGH 4-3    Helping Asian American Females
Understand U.S. Perspectives**

Consider how females are perceived in the Asian culture—they receive less respect than males and generally are valued less. They do not receive opportunities accorded to males and often show less motivation toward success in ventures outside the home. What problems might Asian American females experience in U.S. school systems because of their culture's perspective toward females? How can educators help Asian American females to understand U.S. perspectives toward females—equality and respect?

---

## Socioeconomic Status

The accumulation of wealth allows people more options, opportunities, and increased amounts of leisure time. A change in economic circumstances also influences a person's social expression, values, and patterns of thinking and behaving. A learner's socioeconomic status is undoubtedly one of the most significant factors affecting his or her learning and achievement. Educators can readily understand the educational and social implications of a learner's socioeconomic status and the danger of basing curricular and instructional decisions on stereotypical beliefs and assumptions.

Trying to determine the socioeconomic level of Asian Americans proves difficult at best, because of the diversity among the Asian cultures and the lack of current information on their earning power and social class. Educators must be careful not to rely on the model-minority stereotype by assuming that all Asian Americans experience social and economic success—at least not according to the common U.S. perception of success as the accumulation of material wealth. In all likelihood, some Asian Americans—like members of other cultures—have achieved socioeconomic successes, and others have not.

Some immigrants received high levels of education in their home countries and have come to the United States to seek greater professional opportunities. For example, over 40 percent of foreign-born Filipinos have received bachelor's degrees and over one-quarter are employed in professional, managerial, and executive positions. The average family income of immigrant Filipino families is $48,000, well over the immigrant average of $35,000 (Fuligni, 1997).

## Families

Childrearing techniques of Asian American families, founded in cultural expectations, emphasize loyalty to the family. The culture sends a powerful message of the importance of not bringing embarrassment or shame to the family. The inculcation of guilt and shame is the principal technique that controls the behavior of family members. Parents emphasize their children's obligation to the family and their responsibility for abiding by family expectations. Adults consider children who act contrary to the family's wishes as selfish, inconsiderate, and ungrateful. The behavior of individual members is a reflection on the entire family. For ex-

---

**FOLLOW THROUGH 4-4**   **Helping Asian American Families Understand U.S. Schools**

Asian American families, especially first-generation, might not understand U.S. schools. These families have traditionally placed greater value on sons than on daughters and feel considerable shame when children's achievements or behavior does not meet the family's expectations. List several ways—such as parent education programs or orientation sessions—in which you can help Asian American families to better understand U.S. schools.

---

ample, aberrant behavior is great shame and is usually hidden from the public and handled within the family. Outstanding achievement in some aspect of life is a source of great pride for the child and for the entire family as well. Such a standard of morality sometimes causes confusion for children who are attempting to satisfy the expectations of two cultures, but it emphasizes the importance of unity and honor in the Asian American family (Sue & Sue, 1983).

Asian American children and adolescents learn early in life that the family is the primary unit and that considerable value should be placed on family solidarity, responsibility, and harmony. Communication with adults is usually one-way, primarily adults speaking to children. They also learn loyalty to authority (Rivera & Rogers-Adkinson, 1997).

In summary, the family is central to the Asian culture. Individual conflicts may arise, because parents and family reflect traditional ways and children see another way of life (Kitano, 1989). Case Study 4-2 looks at the powerful influence of the Asian American family and shows what educators can do to learn about families.

---

**CASE STUDY 4-2**   **Understanding the Family**

Mr. Jones looked at the research on Asian American families. Without a doubt, the family plays a major role in determining learners' attitudes, behavior, and academic achievement. He read the following (Hartman & Askounis, 1989): "The family is the primary socializing influence in the Asian culture; parents are responsible for interpreting appropriate and inappropriate behaviors" (p. 110).

He wondered how we, as educators, can better understand the Asian family and its influence on children and adolescents. He jotted down a list to consider.

1. Meeting families firsthand (in their homes, if possible) is the best means of learning family values, customs, and traditions.

2. Arrange small group sessions with families (both immediate and extended), perhaps at Parent Teacher Association (PTA) meetings or other school functions, to learn what families expect of schools and children and to explain school expectations to parents.

3. Learn about families from a variety of Asian cultures for a better understanding of intracultural and individual differences.

4. Learn about generational differences among families, for example, variations in first-, second-, and third-generation immigrant families in the United States.

5. Learn about families from differing socioeconomic groups to gain an understanding of values, traditions, and beliefs.

Family allegiance and respect for parents and family play a significant role in the value system, achievements, and behavior of the developing Asian American child. In many east and southeast Asian cultures, Confucian ideals, which include respect for elders and discipline, are a strong influence. Most Asian American parents and families teach their children to value educational achievement, respect authority, feel responsible for relatives, and show self-control. Asian American children tend to be more dependent, conforming, and willing to place family welfare ahead of their own individual wishes than are other American children (Feng, 1994).

Asian American parents seem to structure their children's lives for academic success more than Caucasian parents do. Asian parents are more likely to decide whether their children should go to college, to discuss SAT/ACT plans and preparation with their children, and limit television and video games. In general, it appears that Asian parents organize and structure their children's lives to facilitate academic success. Another important point, however, needs to be explained. People often have an authoritarian image of Asian parents. That is, Asian parents are less likely to be involved in children's actual academic activities. For example, they are less likely to decide what classes their children should take and to check on the completion of homework. They help their children with homework less often and discuss school progress less.

Researchers have concluded that Asian parents structure their children's lives for success, yet leave the actual work and achievement to the children themselves. On the other hand, Asian American parenting practices are more like a combination of "authoritarian" and "permissive" styles (Asakawa & Csikszentmihalyi, 1998, p. 160).

In the traditional family, age, sex, and generational status are the primary determinants of the child's role behavior. Ancestors and elders are greatly revered and respected and are actively involved with childrearing. Families are patriarchal. The primary duty of the son is to be a good son, and his obligations as a good husband or father come second to his duty as a son. The role of the female in the family is that of subservience to the male, the performance of domestic chores, and the bearing of children (Sue, 1989). Such generalizations may vary depending on socioeconomic class and generational status.

## Religion

The recent influx of Indochinese, Chinese, Koreans, and other groups has increased the religious pluralism in the United States. Laotians and Cambodians are primarily Buddhists, as are the Vietnamese. Some Vietnamese, however, are Taoists or Roman Catholic. Some embrace the philosophy of Confucianism, as do the majority of Korean immigrants. Most Koreans are likely to be Buddhists. A minority, however, are Protestant, and a smaller, but still significant, group are Roman Catholic. The majority of Hong Kong immigrants are Buddhists; some are Taoists. Many of these immigrants are also likely to adhere to the teachings of Confucius (Gollnick & Chinn, 1998).

Asian Americans tend to practice values such as respect for ancestors, filial piety, and avoidance of shame. These moral principles define a person's obligation, duty, and loyalty to others. Good performance and achievement bring honor to the family. Shame and dishonor are powerful preventives to unacceptable behavior. This standard of morality may seem harsh and rigid to the outsider, but to many Asian Americans it maintains honor and harmony in the family (Lum, 1986).

## Language

Unquestionably, the considerable emphasis placed on education, the promise that education holds for successful students, and the parents' insistence that children abide by family wishes have contributed to the success of many Asian American children. Language, however, appears to be an area of difficulty for them. In one school district in California, the number of Asian American children with limited English skills grew from 8 percent to 42 percent in just seven years (Divoky, 1988).

For a better understanding of Asian American learners, educators should recognize the problems Asian Americans have with English. Without doubt, the language barriers and problems confronting Asian American learners make achievements and educational attainments even more significant. Although many Asian American parents encourage the use of English, many adolescents still live in homes where the native language is the primary language. This results in learners who speak and understand two languages.

Understanding the spoken word and being understood while speaking English often pose difficult situations for Asian American learners, especially in school systems that forbid learners from speaking their native languages. For example, of the 4.1 million Asians five years and older, the 1990 U.S. Census found that 56 percent did not speak English "very well," and 35 percent were linguistically isolated.

Percentages of Asians reporting "do not speak English very well" were as follows: Chinese, 56; Filipino, 60.4; Japanese, 57.7; Asian Indian, 31.0; Korean, 63.5; and Vietnamese, 65 (U.S. Bureau of the Census, 1993a). Even with these difficulties, many Asian American children have, however, overcome many language problems, and have demonstrated educational successes. Educators, however, need to recognize the tremendous diversity in Asians' ability to speak English.

Not only must educators in multicultural settings understand (and be understood in) verbal interactions with Asian Americans, but they must also make an equal effort to understand nonverbal communication. Several examples of

---

**FOLLOW THROUGH 4-5   Identifying Asian American Language Problems**

Discuss with a group of Asian American learners how language affects their lives and progress in school. What language problems exist? What are their opinions about forsaking their native languages and adopting English? How can educators and language specialists assist these learners?

---

**FOR ADDITIONAL INFORMATION**   **Internet Addresses**

**NAAAP National Home Page**
http://www.naaap.org/   Provides a look at the National Association of Asian American Professionals (NAAAP), an all-volunteer organization that promotes the personal and professional development of the Asian American community.

**Korea WebWeekly**
http://www.kimsoft.com/korea.htm   Provides information on many Korean aspects such as history, culture, economy, and politics.

**Asian Americans**
http://www.va.gov/womencon/one-VA/asian.htm   Provides a look at Asian Americans

who have won the Congressional Medal of Honor and other Asian American men and women who have served the nation.

**Perceptions: Asian Americans**
http://www.askasian.org/frclasrm/lessplan/1000074.htm   Provides information adapted from Chinese Communities in America.

**Asian Americans—Tables, Figures, Boxes**
http://www.prb.org./pubs/bulletin/bu53-2/tfb.htm   Provides a summary of Asian Americans' diversity and increasing numbers.

---

nonverbal behavior that adolescents learn show the distinctive differences among cultures. First, the forward and backward leaning of the body indicates feelings: A backward lean indicates a withdrawal from a conversation or topic, and a forward lean lets the speaker know that the listener is polite, concerned, and flexible. Other notable differences include Japanese American females expressing anxiety through hurried speaking and Japanese American males expressing anxiety though silence (Bond & Shiraishi, 1974). For educational efforts to be most effective, educators and Asian American learners should work actively to understand each others' verbal and nonverbal behaviors.

## Asian American Learners in the School

When they first enter the United States, children often experience a clash between their cultures and the expectations of their new homes and schools. Several distinct differences exist between Asian and European American expectations and attitudes toward schools and teachers.

First, teachers in Asia are accorded a higher status than teachers in the United States. The informality between American teachers and students may seem confusing to Southeast Asian children and appalling to their families. Second, their cultural backgrounds and values cause Asian children to expect considerable structure and organization.

Obvious differences in values may include: (1) The high value of self-effacement and saving face; students wait to be answered or to participate unless the teacher requests otherwise. Having attention drawn to oneself—the teacher putting a child's name on the board for misbehaving for example—can bring considerable distress. (2) Asian social values call for children to listen more than they speak and to speak in a soft, well-modulated voice. In the United States this characteristic is often perceived as shyness. Asian adults teach children to be modest in dress, manner, and behavior (Feng, 1994).

Eaton and Dembo (1997) examine motivational beliefs of Asian Americans in Implementing Research 4-2.

The European American emphasis on individualism may present challenges for Asian American learners who seek to satisfy the demands of contemporary society while feeling loyalty to Asian American family traditions. Educators need to

---

**IMPLEMENTING RESEARCH 4-2    Motivational Beliefs of Asian Students**

Maintaining that Asian American students outperform their non-Asian counterparts on many commonly accepted indices of educational achievement, Martin Eaton and Myron Dembo (1997) explored the differences in motivational beliefs of 154 Asian American students and 372 non-Asian ninth graders. Their investigation demonstrates that Asian American and non-Asian American students differ in their types of beliefs explaining their achievement behavior. The fear of academic failure best predicted Asian American students' achievement behavior and least explained non-Asian students' performance. The fear of academic failure stems from the emphasis Asian American parents place on children's academic success. Low performance elicits family criticism and shame. Parental pressure, therefore, serves as one of the primary catalysts behind Asian American students' motivational behavior.

Another interesting finding is that Asian Americans demonstrate the consequences of failure avoidance rather than success-approach tendencies. Eaton and Dembo call into question Western theories of motivation that stress individualism, personal choice, and responsibility. For example, children in the United States learn to "stand out" (p. 438), to make their individuality salient, whereas Asian children learn to "stand in" (p. 438), to become so identified with the group that individuality is not noticed.

**Implementing the Research**

1. Educators should recognize the motivational beliefs of Asian students but also acknowledge students' individuality—not all Asian American students are alike or share similar motivational beliefs. Also, educators need to understand that many non-Asian students have a strong desire to be successful in school to please parents. Considerable crossover exists and deserves to be recognized.
2. Educators should encourage all students to succeed, but should avoid making Asian Americans stand out or excel at the expense of their peers.
3. Educators should capitalize on Asian American students' desire to please their parents by using it as a motivational device and also by involving Asian parents in the educational process whenever possible.

---

*Source:* Eaton, M. J., & Dembo, M. H. (1997). Differences in the motivational beliefs of Asian American and non-Asian students. *Journal of Educational Psychology, 89*(3), 433–440.

understand the Asian American's strong regard for the father as head of the family, the value placed on sons rather than daughters, and the respect for the older family members. Maintaining loyalty to family tradition while building an identity and life in a European American society that emphasizes individuality may prove troublesome for Asian American children and adolescents.

It is important that educators understand Asian American parents' perceptions of school behavior and achievement. Asian Americans come from cultures that often view children's behavior as the result of a lack of will or attributable to supernatural causes. Cases of school failure have resulted in parents' complaining that children are lazy and lack character.

Rather than looking for educational reasons, parents often believe that the solution lies in increasing parental restrictions, more homework, and other negative sanctions designed to promote character development. Asian parents consider hard work, effort, and developing character the best avenues to improving behavior or school work. As educators quickly realize, such beliefs can be particularly acute for Asian American children with limited intellectual (or other) abilities (Kitano, 1989).

Even greater challenges may confront the Asian American adolescent who happens to be female. Experiencing the cultural conflict between traditional Asian values and contemporary European American values can cause females to question their role in life and the cultural value placed on their sex. Will they continue to have second-class status in the Asian American family, or should they seek the more equitable standing girls have in the European American family? Because some acculturation will probably occur, the female may be faced at some point with the task of having to make cultural comparisons and attempting to reconcile the differences for herself.

## Achievement Levels

Although Asian Americans undoubtedly have attained enviable accomplishment in U.S. schools, it is unrealistic to expect all Asian Americans to attain such achievement levels. Not all Asian immigrant children are superior students who have no problems at school. Some have learning problems; some lack motivation, proficiency in English, and financial resources; and some have parents who do not understand the American school system because of cultural or language barriers (Yao, 1988).

Lee and Rong (1988) sought to determine whether the reasons for Asian American successes included superior intelligence, concentration, or hard work. They concluded that Asian American children have an ability to hold a particular problem in mind until they reach a solution. In fact, they believe that Asian American children are not far above their peers in native abilities, but that concentration and hard work make up for any deficiencies (Lee & Rong, 1988).

Asian Americans and their educational aspirations are the topics explored in Implementing Research 4-3.

---

**IMPLEMENTING RESEARCH 4-3    Asian Americans and Educational Aspirations**

Kim, Rendon, and Valadez explain how the media's portrayal of Asian Americans as the model minority has led to the neglect of the development of programs and services for Asian American students in need. Their study focused on tenth-grade students from six Asian cultures: Chinese, Filipino, Japanese, Korean, Southeast Asian (Vietnamese, Laotian, Cambodian, and Thai), and South Asian (Asian Indian and Pakistani). They sought to determine (1) differences among the six Asian groups in their educational aspirations, math performance, and socioeconomic characteristics; (2) educational aspirations as related to student-level factors such as track placement, demographic characteristics, parental expectations, and academic self-concept; and (3) educational aspirations as related to school-level factors such as type of school, academic climate of school, racial composition, and location of school. In general, they hope to understand educational realities of Asian American students, develop programs and services for Asian Americans, and improve higher-education opportunities for Asian American students.

They concluded that Asian Americans are not a homogeneous group in terms of academic performance, educational aspirations and attainment, and socioeconomic characteristics. They found considerable differences and concluded the most apparent fact about Asian Americans is their diversity. Although a large number of Asian American students are successful, significant numbers also need assistance, support, and encouragement from counselors and teachers. The purpose of the study was to not undermine the educational needs and aspirations of Asian American students, but rather to acknowledge the reality of Asian American students and to help professionals understand the difficulties and problems Asian American students face academically as well as personally.

**Implementing the Research**

1.  Educators need to understand that the stereotype or myth of all Asian Americans being a "model minority" is not true. Although some Asian Americans have demonstrated enormous success, others continue to struggle and deserve the attention of professionals.

2.  Educators need to understand the fallacy of assuming too much homogeneity among Asian Americans, who are very diverse and deserve consideration, both culturally and as individuals.

3.  Educators need to develop educational programs designed to address the unique needs of specific Asian American groups, which will require learning about individual Asian cultures (such as cultural characteristics, strengths, weaknesses, and needs) and the design of culturally appropriate educational and intervention programs.

*Source:* Kim, H., Rendon, L., & Valadez, J. (1998). Student characteristics, school characteristics, and educational aspirations of six Asian American groups. *Journal of Multicultural Counseling and Development,* 26(3), 166–178.

Trying to meet the high expectations of parents and educators can result in considerable frustration. Although successful Asian American students credit their families for making sacrifices for their futures, others feel resentment (Divoky, 1988): "My parents will not let me stay after school to play soccer," a tenth-grade

Cambodian immigrant stated. "They say I have to study. I study and I study and I study. . . . If I don't have homework, still I study. They make me do it over and over again. They really want me to do well, but they don't understand about schools here." (p. 221)

Implementing Research 4-4 examines Asian Americans students' self-beliefs, academic background, and achievement.

---

**IMPLEMENTING RESEARCH 4-4  Self-Beliefs, Academic Background,
Achievement of Asian American Students**

J. Daniel House investigated the efficacy of attitudes toward self and school, academic self-concept, parental characteristics, and prior education as predictors of Asian Americans' academic performance. While House's research and conclusions focused on post-secondary achievement, his findings have relevance to educators (especially secondary educators) of children and adolescents. House studied nearly 400 students, with a mean age of 18, to study factors that influenced academic achievement.

In his review of the research, House offered several interesting findings: (1) the perception of future opportunities was related to attitudes toward school; (2) parental influence appears to contribute to Asian American students' high school achievement; (3) a higher proportion of Asian American students' parents have advanced degrees (in comparison to other ethnic groups), (4) results from a study of middle school students found Asian American students had higher educational goals than students from other ethnic groups.

His first finding was that initial attitudes such as academic self-concept, achievement expectations, motivational attitudes, and self-efficacy beliefs are significant predictors of Asian Americans' academic performance. His second finding was that academic preparation (such as the high school curriculum) is a significant predictor of first-year grade performance in postsecondary school education. Furthermore, Asian American parents' education significantly correlates with high school curriculum taken by students. Asian American students who took more units of academic study during high school tend to have parents with higher levels of educational attainment.

**Implementing the Research**

Educators, especially middle and secondary educators, should:

1. Place priority on factors such as attitudes toward school, achievement, and academic self-concept as a means of eventually influencing academic achievement.
2. Focus on future goals and career possibilities, so students will see the relationship between educational efforts now and future life goals.
3. Involve Asian American parents and families (just as with other parents and extended family members) in the education of their children and adolescents.
4. Instill high expectations that reflect and reinforce parents' efforts and cultural perceptions of academic success.

---

*Source:* House, D. J. (1997). The relationship between self-beliefs, academic background, and achievement of adolescent Asian American students. *Child Study Journal, 27*(2), 95–110.

## Language Problems

Language poses a major barrier to children in a land where few people can speak or write a language other than their own. As one Vietnamese girl observed (First, 1988), to be successful in the United States, "You have to know English" (p. 206). Educators who work with Asian American learners readily recognize the language and communication problems. One of the authors recently taught a Japanese American learner who excelled over all others in the class. Her language problems, however, required that she study far longer and more diligently than her classmates. During tests and other written work, she relied extensively on her Japanese-English dictionary and requested extra time. Despite all her language difficulties, her persistence and determination overcame her deficiencies in English. Case Study 4-3 tells of Keigo, her language problem, and what her teacher might do to help her.

Japanese American and Chinese American boys and girls scored lower than European American children on the verbal sections of an achievement test. The reasons for language difficulties may include that Asian Americans often come from bilingual backgrounds and that cultural traditions and customs often restrict or impede verbal communication. Many Asian American families, for example, encourage one-way communication; that is, parents speak to children.

Educators working in multicultural settings with such children can avoid several of the pitfalls that may lead to stereotypical thinking. Educators must remember that Asian American students may be communicating in a second language. Although English may be the predominant language, these children may continue to hear their parents' native language (Sue, 1981).

---

### CASE STUDY 4-3   The Language Problem

Keigo, an Asian American fourth-grader, has a language problem that interferes with several aspects of her life. She often cannot understand her teachers, and she has a hard time making friends. Her language at home and in her community does not pose a problem. Her parents and neighbors speak either their native language or a form of English. At school, Keigo's language deficiency results in her having to study harder and having few friends.

Keigo's teacher can take several approaches to helping her improve her language, make better use of her study time, and improve her friendships. It is important at the outset to avoid a "blame the victim" perspective, in which Keigo would be at fault for her lack of fluency in English. The teacher and the school as a whole should understand Keigo's situation and try to help her overcome the language barriers. First, the teacher should make arrangements with the school's language specialist to meet with Keigo and determine the extent of her problem and possible remediation efforts. Second, Keigo's teacher might consider placing her in a cooperative learning team in which other students can help her understand. Third, the teacher might place Keigo and other children with language difficulties in a group that receives extra attention.

Whatever means the teacher uses to help Keigo, it is important that the teacher understand Keigo and her problem rather than simply hope that the problem will disappear on its own.

---

**FOLLOW THROUGH 4-6**   **Addressing Asian American Language Problems**

Suggest several ways educators can address Asian Americans' language problems. What language programs will most effectively help Asian Americans? What other efforts might educators implement to help Asian Americans overcome language obstacles?

---

## Learning Styles: Cultural Considerations

The adjustment of the Asian American learner's cognitive learning styles to the U.S. school system deserves attention. Asian children tend to need reinforcement from teachers, and they work efficiently in a well-structured, quiet learning environment in which there are definite goals. Asian learners seldom reveal their opinions or their abilities voluntarily or dare to challenge their teachers.

Even when they know an answer to a teacher's question, they may choose to sit quietly as though they do not know. Older children may perform well in rote memorization and mathematics operations but may do poorly with creative writing or analytical commentary. Asian children tend to seek teachers' approval and to make their decisions based on what teachers think is best, thus becoming more dependent on teachers for help with schoolwork and guidance in classroom behavior (Yao, 1985).

Some factors are clear concerning Japanese learners: Their mothers are intensely involved in the children's learning, families celebrate the starting of school, and parents introduce children to mathematics concepts earlier in life. In Japan, children must learn a great deal of material quickly, learners must pass strict examinations, teachers teach moral values and character, schools set curfews and dress codes, and children spend more time in school. Although these factors do not represent learning styles per se, they do show how Japanese regard school, and they show that learners work conscientiously and diligently to achieve.

## School Practices Impeding Asian Americans' Progress

Educators who fail to understand Asian Americans' cultural backgrounds and their school-related problems may actually contribute to their difficulties in U.S. schools. Looking at Asian Americans from a European American perspective may promote learning experiences and expectations that are not compatible with Asian American expectations.

What school practices might interfere with the Asian American academic achievement or psychosocial development?

**1.** Providing predominantly verbal teaching and learning experiences that place Asian American learners at a disadvantage.

**2.** Failing to make school expectations clear to learners and their parents.

**3.** Expecting Asian American learners to participate in discussion and sharing times, which may jeopardize their (as in their family's) name or reputation.

**4.** Basing academic and behavioral expectations on stereotypical images of Asian American learners as "model" learners.

---

**CASE STUDY 4-4 "She Will Not Volunteer!"**

Mrs. Bush complains, "I do not know what to do. Those Asian Americans just will not volunteer or show any interest at all. I asked for volunteers to participate in a group discussion and not a hand was raised. Are they totally uninterested? I am at my wit's end. I just don't know how to motivate these students."

This perception of Asian Americans may be all too common in American schools. This problem results, however, more from the teacher's lack of understanding than from Asian Americans being noncommittal toward their education.

The teacher needs to understand that Asian Americans, because of their cultural backgrounds, are reluctant to bring attention to themselves or to stand out among peers. Although the teacher might want to talk with an Asian American student (alone, rather than in front of the class, where the conversation might seem like a reprimand) about class participation, the teacher should not force or coerce the student into participating in an activity that may be culturally or personally threatening.

---

Understanding Asian American learners and their cultural backgrounds and diversity places these practices in proper perspective. Although educators should recognize and appreciate their accomplishments, Asian Americans deserve individual consideration of their differences, abilities, motivation, and attitudes.

Case Study 4-4 shows that Mrs. Bush does not understand her Asian American students and what she might do to improve her cultural understanding.

Suggestions for understanding and teaching Asian American learners include:

**1.** Avoid reprimanding or disciplining the Asian American learner in front of peers. Having one's name written on the blackboard or on other public displays may be far more damaging to the Asian child than to the European American child (West, 1983).

**2.** Avoid thinking that all Asian Americans are high achievers who reach excellence in all academic areas and who model impeccable behavior.

**3.** Help the Asian American family to understand the U.S. school system and its expectations of learners and their families. Also, try to understand how the Asian family perceives teachers; that is with high respect. As the teacher earns the family's respect, the teacher gains its assistance and support.

**4.** Understand that behavior (at least to European American teachers) that may seem to indicate indifference or lack of interest (for example, looking the other way or not volunteering to answer) is appropriate for Asian learners. For example, Asian culture teaches learners to listen more than they speak and to speak in a well-modulated voice.

**5.** Other culturally specific traits that a teacher should understand include: Asian American learners may be modest in dress; girls might be quieter than boys; girls might not want to reveal their legs during physical education activities; and problems might result when assigning girls and boys as cooperative learning partners (West, 1983).

---

**FOLLOW THROUGH 4-7   Determining Differences in Asian American Learners**

Observe a group of Asian American learners doing schoolwork to determine their learning habits, such as time on a given task, individual versus cooperative work, and reliance on bilingual dictionaries. How do they differ from European American learners? What could you, as an educator in a multicultural setting, do to help these learners?

---

### Promoting Self-Esteem and Cultural Identities

Asian American children have special needs that responsive educators should address. In a school system that might seem different, and perhaps even oblivious to their needs, these learners need teaching and learning experiences that reflect their cultural and social experience. Learners in formative developmental stages may begin to question their self-worth and their cultural worth. Responsive multicultural educators need to focus their efforts in several directions that will improve the self-esteem of Asian American learners.

First, the actual effect of the school experience on the Asian American learner deserves consideration. Attending a school that appears to direct attention toward the majority culture can cause Asian Americans to question their place in the school. Educators can focus attention in several directions: recognizing Asian Americans as integral and worthy learners in the school system; recognizing the Asian culture as worthy; and directly addressing the concerns of Asian Americans, for example, teachers who often have high expectations based on the model minority stereotype.

Second, educators can respond by understanding the cultural differences that affect Asian Americans and their academic and social progress in U.S. schools. For example, Asian Americans strive toward the accomplishment that brings pride to the family, in contrast to European Americans, who work for individual acclaim. The custom of many European Americans is to question the teacher, volunteer for an academic activity, or assertively raise their hands to answer a teacher's question. Such traits are in opposition to Asian beliefs. Teachers need to understand these cultural differences and then respond with appropriate teaching behaviors, rather than expect learners of all cultures to respond in a similar fashion.

Specifically, educators can:

1. Read aloud culturally appropriate children's books about Asian Americans.
2. Convey a sense of welcome that makes children feel wanted, a part of the class, and an integral presence in the classroom.
3. Encourage them to make a "Me" collage that demonstrates both the individual and the Asian culture.
4. Encourage learners to engage in "open-ended writing" in which they can probe their feelings and express them without fear of sharing.
5. Teach learners to write about "What I Like about My Life" (and perhaps culture) or "Ten Things about Me," in which learners can feel free to express opinions and emotions (Tiedt & Tiedt, 1995).

Third, responsive multicultural educators need to engage in direct activities to improve the self-esteem of Asian American learners. Such activities include specifically addressing their needs, asking about their families (using extreme caution not to make the learner feel uncomfortable or think that the teacher is prying), genuinely and truthfully conveying to the learner that other students would benefit from knowing more about the Asian culture, and letting the students know that their presence is understood, accepted, and appreciated by both school personnel and other children and adolescents.

Educators should remember the importance of the family in efforts to improve self-esteem. Asians generally have close-knit families, and Asian people's feelings about themselves usually include a consideration of their feelings about the family (and vice versa).

---

**CULTURAL PORTRAIT   Mina—An Asian American Learner**

Mina, a ten-year-old Asian American girl, attends a large urban elementary school whose population is approximately half Caucasian, one-fourth African, and one-fourth Asian and Hispanic. Mina makes about average grades but does not make the high grades that her family and teachers expect. Her problem with the English language is probably the major factor for her grades not being among the highest, but other factors also contribute: her family and teachers have expectations that are unrealistically high; she does not to want to volunteer for special assignments; she does not want to raise her hand to answer; and she does not always understand the European American learner's attitude toward school, teachers, and people. Mina feels a little lost. Her teachers are either European or African American. They are friendly and appear to want to help her, but they do not seem to understand her and the way she believes children should act around adults, especially teachers. She perceives the school as being oriented toward European American expectations, and perhaps a little toward the African perspective, yet very little toward the Asian or the Hispanic expectations. While she feels somewhat frustrated with this arrangement, she also realizes that she has to do her best schoolwork and that her behavior must be exemplary. Otherwise her family might feel shame or disappointment.

*How Mina's Teacher Can Respond*

Responding to Mina's psychosocial and intellectual needs first requires understanding her as an individual learner and then as a member of the Asian American culture. After a determination of her strengths and weaknesses, her teacher should focus attention in several directions.

1. Help Mina to understand both the Asian culture and the American culture.
2. Maintain high (but not unrealistic) expectations for Mina, and avoid relying on cultural stereotypes.
3. Understand that Mina's reluctance to volunteer or raise her hand during class is a reflection of her cultural background and that it does not indicate indifference.
4. Provide appropriate multicultural experiences that teach learners of all cultures about the Asian culture, its diverse characteristics, and its many contributions.
5. Assign a professional in the school to be an adviser or mentor who will help Mina deal with daily school routines.
6. Meet with Mina's family to explain the philosophy and expectations of American school systems, and work to gain the understanding, respect, and support of Mina's family.
7. Decide how special service personnel, that is, guidance counselors, speech and language specialists, and other school support personnel, can assist Mina.

---

**FOLLOW THROUGH 4-8    Promoting Self-Esteem and Cultural Identities**

Asian Americans' different cultural traditions, language difficulties, and different family values can result in lower self-esteem and negative cultural identities. What signs of lower self-esteems or confused or negative cultural identities might educators look for? Name several ways educators can help Asian Americans develop positive self-esteems and cultural identities.

---

## Summing Up

Educators planning educational experiences for Asian American learners should:

**1.** Reflect on both historical and contemporary Asian cultural experiences and plan teaching and learning experiences accordingly.

**2.** Undertake objective assessments, rather than believing all learners are members of a "model minority."

**3.** Understand that language warrants understanding because of its cultural basis (and its cultural value) and because of the problems many Asian Americans have with the English language.

**4.** Understand that positive self-esteem and cultural identities are crucial to Asian learners' psychosocial development and general outlook on life. Plan appropriate activities.

**5.** Recognize that students have their distinct culture with its unique cultural characteristics, rather than grouping all Asian American learners into one "Asian" culture.

**6.** Consider the tremendous diversity among learners—individual, generational, socioeconomic, urban, and rural—rather than categorizing all Asian American learners into one homogeneous group.

**7.** Exercise extreme caution by not expecting all Asian American learners to be high achievers.

**8.** Recognize the family and its powerful influence (e.g., the injunction against bringing shame and embarrassment on the family) on children and adolescents.

## Suggested Learning Activities

1. Select an Asian American learner and evaluate his or her language problem. Specifically, (1) diagnose the exact problem, (2) list several educational areas on which the problem might have an effect, and (3) devise a remediation plan.

2. Complete a case study of a high-achieving Asian American student. Specifically, (1) outline outstanding accomplishments, (2) address how the family has contributed to successes, (3) describe any problems or frustrations the student may experience, (4) explain how one can account for outstanding achievements, even though language problems

exist, and (5) ask how schools can address the student's problems. Show why it is imperative that educators not base teaching and learning experiences on the "model minority" stereotype.

3. Survey several educators who have taught Asian American students. Develop a survey designed to determine the strengths and weaknesses of Asian American learners, the educators' opinions of Asian American attitudes and achievements, and how schools respond to meet the individual needs of Asian American learners. What efforts can be made to educate parents and gain their support? Generally speaking, what approaches can you suggest to educators who work with Asian American learners of varying cultural backgrounds and individual differences?

## Suggestions for Collaborative Efforts

Form groups of three or four that, if possible, represent our nation's cultural and gender diversity. Working collaboratively, focus your group's attention toward the following efforts:

1. Have each member of your group select an Asian American learner: a Japanese American, a Chinese American, a Filipino American, and a Korean American. After getting to know these learners and their families, show similarities and differences among the four cultures. Specifically consider cultural characteristics, families, academic achievement, socioeconomic accomplishments, and any other area in which similarities and differences are evident.

2. Choose two to three learners of similar cultural backgrounds but of differing generational or socioeconomic status. Compare the similarities and differences that reflect the effects of socioeconomic class or generational differences. How does your group think educators can most effectively determine and address generational differences?

3. Educators often experience difficulties locating children's books that focus on Asian American learners and themes. Consult recent publishers' catalogs and make a list of current children's books that appear to provide accurate descriptions of the Asian American culture. Check with textbook publishers to determine what efforts are being made to make textbooks more reflective of our increasingly multicultural society.

## Expanding Your Horizons: Additional Journal Readings and Books

Chang, J. I. (1997). Contexts of adolescent worries: Impacts of ethnicity, gender, family structure, and socioeconomic status. (ERIC Document Reproduction Service No: ED 417 003).

*Chang compared the worries of Caucasian adolescents and minority adolescents (Native American, African American, Hispanic American, and Asian Americans). Minority females worry more than males and Caucasian females, about grades, relationships with parents, and appearances.*

Eaton, M. J., & Dembo, M. H. (1997). Differences in the motivational beliefs of Asian American and non-Asian students. *Journal of Educational Psychology, 89*(3), 433–440.

*Eaton and Dembo explained Asian Americans' fear of academic failure and how this fear contributes to their academic success.*

Espiritu, Y. L. (1997). Race, gender, and class in the lives of Asian Americans. *Race, Gender, and Class,* 4(3), 12–19.

*Espiritu maintains that because of their racial ambiguity, Asian Americans have been described as being both like black and white people.*

Kim, H., Rendon, L., & Valadez, J. (1998). Student characteristics, school characteristics, and educational aspirations of six Asian American groups. *Journal of Multicultural Counseling and Development,* 26(3), 166–178.

*These authors studied differences in educational aspirations, math performance, and socioeconomic characteristics of six Asian American groups.*

Lee, O. (1997). Diversity and equity for Asian American students in science education. *Science Education,* 81(1), 107–122.

*Lee addresses issues of diversity and equity with Asian American students in science education and discusses current reforms in science education, with a focus specifically on Asian Americans.*

Low, J. M., & Wong, P. L. (1998). Effects of a Hmong intern on Hmong students. *Multicultural Education* 5(4), 12–16.

*Low and Wong tell of the effects of an intern on students and focus on teacher beliefs and values that must exist to implement and sustain effective instructional programs for language minority students.*

Park, C. (1997). Learning style preference of Asian American (Chinese, Filipino, Korean, and Vietnamese) students in secondary schools. *Equity and Excellence in Education,* 30(2), 68–77.

*Park studied the learning style preference of Chinese, Filipino, Korean, and Vietnamese students and makes comparisons between Asian and Anglo groups and between Asian groups.*

Wrigley, T. (1997). Raising achievement for Asian pupils. *Multicultural Teaching* 16(1), 21–25.

*Wrigley analyzes management, pedagogy, curriculum, and resources to determine how teachers can raise the achievement of Asian students experiencing marginal academic success.*

## Expanding Your Students' Horizons: Appropriate Asian American Books for Children and Adolescents

Bell, William. *Forbidden City: A Novel of Modern China.* Bantam, 1990.

Betancourt, Jeanne. *More Than Meets the Eye.* Bantam, 1990.

Chang, Margaret, and Raymond Chang. *In the Eye of War.* Macmillan, 1990.

Chandler, David P. *The Land and People of Cambodia.* HarperCollins, 1991.

Demi. *The Empty Pot.* Henry Holt, 1990.

Demi. *The Stonecutter.* Crown, 1995.

Edmonds, I. G. *Ooka the Wise: Tales of Old Japan.* Linnet Books, 1994.

Garland, Sherry. *Vietnam: Rebuilding a Nation.* Dillon, 1990.

Haugaard, Erik Christian. *The Boy and the Samurai.* Houghton Mifflin, 1991.

Heo, Yumi. *One Afternoon.* Orchard, 1994.

Ho, Minfong. *Rice without Rain.* Lothrop, Lee and Shepard, 1990.

Hong, Maria. *Growing Up Asian.* Tupelo, 1993.

Jaffe, Nina (retold by). *Older Brother, Younger Brother.* Viking, 1995.

Johnston, Tony. *The Badger and the Magic Fan: A Japanese Folk Tale.* Putnam, 1990.

Kline, Suzy. *Horrible Harry's Secret.* Viking, 1990.

Lee, C. Y. *The Second Son of Heaven: A Novel of Nineteenth Century China.* William Morrow, 1990.

Mahy, Margaret. *The Seven Chinese Brothers.* Scholastic, 1990.

Major, John S. *The Land and People of Mongolia.* HarperCollins, 1990.

Mayberry, Jodine. *Filipinos.* Franklin Watts, 1990.

Okimoto, Jean Davis. *Molly by Any Other Name.* Scholastic, 1990.

Patent, Gregory. *Shanghai Passage.* Clarion, 1990.

Pitkanen, Matti A., and Reijo Harkonen. *The Children of China.* Lerner/Carolrhoda, 1990.

Say, Allen. *The Inn-Keeper's Apprentice.* Puffin, 1996.

Scarboro, Elizabeth. *The Secret Language of the SB.* Viking, 1990.

Schlein, Mariam. *The Year of the Panda.* HarperCollins, 1990.

Stamm, Claus. *Three Strong Women: A Tall Tale from Japan.* Viking, 1990.

Tan, Amy. *The Hundred Secret Senses.* Putnam and Sons, 1995.

Tompert, Ann. *Grandfather Tang's Story.* Crown, 1990.

Turner, Ann. *Through Moon and Stars and Night Skies.* HarperCollins, 1990.

Waters, Kate, and Madeline Slovenz-Low. *Lion Dancer: Ernie War's Chinese New Year.* Scholastic, 1990.

Wong, Janet S. *Good Luck Gold and Other Poems.* McElderry, 1994.

Yep, Laurence. *The Rainbow People.* Harper & Row, 1989.

Yep, Laurence. *Hiroshima.* Scholastic, 1995.

## Answers to the Culture Quiz: Asian Americans

| | | | |
|---|---|---|---|
| **1.** b | **3.** f | **5.** c | **7.** h |
| **2.** a | **4.** e | **6.** d | **8.** g |

# Chapter 5

---

# Understanding European
American Children
and Adolescents

Understanding the materials and activities in this chapter will help the reader to

- Describe European Americans, their origins, and who they are today.
- Identify several stereotypes of European American learners and how these stereotypes adversely affect peers' opinions as well as educators' perceptions of their propensity toward academic success and behavior.
- Describe European Americans' cultural, gender, socioeconomic, family, religious, and language diversity.
- Describe European American learners and show how teaching and learning practices can reflect knowledge of cultural differences and learning styles.
- Suggest appropriate readings, activities, and collaborative activities for gaining a better understanding of European Americans.

## Overview

The African, Asian, and Hispanic, and Native Americans cultural groups make up a sizable percentage of our nation's diversity. Likewise, their differences, traditions, customs, language, and dialects enrich the United States in many ways. Another cultural group, however, also contributes to the nation's diversity. The various European American cultures bring a plethora of differences that perceptive educators will want their students to understand and appreciate. As Asian and Hispanic

Americans originate from many places, European Americans originate from scores of locations such as France, Germany, Greece, Hungary, Ireland, Italy, Poland, and Portugal as Chapter 1 indicated. This chapter focuses on European Americans and their cultural, gender, socioeconomic, family, religious, and language diversity. To avoid overgeneralizing, we will discuss specific cultural groups whenever possible.

## Origins

The hundred-year period from 1830 to 1930 was a century of mass immigration in the history of the United States. Many millions of people uprooted themselves, primarily from crowded places of Europe, and flowed outward to less crowded areas such as the United States. About 32 million left Europe for the United States, contributing enormously to the nation's expansion and industrial growth. The primary reason for this massive transfer of people from the Old World to the New World was the social and economic strain on the rural systems of Europe. More specific causes included large populations; the lack of farming land for all people; and the abolition of feudalism, which ended peasant privileges (Alba, 1985).

In the colonial days, most of America's immigrants came from Great Britain and Ireland and a few from Germany, France, the Netherlands, Belgium, and Luxembourg. During the early nineteenth century, Germans (mainly tradesmen, farmers, weavers, tailors, shoemakers, and carpenters) began coming in ever-increasing numbers. The French, Norwegians, and Swedes also began moving to the United States, feeling the push of economic pressures at home and the pull of prospective free land and good wages in the New World. Italians began arriving in 1890, and from 1900 until the start of World War I, about a quarter of all immigrants were Italians. After World War II, many Germans arrived in the United States (U.S. Bureau of the Census, 1993d).

The United States in the last thirty years has experienced a surge of immigration unseen since the turn of the century. The foreign-born population of this nation reached a record high of 19.9 million in 1990. The proportion of immigrants from Europe—more than 80 percent in 1900—was only 22 percent in 1990. Two-thirds of present-day foreign-born Americans were born in Latin American and Asia, coming from countries as diverse as Mexico, China, El Salvador, Korea, and the Philippines (Fuligni, 1997).

As Chapter 2 indicated, the European American people came from a wide array of places—western and southern portions of Europe as well as the eastern portion and the Soviet Union. Greeks, Italians, Poles, Irish, French, and Germans are well known in the United States, but other people from the Netherlands, Portugal, Spain, and Switzerland are less known. Each cultural group brought its own cultural characteristics, language, traditions, and customs, which contributed to the already rich diversity of this nation. They came to America for a number of different reasons: some planned to earn money and return to their home country, whereas others planned to make America their home.

Although the number of European cultures makes it impossible to discuss them all, it is interesting to examine a few cultures and immigrants' reasons for coming to the United States. Such a discussion is limited to census information and recent books written on the European people; the same information is not available for all cultural groups.

Greek immigration began in the 1880s when the Greek economy failed to show signs of improvement. These early immigrants came from the Peloponnesus and Tripoli, both agricultural and pastoral regions that were economically depressed. In fact, the Greek government actually encouraged young men to emigrate so they could send money back to Greece (Scourby, 1984).

The majority of Poles came to the United States as a result of mass migration during World War II. The immigrating Poles were a diverse group. Some were women and children without an occupational designation; others were blacksmiths, carpenters, locksmiths, miners, dressmakers, shoemakers, and tailors. There was concern about how Polish immigrants would sustain themselves in their new land. Three percent entered with fifty dollars in their possession, having spent most of their money on transportation. Only about one-fourth had others, usually relatives, to cover the cost. Another problem, language, confronted Poles as they entered the English-speaking nation (Lopata, 1994). They worked in the steel mills and coal mines of Pennsylvania, Ohio, and Indiana; in the automobile factories of Detroit; and in the stockyards of Chicago. Many changed their names to survive and hide their native origins.

---

**THE CULTURE QUIZ   European Americans**

*Directions:* Match the individuals with their contributions or achievements by placing the appropriate letter before each name.

_____ **1.** Lucas Miltiades Miller

_____ **2.** Bruno Bettelheim

_____ **3.** Hannah Arendt

_____ **4.** Stan Ulam

_____ **5.** Thomas F. W. Barth

_____ **6.** Karen Horney

_____ **7.** Camillo Artom

_____ **8.** Salvador Dali

_____ **9.** Felix Bloch

_____ **10.** John von Neumann

**a.** German political philosopher and editor

**b.** Polish mathematician who immigrated to the United States and worked in basic and applied mathematics

**c.** First American of Greek descent to be elected to the U.S. Congress

**d.** Nobel Prize–winner and physicist from Switzerland who taught at Stanford

**e.** Italian biochemist who worked at Bowman Gray Medical School

**f.** Spanish painter who moved to France and eventually to the United States; a surrealist

**g.** Austrian psychologist and psychoanalyst who worked at University of Chicago

**h.** Hungarian mathematician who taught at Princeton

**i.** Geologist from Norway

**j.** German psychoanalyst, a founder of the American Institute of Psychoanalysis

(Answers to the Culture Quiz are located at the end of the chapter.)

More than 5 million immigrants from Italy arrived in America between 1820 and 1870, and more than 4.5 million came during the century of mass immigration, 1830–1930. Only the number of arrivals from Germany was larger. The Italian immigration was concentrated tightly into a small period of time—more than 4 million arrived between 1890 and 1921, and in fact, 2 million arrived during a single decade, 1901–1910. The peak year of Italian immigration was 1907 when nearly 300,000 came to the United States. Although it is difficult to pinpoint exact regions from which they came, many Italian immigrants came from Mezzogiorno. Between 1899 and 1910, when more than 2,200,000 immigrants came, perhaps as many as 80 percent came from the Mezzogiorno region (Alba, 1985).

Abrams (1993) reported that significant numbers of Jews migrated to Israel and to the United States from the former Soviet Union. With the crumbling of the Soviet economic system, came the resurgence of anti-Semitism. Although the majority of Jewish people are choosing Israel as their new home, 40,000 immigrated to the United States in 1989.

These Jewish people, however, are not the first to arrive in the United States from the former Soviet Union. In the 1970s, some Jewish people arrived in the United States from the Soviet Union after the Six Day War and the Leningrad Trial.

---

## FOR ADDITIONAL INFORMATION    Associations

European American Chamber of Commerce, 801 Pennsylvania Ave., NW, Washington, D.C. 20004.

This association works to promote U.S. and European trade by conducting seminars, studies, and educational programs.

Society for the Preservation of the Greek Heritage, 5125 MacArthur Blvd., NW, Washington, D.C. 20016. As the name suggests, the association works to preserve the natural and cultural heritage of Greece. It consists of professional, business, and academic groups and publishes a quarterly newsletter.

American Hungarian Library and Historical Society (AHLHS), 213 E. 82nd St., New York, NY 10021. The AHLHS maintains a collection of Hungariana and sponsors a library. It is affiliated with the American Hungarian Foundation and holds an annual meeting.

Irish Heritage Foundation (IHF), 2123 Market St., San Francisco, CA 94114. The IHF includes individuals interested in Irish culture, history, and education. It maintains a library and publishes a monthly newsletter.

American Institute of Polish Culture (AIPC), 1440 79th St. Causeway, Suite 117, Miami, FL 33141. The AIPC includes professionals, students, artists, and writers. It works to further knowledge and appreciation of the history, science, art, and culture of Poland.

French-American Foundation (FAF), 41 E. 72nd St., New York, NY 10021. The FAF works to strengthen relations between the United States and France by promoting exchange of specialists, internships, study tours, and conferences.

American Academy for Jewish Research (AAJR), 3080 Broadway, New York, NY 10027. Founded in 1919, the AAJR consists of scholars, rabbis, and learned laymen interested in promoting Jewish learning and research. The association publishes an annual journal, which contains articles on Judaica and related subjects.

American Jewish Historical Society (AJHS), 2 Thornton Rd., Waltham, MA 02154. The AJHS comprises individuals and institutions interested in American Jewish history. The association maintains a reference library, gives various awards, and publishes a quarterly journal.

---

**IMPLEMENTING RESEARCH 5-1    White Americans: The New Minority?**

Warren and Twine explain the common belief that whites will be a minority as immigrants increasingly enter our nation. The Immigration Act of 1965 changed immigration patterns, and U. S. policies no longer favored privileged European immigrants. People from many other cultural groups were allowed to enter the United States. Asian and Latin American immigrants are now the majority in some California cities.

Still Warren and Twine question whether whites are really becoming a minority because "whiteness" is not a fixed racial category. As they say, "racial categories are not etched in stone, but are malleable" (p. 215). For example, races other than the traditional white or Anglo-Saxon races are being included in the designation. At one time in American history, the Irish people were not considered white—they were considered as a separate race and members of an "inferior Celtic race" (p. 219) that could be physically distinguished from the "superior Anglo-Saxon race" (p. 220). Now the Irish are considered white by the Census Bureau and everyone else.

Warren and Twine raise several questions: How did the expanding white category come to include previously defined nonwhites? How did the Celts, Slavs, and Mediterraneans come to be included in the white race? When were these groups allowed to blend, intermarry, and move up the socioeconomic ladder? The authors do not answer these questions, but they do contend that the answers rest in large part with the way whiteness is defined in the United States.

**Implementing the Research**

Multicultural educators should:

1.    Realize that racial categories are not fixed. It is sometimes difficult to place people in specific categories. In fact, some people might be confused about where they "belong."
2.    Realize the struggles that many cultural groups have experienced throughout American history, such as the Irish, Chinese and Japanese Americans, and African Americans, just to name a few. Many have been treated harshly because of their skin color or cultural background.
3.    Understand and accept all people as worthy of respect, whatever their cultural backgrounds and whether they are considered majority or minority.

---

*Source:* Warren, J. W., & Twine, F. W. (1997). White Americans: The new minority? Non-blacks and the ever-expanding boundaries of whiteness. *Journal of Black Studies 28*(2), 200–218.

At first, nearly all left for Israel; but after 1972, a rising proportion chose other countries. The majority of the 90,000 Soviet Jews who chose the United States came from Russia, Byelorussia, and Ukraine, those republics most heavily under the rule of the Soviet regime. These Jews had had their Jewish heritage systemically denied through the closing of synagogues, the banning of the study of Hebrew and Yiddish, and the virulent anti-Israel, anti-Zionist propaganda of the Soviet regime (Abrams, 1993).

**FOLLOW THROUGH 5-1    Will Whites Become a Minority?**

In a group of three or four, discuss Warren and Twine's question: Are whites really becoming a minority because whiteness is not a fixed racial category? A number of demographic studies suggest whites will become a minority—what does your group think?

**USING CHILDREN'S LITERATURE    The European American Experience**

Zheleznikov, Vladimir. *The Rainbow People,* HarperCollins, 1990. A young girl comes to live with her grandfather in Russia. This is a powerful story of an individual against a group.

Lingard, Joan. *Tug of War,* Dutton/Lodestar, 1990. The Germans are retreating from Russia, and the Petersons are on the enemy list.

Pettepice, Thomas, and Aleksin, Anatoly (Eds.), *Face to Face,* Putnam/Philomel, 1990. This is the first collection of American and Russian short stories published simultaneously in both countries.

## European Americans Today

European Americans today live in many geographical areas of the United States. Available data from the U.S. Census Bureau do not indicate the cities where European Americans have selected to live. Some evidence, however, suggests that immigrants to the United States tend to settle near their port of entry. More than two-thirds of those who came from Italy, for example, live in the northeastern part of the country where they arrived (U.S. Bureau of the Census, 1993d).

Table 5-1 shows selected cultural groups and their immigration numbers in 1980 and 1995. Table 5-2 on page 120 shows the immigrant numbers of the top five

**TABLE 5-1    Numbers of German, British, and Italian Immigrants to the United States, 1980 and 1995**

|                 | 1980[1]   | 1995[2]     |
|-----------------|-----------|-------------|
| Germany         | 849,000   | 620,000     |
| United Kingdom  | 669,000   | 1,200,000   |
| Italy           | 832,000   | 220,000     |

[1]From *We the American . . . foreign born,* p. 3. by U.S. Bureau of the Census, 1993d, Washington, D.C.
[2]U.S. Bureau of the Census. (1997a). *Statistical abstracts of the United States* (117th edition). Washington, D.C.

TABLE 5-2   The Five European Cultural Groups with the Largest
            Numbers of Immigrants to the United States, 1995

| | |
|---|---|
| Soviet Union (former) | 54,500 |
| Poland | 13,800 |
| Germany | 6,200 |
| Ireland | 5,300 |
| Romania | 4,900 |

*Source:* U.S. Bureau of the Census. (1997a). *Statistical abstracts of the United States* (117th edition). Washington, D.C.

European cultural groups in 1995. Of the forty groups with more than 100,000 foreign-born persons in 1990, fourteen declined in size from the previous census. Italians, followed by Scottish, Hungarians, Germans, and Greeks had the largest declines (U.S. Bureau of the Census, 1993d).

Case Study 5-1 acknowledges the tremendous cultural diversity of our nation and shows how one school offered a response.

---

**CASE STUDY 5-1   School of Many Cultures**

Eastside Elementary School is in an urban area of California. Its diversity reflects many different cultures, each with its own traditions and customs and many with their own languages. Many students are first- and second-generation Americans who live in cultural enclaves or areas where they feel comfortable with others who share their culture and language.

Teachers and administrators at Eastside Elementary School have had many challenges. First, about half the teachers had taught only middle-class (mostly white) children before coming to Eastside. Not only did they experience culture shock, they also had to change their teaching styles. Second, language has posed a problem. One administrator commented that twelve different languages are spoken in the school. Various school committees work diligently to find ways to foster language diversity in the schools *and* provide English as a second language.

Third, they have had to address communicating with parents, many of whom have con-

siderable difficulty with English. Fourth, Eastside implemented curricular experiences and teaching strategies to reflect cultural diversity. This planning required special training, which the teachers gained through contract courses with the nearby university and through in-service courses at the school.

The educators at Eastside have met these and other challenges with varying degrees of success. The important point is that they have realized that the changing cultural composition of the student body requires them to change the school; no longer can educational experiences reflect only the learning needs and styles of 15 percent of the student population. Likewise, the effort involves all those associated with the school—students, educators, parents, and other community members. Eastside's educators are taking a comprehensive approach, one that requires deliberate effort and dedication. The result is an excellent example of a school addressing our nation's multicultural population.

## *Stereotyping of European American Children and Adolescents*

European cultures are not immune to the stereotyping that has dogged Native, African, Asian, and Hispanic cultures. Alba (1985) writes of the the stereotyping of Italian Americans and suggests that all European groups have been considered in terms of undesirable characteristics. Italians have been stereotyped as being swarthy, bearing signs of physical degradation (such as their foreheads), having criminal tendencies, and being prone to passion and violence. Jews are stereotyped as stingy, shrewd, and intellectual (Atkinson, Morten, & Sue, 1993). Germans are often characterized as evil, incompetent, or mad (Winawer-Steiner & Wetzel, 1996). Readers know that the unfair and dangerous list could continue.

## *Cultural Characteristics*

The most valid cultural descriptions of European Americans come from considering individual cultures.

Greek Americans are confident that they alone know the causes of their problems and how best to solve them. If they feel powerless, they are likely to either overdo attempts to control their families or to sink into fatalistic resignation. If misfortune comes their way, they assume that the causes of the problems come not from themselves but from somewhere outside the family, such as the malice of neighbors or the envy of competitors.

Greek Americans take tremendous pride in individual achievement and consider themselves as individuals (Welts, 1982). Welts believes that Greek Americans may have difficulty in cooperating with others, especially in business deals. They prefer a competitive atmosphere and are usually unwilling to put aside their individual interests for the sake of the group.

Case Study 5-2 on page 122 looks at Helen, a Greek American girl, and the concerns she faced.

Italian Americans have a strong allegiance to family, and tend to live where they grew up. They believe young people should learn from their elders and have an allegiance to a church. They are suspicious of strangers and expect filial obedience (Alba, 1985). Alba comments that some of these tendencies (e.g., suspiciousness of strangers) decrease with education and advancing occupational position.

---

**FOLLOW THROUGH 5-2   Clarifying Stereotypes and Their Harmful Effects**

Stereotypes, as harmful as they are to interpersonal relationships and to decisions about educational practice, persist. Name some of the more common stereotypes about the various European cultures—how might these stereotypes affect teaching and learning decisions? How might educators educate themselves and others about stereotypes?

### CASE STUDY 5-2   Helen—A Greek American Girl

Helen, an eleventh-grader, was a second-generation Greek American. She was personable, intelligent, spoke excellent English, and was an all-around good student. She spoke of wanting to teach in an elementary school when she finished college. While Helen was sociable and others liked her, she did not have any close friends. In fact, she perceived several of her teachers as friends and spoke with them at length whenever she could.

While Helen was Americanized in many ways, her parents and extended family members held onto Greek values, customs, and traditions. They continued to speak Greek in their home on many occasions. Once the teacher telephoned Helen's home and asked to speak with her. The father spoke English with such an accent and with such difficulty that the teacher could not understand why Helen could not come to the phone. The next day, Helen asked the teacher whether she had called and ex-plained that she had not been at home. The teacher perceived that Helen was uncomfortable that she had called and did not call Helen at home again.

The family owned a fast-food restaurant, which had been in business for nearly twenty-five years since the father brought his family from Greece. All family members worked at some time; Helen probably worked the least because she committed so much of her time to schoolwork.

The teacher had a genuine respect for Helen's Greek background, but she wondered how Helen considered her diversity. Did she feel accepted? Did her parents and family members' continuing to speak Greek bother her? Did she intentionally avoid working in the restaurant? The teacher did not take any specific action, but she wondered about Helen's feelings and wondered about her own decision not to discuss Helen's diversity with her.

Greek Americans value frugality, careful saving, and wise use of financial resources; they often work two jobs. Scourby (1984) describes Greek Americans in several ways: they have clearly defined status and roles in work situations; they practice patriarchal control and have deeply binding extended kinship networks; they value interdependence among people (rather than individualism); and they demonstrate a strong need to defend family honor and, generally speaking, have a love of *philotimo* or honor.

### USING CHILDREN'S LITERATURE   The European American Experience

Hollinger, Peggy. *Greece.* Franklin Watts, 1990. This book looks at Greece and the Greek people—their education, religion, and family life.

Rosen, Billi. *Andi's War.* Dutton, 1991. Hostility between countrymen remains in Greece even after World War II.

Ian, James. *The Netherlands.* Franklin Watts, 1990. This book looks at the history, art, food, and other topics of the Netherlands.

Roberts, Elizabeth. *Europe 1992: The United States of Europe.* Franklin Watts, 1990. Roberts looks at the Single European Act, which proposes that twelve countries establish an area without internal frontiers.

## Gender

While not an area of extensive research in the European American culture, gender differences exist in European American males and females, just as they do in all cultures. Girls and boys have different learning styles, worldviews, perceptions of motivation and school success, and learning strategies. For example, an educator cannot conclude that a cooperative, seemingly passive female is not motivated, because boys show different signs of motivation and competitive behaviors. The educator's challenge is to recognize that girls and boys are different, make an attempt to know individual females, and plan strategies to which females can relate.

## Socioeconomic Status

Describing the socioeconomic status of the many European cultures is nearly impossible. Just as with other cultures we discuss in this book, many variations exist among European cultures. There are both wealthy and poor European Americans, just as with all cultures. Many criteria determine a person's socioeconomic status: Is the husband or father present? Does the wife work? How many children are in the family? Are the people living in a part of the country where the cost of living is high or low? How well does the family manage its money?

## Families

An educator should approach any discussion of family characteristics with considerable caution. Family patterns differ according to time of immigration, region of origin, economic class, and religious background. Many factors influence how a family lives, the roles of the husband and wife, perspectives on and treatment of children, and the importance of extended-family members. While preservice and

---

### FOR ADDITIONAL INFORMATION

For additional information on children's books, we refer readers to *Our Family, Our Friends, Our World: An Annotated Guide to Significant Multicultural Books for Children and Teenagers* by Lyn Miller-Lachmann (Providence, NJ: R. R. Bowker, 1992). This bibliography comprehensively explores multicultural books from all over the world, divides books into age groups, and provides a brief summary of each.

---

### FOLLOW THROUGH 5-3   Helping Learners from Lower Socioeconomic Groups

List ways that coming from a lower socioeconomic group might influence a learner's motivation, perceptions of school success, or value placed on education. Do schools genuinely address the learning needs of the poor? What steps do you or your group recommend for schools to better meet the needs of learners from lower socioeconomic groups?

in-service teachers need information about European families, providing a description of these families risks stereotyping. To avoid stereotyping, we attempt to use only the most objective information and the most widely accepted resources.

In the German American family, the husband or father is the head of the household and leader of the family. Traditionally the father, although sometimes sentimental, has a stern side. He is usually self-controlled, reserved, strict, and stubborn. Somewhat distant, the husband or father is often less emotionally available to the children than their mother. The German American woman, regarded as hardworking, dutiful, and subservient, adopts her husband's family and friends and gains his social status. Her contributions center mainly around household and family duties. Today the wife's main tasks continue to focus on the house and the family. In fact, how her husband and children look can be a source of pride to her (Winawer-Steiner & Wetzel, 1996).

Implementing Research 5-2 looks at immigrant families and the changes they might face on their migration to the United States.

The Greek American family maintains strict sex roles. Men provide economic necessities, and women cater to men's desires and wish to be good wives. Men are authoritarian fathers and husbands. Often appearing emotionally distant, they are parsimonious with praise and generous with criticism. They often tease their children (some say to toughen them), and children learn that teasing is part of being loved. Other male characteristics include revering their mothers, valuing the family honor, and believing the women's place is in the home. Women expect to comply with tradition and view motherhood as a fulfillment. They prefer male children over female, even in the urban areas of the United States. Having a son is a mother's main source of prestige. Parents feel that some emotions such as uncertainty, anxiety, and fear are weaknesses that should be hidden from their children (Welts, 1982).

Irish American women have traditionally dominated family life and primarily found their social life through the church. They have enjoyed a greater amount of independence relative to women in other cultures. More Irish women have immigrated to the United Stated than Irish men. Irish families often pay as much attention to the education of their daughters as of their sons. Traditionally, fathers have been shadowy or absent figures, and husbands dealt with wives primarily by avoidance.

Discipline is maintained by ridicule, belittling, and shaming. Children are generally raised to be polite, respectful, obedient, and well behaved. Parents rarely praise or center attention on their children (McGoldrick, 1982).

For Italians, the family is the training ground for learning to cope with a difficult world. The father has traditionally been the family's undisputed head, often authoritarian in his rule and guidelines for behavior. He usually takes his responsibilities to provide for his family very seriously. As the ultimate authority on living, he offers advice on major issues.

The mother provides the emotional sustenance. While yielding authority to the father, she traditionally assumes responsibility for the emotional aspects of the family. Her life centers around domestic duties, and she is expected to receive her primary pleasure from nurturing and servicing her family. Concerning children,

**IMPLEMENTING RESEARCH 5-2   Immigrant Families**

The enormous immigration to the United States is causing us to try to understand the complex ways in which the new arrivals construct their family lives here. Along with the increasing interest in gender and generation, there is a growing literature on the position of women and children in immigrant families. There is also an awareness that the family is not just a haven in a heartless world but a place where conflict and negotiation occur.

Nancy Foner (1997) examined the way family and kinship patterns change in the process of immigration. Offering an interpretative synthesis, Foner emphasizes the way first-generation immigrants to the United States fuse together the old and the new to create a new family life. The family is seen as a dynamic interplay between structures, culture, and agency. New immigrant family patterns are shaped by the cultural meanings and social practices immigrants bring with them from their home countries as well as by social, economic, and cultural forces in the United States.

Immigrants do not exactly reproduce their old cultural patterns when they move to a new land, but cultural patterns continue to have a strong influence. Immigrants bring with them a "memory of things past" (p. 965) that operates as a filter through which they view and create new lives in the United States.

**Implementing the Research**

Directions that educators of children and adolescents can take include:

1.  Understanding the problems and challenges that immigrant students might face as their families reconstruct their lives, giving up some cherished customs and holding onto others.
2.  Addressing the conflict that students might face when their families' expectations differ from those of their peers' families. They may face similar conflict when depictions of family in curricular materials conflict with their own understanding.
3.  Planning for parent conferences and parent involvement activities with immigrant parents who might not understand U.S. perceptions of parents' roles in home and school settings.

*Source:* Foner, N. (1997). The immigrant family: Cultural legacies and cultural changes. *International Migration Review, 31*(4), 961–974.

**FOLLOW THROUGH 5-4   Understanding Families from Culturally Different Backgrounds**

Use considerable caution when making generalizations about families from culturally different backgrounds. For example, although we might be able to say that Greek American families share similar cultural characteristics, we certainly cannot say that all Greek American families are alike. What factors determine what a family is like? How do factors such as generational status and socioeconomic background affect what families are like?

there is marked difference between sons and daughters. Sons are given much more latitude in what they do. The family expects a daughter, rather than a son, to assume major responsibility for an aging or sick parent. The extended family plays a central role in all aspects of Italian family life, including decision making (Rotunno & McGoldrick, 1982).

A major characteristic of the Polish American family is its respect for individual family members. The father and husband is the acknowledged leader of the household. The family is to respect and obey his wishes. Children are raised in a strict tradition of discipline, and they are to give their fathers unquestioned obedience. They are disciplined physically, sometimes harshly. Second-generation children have grown and become acculturated, but the practice of physical discipline continues (Mondykowski, 1982). Case Study 5-3 describes a Polish American elementary school girl and her parents' wishes to teach her the Catholic faith.

In the Portuguese American family, the man maintains great physical and emotional strength to combat life's difficulties. Family members tend to keep feelings to themselves to avoid the loss of respect or power. The father expects to receive respect and obedience from his children. Virtue and purity are desirable feminine qualities for the Portuguese woman. Her role includes loving, honoring, and obeying her husband and caring for her family's many needs. Children are to be seen and not heard. They receive most physical and emotional attention from their parents from infancy to about school age. Girls tend to receive overt displays of affection from both parents; the parents, especially the father, often don't give to boys in the same way (Moitoza, 1982).

---

### CASE STUDY 5-3   A Polish American Elementary School Girl

Linnet was a Polish American sixth-grader who attended an all-Catholic elementary school in the North. Her parents worked in factories and had saved diligently to send Linnet to the parochial school. They did not have any quarrel with or criticism of the public school, but they wanted their daughter to have religious training in a strict Catholic environment.

Linnet's grandfather had come to America and worked at any job he could find to survive. His language and his lack of knowledge of U.S. customs posed major problems. He thought several times of returning to Poland but did not have the money for the return trip. Finally, despite the reluctance of employers to employ a Polish man, he landed a job and worked for many years. Linnet's father had been luckier. When he finished the tenth grade, he took a job in a factory and worked there for many years.

Even though Linnet was only in the sixth grade, her parents and she planned for her to go to college when she completed high school.

Linnet studied diligently, learned the Catholic faith, and lived a strict life, both at home and at school. Her parents had high expectations for her academic achievement and behavior. Likewise, the nuns at school required strict obedience and hard work. Her school was predominantly Polish, but there were some Italians and a mixture of other cultures. In her school, Linnet learned to respect her cultural background and religion as well as to respect the cultural differences of others. She was growing up with an understanding of her Polish heritage, a solid grasp of Catholicism, and a fairly clear (especially for a sixth-grader) understanding of the value of education.

## Religion

As with other descriptors, European Americans' religion deserves careful consideration. A culture's religion often depends on its specific geographical origin and degree of acculturation.

Italian Americans are predominantly Catholic. One survey showed that 90 percent of the respondents had been raised as Catholics, and 80 percent called themselves Catholic at the time of the survey. Because the church has stood for tradition, family, and community, Italians continue to offer their support to the church (Alba, 1985). Similarly, Polish Americans have a powerful allegiance to the Catholic church (Lopata, 1994).

By 1923, there were about 140 Greek churches in the United States. Each community of Greeks formed a board of directors whose function was to build a Greek Orthodox church. Some attempts were made to unite the Greek church with other Eastern churches into an American Orthodoxy, but this consolidation did not materialize. The church seems inextricably intertwined with its role as transmitter of the Greek heritage (Scourby, 1984).

For most newcomer Jews, their primary motivation in leaving the Soviet Union was fear of anti-semitism rather than the desire for religious freedom. Most Soviet Jews view themselves as culturally Jewish. They are interested in the Jewish past expressed in history and literature, but they are not sure which religious practices have meaning (Abrams, 1993).

## Language

As Table 5-3 indicates, considerable variation exists in European Americans' ability to speak English. For example, census information suggests most learners from Germany and the United Kingdom have little difficulty with the English language. On the other hand, over half of the Italians living in this country experience difficulty with the language. (Census documents do not provide information on language for the other European groups.) Without doubt, considerable diversity exists within the three groups. Several factors influence learners' ability to speak English—for example, whether their parents and families live in "language enclaves" where people speak native languages, whether the parents speak the native language in the home, whether parents are trying to learn to speak English,

**TABLE 5-3　English Proficiency among Non-Native Speakers**

| Cultural Group | Do not speak English "very well" | Speak English "very well" |
|---|---|---|
| Germans | 22.6% | 77.4% |
| United Kingdom | 15.7% | 84.3% |
| Italians | 53.5% | 46.5% |

*Adapted from:* U.S. Bureau of the Census. (1993d). *We the American . . . foreign born.* Washington, D.C. p. 6.

---

**FOLLOW THROUGH 5-5    Helping Learners with Language Challenges**

Consider Table 5-3, English Proficiency among Non-Native Speakers. Educators can expect to experience problems when considering the following cultures not speaking English "very well": Germans 22.6 percent, United Kingdom 15.7 percent, and Italians 53.5 percent. While the language barrier might not be as serious for them as it is for some of the Asian and Hispanic groups, it nonetheless presents a challenge to educators. How might language problems be addressed? How can we help the children and adolescents? What can be done to help educators?

---

**FOR ADDITIONAL INFORMATION    Internet Addresses**

**Teacher Talk Home Page**
http://education.indiana.edu/cas/tt/tthmpg.html    Provides information from the Center for Adolescent Studies at the School of Education, Bloomington, Indiana.

**Immigration**
http://www.colorado.edu/libraries/govpubs/colonumb/immdef.htm    Provides a look at the Statistical Yearbook of the Immigration and Naturalization Service.

**Immigration Basics**
http://ilw.com/thal/immigrat.htm    Provides information that explains the three ways foreign-born individuals can come to the United States legally.

**Welcome to America Immigration Report**
http://www.uslawyer.com/    Provides periodic updates on immigration reports.

---

and the school's efforts to provide programs in English as a second language (and show appreciation for native languages). Table 5-3 looks at selected cultural groups and their ability to speak English.

## *European American Learners in the School*

Educators probably better understand European American learners than, say, Asian or Hispanic learners. However, there still exists a need to understand immigrant learners and their cultural backgrounds and individual differences. Special concerns for educators include language differences, parents' and families' reluctance to attend conferences and other school meetings, students' learning styles, perceptions of motivation and school success, cooperation versus competition, and differences in behavior expectation and management. The U.S. school system traditionally has directed attention toward the white middle-class male. Although some European Americans might fall into this category, it is still imperative that educators understand learners' cultural diversity and individual traits.

Implementing Research 5-3 looks at adolescent achievement and immigrant families.

**IMPLEMENTING RESEARCH 5-3**  Adolescent Achievement and Immigrant Families

The increase in immigrant families in the United States has resulted in an increased number of immigrant children in schools. Many of them come from homes where English is not spoken; others come from situations where poverty or war interrupted their schooling. Not many immigrant parents know how American schools work; some parents themselves have received little formal education. Many immigrant families move to large cities that have troubled school systems.

Only a few studies have examined immigrant adolescents' educational adjustment to United States schools. Some of these studies, however, suggest that European students do not have as many difficulties in schools as some might expect. Andrew Fuligni examined the relative impact of family background, parent attitudes, peer support, and adolescents' own attitudes and behaviors on the academic achievement of students from immigrant families. He also tried to understand the differences in educational adjustment among immigrant students themselves.

Fuligni reported some children of immigrant families:

1.  Perform as well as if not better than native-born students in schools.
2.  Receive significantly higher grades than their peers from native families despite coming from families who had less education and among whom English was less frequently spoken.
3.  Receive higher grades in both mathematics and English courses than students from native-born families.
4.  Receive lower grades during the latter years of secondary schooling (as do students from native-born families) but still receive higher grades than other students at all three grade levels during middle and high school.

## Implementing the Research

Perceptive middle and secondary educators will:

1.  recognize the dangers of stereotyping immigrant children and adolescents as being slow learners who are plagued with language and school adjustment problems;
2.  recognize and plan appropriate educational experiences for adolescents who *do* experience learning problems and school adjustment difficulties—immigrants make up a diverse group and although significant numbers succeed in American schools, others need appropriate assistance;
3.  provide parents and families with appropriate parent education experiences, especially those who do not understand the American school system and who want to know additional ways to help their adolescents succeed in school; and
4.  provide educational experiences that reduce the decline in academic achievement during the latter years of secondary schooling.

*Source:* Fuligni, A. J. (1997). The academic achievement of adolescents from immigrant families: The roles of family background, attitudes, and behavior. *Child Development, 68*(2), 351–363.

---

**FOLLOW THROUGH 5-6    Helping Immigrant Learners Succeed Academically**

Consider Implementing Research 5-3 on adolescent achievement and immigrant families. While educators must avoid assuming that all immigrant children and adolescents experience lower academic achievement, programs should be carefully designed and implemented to help those who do. Name four or five specific directions they can take to address immigrants' learning (and social) needs as well as increase their academic achievement.

---

## Learning Styles: Cultural Considerations

Very little research has focused on learning styles of European American learners. One study (Dunn, Gemake, Jalali, Zenhausern, Quinn, & Spiridakis, 1990) included a European American group in an examination of the learning styles of four cultural groups—Chinese, Mexican, African, and Greek—in the fourth, fifth, and sixth grades. Researchers' suggestions included providing all groups with quiet areas and student interaction areas, providing conventional and informal seating arrangements, and allowing learners to work alone.

Contemporary educators need to remember that students from European American cultures (as well as from other cultures) may:

1. perceive educational situations (e.g., competition and demonstration of motivation) differently;
2. perceive the world differently, such as focusing on the whole rather than the parts; or
3. prefer to learn using visual, perceptual, and spatial modes rather than words.

Directions for educators in pluralistic schools include:

1. Accept professional responsibility to recognize that students learn in different ways.
2. Plan culturally appropriate learning experiences.
3. Provide classroom environments that reflect culturally diverse learners' needs and expectations, such as cooperativeness over competition.
4. Provide bias-free curricular materials that allow students to learn using visual, perceptual, and spatial styles.
5. Maintain familiarity with the research and scholarly writing about learning styles among learners from culturally different backgrounds.

---

**FOLLOW THROUGH 5-7    Determining and Addressing Learning Styles**

From a number of sources, such as journals and testing manuals, determine how educators can most effectively determine students' learning styles. What tests or inventories can be used? What are some ways to address students' differing learning styles?

## School Practices Impeding European Americans' Progress

What school practices might impede European American learners' progress? It sounds ironic to even suggest school practices would interfere with students' learning and overall school progress, especially because a major goal of schools is to teach. Schools, however, still often have practices that do not contribute to the academic achievement and overall development of all learners.

First, policies toward language might be a detrimental factor. Some schools forbid learners to speak their native languages. For example, the school might not allow one Greek American child to teach another Greek American child their native language. Also, some schools fail to provide adequate English as a second language programs. As a result learners are taught in a language that they do not fully understand.

Second, perhaps because of language difficulties or teachers' perceptions, the school sometimes places European Americans in a group that is academically too high or too low for their abilities. Third, teachers sometimes fail to realize that learners in various cultures have differing learning styles and perspectives of motivation and school success.

Case Study 5-4 examines a school that was reluctant to change and the problems that resulted for both students and educators.

## Promoting Self-Esteem and Cultural Identities

As other chapters on the various cultures have indicated, perceptive educators, especially those teaching in multicultural settings, need to be aware of the importance to children and adolescents of the formation of self-esteem and positive

---

**CASE STUDY 5-4    A School Reluctant to Change**

The high school was located in an aging part of town, a section that had at one time been a prosperous middle-class neighborhood. Over the previous ten to twelve years, several demographic changes occurred: Many people moved out of the neighborhood, several businesses closed, and large numbers of first- and second-generation immigrants moved into the neighborhood. In other words, the neighborhood and school's student population changed, yet the school remained the same.

A number of factors could be cited for the school's lack of response: poor leadership, failure to recognize the changing demographics, and an outright refusal to change. Regardless of the reason, the school's efforts did not reflect the cultural diversity of the student population. The school failed to make its curriculum multicultural, failed to realize that learning styles could change over ten to twelve years, failed to provide an appropriate classroom management system reflective of learners' expectations, and failed to try to involve parents and families.

In essence, the school was stuck in the mid-twentieth century. The educators knew the student population had changed, but they did not try to meet the needs of a different population. Students and educators both struggled with the situation, often to the point of extreme frustration.

cultural identities. Cultural differences play significant roles in a young person's degree of self-worth and self-image. For example, a student from a culture different from the teacher's and from a lower socioeconomic level may, indeed, consider his or her differences as inferior or wrong. Perceptive educators recognize the disastrous consequences such feelings can have on children's and adolescents' sense of personal worth.

Scholars can take special steps such as the following two to promote positive self-esteem and cultural identities:

**1.** Educators, perhaps through academic and extracurricular programs, can help European American children and adolescents understand "culture," recognize how culture affects peoples' lives, and understand that they cannot place values on culture.

**2.** Educators can work toward providing all children and adolescents with accurate and objective materials and lead discussions about culture and cultural differences that dispel as many myths, distortions, and stereotypes as possible.

Gender Perspectives 5-1 shows how females' self-esteem deceases as they progress through the school years.

---

### GENDER PERSPECTIVES 5-1    Gender Gap in Self-Esteem

Research suggests females have much lower self-esteem than males, especially among 10- to 14-year-olds. Backes administered a self-esteem scale to 1,205 students in grades 6–8. Selected results included:

| Item | 6 | 7 | 8 |
|---|---|---|---|
| I'm pretty sure of myself. | 84.4% | 83.4% | 75.0% |
| I often wish I were someone else. | 48.1% | 36.4% | 46.0% |
| There are lots of things about myself I'd change if I could. | 56.1% | 56.2% | 67.6% |
| I'm proud of my schoolwork. | 71.7% | 67.7% | 50.0% |
| I have a low opinion of myself. | 21.2% | 24.0% | 36.9% |

Backes's survey provides clear evidence that educators need to recognize gender differences in self-esteem and help females increase their self-esteem. Interventions designed to improve females' self-esteem require the involvement of teachers, administrators, and parents: working to address bias in classroom interaction patterns and to develop gender-fair curricula; providing girls equal opportunities to enroll in mathematics and science courses; giving equal and equitable attention to females' activities; including a focus on improving the self-esteem and achievements of females; avoiding perpetuation of the myth of the superiority of males in society; and dealing directly with issues of power, gender, politics, and maltreatment of females.

---

*Source:* Backes, J. S. (1994). Bridging the gender gap: Self-concept in the middle grades. *Schools in the Middle, 3*(3), 19–23.

**CULTURAL PORTRAIT   Anna—An Italian American Girl**

Anna is a nine-year-old, second-generation Italian American girl living in a large urban area. She lives with her father, mother, and grandmother (her father's mother). Anna attends an overcrowded city school, which has a cultural composition fairly representative of that of the nation. A number of European American cultures are represented and significant numbers of African and Hispanic American students as well. Anna feels fairly safe in her school except when fights break out. The school's security guards have done a good job of curtailing fights.

Anna's teacher, Ms. Taylor, is a white American who has tried to understand Anna and her family traditions. Anna and Ms. Taylor get along, but Anna does not want her teacher to meet her parents unless absolutely necessary. Anna has a problem or conflict between her family and her school; her parents do not understand what the school is trying to do. Their English is not very good; in fact, they continue to speak Italian at home. Sometimes, Anna's schoolwork makes little sense to them, and they usually do not understand written correspondence from the school. Anna tries to interpret the English and explains the meaning of the correspondence to her parents.

Anna's schoolwork is usually pretty good. She does all right in reading (in fact, she works diligently) and other school subjects. Her weakest subject is mathematics, and although she studies daily, her grades in math are not as high as her other grades. She wants to improve, to satisfy both her teacher and her parents.

Anna has one or two friends but no one she can really call a best friend. She is sociable with people once she gets to know them, but she is a little quiet (perhaps a little suspicious) at first around strangers.

*How Anna's Teacher Can Respond*

Ms. Taylor can respond to Anna's learning and individual needs in several ways. She can:

1. arrange for important school correspondence to be translated into Italian, so Anna's parents will have a better understanding of the school's roles and objectives;
2. speak with Anna's parents if they attend a parents' meeting, make them feel comfortable, accept the fact that they might view her with suspicion, and let them know that she wants to help Anna;
3. arrange for Anna to have tutoring or additional assistance in mathematics—Anna wants to do better, and she deserves the opportunity; and
4. help or at least provide opportunities (e.g., cooperative learning) for Anna to make closer friends with whom she can speak and socialize.

---

**FOLLOW THROUGH 5-8   Determining a School's Response to Cultural Diversity**

Design a survey to determine a school's response to cultural diversity. What aspects do you want to consider? You might list six to eight broad categories (such as Curriculum Efforts) and then add subcategories (such as Library Materials and Textbooks). Remember, efforts to instill multiculturalism should be comprehensive rather than changing just two or three aspects of the school.

## Summing Up

Educators planning educational experiences for European American learners should:

**1.** Perceive European American learners as an integral part of our nation's diversity even though little attention and research has been focused toward this group.

**2.** Recognize the futility of past educational practices, in which language programs were inadequate and cultural differences in motivation and learning went unrecognized.

**3.** Recognize that girls and boys have different perceptions of motivation and school success and perceptions of learning strategies.

**4.** Realize that cultural characteristics vary among European Americans and that people also differ according to generational status and age, social class, and gender.

**5.** Understand that European Americans vary widely in their ability to speak English and that the need is strong for methodically planned language programs.

**6.** Consider European American language differences, learning styles, perceptions of motivation and school success, cooperation versus competition, and differences in behavior expectation and management.

**7.** Be aware how important it is for European American children to develop positive self-esteem and cultural identities.

## Suggested Learning Activities

**1.** Interview a first- or second-generation Greek, French, or German American student to determine the problems or special challenges he or she faces in school. If possible, meet with the family as well to learn what problems they experience with the schools. Then, list problems on the left side of your paper and possible solutions on the right.

**2.** Read a book such as H. Z. Lopata's *Polish Americans* (1994) or A. Scourby's *The Greek Americans* (1984) to learn of the hardships and discrimination that many European Americans have experienced. In many cases, the hardships of the past are no more; however, different forms of hardships and discrimination exist. Read several current periodicals (e.g., newspapers, popular magazines) and make a list of difficulties many European Americans are experiencing today. How might schools help remedy these situations?

**3.** Language problems continue to plague many European American learners: They cannot speak the language of the school but are forbidden to speak their native languages in school. Their parents cannot understand the school's language, and the school might show little appreciation for native languages. Yet, in all candor, educators feel they should use the language of the nation or the language most students speak. The dilemma challenges many schools in our nation. Think about and write a brief proposal (no matter how radical and forward-looking!) to address this challenge.

## *Suggestions for Collaborative Efforts*

Form groups of three or four that, if possible, represent our nation's cultural and gender diversity. Work collaboratively, and focus your group's attention on the following efforts:

1. Have each member of your group interview four or five students from different European cultures, preferably first- and second-generation. As a group project, design an interview to learn about differences in cultural characteristics, language, family (be careful, some cultures may feel you are prying), social class, and gender. What differences do you find among cultures? Did you find intracultural differences? Were there significant gender differences? What role does social class play in determining what a person is like? Last, what differences did you find between first- and second-generation European Americans?

2. We hear that people from different cultures are "lazy," others "dumb," some "swarthy," and others "stingy." Some are "model minorities," and others are prone to passion and violence. Being careful to respect class members' feelings and cultures, make a list of stereotypes (perhaps on the board as a class project). To show stereotypes are myths and often the result of hate mongering, hypothesize how these stereotypes might have begun. How can stereotypes affect the person being stereotyped and the person harboring the stereotype? How should we as educators respond when we hear someone describe another person in stereotypical terms?

3. Assign individual members of your group to review catalogs of children's books (check with your children's literature professor or the college or school library) to learn titles of new books by European American authors or about European American children and adolescents. Before beginning, decide on certain criteria: whether your group wants lists for elementary-, middle-, or high-school-age youngsters; books published in the last three years or older; and other criteria your group considers important. Have each member prepare a bibliography, and compile your efforts.

## *Expanding Your Horizons: Additional Journal Readings and Books*

Cohen, E. G., & Lotan, R. A. (Eds.) (1997). *Working for equity in heterogeneous classrooms: Sociological Theory in Practice.* New York: Teachers College Press.

*The editors provide a wealth of information on equity, organization, raising expectations, testing, teachers as learners, and administrators.*

Fuchs, D., & Fuchs, L. S. (1998). Competing visions for educating students with disabilities: Inclusion versus full inclusion. *Childhood Education* 74(5), 309–316.

*Fuchs and Fuchs discuss the differences between inclusion and full inclusion and outline the continuum of services for the disabled.*

Gillette, M. D., & Chinn, P. C. (1997). Multicultural education: Responding to a mandate for equitable educational outcomes. *Teacher Education and Practice,* 13(1), 1–13.

*To address the diverse needs of students, educators need to infuse the school setting with multicultural education, instruction, evaluation, and support services.*

Lucero, E. L. (1997). Promoting multiculturalism in the early grades. *Principal, 76*(5), 5–6; (8)10–11.

*Rather than wait for negative incidents to occur, schools need to identify and address prejudice by using a video-based curriculum.*

Lundy, B., Field, T., McBride, C., Field, T., & Largie, S. (1998). Same-sex and opposite-sex best friend interactions among high school juniors and seniors. *Adolescence, 33*(130), 279–289.

*These authors studied eighteen adolescents in the eleventh and twelfth grades and offered conclusions about gender differences in peer intimacy.*

## *Expanding Your Students' Horizons: Appropriate European American Books for Children and Adolescents*

**United Kingdom**

Bawden, Nina. *The Finding.* Lothrop, Lee & Shepherd, 1985.

Foreman, Michael. *War Boy: A Country Childhood.* Brown/Arcade, 1990.

Cross, Gillian. *Chartbreaker.* Holiday House, 1987.

**Ireland**

Moran, Tom. *A Family in Ireland.* Lerner, 1986.

MacDonald, Michael. *Children of Wrath: Political Violence in Northern Ireland.* Basil Blackwell, 1986.

Meyer, Carolyn. *Voices of Northern Ireland: Growing Up in a Troubled Land.* Harcourt Brace Jovanovich, 1987.

**Germany**

Hartling, Peter. *Old John.* Lothrop, Lee & Shepard, 1990.

Matas, Carol. *Lisa's War.* Scribner, 1989.

Watkins, Paul. *Night Over Day Over Night.* Knopf, 1988.

**France**

Roth-Hano, René. *Touch Wood: A Girlhood in Occupied France.* Penguin, 1989.

Harris, Jonathan. *The Land and People of France.* HarperCollins, 1989.

Sullam, Joanna. *Villages of France.* Rizzoli International, 1988.

**Portugal**

Wain, John. *The Free Zone Stops Here.* Delacorte, 1984.

DeSkalon, A., and Stadtler, Christina. *We Live in Portugal.* Franklin Watts, 1987.

Lye, Keith. *Take a Trip to Portugal.* Franklin Watts, 1986.

**Sweden**

Cohen, Peter. *Olson's Meat Pies.* Farrar, Straus, & Giroux, 1989.

Lindgren, Astrid. *Lotta's Bike.* Lerner/Carolrhoda, 1990.

Peterson, Hans. *Erik Has a Squirrel.* Farrar, Straus, & Giroux, 1989.

**Spain**

Miller, Arthur. *Spain.* Chelsea House, 1989.

Wuorio, Eva-Lis. *Detour to Danger.* Delacorte, 1981.

Woods, Geraldine. *Spain: A Shining New Democracy.* Dillon, 1987.

**Europeans in General**

Ayer, Eleanor. *Parallel Journeys.* Athenum, 1995.

Banks, L. R. *One More River.* Morrow, 1992.

Bitton-Jackson, Livia. *I Have Lived a Thousand Years: Growing up in the Holocaust.* Simon & Schuster, 1997.

Dalokay, Veda. *Sister Shako and Kolo the Goat.* Lothrop, Lee & Shepard, 1994.

Heese, Karen. *Letters from Rifka.* Holt, 1993.

Karas, Phyllis. *The Hate Crime.* Avon, 1995.

Laird, Elizabeth. *Kiss the Dust.* Dutton, 1993.

Morpurgo, Michael. *The Ghost of Grania O'Malley.* Viking, 1996.

## *Answers to the Culture Quiz: European Americans*

| | | | | |
|---|---|---|---|---|
| **1.** c | **3.** a | **5.** i | **7.** e | **9.** d |
| **2.** g | **4.** b | **6.** j | **8.** f | **10.** h |

$Chapter$ $6$

# Understanding Hispanic American Children and Adolescents

Understanding the material and activities in this chapter will help the reader to:

- Describe the cultural, gender, socioeconomic, familial, and language characteristics of Hispanic American children and adolescents.
- Understand the dangers of stereotyping Hispanic American learners and know how to respond appropriately in teaching and learning situations.
- List and describe the educational characteristics and problems of Hispanic American learners.
- Name several practices that impede the educational process of Hispanic American children and adolescents.
- List several points that educators of Hispanic American children and adolescents should remember.
- Incorporate practical activities, suggest appropriate children's literature, implement research findings, and respond appropriately to school situations involving Hispanic American learners.

## Overview

Understanding Hispanic American children and adolescents requires knowledge of their families, their religion, their language, and their culture's contributions. "Knowing, understanding, and appreciating" Spanish-speaking learners are prerequisites, yet not enough: Educators must also understand the relationship of the cultural characteristics of Hispanic learners, their differences as learners, and their school-related problems. Educators' emphasis should be on understanding cultural diversity and demonstrating genuine appreciation of and respect for Hispanic cultures.

## Origins

Hispanic Americans as a group include people who are Mexican Americans, Central and South Americans, Chicanos, Spanish Americans, Latin Americans, Puerto Ricans, Cubans, Guatemalans, and Salvadorans (U.S. Bureau of the Census, 1993e). All these Hispanics share many values and goals but are different in many aspects. In some ways, Hispanics are a single cultural group with a fairly common history and the sharing of language, values, and customs, but in other ways are a significant heterogeneous population that is an aggregate of distinct subcultures.

Tremendous cultural diversity exists among Hispanic Americans, such as the differences between Mexican Americans and Cuban Americans, among genera-

---

**THE CULTURE QUIZ   Hispanic Americans**

*Directions:* Match the individuals with their contributions or achievement by placing the appropriate letter before each name.

_____ **1.** Eliana Schippel

_____ **2.** Pauline Gómez

_____ **3.** Isabel Schon

_____ **4.** José Pedro Greer

_____ **5.** Caesar Chavez

_____ **6.** Henry G. Cisneros

_____ **7.** Juan Ramon Jimenez

_____ **8.** José Aruego

_____ **9.** Lupe Angiano

_____ **10.** Helga Silva

**a.** First person of Mexican descent to win election as mayor of a major United States city

**b.** Prepared report, "The Children of Mariel," which examined programs designed to cope with 15,000 non-English-speaking students

**c.** Leading spokesman for Mexican American farmers in the 1960s—led strike against grape growers

**d.** An illustrator with a law degree, a sense of history, and a talent for making children laugh

**e.** Former alcoholic who runs an alcoholic treatment program—La Posada—in Dallas

**f.** Born blind; founded the Nation Federation of the Blind in New Mexico

**g.** Reviewed recently published children's books and pointed out how stereotypes and misconceptions continue

**h.** Operates free clinic in Miami—Camillus Health Concerns; 200 volunteers and 12 staff members

**i.** Responsible for creating several Hispanic women's groups

**j.** Winner of 1956 Nobel Prize for literature

(Answers to the Culture Quiz are located at the end of the chapter.)

tions, and among people living in different geographic locations in the United States. Although this section examines only several Hispanic cultural characteristics, educators should learn about individual students and their respective cultural characteristics.

## Hispanic Americans Today

In 1990, there were 22.4 million Hispanics in the United States, almost 9 percent of the nation's nearly 250 million people. The Hispanic population grew by 53 percent between 1980 and 1990 and by 61 percent between 1970 and 1980. The Mexican American population nearly doubled between 1970 and 1980 and nearly doubled again by 1990. Both the Cuban American and Puerto Rican American populations grew at a rate at least four times faster than the rest of the nation. Other Hispanic populations grew dramatically between 1980 and 1990, partly as a result of the large influx of Central and South American immigrants during this time. In 1993, 54 percent of all Hispanic Americans resided in two states, Texas and California (U.S. Bureau of the Census, 1993e).

Olsen (1988) describes the effects of today's unprecedented racial and ethnic diversity in California classrooms. Referring to both Southeast Asian and Hispanic learners, Olsen reports issues affecting California learners as being demographic changes, changes resulting from war, "undocumented children," cultural changes, language and academic needs, and the problems of coping with a strange educational system.

As children learn about Hispanic culture and people, teachers can suggest developmentally appropriate children's informational books and biographies.

---

**USING CHILDREN'S LITERATURE   Informational Books and Biographies**

Hewitt, Joan. *Getting Elected: The Diary of a Campaign.* Dutton/Lodestar, 1989. Written for students in grades 4 to 6, this book features Gloria Molina, the first Chicana elected to the California Assembly.

Morey, Janet, and Wendy Dunn. *Famous Mexican Americans.* Dutton/Cobblehill, 1989. Probably best for grades 7 through 9, this book focuses on the lives and contributions of fourteen noted Mexican Americans.

Sumption, Christine, and Kathleen Thompson. *Carlos Finlay.* Raintree, 1990. Written for students in grades 4 to 6, this story tells of a Cuban-born

scientist, a medical doctor, who developed the theory for the cure of yellow fever.

Munson, Sammye. *Our Tejano Heroes: Outstanding Mexican-Americans in Texas.* Eakin, 1989. Students in grades 4 to 6 will benefit from this book of biographies, husband and wife teams, and families.

Garza, Carmen Lomas, and Harriet Rohmer. *Family Pictures/Cuadros de familia.* Children's Book Press, 1990. For grades kindergarten through 3, this book introduces readers to one of the country's finest artists of Mexican American heritage.

---

## Stereotyping of Hispanic American Children and Adolescents

As with other learners, Hispanic American children and adolescents may experience "double jeopardy" if educators label learners and base teaching and learning decisions on cultural stereotypes. In essence, teachers may perceive children and adolescents erroneously as exhibiting undesirable behavior, while feeling Hispanic Americans have tendencies toward emotional and violent behavior.

Educators do learners a terrible injustice when educational decisions are based on such stereotypes as the Hispanic American learner is not as "well-behaved" as the Asian American learner, is not as "intelligent" as the European American, and is not as "docile or peaceful" as the Native American learner. In fact, such stereotypes become self-fulfilling prophecies; Hispanic learners may achieve and behave in accordance with the educator's stereotyped academic and behavior expectations.

What action should educators take? All school personnel should seriously examine the validity of their cultural "baggage" and work toward an objective understanding of Hispanic American children and adolescents. Educators can acquire a more enlightened picture of Hispanic American learners by meeting Hispanic Americans firsthand, learning their proud and diverse history, becoming acquainted with their parents and extended families, understanding the culture's contributions, and understanding their allegiance to the Spanish language. It is also helpful to understand what being a Hispanic American child or adolescent is really like and to realize the potentially disastrous consequences of basing educational programs on cultural misperceptions. As Case Study 6-1 indicates, teachers also must accept the often difficult responsibility for changing other children's cultural attitudes.

---

**CASE STUDY 6-1    Name-Calling**

Nine-year-old Juan wonders what his second day at his new school will be like. He quickly recognizes that most children are either white or black. During the first classes of the day, Juan notices that no one seems to want to be his friend, but he thinks things will improve during recess. At recess, however, the other children still do not pick him when choosing teams for kickball. Finally, he hears three children laughing, and although he could not hear exactly what they said, he did hear "wetback." Juan is angered and hurt; he feels like crying, but wonders whether he should fight. The teacher sees and hears the entire episode.

Juan's teacher recognizes how damaging such a situation could be for Juan's self-esteem and Mexican American identity. Although she

does not want to call a great deal of attention to the situation, she does want to respond appropriately. She feels that several steps are in order.

1. She will have a class discussion on name-calling; she will show how name-calling labels or stereotypes children and how derogatory names can hurt.
2. She will plan activities to involve Juan so that students can know him as an individual and learn about the contributions he can offer the class.
3. She will integrate multiculturalism into her curriculum so that all students can understand and value each others' cultural heritages.

## Hispanic American Children and Adolescents

Educators who plan and implement a multicultural curriculum can benefit from knowledge, understanding, and appreciation of Hispanic learners and their culture. Steinberg, Blinde, and Chan (1984) concluded that studies of Hispanic youngsters do not sufficiently differentiate among the different Spanish-speaking ethnic groups. Differing cultures, generational, socioeconomic, and acculturation factors exist that educators must consider to understand Hispanic American learners.

America now has slightly more Hispanic children than African American children. There are 10.5 million Hispanic children under age 18; in contrast, there are 10.4 million non-Hispanic black children. Hispanic children are the fastest-growing youth population, and this increase should continue well into the next century. As a result, by 2020, projections show that more than one in five children will be of Hispanic origin (Hispanic youth edging past blacks in number, 1998).

### Cultural Characteristics

A cultural description of Spanish-speaking peoples should include an understanding of certain values and traits (Gonzalez, 1989; Christensen, 1989). Educators can gain considerable insight into the culture by understanding several unique characteristics (see Table 6-1). Hall (1981) points out that Hispanic Americans who are not members of an elite group tend to avoid any competition or activity that will set them apart from their own group. To stand out among one's peers is to place oneself in great jeopardy and is to be avoided at all costs.

"Machismo" plays a significant role in the Puerto Rican culture and significantly influences the behavior and attitudes of adolescent males during this time

**TABLE 6-1   Selected Characteristics of Hispanic American Children and Adolescents**

| Category | Characteristics |
|---|---|
| Behavioral/ emotional expressiveness | Restraint of feelings, particularly anger and frustration |
| Verbal | Limited verbal expressions toward authority figures |
| Nonverbal | Preference for closer personal space; avoidance of eye contact when listening or speaking to authority figures |
| Concept of time | Present time perspective; relaxed about time and punctuality; and immediate short-term goals |
| Social orientation | Collective, group identity; interdependence; cooperative rather than competitive; emphasis on interpersonal relations |

*Developed from:* Rivera, B. D., & Rogers-Adkinson, D. (1997). Culturally sensitive interventions: Social skills training with children and parents from culturally and linguistically diverse backgrounds. *Intervention in School and Clinic, 33*(2), 75–80.

---

**FOLLOW THROUGH 6-1**   **Understanding the Hispanic Culture**

It is important that educators of Hispanic children and adolescents understand and appreciate important concepts of the Hispanic culture. On understanding these cultural characteristics, try to identify related behaviors in Hispanic learners.

*corazon:* heart
*sensibilidad:* sensitivity
*afecto:* warmth and demonstrativeness
*dignidad:* dignity
*respecto:* respect
*machismo:* biological superiority of the male

---

of identity formation. It suggests a clear-cut distinction between the sexes; males can enjoy rights and privileges denied to females.

Used as a flattering term among Hispanic Americans, Hispanic American boys and girls learn that *machismo* refers to the male's manhood, to the courage to fight, to the many traits of honor and dignity, to keeping one's word, and to protecting one's name. On a more subtle level of analysis, machismo also includes dignity in personal conduct, respect for others, love for the family, and affection for children. Many children are taught early that European Americans are not trustworthy. Mexican Americans, for example, often teach their children to look toward European Americans with fear and hostility. Children who are taught such attitudes have difficulty believing that European American professionals have their best interests at heart (Fitzpatrick, 1987).

---

**FOLLOW THROUGH 6-2**   **Determining Learning Opportunities about Hispanic Learners**

Educators have realized for many years the advantages of knowing as much as possible about learners. When teaching students from culturally different backgrounds, however, educators must understand learners' cultural backgrounds so as to make the most of learners' opportunities to improve learning experiences and self-esteem. What can educators do to learn about Hispanic learners' cultural backgrounds?

1.  Read objective literature about the Hispanic culture to learn about its historical background.
2.  Understand Hispanic peoples' contributions and cherished cultural traits and how they are different from and similar to the majority culture and other minority populations.
3.  Learn about Hispanic families—both immediate and extended—and understand the value Hispanic people place on the family.
4.  Get to know individual Hispanic learners. Don't just generalize about them.
5.  Visit Hispanic learners in their homes to learn firsthand about their home lives.

---

Although acculturation undoubtedly affects Hispanic learners, many would not agree that the European American ideas of self-advancement and equality within the family are necessary to sustain the ideals of freedom, democracy, and progress (Mirande, 1986).

Implementing Research 6-1 proposes that language plays an instrumental role in the education of Latino youth, especially in their communities.

In general, group-oriented Mexican American children are likely to change their own behavior to adapt to an interpersonal challenge rather than try to change

---

**IMPLEMENTING RESEARCH 6-1   Latino Youth—Home, Communities, and School**

Ana Celia Zentella (1997) maintains that language plays an instrumental role in determining why, what, and how Latino youth learn in their communities. In fact, Zentella contends that English–Spanish bilingualism is a fundamental and often overlooked resource for building bridges between communities, homes, and schools.

In most U.S. classrooms, educators allow only standard English. Less than one-half of the population has access to bilingual programs, and these emphasize standard Spanish. Thus, the educational system fails to tap the diverse linguistic abilities that Latinos learn in their communities. Diminished competence in Spanish among Latinos in the United States results in the erosion of the sense of unity among families and communities. In other words, children who cannot understand Spanish miss family interactions, the transmission of community, family history, and cultural values.

Zentella recommends that community-based institutions (CBIs) provide Latino youth with feelings of cultural acceptance that they need. CBIs could also address the problems of at-risk youth more successfully than schools because they are less threatening than schools and are "user friendly" (p. 127): They are smaller in size, have simpler organizational structure and more flexible schedules, and are more diverse and more community-based. Zentella maintains that unfortunately most CBIs and Latino communities conduct youth activities in English. Bilingualism is not a priority, despite the significant role that Spanish plays in Latino youth achieving goals.

**Implementing the Research**

1. Both elementary and secondary educators should involve the family and community in the education of Latino youth. This sense of community can contribute to academic achievement as well as overall success in U.S. schools.
2. Students enrolled in effective bilingual programs will develop a sense of unity among families and communities and will understand Spanish family interactions, the transmission of community, family history, and cultural values.
3. Educators working in community-based institutions should allow and, in fact, encourage the use of Spanish, so youth can gain a sense of respect for both languages as well as for their cultural heritages and backgrounds.

---

*Source:* Zentella, A. C. (1997). Latino youth at home, in their communities, and in school. *Education and Urban Society, 30*(1), 122–130.

---

**FOR ADDITIONAL INFORMATION**

Association of Hispanic Arts (AHA), 200 E. 87th Street, New York, NY 10028. Founded in 1975, AHA promotes the general concept of Hispanic arts, specifically dance, music, art, and theatrical performances.

Hispanic Institute for the Performing Arts (HIFPA), P.O. Box 32249, Calvert Station, Wash-ington, D.C. 20007. Begun in 1981, HIFPA seeks to promote a better understanding of Hispanics by conducting educational and cultural activities.

---

situations. They are less assertive in expressing themselves to peers and adults and rely on authority figures to resolve interpersonal problems (Rotheram-Borus & Phinney, 1990).

Readers who want a better understanding of Hispanic children and adolescents and the contributions of the Hispanic cultures may want to write to the listed organizations.

## *Gender*

In Hispanic American culture, just as in other cultures, females differ from their male counterparts. Although males and females both experience similar frustrations, such as discrimination and prejudice and sometimes poverty and lower standards of living, Hispanic American females are different from males in other ways. For example, Hispanic American females usually prefer cooperative learning environments over competitive classrooms in which many boys learn best. Likewise, Hispanic American females, because of their families' adherence to strict gender roles, are often less vocal and take less assertive stands than males do (Grossman & Grossman, 1994).

It is important to note, however, that because of acculturation and females taking steps to improve themselves economically and socially, some Hispanic American females are adhering less and less to traditional gender expectations. In any event, perceptive educators who work with Hispanic American females will want to bear in mind the gender-role differences among Hispanic cultures and among individual females.

---

**FOR ADDITIONAL INFORMATION**

The Hispanic Policy Development Project, Suite 310, 1001 Connecticut Avenue, NW, Washington, D.C. 20036. This organization examines the problems of Hispanic youth living in the United States today and suggests public and private strategies for helping these youth.

---

## Socioeconomic Status

In 1990, over 1 million Hispanic American families lived in poverty—just over two of every ten Hispanic families, compared with less than one of every ten non-Hispanic families. About 30 percent of Puerto Rican families, 33 percent of families from the Dominican Republic, about 10 percent of families from Spain, 11 percent of Cuban families, 23 percent of Mexican families, and 21 percent of Central American families were below the poverty level in the United States in 1990. Poverty rates are also disturbing for Hispanic children and adolescents. About 18 percent of Hispanic children under eighteen years of age lived in poverty, compared with 17 percent of non-Hispanic children (U.S. Bureau of the Census, 1993e).

Fitzpatrick (1987), referring to Puerto Rican Americans, contends that the continuing level of poverty is a puzzling concern. Although the second generation in the United States has improved in socioeconomic terms, poverty and its effects continue to be widespread. Two interrelated factors contribute to this cycle of poverty among Hispanic Americans: The unemployment rate among Puerto Rican males is twice that of European Americans, and the number of female-headed households continues to increase.

Are there indications that the socioeconomic status of Hispanic American children and adolescents will improve? One could provide an affirmative answer to this question if Hispanics work to improve their educational levels and English skills. These improvements will allow them to venture from Spanish-speaking communities into mainstream U.S. society. Although educators should recognize (and respond appropriately to) the effects poverty often has on academic achievement, it would also be a serious mistake to categorize all lower socioeconomic Hispanics into unmotivated or underachieving academic groups.

## Families

A basic feature of the Hispanic American family is the extended family, which plays a major role in each family member's life. These are families with strong bonds and frequent interaction among a wide range of kin. Grandparents, parents, and children may live in the same household or nearby in separate households and visit one another frequently. A second feature is the emphasis on cooperativeness and on placing the needs of the family ahead of individual concerns. This aspect of Hispanic family life has led to the erroneous conclusion that the family impedes individual achievement and advancement. Observers of the Hispanic American culture must distinguish between being cooperative and respectful and being docile and dependent (Mirande, 1986). Generally speaking, Hispanic American children and adolescents learn to show respect for authority, the patriarchal family structure, and extended family members (Rivera & Rogers-Adkinson, 1997).

More than one-third (36 percent) of Hispanic households were married couples with children in 1997; only a quarter of non-Hispanic households were

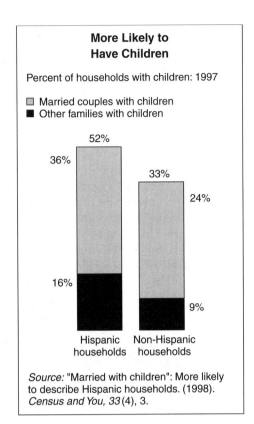

FIGURE 6-1    **Percentage of Households with Children**

married couples with children. Children lived in more than half (52%) of the 8.2 million Hispanic households. Only about one-third (33%) of the 9.3 million non-Hispanic households included children ("Married with children": More likely to describe Hispanic households, 1998). Figure 6-1 shows the number of households with children.

Hispanic American children learn early the importance of (1) a deep sense of family responsibility, (2) rigid definitions of sex roles, (3) respectful and reverent treatment of the elderly, and (4) the male's position of respect and authority in the family. Although some of the male's authority appears to be relaxing as the woman's role is redefined, women in the Hispanic American culture continue to occupy a subordinate position. Fathers have prestige and authority, and sons have more and earlier independence than do daughters (Lum, 1986).

Latino and Chicano families value the extended family structure and interaction in their daily lives. Parents often arrange for godparents or "companion parents" for the child, thus demonstrating the value Hispanics place on adults other than the immediate parents. These *compadres* also have a right to give advice and correction and should be responsive to the child's needs (Fitzpatrick, 1987).

---

**FOLLOW THROUGH 6-3   Getting to Know Hispanic Families**

Learning about the Hispanic learner's family might be one of the best ways to improve the child's academic achievement and self-esteem. Educators can do several things to learn about Hispanic families.

1. Invite families to school on special occasions just to visit. While the family learns about the school and its policies and expectations, teachers can become acquainted with the families.
2. Request that students write a story or essay about their families. Be sure to emphasize including parents, grandparents, brothers and sisters, cousins, and other relatives living in the home. Keep an open mind, and remember the importance of the extended family. Tell students before they write the story whether or not their stories or essays will be shared with the class.
3. Educators who teach in areas with great numbers of Hispanics may want to schedule a day for only Hispanic families to visit. Have individual meetings to determine how the family influences school achievement and attitudes toward school. (If possible, speak Spanish to families with limited English-speaking skills.)
4. Schedule individual meetings with Hispanic students to discuss their families, but be careful that students understand the purpose of these discussions. Allow and respect a learner's privacy.

---

**FOR ADDITIONAL INFORMATION**

Puerto Rican Family Institute (PRFI), 116 W. 14th Street, New York, NY 10011. This organization was established in 1960 for the preservation of the health, well-being, and integrity of Puerto Ricans and other Hispanic families in the United States.

Chicano Family Center (CFC), 7145 Avenue H, Houston, TX 77011. Founded in 1971, the CFC seeks to enhance understanding and appreciation of the Chicano culture.

---

## *Religion*

Religion plays a central role in the lives of Hispanic Americans. The Spanish colonial experience brought about a distinct culture of which the Catholic faith was an important part. Catholicism was brought by the Spanish to the United States. The first mass on what is now U.S. soil was celebrated at Saint Augustine, Florida, in 1565. Spanish missionaries were active in the Southwest as early as 1539, and California missions were founded between 1770 and 1782 (Fitzpatrick, 1987).

Fitzpatrick (1987) believes that Hispanics make up 40 percent of the current Catholic membership. Numbers from *The Gallup Report* substantiate the belief that Hispanics predominantly adhere to the Catholic faith: Protestants account for 18 percent; Catholics, 70 percent; others and those not claiming a religious preference, 12 percent (*Religion in America*, 1985).

## Language

Hispanic people in the United States speak many Spanish dialects, depending on where the speakers live, how long they have lived in this country, and where they came from originally. Spanish in the Southwest is different from Spanish in the Midwest, the Northeast, and Florida. Even in New York City, there are important cultural and linguistic differences between speakers from Puerto Rico, Cuba, the Dominican Republic, Colombia, Ecuador, Peru, Mexico, Venezuela, Bolivia, and other South American areas (Tiedt & Tiedt, 1995).

Some Hispanic American learners' language poses a problem outside the immediate neighborhood, because they tend to retain the native tongue rather than make a cultural transition to English. Instead of making an attempt to learn English, many do not perceive a need to develop proficiency in English and continue to risk survival in a predominantly English-speaking world. Language difficulties that learners experience may have a major impact on self-esteem and the developing identity.

Nonverbal language, as in other cultures, also plays a major factor in the Hispanic American culture, and professionals of other cultures must recognize and understand this. Although a complete list of nonverbal behaviors is impossible and would deny individual and intracultural differences, several examples will serve to indicate their significance. Many Hispanic Americans stand close together while communicating, touch to communicate, and often avoid eye contact. Other examples may include behaviors unique to boys and girls, for example, boys' assertion of "potential manhood" and girls' tendency toward a retiring and reserved attitude (Padilla, 1981).

---

### FOR ADDITIONAL INFORMATION    Internet Addresses

**Hispanic Americans Denied Equal Educational Opportunity**
http://www.gseis.ucla.edu/courses/ed191/assignment1/1996hispanic.html    Provides a report entitled "Our Nation on the Fault Line: Hispanic American Education."

**Background—Hispanic Americans and the Business Community**
http://www.aspeninst.org/dir/Polpro/HABC/Hispanicbkgd.html    Provides a summary of the Aspen Forum to discuss issues involving Hispanic Americans and society.

**Association of NIST Hispanic Americans**
http://www.nist.gov/director/groups/anha.htm    Provides a look at the work of the National Institute of Standards and Technology.

**Hispanic Americans**
http://libby.rbls.lib.il.us/dpl/hispanic.htm    Provides an examination of Hispanic Americans who have made valuable contributions.

## Hispanic American Learners in the School

On reaching an understanding of the social and cultural characteristics of Hispanic American children and adolescents, educators can proceed with understanding the learner in the Hispanic culture. Santiestevan (1986) maintains that "Nationwide, United States Hispanics agree that the single most crucial problem they face today is education" (p. 396).

This section considers Hispanic American learners and looks for answers to several questions related to their educational progress. What special school-related problems do Hispanic learners experience? Do European American expectations and stereotypes penalize Hispanic learners? Are Hispanic learners labeled? How do learning styles of Hispanics differ? What school practices might impede Hispanics' progress? As we explore these and other questions, we caution readers to consider the intracultural, generational, and socioeconomic differences between individual learners when reaching educational decisions.

Implementing Research 6-2 on page 150 looks at educational aspirations of African and Hispanic American youth.

### Educators' Understanding of Hispanic Americans

In her essay on Hispanic children, Valero-Figueira (1988) wrote:

> *There is among Hispanic and other linguistically and culturally different groups a new and not-so-young population that must be considered. They are the immigrant children from countries of war, who come to the United States and are expected to attend school and learn the language and subject matter just as any other child would. Many of these children are not performing well in school . . . where a different language is spoken and things are done in a way that is foreign to them.* (p. 48)

Before getting to know the strengths and weaknesses of learners, teachers and other school personnel need to know the individual.

Implementing Research 6-3 on page 151 examines Latino youth gangs and the meaning of school.

### Achievement Levels

The news media periodically raise several issues concerning the level of educational achievement of Hispanic American students, such as the relatively low number of Hispanic American students eligible for college. By the senior year, only 31 percent of Hispanic American high school students are enrolled in college preparatory courses. Of the Hispanic students graduating from high school, only about 10 to 15 percent are academically qualified to enter state universities

---

**IMPLEMENTING RESEARCH 6-2**   **Educational Aspirations of Minority Youth**

Grace Kao and Marta Tienda (1998) analyze how educational aspirations are formed and maintained from eighth to twelfth grade. They conclude that ethnic groups differ in the extent to which educational aspirations are maintained. They also found that family socioeconomic status contributes to ambitious aspirations in eighth grade and also to the maintenance of high aspirations during the high school years. Because African and Hispanic American youth are less likely to maintain their high aspirations throughout high school, owing to their lower family socioeconomic status, Kao and Tienda conclude that their early aspirations are less concrete than those of white and Asian American students.

Kao and Tienda also believe an ethnic group can compensate for the liabilities of minority group status by overachieving scholastically; on the other hand, the lack of opportunity can lead to educational underperformance if a racial or ethnic group becomes skeptical about the value of educational success as a means of upward mobility.

The researchers theorize about why, despite their high educational aspirations, African and Hispanic youth underachieve scholastically, but Asians overachieve relative to their ability and material resources. Some students believe their parents' financial status makes college an impossible dream, and others believe they can obtain a full scholarship simply because they are Hispanic or athletes. They conclude that the lack of information about college and admissions procedures may also drive some ambivalent students not to apply.

**Implementing the Research**

1. Educators need to recognize that the differences in educational aspirations among ethnic groups call for a methodical plan to remedy this situation.
2. Educators need to provide informational sessions for all students (and especially African and Hispanic Americans) to inform them about colleges, admission procedures, and financial packages.
3. Adolescents who think they might receive college scholarships simply because they are Hispanic or athletes should be informed of the keen competition for scholarships, both academic and athletic.
4. Educators who understand the relationship between socioeconomic status and educational aspirations should be careful to avoid making assumptions based on students' ethnicity.

*Source:* Kao, G., & Tienda, M. (1998). Educational aspirations of minority youth. *American Journal of Education 106*(3), 349–384.

in California (*Closing the Educational Gap for Hispanics,* 1987). Goldenberg (1987) described Hispanic Americans' academic achievement this way:

> *Hispanic students score lower than do their white, middle-class counterparts on tests of academic achievement. They are more likely to fail one or more grades in school, be placed in special education, and drop out altogether. Attitudes toward school are negative, with Hispanic students reporting a higher degree of alienation and disenchantment with school and school personnel. (p. 149)*

**IMPLEMENTING RESEARCH 6-3**    Latino Youth Gangs and the
                                 Meaning of School

Tellez and Estep (1997) maintain that despite widespread condemnation of gangs, few studies direct attention to gangs in schools, particularly Latino gangs. These researchers interviewed eight male former or active gang members to determine their schooling experiences and found they did well in school when they had a "good" (p. 69) teacher and that they had a favorite subject in school. Tellez and Estep suggest that the school curriculum can make a difference in helping gang members through secondary schooling and on to more traditional lifestyles.

Schools take several approaches to gang membership. They ignore the gangs, get tough on gangs, or provide self-esteem training that supposedly prevents gangs.

**Implementing the Research**

On the basis of their research, Tellez and Estep conclude and suggest:

1. *Teachers.* A great majority of teachers understand little about gang life or how to encourage gang members to stay in school.
   *Implementation suggestion:* Provide in-service training (and other training in diversity) for teachers by Latino experts who know Latinos' cultural backgrounds, strengths, and challenges.

2. *Curriculum.* The curriculum has few ideas interesting to Latinos and never addresses their lived experiences.
   *Implementation suggestion:* Revisit the curriculum to determine how it can be changed to reflect Latino experiences, especially those of Latino adolescents who might be prone to join gangs.

3. *Dropping out.* All the Latino interviewees had dropped out, except for the 12-year-olds.
   *Implementation suggestion:* Conduct additional studies (as Tellez and Estep have done) to determine other reasons that Latino gang members drop out of school. Plan school programs and curricular experiences that might keep them in school and career education options to capture their interest.

4. *Segregation.* Most interviewees went to schools that many other Latino gang members attended. They should have had more opportunities to attend more diverse schools.
   *Implementation suggestion:* Study the possibility of sending some Latino students to magnet schools (again as Tellez and Estep recommend in an effort to have a more diverse student body and for students to see options and life possibilities other than dropping out of school.

*Source:* Tellez, K., & Estep, M. (1997). Latino youth gangs and the meaning of school. *The High School Journal, 81*(2), 69–81.

Teachers should not let stereotypes and erroneous conclusions interfere with their academic and behavior expectations of Hispanic learners.

Case Study 6-2 on page 152 underscores the necessity of perceiving Hispanic American learners objectively and as individuals.

---

**CASE STUDY 6-2    Basing School Expectations on Long-Held Beliefs**

"Hispanic students always experience learning problems in American schools," Mrs. Miller was saying in the teachers' workroom. "They have so many problems—language, poverty, and those big families! What more can you expect? It has always been that way."

One of the professionals in the workroom should explain to Mrs. Miller the danger and futility of such statements. Expecting poor academic achievement as a result of language problems and poverty may set the stage for students' failure. Without doubt, Mrs. Miller needs a better understanding of Hispanic cultural heritages, more recognition of the differ-

ences within the Hispanic cultural heritages, more recognition of the differences within the Hispanic culture, and more objectivity with regard to Hispanic students. Mrs. Miller should also understand individual differences resulting from generational factors, geographic origins, and socioeconomic factors.

In general, Mrs. Miller continues to perpetuate a European American–oriented philosophy in an increasingly multicultural society. Though unfortunate, far more serious consequences exist for learners from different cultural backgrounds, in this case, the Hispanic American learners in the school.

---

**FOLLOW THROUGH 6-4    Teaching Hispanic American Learners**

1. Meet the learner's family, both immediate and extended, if possible.
2. Administer an "interest inventory" to determine the areas in which learners might have the most motivation.
3. Administer appropriate diagnostic instruments to determine learners' strengths and weaknesses. Be sure instruments take into account Hispanic learning styles.
4. Talk with Hispanic children or adolescents to learn more about the Hispanic culture, the family, areas of interest or confusion, fears, expectations, and any other factors that might help in planning culturally and developmentally appropriate instructions.
5. Seek the advice and input of other professionals in the school (speech correctionists, guidance counselors, and remedial, resource, and gifted teachers) who have knowledge of the Hispanic learner.

---

**FOLLOW THROUGH 6-5    Enhancing Hispanic American
                         Learners' Academic Records**

It is time for school systems to do their part to enhance the Hispanic learner's academic record by:

1. considering the Hispanic learner objectively and avoiding labels;
2. developing a more individualized instructional program that recognizes Hispanic learning styles;
3. implementing a curriculum that recognizes, respects, and builds on Hispanic learners' cultural diversity; and
4. involving parents by explaining the role and purposes of schooling and by showing what they can do to help their children in school.

## Language Problems

Undoubtedly, many of the problems Hispanic American learners experience stem from their difficulties with English. Hearing Spanish spoken at home, yet feeling pressure to communicate in English at school, often results in academic and behavioral problems, lower self-esteem, negative cultural identities, and a general pessimism toward teachers and schools.

The number of school-age children who speak a language other than English at home and have difficulty speaking English has increased from 1.3 million in 1979 to 2.4 million in 1995, about 5 percent of all children in those age groups (*Hispanic youth edging past blacks in number*, 1998).

Olsen (1988) reports that 9 percent of the children with limited English proficiency in California are not receiving native-language support and are not involved in an English language program. Olsen (1988) reports the following words of a young boy called Socorro:

> *I just sat in my classes and didn't understand anything. . . . Sometimes I would try to look like I knew what was going on; sometimes I would just try to think about a happy time when I didn't feel stupid. My teachers never called on me or talked to me. I think they either forgot I was there or else wished I wasn't. I waited and waited, thinking someday I will know English. (p. 216)*

Implementing Research 6-4 on page 154 looks at language-minority Latino students and their education achievement.

Case Study 6-3 shows the importance of being understood and what Mr. Donaldson did to help Maria.

---

**CASE STUDY 6-3    The Importance of Understanding**

Mr. Donaldson, an elementary school teacher, had a fourth-grade child whose lack of proficiency in English left her virtually unable to learn. Rather than being a meaningful learning experience, the school day became a time of boredom and frustration. Devastating consequences awaited Maria (and other, similar learners with culturally diverse backgrounds), who felt "stupid" or that teachers forgot she was there or else wished she were not. Even though language proficiency takes time and effort, Maria needed to feel that teachers and other school personnel cared and wanted to help her. Mr. Donaldson decided to take several steps to help Maria have meaningful school experiences:

1. request that the bilingual (or other) language specialist meet with Maria to determine an immediate plan of action;

2. arrange for a professional, perhaps an aide, to work closely with Maria to show a sense of caring and concern;

3. call on or talk to Maria about anything: school, the Hispanic culture, or activities in the playground; and

4. administer an "interest inventory" to learn about Maria's interests, likes, and dislikes, then plan instruction and communication accordingly.

---

**IMPLEMENTING RESEARCH 6-4**   Language-Minority Latino Students and Education Achievement

Questioning why some minority students experience success in school while others do not, Rumberger and Larson (1998) looked at the extent of differences in educational achievement among Mexican American language-minority students in a large, urban middle school. They assessed the students from sociocultural and socioeconomic perspectives to determine social and academic behavior on educational achievement. They found that bilingual students who were fluent English proficient (FEP) had better grades and a higher rate of academic stability and were more likely to complete a quarter of high school credits by the end of the ninth grade than were students from limited English proficiency (LEP) backgrounds.

Rumberger and Larson concluded that research supports the notion that attitudes and behaviors result from students' interaction with their environment—that is, low-income minority students have fewer opportunities to develop relationships with teachers, administrators, and other institutional agents who can provide support and resources necessary for school success. Even if students have the motivation for school success, they may not always have access to the resources that can help them succeed. The authors also conclude that schools must actively address how to increase both the academic and social engagement of their students.

**Implementing the Research**

1. Schools should focus on the academic curriculum as well as emphasize improving skills such as note taking, time management, and organization as well as monitoring students' work over a period of time.
2. Schools should recognize the importance of a social support system (teachers, administrators, and peers who are good role models) to engage students socially and reduce problematic behaviors.
3. Educators need to consider language-minority students objectively—many differences exist that will influence academic achievement and social support systems.
4. Educators should base educational experiences on the belief that although achieving proficiency in English is necessary, it is not a sufficient condition for Latino students' success in schools.

---

*Source:* Rumberger, R. W., & Larson, K. A. (1998). Toward differences in educational achievement among Mexican American language-minority students. *Sociology of Education, 71,* 69–93.

Children who feel pressure to speak Spanish at home and English at school may develop problems in both languages, may become bilingual, or may avoid English-speaking situations. Such a situation can result in dual cultural identification, additional language conflicts, and chronic anxiety (Padilla, 1981). In the Southwestern United States, many Hispanic American people live in Spanish-speaking communities isolated from English-speaking communities. In fact, children often enter the English-speaking world for the first time when they begin their public school education. Then, to make matters worse, these children are often threatened with punishment in school environments for speaking Spanish (Vontress, 1976).

---

**FOLLOW THROUGH 6-6   Appreciating Hispanic Names**

Names and their meanings are special to learners of all cultures and ages. Teachers, other school personnel, and students should understand the special meaning and value Hispanic cultures place on names.

Soledad (solitude)
Concepcion (conception)
Salvador (savior)
Dolores (sorrows)
Mercedes (mercies)
Jesus (Jesus)

---

*Source:* Tiedt, P. L., & Tiedt, I. M. (1995). *Multicultural teaching: A handbook of activities, information, and resources.* Boston: Allyn & Bacon.

## *Learning Styles: Cultural Considerations*

As we mentioned in the previous chapters on children and adolescents of various cultures, educators can determine learning styles by observing learners' overt behavior (Keefe, 1987). What cultural or sociological elements should educators consider in the Hispanic American learner? Learners can provide clues while demonstrating any number of behaviors. Some learners work and achieve when left alone; distractions such as the presence of other people, movements, or sounds create disturbances. Other children learn best when among peers working on case studies, small-group activities, or team learnings (Dunn & Dunn, 1979).

Determining the most appropriate learning styles for Hispanic Americans requires that educators, whether regular classroom teachers or remedial and resource teachers, observe both individual and cultural differences that may affect learning styles.

---

**FOLLOW THROUGH 6-7   Helping Second-Language Learners**

Educators can help second-language learners through bilingual programs, English as a second language (ESL) programs, English remediation classes, and instruction in Spanish for at least part of the day. Other suggestions include:

1. Read aloud to students.
2. Respect students' efforts.
3. Provide opportunities for oral communication.
4. Provide opportunities for students to speak and write.
5. Use a variety of methods and materials, such as small-group speaking situations, tapes, choral speaking, and records.
6. Respect the student's native language.

Effective multicultural educators should look at specific Hispanic cultural characteristics to determine their potential effects on learning. Case Study 6-4 looks at several cultural characteristics that may affect learning styles. As in other chapters on cultural diversity among learners, we urge educators to use caution by considering both the culture and the individual within the culture.

---

**CASE STUDY 6-4   Cultural Characteristics and Learning**

Mr. Smith, an Anglo teacher in his fourth year of teaching, received his class roll for the upcoming school year and learned that nearly half his class was Hispanic. Although he had some background in providing educational experiences in multicultural situations, he was unsure how to relate Hispanic cultural characteristics to learners' teaching/learning experiences. Mr. Smith met with colleagues to discuss the challenge and received the following suggestions:

| Cultural Characteristic | Implications for Learning |
|---|---|
| "Personalism"—wanting personal contact | Learner needs opportunities to have first-hand contact with teacher and others in school |
| "Machismo"—biological superiority of the male | Sexes may feel uncomfortable working with each other; may feel that the male must lead and reach decisions |

| Cultural Characteristic | Implications for Learning |
|---|---|
| Does not want to be set apart as excelling | Provide opportunities for group work so group will excel, not individual |

These characteristics and implications are only representative, but Mr. Smith saw that learning could and should be based on the cultural characteristics of learners.

---

**FOLLOW THROUGH 6-8   Improving Performance through Understanding Learning Styles**

Give Hispanic students better understanding of their personal learning styles and you provide them an excellent means of improving their learning performance. As learners better understand how they learn, perceptive educators can also gain insight into how they should plan and implement learning experiences. Learners can ask themselves several questions:

1. Do you prefer to (a) think through a learning experience to reach a conclusion or (b) be told the conclusion and then think out how the conclusion was reached?
2. Do you think your most effective learning experiences are in the morning, the afternoon, or at night?
3. Do you prefer a quiet learning environment, or can you learn better when there is background noise?
4. Do you prefer teaching and learning experiences that require you to see, listen, or feel?
5. Do you prefer to study and learn alone or with a friend?

These represent only a few determinants of learning styles. "For Additional Information" lists sources for learning more about learning styles.

## School Practices Impeding Hispanic Americans' Progress

Is it possible that well-meaning teachers, either European American or of another culture, actually encourage school practices that may prove detrimental to Hispanic students? A look at many American schools causes one to answer in the affirmative. The already somewhat overwhelmed Hispanic child or adolescent may be even more startled at the verbal emphasis in America's schools. The extreme verbalism that characterizes U.S. schools can have profound consequences for learners with limited English-language skills.

A second, related detrimental practice is well-meaning teachers' forbidding Hispanic students to speak Spanish and actually punishing them for it. Understanding such a situation is difficult for learners who are proficient in Spanish but are experiencing considerable difficulty with their second language.

A third practice involves an entanglement of values and cultural orientations. Believing in the American cultural tradition of excelling among one's peers, teachers often motivate learners by encouraging Hispanic learners to excel above others in the class. Causing oneself to stand out among one's peers goes against Hispanic cultural traditions and expectations.

Another problem results when teachers from European American and other cultural groups have stereotypical beliefs of Hispanic learners. How many educators believe that Hispanic learners are slow, violent, prone to emotional, erratic behavior, and generally speaking, unable to perform academically in American schools? So (1987) believed that European American teachers harbored biases against Hispanic American students. In his research, So concluded that European American teachers assigned a good or bad label to students and then gave different treatment to some students. The students began to accept the teacher's label and responded appropriately. Such practices can also affect students' motivation and academic achievement.

---

**FOR ADDITIONAL INFORMATION**

Learning styles, especially with multicultural learners, have considerable potential for teachers and learners. The following resources are recommended for teachers who wish to match teaching and learning activities with the students' learning styles.

Dunn, R., Beaudry, J. S., & Klavas, A. (1989). Survey of research on learning styles. *Educational Leadership, 46*(6), 50–58. In this theme issue dealing with diversity, Dunn, Beaudry, and Klavas comprehensively survey the research on learning styles.

Keefe, J. W. (1987). *Learning Style: Theory and Practice*. Reston, VA: National Association of Secondary School Principals. This succinct forty-eight-page monograph provides an overview of learning styles and focuses on assessment and application.

*Theory into Practice, 23,* (Winter, 1984). This entire issue deals with learning styles and provides twelve excellent readings, which range from the theoretical to practical application.

---

**IMPLEMENTING RESEARCH 6-5    Hispanic Representation in
Young Adult Literature**

Arlene Barry (1998) maintains that the lack of Hispanic representation in popular books seems odd, particularly considering their current proportion in the population as well as the predictions for continued growth. The author provides such statistics as the following: Hispanic children appear in only 10 percent of the Newbery Medal books; of the nearly 5000 children's books published each year in the United States, only 2 percent represent the Hispanic culture; Puerto Ricans are virtually invisible in children's books; and Mexican Americans are often underrepresented and misrepresented in children's literature.

It is important for students to have their culture represented in books they read. Multiethnic literature increases minority children's self-esteem and encourages the development of respect across cultures. Through multiethnic literature, minority children learn about the valuable contributions their culture has made to the United States and the world. Also, they can see similarities between cultures.

Reasons for poor representation of Hispanics include the possibility that they have not had a social advocate for their positive representation, as did African Americans. Additionally the Hispanic community has lacked political and commercial influence, there are not many Chicano writers of young people's books, and publishers may be less willing to publish books about the cultures or experiences of small subgroups within the larger Hispanic culture.

**Implementing the Research**

Educators at all levels need to realize the dearth of books for young people that positively represent Hispanic characters. Young people need to see their culture represented in books and curricular materials, so as to increase their self-esteem as well as promote their cultural identity. The same holds true for young people of all cultures. To show their commitment to literature and curricular materials where cultural representation is the norm rather than the exception, educators can (1) purchase *only* literature that has cultural representation, (2) become advocates for cultural representation by encouraging book publishers to provide fair representation, and (3) compile lists of books and curricular materials to be shared with other teachers (and the library media specialist) in the school.

*Source:* Barry, A. L. (1998). Hispanic representation in literature for young adults. *Journal of Adolescent and Adult Literacy, 41* (8), 630–637.

In Implementing Research 6-5, Arlene Barry asks why, if Hispanics are the fastest-growing minority in the United States, are they underrepresented in young adult literature?

## *Promoting Self-Esteem and Positive Cultural Identities*

The educator's role in promoting self-esteem and positive cultural identities among learners will always be of paramount importance. Purkey and Novak (1984) have clearly demonstrated the relationship between self-esteem and school achievement. Emphatically stated, a student who feels "worthless," "not so good," and "inferior" will experience academic difficulties despite the teacher's most conscientious efforts. Drill, memorization, and worksheets cannot overcome learners' feeling that they (or their culture) are inferior.

Although the problems associated with speaking one's mother tongue in a predominantly English-speaking environment deserves consideration, allowing (or

---

**FOLLOW THROUGH 6-9    Respecting Hispanic Cultures**

Answer these questions about your school.

1. Is genuine respect shown for Hispanic learners and their culture?
2. Are efforts made to understand the cultural assets and contributions of Hispanic learners?
3. Are Hispanic people employed by the school and in what positions? Do Hispanics serve on committees and in decision-making capacities?
4. Are efforts under way to teach cultural understanding and acceptance?
5. Do teachers provide learners with chances to feel that the school appreciates their culture and individuality?
6. Do any policies (either overt or covert) limit opportunities to participate, for example, in extracurricular activities?
7. Are there efforts to diagnose and remediate specific learning problems of Hispanic learners?

Try these exercises.

*Choosing Names:* Ask children how they got their names—from a relative or more than one relative?

*Surnames:* What are they? Where do they come from? Discuss the origins of Castaneda, Chavez, Feliciano, and Vasquez.

*Family Roots:* Students can ask their families about family history and write information on a chart.

> Name
> Birthplace
> Date
> Mother
> Father
> Brothers
> Sisters

*Family Tree:* Have children construct a family tree using the information they collected under "Family Roots." Learning more about one's self and family has the potential for allowing learners to see the uniqueness or special qualities of all people and families.

---

*Source:* Tiedt, P. L. & Tiedt, I. M. (1995). *Multicultural Teaching,* 56, 60, 83. Boston: Allyn & Bacon.

## CULTURAL PORTRAIT    Carlos—A Hispanic American Learner

Carlos S., a twelve-year-old boy of Spanish origin, is one grade level behind in his public elementary school, which is composed predominantly of black and Hispanic American children. A small percentage of Anglo students attend Carlos's school; while the majority of the teachers are Anglo, a few are black, and one is Hispanic. Carlos lives in a lower-socioeconomic Spanish-speaking neighborhood near the school. Carlos has several problems: His family speaks Spanish at home, but he is forbidden to speak Spanish at school. His difficulty with the English language has resulted in lower reading grades and achievement test scores (hence, the grade level behind), and he sees older boys dropping out of school and wonders when he can end his frustrations with school.

Carlos admits his frustrations to his best friend, another Hispanic American boy: Why does the teacher keep asking him to excel? Why does she say ignore blacks and Anglos when they pick on Hispanic children? Why doesn't she allow him to speak Spanish when his family (including his grandparents, aunts and uncles, and cousins) continues to speak Spanish? Carlos knows he has problems, and he thinks his teachers have almost given up on him.

*What Carlos's Teacher Can Do*

Carlos's situation calls for immediate attention. First, whenever possible, Carlos needs to be allowed to speak Spanish. This is the language in which he is most proficient, and he cannot understand the reason for not being allowed to speak a language that both his family and his friends speak. Second, Carlos needs English-language instruction from qualified professionals who understand second-language instruction and who understand the problems Hispanic learners face. Third, Carlos needs appropriate diagnostic testing to determine his strengths and weaknesses, and carefully planned remediation to address his weaknesses.

Equally important is that the teachers in Carlos's school understand the Hispanic culture and situations of students like Carlos. Additionally, because the cultural diversity of the school population is not reflected in the teaching staff, the curriculum and learning environment probably reflects an Anglo perspective. More effort should be directed toward making Carlos's school more multicultural in nature and, in this case, more understanding and accepting of Hispanic American learners.

even encouraging) Hispanic children to read appropriate children's literature written in Spanish might enhance their self-esteem and cultural identities.

Specifically, what can educators do to promote positive feelings of self-worth and cultural identity? First, all efforts should be genuine and honest; learners will detect hypocrisy if teachers say one thing but demonstrate another. Second, educators should plan programs that teach about the Hispanic culture and the proud history and accomplishments of the Spanish-speaking people. Third, rather than having "Spanish Art, Music, and Foods Week," educators must develop a curriculum that shows an appreciation for cultural diversity and that fully incorporates the Hispanic culture into all areas of the school curriculum. Last, educators can use literature and any other method or activity that improves learner self-esteem, enhances cultural identities, and increases the appreciation of cultural differences.

## Summing Up

Educators who plan teaching and learning experiences for Hispanic American children and adolescents should

1. Provide an educational environment in which Hispanic American children and adolescents feel that educators and other significant adults and peers respect their Spanish culture and background.
2. Allow Spanish to be spoken in schools, because it is the language spoken at home and in the neighborhoods, although learners should be taught to speak English.
3. Understand that language problems and differences are partly responsible for most academic problems.
4. Consider differences in learning styles when planning and implementing education programs.
5. Promote positive feelings toward learners' selves and their culture, because learners' self-esteem and cultural identities influence school achievement and social development.
6. Understand and appreciate cultural diversity to the degree that Hispanic learners do not feel their culture, socioeconomic class, families, religion, and language are wrong or inferior.
7. Use utmost caution not to label Hispanic learners on a basis of myth, stereotypes, prejudices, racism, or any other form of discrimination.
8. Use test data carefully, and remember that achievement tests, intelligence tests, and other measurement instruments might have a cultural bias toward European American standards and cultural expectations.

## Suggested Learning Activities

1. Choose a typical Spanish-speaking student (from any of the Spanish-speaking cultures) and write a case study that explores individual and cultural characteristics. Consult with the school guidance counselor to better understand the child and his or her culture. After listing specific individual and cultural characteristics, plan an educational program that will meet the needs of this child.

2. Observe the overt learning behaviors of a Hispanic child to determine learning style. Consult with a remedial or resource teacher for help in interpreting the behaviors. After specifically determining the child's learning styles, tell how educators can plan appropriate learning opportunities based on these styles.

3. Choose a low-achieving Hispanic American student and assess his or her language proficiency. To what extent is the student's lower academic achievement a product of poor English skills? Interview the student to determine whether the immediate and extended families speak Spanish or English. In what ways can the school's speech cor-

rectionist (working with language development specialists) assist this child? Plan an instructional program that addresses the student's problems with language and academic achievement.

## Suggestions for Collaborative Efforts

Form groups of three or four that, if possible, represent our nation's cultural and gender diversity. Working collaboratively, focus your group's attention toward the following efforts:

1. Survey a group of Puerto Rican American and Mexican American children. Have each member of your group focus on a specific difference—cultural, language, religion, or familial. What similarities and differences exist? Also suggest ways educators can address intracultural differences within varying Spanish-speaking cultures.

2. With the increasing Spanish-speaking populations, it is becoming easier for Hispanic people to live in sections in which Spanish continues to be the mother tongue. Have each member of your group examine a specific language aspect. What language is spoken during recess, lunch times, or other breaks during the school day? Do teachers allow Spanish to be spoken in the classroom? Do teachers see the advantages of having one learner help another while speaking in Spanish? What language is spoken in the home? When parents and guardians speak to children in school, what language is spoken? Does the learner live in a predominantly Spanish-speaking neighborhood? What attempts have you made to understand the beauty of the Spanish language and to realize the language problems some students might experience?

3. Increasingly, the Spanish language will be spoken in the United States, especially because all demographic predictions suggest the Hispanic population will continue to increase. Some people feel that the United States should accept Spanish as the official second language; other people argue that English should be the only official language of the nation. In your group, discuss issues related to Spanish being increasingly spoken in the United States: whether Spanish should be accepted in an English-speaking country; whether schools should teach Spanish as well as English; whether instruction should occasionally be in Spanish; the implications for our society and schools; and other issues that your group feels are significant.

## Expanding Your Horizons: Additional Journal Readings and Books

Barry, A. L. (1998). Hispanic representation in literature for young adults. *Journal of Adolescent and Adult Literacy, 41*(8), 630–637.

*In this helpful article Barry calls for more Hispanic representation in books and provides appropriate titles and authors.*

Basen-Enquist, K., Tortolero, S., & Parcel, G. S. (1997). HIV risk behavior and theory-based psychosocial determinants in Hispanic and non-Hispanic white adolescents. *Journal of Health Education, 28*(4), S-44–S-50.

*These researchers studied students in a Texas high school to assess differences in HIV risk behavior among Hispanic and non-Hispanic white adolescents and offer implications for instructional design.*

Guinn, B. (1997). Health locus of control and HIV/AIDS knowledge among Mexican American young adolescents. *Journal of Health Education, 28*(4), S-13–S-16.

*Guinn investigated the perceived control over health and health behaviors in relation to HIV/AIDS knowledge among Mexican American adolescents and found that intervention programs should emphasize family, role models, and community leaders.*

Hispanic youth edging past blacks in number. (1998). *Census and You, 33*(9), 3.

*This census article provides specific demographic data on Hispanic and African Americans and explains that Hispanics are the fastest-growing population—their growth is expected to continue during upcoming decades.*

Isom, B. A., & Casteel, C. P. (1997/1998). Hispanic literature: A fiesta for literacy instruction. *Childhood Education, 74* (2), 83–89.

*This article shows how several Hispanic books can contribute to critical thinking, creative thinking, and metacognition.*

The Hispanic Development Project. (1997). *The challenges of change.* New York: Author.

*This excellent report looks at backlashes, demographic realities, advertising, employment, and looking toward the future.*

## Expanding Your Students' Horizons: Appropriate Hispanic American Books for Children and Adolescents

Bachelis, Faren. *The Central Americans.* Chelsea House, 1990.

Becerra de Jenkins, Lyll. *So Loud a Silence.* Lodestar, 1996.

Bvelpre, Pura. *Firefly Summer.* Arte Publcio. 1996.

Bierhorst, John. *The Mythology of Mexico and Central America.* Morrow, 1990.

Cisneros, Sandra. *The House on Mango Street.* Random House, 1991.

Codye, Corinn. *Vilma Martinez.* Raintree, 1990.

Cofer, J. O. *An Island Like You: Stories from the Barrio.* Orchard, 1995.

Cullison, Alan. *The South Americans.* Chelsea House, 1991.

Delacre, Lulu. *Arroz CON LECHE.* Scholastic, 1990.

Delacre, Lulu. *Las Navidades.* Scholastic, 1990.

De La Garza, Phyliss. *Chacho.* New Readers, 1990.

Dwyer, Christopher. *The Dominican Americans.* Chelsea House, 1991.

Fernandez, Roberta. *Intaglio: A Novel in Six Stories.* Arte Publico Press, 1990.

Gleiter, Jan, and Kathleen Thompson. *Jose Marti.* Raintree, 1990.

Hargrove, Jim. *Diego Rivera: Mexican Muralist.* Children's Press, 1990.

Hewitt, Joan. *Hector Lives in the United States Now: The Story of a Mexican American Child.* HarperCollins, 1990.

Hurwitz, Johanna. *Class President.* William Morrow, 1990.

Lynn, Joseph. *Coconut Kind of Day: Island Poems.* Lothrop, Lee & Shepard, 1990.

Lopez, Tiffany Ana. *Growing Up Chicana/o.* Tupelo, 1993.

Lynn, Joseph. *A Wave in Her Pocket: Stories from Trinidad.* Clarion, 1991.

Myers, Walter Dean. *Toussaint L'Ouverture: The Fight for Haiti's Freedom.* Simon and Schuster, 1996.

Orr, Katherine. *My Grandpa and the Sea.* Lerner/Carolrhoda, 1990.

Paulsen, Gary. *The Crossing.* Dell, 1990.

Paredes, Americo. *George Washington Gomez.* Arte Publico Press, 1990.

Roe, Eileen. *Con Mi Hermano/With My Brother.* Bradbury, 1991.

Shute, Linda. *Rabbit Wishes.* Lothrop, 1995.

Soto, Gary. *Baseball in April and Other Stories.* Harcourt Brace Jovanovich, 1990.

Soto, Gary. *Local News: A Collection of Short Stories.* Harcourt Brace Jovanvich, 1993.

Sumption, Christine, and Kathleen Thompson. *Carlos Finlay.* Raintree, 1990.

Talbert, Marc. *Heart of a Jaguar.* Simon and Schuster, 1995.

Temple, Frances. *Tonight, by Sea.* Orchard, 1995.

Thompson, Kathleen. *Sor Juana Ines de la Cruz.* Raintree, 1990.

Velasquez, G. *Juanita Fights the School Board.* Piñata, 1994.

Velasquez, G. *Maya's Divided World.* Piñata, 1995.

Velasquez, G. *Tommy Stands Alone.* Piñata, 1995.

## Answers to the Culture Quiz: Hispanic Americans

| | | | | |
|---|---|---|---|---|
| **1.** e | **3.** g | **5.** c | **7.** j | **9.** i |
| **2.** f | **4.** h | **6.** a | **8.** d | **10.** b |

$$Chapter \quad 7$$

# Understanding Native American Children and Adolescents

Understanding the material and activities in this chapter will help the reader to:

- Describe the cultural, socioeconomic, and familial characteristics of Native American children and adolescents.

- Explain special problems and challenges that confront Native American children and adolescents.

- Describe Native American learners and their development, achievement levels, language problems, and learning styles.

- List several educational practices that impede the Native American learners' educational progress.

- Offer several suggestions and strategies for improving Native American learners' self-esteem and cultural identities.

- List several points that educators of Native Americans should remember when planning teaching and learning experiences.

- Suggest appropriate children's literature, implement research findings, and provide culturally appropriate experiences for Native American learners.

## Overview

Native American children and adolescents have special needs that warrant educators' understanding: cherished and unique cultural characteristics, language problems, familial traditions, and learning problems, which present schools with special challenges. Yet teacher education programs traditionally have not prepared prospective teachers to understand multicultural populations and the special characteristics and learning problems of Native American learners or, in reality, any other multicultural group. This chapter examines Native American learners—their culture, language issues, families, achievement levels, learning styles, and overall school programs.

## Origins

Banks (1987) contends that scholars do not know exactly when people first came to the Americas. While many archaeologists have concluded that the lack of fossils rules out the possibility of men and women having evolved in the Western hemisphere, some Native American groups believe that they originated in the Americas. Archaeologists believe that the ancestors of Native Americans came from Asia (Banks, 1987).

Whatever explanation of origins one accepts, it is a fact that these people, who are today known as Indians, American Indians, or Native Americans, have continuously occupied North America for 30,000 years or longer (Dorriss, 1981). Whites came to the Americas and began a crusade of taking Native American land and using it for their own purposes. Native Americans are unique among minorities: They did not immigrate to the Americas. Native Americans faced the problem of whites coming to their land and expecting them to relinquish cherished cultural traditions (Banks, 1987).

## Native Americans Today

Native Americans number more than 500 tribes of varying sizes. The larger tribes (those with more than 100,000 members) include the Cherokee, Navajo, Chippewa, and Sioux. Tribes in the range of 50,000 people include the Choctaw, Pueblo, and Apache. Fourteen tribes have populations between 10,000 and 21,000. Most tribes have less than 10,000. Nearly one-half of Native Americans today live west of the Mississippi River. In fact, more than half of the Native American population lived in just six states in 1990: Oklahoma, California, Arizona, New Mexico, Alaska (with large numbers of Aleuts), and Washington.

The U.S. Bureau of the Census offers other facts about Native Americans and their demographics. First, they are a young and growing population. Thirty-nine percent of the Native American population (which also includes Eskimos and Aleuts) was under twenty years of age in 1990, compared with 29 percent of the nation's total population. Second, their educational attainment improved during the 1980s. Increasingly, Native Americans are finishing high school, and about 9 percent completed a bachelor's degree or higher. Third, more Native Americans

---

**FOLLOW THROUGH 7-1    Learning about Native Americans—
Their Tribes and Individuals**

The Native American population represents many different tribes and peoples—it is difficult to offer generalizations and conclusions. Bearing in mind tribal and individual differences, suggest four or five ways you could learn about the Native American students in your class.

---

lived below the poverty lines. Fourth, about 22 percent, or about 437,431, lived on reservations and trust lands in 1990 (U.S. Bureau of the Census, 1993c).

Over the past three decades, Native Americans have been progressively moving off reservation lands. As a result, over 70 percent of Native Americans live in non-Indian communities. Movement from reservation to off-reservation settings can harm family relationships and increase the likelihood of risk-taking behaviors that endanger health and well-being. Because educational behaviors and attitudes may result from other stresses in students' lives, off-reservation adolescents may be even more prone to educational problems than their on-reservation peers (Machamer & Gruber, 1998).

The following exercise provides an opportunity for readers to test their knowledge of Native Americans, both historical and contemporary. As readers consider their success on the exercise, they should realize that neither social studies texts nor the contemporary media have given widespread attention to the contributions and accomplishments of Native Americans. Readers will have to make a deliberate and planned effort to enhance their knowledge of Native Americans and their contributions to U.S. society.

As Implementing Research 7-1 shows, professionals who have a genuine understanding of the Native American population are better prepared to address the unique issues these people face.

## *Stereotyping of Native American Children and Adolescents*

Although stereotypical images often accompany the term *Indian children and adolescents,* this culture and these developmental periods constitute a highly diverse group. Differences in developing children and adolescents vary significantly. Not all Native Americans are slow learners, shy, and undependable; likewise, not all adolescents are rebellious and experience difficult and stressful times. Although some common characteristics emerge from the study of Native American children and adolescents, we must use caution not to oversimplify or ignore individual differences.

Case Study 7-1 on page 170 shows the importance of understanding Native Americans.

## THE CULTURE QUIZ    Native Americans

*Directions:* Match the individuals with their contributions or achievements by placing the appropriate letter before each name.

_____ **1.** Vin Deloria, Jr.

_____ **2.** Watie Strand

_____ **3.** Jim Thorpe

_____ **4.** Ely Samuel Parker

_____ **5.** Kelly Haney

_____ **6.** C. Matthew Snipp

_____ **7.** Susan LaFlesche

_____ **8.** Charles Eastman

_____ **9.** Annie Dodge Wauneka

_____ **10.** Oren Lyons

**a.** First Native American to serve as U.S. Commissioner of Indian Affairs

**b.** A Sioux leader in the fight for Indian rights, wrote *Custer Died for Your Sins*

**c.** Seminole Creek Indian, member of the Oklahoma Senate

**d.** Rural sociologist, a Cherokee Choctaw; wrote *American Indians: The First of This Land*

**e.** The only Native American brigadier general in the Confederate army

**f.** One of the greatest athletes in history; first president of the American Professional Football Association (now National Football League)

**g.** Sioux physician and crusader for Native American rights

**h.** The first female Native American to become a doctor of Western medicine

**i.** Navajo woman who has worked to help her people combat tuberculosis and alcoholism; won the Presidential Medal of Freedom Award in 1963

**j.** Spiritual leader; clan chief of Onondaga branch of the Iroquois; supports nature and environmental issues

(Answers to the Culture Quiz are located at the end of the chapter.)

## USING CHILDREN'S LITERATURE    Informational Books

Aliki. *Corn Is Maize: The Gift of the Indians.* Crowell, 1976. Aliki provides an interesting and excellent history of corn, how it grows, and its first uses. (Reading Level: 2; Interest Level: 5–9.)

Ashabranner, Brent. *To Live in Two Worlds: American Indian Youth Today.* Dodd, Mead, 1984. Ashabranner provides true accounts as Indian youths tell about their own lives. (Reading Level: 7; Interest Level: 11 and above.)

Ashabranner, Brent. *Morning Star, Black Sun: The Northern Cheyenne Indians and America's Energy*

*Crisis.* Dodd, Mead, 1982. This informative text traces the history of the Northern Cheyenne and discusses their fight to save their lands. (Reading Level: 7; Interest Level: 11 and above.)

Poatgieter, Alice Hermina. *Indian Legacy: Native American Influences on World Life and Culture.* Messner, 1981. This text provides readers with an informative account of Native North and South American contributions to democratic attitudes and culture. (Reading Level: 5–7; Interest Level: 9 and above.)

**IMPLEMENTING RESEARCH 7-1   Understanding Native Americans**

Numerous discussions focus on the changing waves of immigrants and their social service needs, but not much has been written about the original inhabitants of North America, the Native Americans. Indigenous peoples hold a unique place in our increasingly multicultural society. Their history in the United States differs from that of people who entered the United States as immigrants. For many Native Americans, a primary goal has been self-preservation through separatism and isolationism rather than seeking a place within the multicultural society. Also, the federal government has specific moral and legal responsibilities toward Native Americans, unlike other groups in the United States. All professionals working with Native Americans need an understanding of the issues specific to the indigenous peoples in a multicultural society.

Hilary Weaver (1998) examined the unique status of indigenous peoples in the United States and explored the implications of addressing their needs. She writes in the journal *Social Work* and primarily for human-service providers, but her theories and implications also pertain to educators of children and adolescents. Weaver contends that cultural competence can be summarized in three major principles: (1) knowledge of the group in question, (2) self-reflection, which allows professionals to recognize biases within themselves and their profession, and (3) ability to integrate knowledge and reflection with practice skills.

Weaver maintains that, given the diversity of Native Americans, professionals need to be knowledgeable about peoples' specific tribes or nations. Accurate information about specific Native American groups can best be obtained from the groups themselves. The practitioner should begin by asking individuals about their cultural background and the role that cultural identity plays in their lives. In fact, most reservations and urban areas have social services and cultural agencies that are willing to provide information to practitioners. Other issues Weaver examines include historical trauma, citizenship, sovereignty, and cultural identity.

### Implementing the Research

Educators working with Native American children and adolescents need to:

1. understand Native Americans' unique status in the United States—they already lived on this land rather than immigrating here;
2. develop the knowledge of Native Americans, the self-reflection needed to recognize bias, and the ability to integrate knowledge and reflection into educational experiences;
3. ask (demonstrating both respect and interest) Native American children and adolescents about their cultural backgrounds, yet be careful to respect students' privacy since, as Weaver states, some Native Americans distrust and feel suspicious about others; and
4. avoid basing perceptions and educational experiences on myth and stereotypical opinions; instead seek accurate and objective information from Native Americans themselves, reservations, social services, and cultural agencies.

*Source:* Weaver, H. N. (1998). Indigenous people in a multicultural society: Unique issues for human services. *Social Work, 43*(3), 203–211.

---

**CASE STUDY 7-1    Accurate Perceptions of Native Americans**

On completing her teacher education program in the East, Ms. Stein joined several friends who went to a Western state in hopes of finding teaching positions. Ms. Stein accepted a position teaching eighth-grade social studies in a school that was predominantly Native American.

Trying to be as objective as possible, Ms. Stein questioned her beliefs about Native American learners. She asked herself and her friends, "Are Native Americans really different? Are they all poor? What will I do about their lower achievement?" She had heard so many stories. She wondered whether they were true and how she should separate facts from stereotypes.

Ms. Stein and her future students are fortunate in at least one aspect—Ms. Stein realizes that she does not know what to believe, and she is willing to question stereotypical generalizations. Miss Stein decided on the following strategy:

1. Speak with several professionals in the school—teachers, administrators, and special-services personnel, such as the speech therapist and the librarian. Obtain an objective cultural portrait; base opinions on objective information about the Native American culture, families, religions, socioeconomic status, and language.

2. Look at each student's permanent record to learn academic strengths and weaknesses.

3. Learn as much as possible about the learners' families and their role in the education process.

4. Read about the Native American culture, its contributions, and its proud heritage.

5. Read nonfiction and basic informational children's books that provide insights into the Native American culture.

6. Talk to Native American learners and express an interest in their cultural backgrounds.

7. Seek information from organizations that promote Native Americans, their overall welfare, and their determination for equality.

---

## Cultural Characteristics

Native American culture plays a major role in the shaping of children and adolescents. Educators must make the extra effort to seek accurate information and to understand American history and the Native American culture from the point of view of the Native American and from the child and adolescent's perspective (Banks, 1987). Educators should also think through their own cultural beliefs and realize the dangers of *cultural substitution* in which Native American learners are expected to change cultural viewpoints to coincide with European American, middle-class ones. Table 7-1 provides a look at selected cultural characteristics of Native American children and adolescents.

Banks (1987) warns that the term *Indian* often connotes stereotypical images in people's minds when, in fact, Native Americans' height, hair texture, and facial features vary greatly, and skin colors range from dark brown to very light. Diversity also includes a wide variety of personality traits, cultural practices, and lifestyles (Lum, 1986).

Native Americans esteem values and beliefs that differ from those of European Americans. European Americans believe that individuals have freedoms as long

**TABLE 7-1    Selected Characteristics of Native American Children and Adolescents**

| Category | Characteristic |
| --- | --- |
| Behavioral/emotional expressiveness | Introverted |
| Verbal | Indirect gaze when listening or speaking |
| Nonverbal | Preference for close personal space |
| Concept of time | Time and place viewed as permanent and settled |
| Social orientation | Group-centered; cooperative rather than competitive |

*Developed from:* Rivera, B. D., & Rogers-Adkinson, D. (1997). Culturally sensitive interventions: Social skills training with children and parents from culturally and linguistically diverse backgrounds. *Intervention in School and Clinic 33*(2), 75–80.

as their actions remain within the law; Native American children are taught that all actions must be in harmony with nature. Other values conveyed to children and adolescents include a degree of self-sufficiency and being in harmony with knowledge they gain from the natural world. Adults teach youth to respect and protect the aged, who provide wisdom and acquaint the young with traditions, customs, legends, and myths (Axelson, 1985).

Achievement in the European American culture may not equate with achievement in the Native American culture and vice versa, and to place a value judgment on one or the other constitutes a serious mistake. Sanders (1987) hypothesizes that this cultural conflict and incompatibility contribute significantly to the academic failure of many Native American children. Native American children function in the average to superior range until the fourth grade. Thereafter, academic achievement typically declines each year so that by the tenth grade, Native American students are doing below-average work.

---

**USING CHILDREN'S LITERATURE    Biographies**

Tobias, Tobi. *Maria Tallchief.* Crowell, 1970. The biography of Maria Tallchief, a world-renowned ballerina born in Fairfax, Oklahoma. (Reading Level: 4; Interest Level: 8–12.)

Fall, Thomas. *Jim Thorpe.* Crowell, 1970. A biography for young children, this story focuses on Jim Thorpe, a great athlete and Olympic hero. (Reading Level: 2; Interest Level: 7–10.)

Grant, Matthew. *Squanto: The Indian Who Saved the Pilgrims.* Publications Associates, 1974. This is an illustrated biography of the Wampanoag who played an important role in the lives of early settlers in New England. (Reading Level: 3; Interest Level: 6–10.)

Brown, Marion Marsh. *Homeward, The Arrow's Flight.* Abington, 1980. The story of the first female Native American to become a doctor of Western medicine. (Reading Level: 6; Interest Level: 9–11.)

Native American tribes, organizations, and communities play vital roles in the improvement of educational opportunities for Native American children. More than one hundred tribes operate Head Start programs that serve 16,548 Native American children. Many public schools, the Bureau of Indian Affairs, and tribal schools also strive to provide special education and culture-related learning designed to assist the development and early education of Native American children (Walker, 1988).

Societal and cultural beliefs and traditions of the Native American people particularly influence developing adolescents and their evolving identities. Adolescents living in Native American families and attending European American schools, whether on or off the reservation, experience degrees of cultural confusion and often question allegiance to a cultural identification. Such a dilemma can pose a particularly serious problem for adolescents who want to retain their rich cultural heritage while seeking acceptance in European American schools and society.

Native American adolescents must also resolve cultural differences surrounding the concept of sharing. Sharing represents a genuine and routine way of life in the Native American culture. Yet this cultural belief, which is so deeply ingrained in the Native American culture, does not equate with the European American custom of accumulating private property or savings.

The accumulation of material possessions is the measure of most people's "worth" and social status, but the Native American considers the ability and willingness to share to be most worthy (Lewis & Ho, 1989). While younger children may wish to share only with adults, an acceptance and allegiance to the cultural tradition of sharing increases as the child or adolescent develops. Adolescence is a unique time to develop a concept of sharing that is congruent with Native American cultural expectations. Case Study 7-2 shows the need for teachers to understand the Native American concept of sharing.

Several reasons exist for adolescents' becoming increasingly cognizant and accepting of this cultural expectation. Adolescents have more advanced intellectual abilities that enable them to recognize that it is possible for two people to want the same thing at the same time, that shared possessions often return, and that sharing can be reciprocal. Developing intellectual skills allows an adolescent to understand the difference between sharing temporarily and donating permanently. The adolescent can understand, as well as make clear to others, his or her intent (Kostelnik, Stein, Whiren, & Soderman, 1988).

Other notable cultural characteristics of Native Americans that become an integral part of children's and adolescents' evolving identity are the tendencies toward patience and passive temperaments. Native Americans are taught to be patient, to control emotions, and to avoid passionate outbursts over small matters. As the Native American adolescent develops an identity, cultural characteristics such as poise and self-containment become ingrained.

These cultural habits conflict with European American impatience and competitiveness and often result in the mistaken perception that the Native American is lazy, uncaring, and inactive (Lewis & Ho, 1989). This demeanor or personality

---

**CASE STUDY 7-2    The Native American Concept of Sharing**

Mrs. Jason was upset with eight-year-old Bill, a Native American, when she learned that he had taken a pencil off another child's desk. The week before he had taken a pencil off her desk. What's wrong with Bill? she wondered. She asked a friend, "I told him about taking other people's things. I just cannot understand him. Why does he continue to take things that do not belong to him?"

Her friend thought that the problem might be more Mrs. Jason's than Bill's. Although Mrs. Jason needs to discuss with Bill that whites can misconstrue taking things as stealing, Mrs. Jason also needs to understand Bill's perception of the situation and his cultural concepts of sharing.

Bill had forgotten his pencil, and in his culture taking another's pencil is not a problem (she had others, didn't she?). He would not have objected if someone had taken his pencil when he had more than one.

When she heard Bill's explanation, Mrs. Jason realized that what she had perceived as stealing was Bill's concept (culturally permissible and encouraged) of sharing. She decided that two steps would be appropriate: First, she needed a better understanding of sharing in the Native American culture, and second, she needed to explain to others in the class that Bill was not stealing their pencils.

---

trait is also demonstrated in Native Americans' tendency to lower their voices to communicate anger, unlike European American adolescents, who learn to raise their voices to convey a message (Kostelnik, Stein, Whiren, & Soderman, 1988).

Noninterference with others and a deep respect for the rights and dignity of individuals constitute basic premises of Native American culture (Banks, 1987). Although such practices may have allowed people of other cultures to think of Native Americans as uncaring or unconcerned, the actual case is quite the contrary. Native Americans are taught early to respect the rights and privileges of other individuals and the responsibility to work together toward a common goal in harmony with nature.

---

**FOLLOW THROUGH 7-2    Understanding the Native American Concept of Sharing**

Talk to Native American children and adolescents about sharing. Learn specifically how they feel and why. See how they perceive European American attitudes toward possessions and ownership.

---

**FOLLOW THROUGH 7-3    Understanding Native American Values and Beliefs**

Learn more about Native American students by asking about their values and beliefs. For example, question how they feel about competition, achievement, and self-sufficiency and ask for their opinions of school rules.

---

## FOR ADDITIONAL INFORMATION

Indian Youth of America, 609 Badgerow Building, P. O. Box 2786, Sioux City, IA 51106. This Native American organization sponsors cultural enrichment projects, summer camp programs, and a resource center in its attempt to improve the lives of Native American children.

Council for Indian Education, 517 Rimrock Rd., Billings, MT 59102. The CIE seeks to improve and secure higher standards of education for American Indian children, promotes high-quality children's literature in the Indian culture, and publishes books about American Indian life, past and present.

Natural Indian Education Association, 1819 H St., NW, Suite 800, Washington, D.C. 20006. This organization designs programs to improve the social and economic well-being of American Indians and Alaskan natives. The primary emphasis is on an exchange of ideas, techniques, and research methods among participants in American Indian education.

---

## Gender

Gender is another difference that makes Native American children and adolescents unique. As in other cultures, Native American females differ from males in their ways of thinking, behaving, and learning. Undoubtedly, Native American females are also taught certain cultural and tribal beliefs from birth that influence their roles. Educators working with Native Americans need to address females' particular gender differences, rather than assuming too much homogeneity between males and females. While research studies focusing specifically on Native American females are virtually nonexistent, it is obvious that gender differences exist (Grossman & Grossman, 1994). As with other differences that multicultural educators work to address, gender differences also deserve consideration.

## Socioeconomic Status

Statistically, Native Americans in the United States are among the poorest economically, the least employed, and the unhealthiest. Their education and income levels are low, and they are among the worst-housed ethnic groups. There are, however, signs of improvement in each area (p. 63).

Civil rights legislation and the strong will and determination of the Native American population are enabling these people to improve their lot in life. Some of their lands contain rich energy resources. Specifically, the Southern Utes in Colorado, the Uinta-Ouray Utes in Utah, and the Blackfeet in Montana have gas and oil reserves, as do the Shoshones and Arapaho in Wyoming. Similarly, the Bannocks and Shoshones, whose reservations are in Idaho, own one of the largest phosphate deposits in the West. The Navajo and Hopi reservations in the Southwest contain vast oil and gas fields as well as uranium reserves (Dorriss, 1981).

Attempting to break the bonds of poverty, other Native Americans today are making notable achievements. With such attitudes as "we never, never give up"

(Dorriss, 1981, p. 40), some Native Americans have engaged in business ventures that have had considerable successes. The Navajo nation produces electronic missile assemblies for General Dynamics; the Choctaws of Mississippi build wire harnesses for Ford Motor Company; the Seminoles in Florida own a 156-room hotel; and the Swinomish Indians of Washington state plan a 60-acre boat basin, an 800-slip marina, and a three-story office and commercial headquarters.

*Newsweek* reports that such aggressive approaches to business were previously unheard of on the reservations. High unemployment, high rates of alcoholism, and poverty-level living conditions have characterized the Native American people for many decades. Critics charge that these successful business ventures have not helped the entire culture: Unemployment affects 35 percent of some tribes, young people often must leave home to find work, and some critics worry that economic development will threaten the cultural identity of Native Americans (*Indian Tribes, Incorporated*, 1988).

## Families

Native American adolescents place a high priority on both the immediate and the extended family. The immediate and extended families, tribe, clan, and heritage all contribute to the child's cultural identity and play a significant role in overall development.

Grandparents retain an official and symbolic leadership in family communities. Children seek daily contact with grandparents, who monitor children's behavior and have a voice in childrearing practices (Lum, 1986). Although the adolescent's social consciousness and awareness doubtlessly cause a transition from a family-centered to a more peer-centered environment, the traditional Native American respect and commitment to the family continues (Lum, 1986).

Adult perceptions of childhood and childrearing practices also influence the developing person significantly. Richardson (1981), for example, contends that the Indian family consider children to be gifts worthy of sharing with others, while the white perception holds that children constitute private property to be disciplined when necessary. In essence, children in the Indian family have few rules to obey, but white children have rules with strict consequences.

Native American parents provide children with early training in self-sufficiency. Whereas European Americans prize individualism, the Native American family places importance on group welfare (Axelson, 1985).

Sanders (1987) provides examples of the Native American emphasis on group welfare in her reports of high school absenteeism. Any crisis in the home or within the family precipitates an absence from school until the crisis ends and the family situation returns to normal. Native American children and adolescents are taught obedience and respect for elders, experts, and those with spiritual power. They also learn the importance of the family as well as responsibility to family members. In fact, supportive nonfamily members are often considered to be an integral part of the family network (Rivera & Rogers-Adkinson, 1997).

---

**IMPLEMENTING RESEARCH 7-2   Families and Educational Risk**

Machamer and Gruber examined adolescent self-reports of family connectedness, educational commitment, and education-related risk taking (i.e., skipping school, earning poor grades, and engaging in substance abuse) in more than 6000 public school students, with a focus on Native Americans. They found that low family connectedness is associated with decreased educational commitment and an increased risk of absenteeism, substance use before and during school hours, and the purchase of alcohol and drugs at school. The youths reported lower levels of connectedness to family and poorer educational performance than their African American and Caucasian peers, as well as higher rates of risk taking. Life in an urban setting, away from the tribe and the extended family, can create unique stress for Native American youth, such as being vulnerable to increased familial stress and encountering cultural conflicts in mainstream educational settings. Machamer and Gruber (1998) conclude that Native Americans have the highest rates of negative aspects of family connectedness, educational commitment, and educational risk taking.

In addition to the loss of extended family, urban Native American adolescents experience conflict resulting from values they hold that are incongruent with those found in mainstream society. Different norms for behavior with authority figures, including averted eyes, no questions or challenges, and discouragement of assertiveness or competition, may make majority-culture classrooms uncomfortable and even threatening for Native American students.

**Implementing the Research**

1. Elementary and secondary school educators should recognize the challenges Native American youth often experience when they move off the reservation—the loss of tribal and extended family relationships.
2. Family connectedness can play a significant role in the educational achievement of Native American youth; therefore, perceptive educators must recognize the need to involve parents (and in some cases, other tribal members) in educational experiences.
3. Educators should not perceive Native American youths' different norms for behavior (such as averted eyes, no questions or challenges, and discouragement of assertiveness or competition) as implications that Native American youth are rude or uninterested.

*Source:* Machamer, A. M., & Gruber, E. (1998). Secondary school, family, and educational risk: Comparing American Indian adolescents and their peers. *The Journal of Educational Research, 91*(6), 357–369.

Implementing Research 7-2 looks at the importance of families in educational risk taking of Native American youth.

Native American childrearing practices and differing cultural expectations for behavior can result in confusion and frustration for the children. Native Americans who confront an incompatibility with their European American counterparts appear to demonstrate growing feelings of isolation, rejection, and anxiety, which can result in alienation, poor self-image, and withdrawal (Sanders, 1987). Such feelings undoubtedly affect the behavior and aspirations of Native American children and adolescents.

---

**FOLLOW THROUGH 7-4    Talking about Parents and Extended Families**

Talk with Native American learners about their parents and extended families. Try to understand the Native American concept of family and the role of extended family members in the lives of children and adolescents.

---

Young people seek social acceptance and approval from older members of the family as well as from younger family members. Unlike adolescents in the European American culture, which emphasizes youth and the self, Native American adolescents place family before self and have great respect for elders and their wisdom. The wisdom of life is received from the older people, whose task it is to acquaint the young with the traditions, customs, legends, and myths of the culture. All members of a family care for the old and consider death an accepted fact of life (Axelson, 1985).

The early training in self-sufficiency that Native Americans receive from their families and other significant adults continues to have an impact during the adolescent years. Although the adolescent continues to recognize the loyalty and dependence on the immediate and surrounding family, adolescents develop independence and confidence in their abilities to deal with the world outside the family. We must consider this attitude of self-sufficiency, however, from the Native American point of view. For example, not sharing with one's fellows and the accumulation of great wealth and possessions would not be included in the Native American self-sufficiency concept. The cultural expectation must be compatible with knowledge of the natural world and in harmony with others. Achieving self-sufficiency and self-gain cannot be at the expense of family or tribal members or at the expense of harming any aspect of the natural world (Axelson, 1985).

## *Religion*

According to Native American belief, the world is interconnected, and everything, including humankind, lives according to the same process. Each being has its power, function, and place in the universe. Every part of nature has a spirit that many tribes believe possesses intelligence, emotion, and free will. Praying, in fact, is praying to one's own power. Because the Great Spirit is everything in all of nature, there is no need to question the existence of a god. Because nature is the essence of God, nature would stop if God no longer lived (Axelson, 1985).

God is the great power above everything. It is "the force which is responsible for action, and which can actually have control over man's destiny" (Zychowicz, 1975, p. 15). God created man, nature, and the universe, and God instructs on how to live on the land. The inner spiritual power, or the word *God*, was "orenda" to the Iroquois, "manitou" to the Algonkian tribes, "alone" to the Powhatans, and "wakan" or "wakonda" to the Sioux. The Sioux also used the expression "wakan tanka," meaning all of the "wakan" beings.

The spiritual God of the Native Americans is positive, benevolent, and part of daily living. God's knowledge and advice are transmitted through traditional Native American wisdom. Ideal action toward God is accomplished by helping others understand and get along with people and by comprehending the natural world of which everything (living and nonliving) is a part. The Native American respects all of nature's objects equally as both physical and spiritual entities (Axelson, 1985).

As in any other culture, the Native American culture contains norms and standards for behavior, but Native Americans are inclined to judge each person as a separate individual, taking into consideration the reasons for actions ahead of the norms of the society. The dominant society judges behavior as right or wrong, good or bad, and considers how things "should" be and not necessarily how they are. The practice of judging the behavior of others is an important value in mainstream society (Axelson, 1985).

For Native Americans there exists a close relationship between spiritual realization and unity and their cultural practices. Catholic and Protestant clergy have sought to Christianize Native Americans, but there has been a continuation of indigenous religious rituals and beliefs in the healing power of nature. Natural forces are associated with the life process itself and pervade everything that the believing Native American does.

Community religious rites are a collective effort that promote this mode of healing and increase inward insight and experiential connection with nature. Native American individuals can utilize the positive experiences resulting from ceremonial events, power-revealing events (omens, dreams, visions), and contact with a tribal medicine man in the healing process. Helping to discover and reinforce the therapeutic significance of Native American religious and cultural events can be a learning task for social workers (Lum, 1986).

## Language

Language and communication, whether verbal or nonverbal, may constitute the most important aspects of an individual's culture and characterize the general culture, its values, and its ways of looking and thinking. Educators should develop a consciousness and appreciation for the many Native American languages and recognize the problems that may result when educators and school children have differing language backgrounds.

The cultural mannerisms and nonverbal communication the Native American child demonstrates add another personal dimension to both culture and language. During the last decade, anthropologists, counselors, sociologists, and teachers have begun to awaken to the urgent need to understand these "silent languages." Gestures, body movements, practices due to attitudes toward time and space, and general social behavior all provide valuable information (Jensen, 1985).

Professionals should recognize communicational differences (both verbal and nonverbal) between Native American and European American children. Native Americans tend to speak more softly and at a slower rate, to avoid direct identification between speaker and listener, and to interject less frequently with encouraging communicational signs such as head nods and verbal acknowledgements (Sanders, 1987).

---

**FOLLOW THROUGH 7-5   Observe Native American Nonverbal Communication**

Observe Native American nonverbal communication patterns. How might communication be misunderstood? Discuss with Native Americans how nonverbal communication is important for all cultures and the importance of considering nonverbal mannerisms not only from one's own cultural perspective.

---

Native American adolescents, like adolescents of all cultures, need the security and psychological safety that a common language provides, yet they experience significant language problems during this crucial period of development. Of the approximately 400,000 Native Americans under twenty-one years of age in 1974, over three-fourths obtained their education on reservations or in special boarding schools off the reservation.

Self-esteem and the identity are formed during the transition from the family-centered world of the immediate and extended home. No longer is communication possible only with elders, parents, and siblings. Native American adolescents' ability to reach out to a wider world depends greatly on the ability to speak and understand the language of the majority and other cultures (Youngman & Sandongei, 1983).

Native American children and adolescents often have to decide which language to speak. This may be an even more difficult task for Native Americans than for other cultures, because Native Americans view language as a crucial aspect of the culture and a cherished gift that should be used whenever possible (Richardson, 1981). Such a belief conflicts with the European American opinion that English is Native Americans' means to success and that English should be the predominant language.

---

**FOR ADDITIONAL INFORMATION   Internet Addresses**

**American Indians**
http://chariott.com/~schmidt/spiel/general/indian.html   Provides information on the Indian Child Welfare Act of 1978, which entitles adoptees of Native American heritage to specific rights.

**SI Antho Outreach subpage: American Indian Resources**
http://www.nmnh.si.edu/anthro/outreach/resource.html   Provides a look at elementary school explorations of Native American cultures and maintains that educational activities focus too much on traditional arts and crafts.

**Choctaw Home Page**
http://www.choctaw.com/   Provides an examination of the Choctaw people and their lives and contributions.

**Anth Outreach Indian Languages**
http://www.nmnh.si.edu/anthro/outreach/indian_html   Provides information on the many American Indian languages north of Mexico as well as in Mexico and Central and South America.

## Native American Learners in the School

Nel (1994) suggests that educators who understand Native Americans' cultural characteristics can help prevent school failure in Native American learners. A significant factor in Native Americans' academic underachievement appears to be feelings of isolation, anxiety, and rejection as they confront the incompatibility of their cultural values with those of their mainstream classrooms. Often forced to renounce their own culture, these learners are torn between two worlds and often withdraw as a result.

Nel (1994) offers several Native American cultural characteristics that often conflict with mainstream school systems:

- Native Americans often place emphasis on generosity, sharing, and cooperation. These cultural characteristics sometimes conflict with mainstream school systems, which emphasize competition.

  Educators can take two directions: (1) reassure Native American learners that mainstream society accepts and encourages personal achievement and that peers will not blame them or think less of them for excelling in classwork or even in the playground, and (2) provide teaching and learning experiences that emphasize teamwork and cooperation.
- Native Americans often experience discomfort when teachers single them out for praise for accomplishments, because they often do not want to excel at others' expense.

  Educators can (1) let students know that praise is a form of acknowledging accomplishments and mainstream schools' students expect it, and (2) offer private recognition and praise for those learners who continue to feel uncomfortable.
- Native Americans' sense of generosity and cooperative efforts makes it difficult not to help a friend in need, for example, a fellow student needing help on a test or graded exercise.

  Educators should understand Native Americans' concept of generosity and should take special care in handling these situations. Educators can (1) avoid situations in which they strictly prohibit lending assistance, and, for situations in which individuals must work alone, (2) try to explain the necessity of working alone, so they can determine individual achievement.
- Native Americans have more flexible concepts of time than do some other cultures; that is, students might not arrive at class on time and might be late with assignments. They often do not regard time and punctuality as important concerns.

  Educators need to take several directions: (1) avoid judging Native Americans using middle-class white perspectives by realizing that students being late or submitting assignments late might not be signs of "laziness" or "unconcern," and (2) help students to understand that their cultural orientations are not wrong but that mainstream U.S. schools and society expect punctuality in many cases.
- Native Americans often demonstrate nonverbal behaviors, that suggest (at least to middle-class mainstream educators) a lack of interest in school or respect for people in authority.

Educators can take at least two directions: (1) understand that learners working slowly, looking unconcerned or unmotivated, and being at ease during supposedly hectic times are not signs of disinterest; instead, Native American learners might be very motivated and interested but do not show traditional middle-class indicators of motivation and interest; and (2) give an impression of being unhurried and at ease when dealing with Native American learners, who do not want to feel they are imposing on others or are consuming their time (Nel, 1994).

Educational and societal factors, as well as the clash of cultures, during these crucial developmental years have the potential for developing feelings of frustration and hopelessness that often result in alienation. Such alienation may have been a factor to the Native Americans' general loss of confidence and decline in motivation. These feelings during adolescence may also result in considerable confusion in the classroom. The Native American adolescent may demonstrate behavior that teachers perceive as excessive shyness, inactivity, or lack of motivation. Adolescents whose teachers misunderstand or culturally misconstrue these characteristics (along with the adolescent's usual steady decline in achievement) may develop feelings of hopelessness and alienation.

Educators can benefit from understanding the Native Americans' predicament in predominantly white schools.

**1.** In contrast to people in other cultures, Native Americans often harbor significant feelings of suspicion and distrust of professionals and institutions and especially of European Americans.

**2.** Communication problems may result in an inability to understand, trust, and build rapport with peers and professionals of other cultures. Differences in "home language" and "school language" or Native Americans' nonverbal communication might hinder educational efforts. Native American learners may appear to be unconcerned with educational progress when, in fact, they may be painfully shy and over sensitive to strangers because of language problems and mistrust of European Americans.

**3.** Native American adolescents develop in an often unique and difficult situation. They must reconcile allegiance to the values and customs of both the Native American and the European American cultures. They also encounter the usual problems of adolescence, for example, the possibility of experiencing role confusion or differences associated with building a positive identity.

**4.** Native American learners have to decide whether the Native American or European American culture (or some "cultural combination") should provide the basis for the identity. They need to attempt proficiency in both the Native American language and English and learn how to maintain harmony with family and nature while surviving in the European American world. They also face the problem of how to accept the vast cultural differences in situations in which the European American is unlikely to attempt cross-cultural understandings or acceptance.

---

**FOLLOW THROUGH 7-6    Examine Curricular Materials for Relevance**

Examine several curricular materials to determine how useful they would be for Native American learners. Do the materials recognize Native Americans and convey a respect for Native American values such as sharing and noninterference with others?

---

In an investigation of study habits and attitudes of Native American learners, Gade, Hurlbert, and Fuqua (1986) studied students in grades seven to twelve. They found a correlation between poor study habits and attitudes, especially in junior high school years and among boys, and teacher evaluations that cited low achievement, insufficient cooperation, and poor work habits.

Gade, Hurlbert, and Fuqua (1986) drew several inferences for professionals in today's schools. First, they emphasize the importance of understanding that study habits and attitudes involve all school personnel, not just classroom teachers. Second, students' poor opinions of teachers and their classroom behaviors and methods indicate the need for recruitment of more Native American teachers and counselors. Third, Native American learners need direct instruction in study skills and attitudes toward their education.

Case Study 7-3 shows how Mr. Thomas realized that the low-achieving students in his classes needed additional assistance and how he helped them.

---

**CASE STUDY 7-3    Helping the Low Achiever**

Mr. Thomas pondered his class—the achievers, the low achievers, and those who seemed to be in a constant struggle just to make passing grades. As Mr. Thomas thought about his students, he also wondered whether his lack of knowledge of how Native Americans learn actually contributed to their learning difficulties. Mr. Thomas asked himself, "What can I do and what should I know about the way Native Americans learn to improve their academic achievement?"

Mr. Thomas went to several authorities on Native American children and adolescents to seek advice on how he could better understand his students, make his teaching more effective, and maximize teaching and learning efforts. Advice he received included:

1. Understand the short-term time orientations of many Native Americans.

2. Understand the need to understand families and involve them in school activities and their children's learning.

3. Understand the need to improve the Native American learners' self-esteem and their belief in their ability to learn.

4. Understand the need for genuinely positive and caring relationships between teachers and students.

5. Understand the need to design curricula that reflect Native Americans' backgrounds and contemporary needs.

6. Understand Native American learning styles and how the curricula and teaching methods can be changed to match students' learning styles.

## Achievement Levels

As stated earlier, several studies suggest that tests and teacher reports show that Native American children function at the average-to-superior range until the fourth grade. After the fourth grade, academic functioning typically declines each year so that by grade ten, Native American learners' academic achievement falls below that of their European American peers. Several complex factors may contribute to this predicament, such as growing feelings of isolation, rejection, and anxiety that Native American learners feel as they confront the incompatibility of their cultural value system with that of their European American peers. These feelings contribute to alienation, poor self-image, and withdrawal (Sanders, 1987).

How can the clash of values between Native Americans and European Americans affect educators? European American teachers view some behaviors that American Indian students exhibit as rude or insulting. For example, if these students avoid the teacher's gaze, do not volunteer answers, or delay response as their cultural background has taught them to do, they are seen as lazy or uncomprehending.

European Americans see Native American students as lacking time-management skills or being self-centered because of their present-time orientation. The Native American concept of time is that what is happening now is more important than what is not happening now; that what is happening now deserves full attention; and that what one will be doing at this time tomorrow will be more important than what one is doing now or what one will not be doing tomorrow (Sanders, 1987).

Whether or not the educational problems Native American adolescents experience are caused by "cultural teachings" or the "cultural differences" in European American schools, the result is the same: Native Americans continue to have one of the highest dropout rates of any ethnic group at the high-school level regardless of region or tribal affiliation (Sanders, 1987). The reasons for dropping out of school include: (1) school rules are not enforced uniformly; (2) factors pertaining to teacher–student relationships, for example, teachers' not caring about students and not providing sufficient assistance; (3) disagreements with teachers; and (4) the content of schooling, which the students perceive as not important to what they want to do in life (Coladarci, 1983).

---

**FOLLOW THROUGH 7-7   Increasing Native Americans' Academic Achievement**

While understanding the reasons for the decline in Native Americans' academic achievement after fourth grade is important, it is even more important to think of strategies for increasing their academic achievement. Suggest a number of steps (e.g., culturally appropriate diagnostic tests, culturally relevant curricular materials, instruction that reflects learning styles) that educators might take to increase Native Americans' academic achievement.

Perceptive educators should demonstrate genuine care, understanding, and encouragement with which Native American learners can identify; ensure that the curriculum addresses Native American needs and provides culturally relevant experiences; and understand the home problems of some Native Americans, such as separations and divorces, unemployment, alcoholism, and child abuse.

## *Language Problems*

That Native Americans speak about 2,200 different languages further complicates the language problem. This broad and diversified language background, albeit personal and sacred to Native Americans, has not provided the rich cultural and language experiences that contribute to European American definitions of school success. Wide-scale differences exist in Native Americans' ability to speak English. In some cases, as few as 4 percent of Native Americans speak "excellent" English; a far greater percentage speak either "good" or "poor" English. Children who have attended English-speaking schools, of course, speak better English than their elders.

Attending a school staffed with European American teachers and facing daily the academic and social problems associated with not being understood and not understanding the language of others significantly affects an adolescent's self-perception. Language may be a contributing factor in the adolescent's tendency to decline in academic achievement. Lack of cognitive and academic skills does not appear to be a major factor (Sanders, 1987). Case Study 7-4 looks at how a fifteen-year-old boy experiences difficulty because of his language problems.

---

**CASE STUDY 7-4    Native American Language Problems**

Harry, a fifteen-year-old boy, has several problems that result, at least in part, from his lack of proficiency in English. He is faced with functioning in a bilingual world.

His family continues to rely on the language it has spoken for centuries, but he must speak English at school. (Some of his friends have been punished for not speaking English.) Meanwhile, his grades are failing, he does not always understand the teacher (and vice versa), and he experiences difficulty as he ventures outside the social confines of his culture.

Harry's teacher, Mrs. Rivers, can take several steps to assist him. She can:

1. Arrange for Harry to visit the language specialist or a bilingual teacher who can determine the extent of his problem and plan an appropriate course of action.
2. Seek the services of the remedial or resource teacher to provide Harry with appropriate remedial assistance.
3. Arrange for Harry to visit the guidance counselor, who may be able to help him widen his circle of friends.
4. Talk with Harry to let him know that she and other school personnel are interested in him as a person and as a learner.

## Learning Styles: Cultural Considerations

Effective education for Native American learners requires consideration of each individual's learning styles—the strategies the learner uses to acquire knowledge, skills, and understanding. Myriad differences exist among the Native American people. To assume that all Native Americans have similar learning styles shows a disregard for nations, tribes, and individuals, as well as for varying educational and socioeconomic backgrounds. Table 7-2 provides a brief overview of several learning areas and their implications for Native American learners.

Although Table 7-2 provides representative examples of learning styles and implications, perceptive educators can see the need to consider individual learners, teaching and communication styles, internal cognitive processes, and the external conditions that affect learning outcomes. Teachers must use appropriate diagnostic instruments and learning style inventories and get to know individual learners and their learning styles.

### School Practices Impeding Native Americans' Progress

Because some techniques taught to educators are incompatible with Native American cultural traditions, it is imperative that educators use strategies that are appropriate for the culture. What specifically should educators avoid?

**1.** Methods that increase positive self-talk, such as "something I like about myself" or "a sport I can play well," often work well with white or black children but not with Native American children.

### TABLE 7-2  Native American Learning Styles

| Area | Implications |
| --- | --- |
| Many Native American learners prefer to learn by visual, perceptual, and spatial rather than verbal means. | Present new or different material in a visual, perceptual, and spatial mode; many students need to improve their skills in the verbal mode. |
| Many Native American learners use mental images rather than word associations to remember or understand words and concepts. | Present metaphors, images, or symbols rather than dictionary-style definitions or synonyms when teaching difficult concepts. |
| Many Native American learners process information in a global, analytic manner; that is, they focus on the whole rather than the part. | Present material in a manner in which overall purpose and structure are clear, rather than in small, carefully sequenced bits. |

*Source:* Swisher, K., & Deyle, D. (1989). The styles of learning are different, but the teaching is just the same: Suggestions for teachers of American Indian youth. *Journal of American Indian Education, Special Issue,* August, 1–11.

**2.** Attempts to convince Native Americans to be competitive (such as being the first, best, fastest, or smartest) are incompatible with their cultural values.

**3.** Educators often expect eye contact and perceive the Native American's tendency to look the other way as a sign of withdrawal, embarrassment, or discomfort.

**4.** Educators and counselors often rely extensively on verbal participation by children in the class. Although verbal interaction is valued by Anglo, African, and Hispanic cultures, it is not valued by Native Americans.

Implementing Research 7-3 examines curriculum issues as related to Native American learners.

---

**IMPLEMENTING RESEARCH 7-3    Curriculum Issues and Native American Students**

Maintaining that pressure is mounting for elementary and secondary educators to create a culturally relevant curriculum, David Davison and Kenneth Miller (1998) describe how mathematics and science curricula can be made more culturally relevant to Native American students. They raise questions such as: Can students of one culture develop meaningful culturally relevant materials for a different culture? Can an activity be relevant to a culture but not to a student?

In answering these questions, Davison and Miller suggest an ethnomathematics and ethnoscience approach. Ethnomathematics represents one way of connecting mathematics and science: viewing mathematical ideas from a cultural context. Native Americans need a mathematics curriculum that is sensitive to their experiential background.

Similarly, ethnoscience can be interpreted as the body of science used by a culture to make the curriculum relevant to the individual. Identifying indigenous plants by their scientific names is consistent with Western scientific procedure, but it ignores aspects of Native American culture such as religion, medicine, and language.

**Implementing the Research**

1. Educators need to recognize that elementary and secondary school curricula have traditionally come and been taught from majority culture perspectives. As schools become increasingly diverse, educators will need to provide culturally relevant curriculum.

2. Mathematics that is culturally relevant to Native Americans could include the use of art designs. Students might investigate art designs by creating their own, using manipulatives such as tangrams or pattern blocks. Also, exponents of loom beadwork can demonstrate rich symmetric geometric patterns.

3. Many educators assert that Native American students learn holistically, so learners might respond to a thematically integrated curriculum format. Using such a format, loom beadwork will be applicable to science and mathematics as well as to other subject disciplines.

---

*Source:* Davison, D. M., & Miller, K. W. (1998). An ethnoscience approach to curriculum issues for American Indian students. *School Science and Mathematics, 95*(5), 260–264.

## Promoting Self-Esteem and Positive Cultural Identities

Educators working with Native American learners readily recognize the many personal and social factors that affect children's and adolescents' self-esteem and cultural identities. Injustice and discrimination, poverty, low educational attainment, and perhaps growing up on reservations, in foster homes, or in a predominantly white society may cause Native American learners to question their self-worth and the worth of their culture.

Although self-esteem scales reveal little difference in the levels of self-esteem between preschool Native American and European American children, other evidence suggests that Native American learners experience conflict on entering school (Little Soldier, 1985).

---

**CULTURAL PORTRAIT   John—A Native American Learner**

Fourteen-year-old John attends school off the reservation. The student population is a mix of Native Americans, some Hispanic Americans, a few black Americans, and some European Americans. Although the school population includes several culturally diverse groups, most teachers are European American, and the school environment and educational program indicate an orientation toward traditional white expectations.

John has several academic and social problems: He makes below-average grades, feels he does not have many friends, and generally feels uncomfortable in school. Everything is rushed, cooperation is second to competition, his teachers feel he is not trying, and the overall curricular emphasis makes little sense to him. He has an interest in the ancient traditions of his people, but his teachers rarely address his cultural needs or, in fact, any of his individual needs. He realizes that his grades need to improve, but he does not always understand the teacher or the way she teaches. Although he has Native American friends, he has few friends among the students of the other cultures. School days are often frustrating for John as he strives to make it through another day.

*What John's Teacher Can Do*

John's teacher can take several specific steps to help him improve his academic and social prog-

ress. First, she can spend some time alone with John to determine his strengths, weaknesses, and interests. Second, she can consult the language specialist to determine whether John's academic (or social) problems are attributable to his using a second language. Third, she can arrange for John to have individual assistance from the remedial specialist. Fourth, she can reassess her teaching techniques to see whether her teaching methods match John's learning styles. Finally, she can build on John's interest in his cultural heritage through appropriate reading and other curricular materials. Reading and studying about his own cultural background might show John that the curriculum values his Native American culture and recognizes his individual needs and interests. Just as important, the teacher will provide a curriculum that gives other learners an appropriate multicultural understanding of the Native American culture.

Almost any number of suggestions could help John and improve his feelings about school and himself. John's teacher should recognize though how important it is to show interest in John and provide firsthand and individual help in improving his academic and social progress.

Laura Stachowski (1998) in Implementing Research 7-4 looks at self-esteem in Native American children and adolescents and suggests how educators can provide self-esteem improvement activities.

One study compared Native American and European American children and concluded that children of various tribes (e.g., Cree, Miccosukee, Seminole) score lower on self-esteem scales (Rotenberg & Cranwell, 1989). Such measures and conclusions, Rotenberg and Cranwell (1989) warn, may be misleading, because the self-esteem scales may be more culturally relevant for European Americans than for Native Americans.

---

**IMPLEMENTING RESEARCH 7-4    Self-Esteem in Navajo Students**

Native American children often have low self-esteem and have difficulty establishing ethnic and tribal self-identity and pride in their culture. Laura Stachowski tells of the American Indian Reservation Project at Indiana University in Bloomington, which places student teachers in assignments at the Bureau of Indian Affairs across the Navajo nation. The participants engage fully in all teacher-related functions of the school.

In this study, participants documented ways to improve Navajo students' self-esteem. One method included encouraging students to make class presentations on stories by a Navajo woman named Luci Tapahonso. This exercise allowed students to legitimize their culture as worthy of study. Another way was a game called Navajo Jeopardy, which allowed students to name their clans with a sense of pride. Bringing in local Navajo artists, historians, and others to talk about their work and their lives was another part of the program. Overall, selected efforts included using culturally relevant teaching units, resources, and materials; using positive reinforcement and other incentives; encouraging students to explore their lives and identities; promoting a sense of community in the classroom; and making presentations to other classrooms and displaying their own work.

The author maintains that the effort to improve Native American students' self-esteem cannot be approached in a hit-or-miss manner. The effort should permeate the entire elementary and secondary school curriculum, directly and subtly.

**Implementing the Research**

Elementary and secondary educators working with Native American students need to:

1. realize the importance of self-esteem in the students' motivation, attitudes toward school, and actual academic achievement;
2. implement teaching units that address Navajo's self-esteem and cultural identities; and
3. understand Stachowski's contention (which is also a major thrust of this book) that providing culturally appropriate educational experiences and promoting learners' self-esteem must be a continuous, planned, methodical effort.

---

*Source:* Stachowski, L. L. (1998). Student teachers' efforts to promote self-esteem in Navajo pupils. *The Educational Forum, 62,* 341–346.

---

**FOLLOW THROUGH 7-8   Involving Native American Children**

Ask young Native American children to make a drawing or a silhouette of a Native American child. Ask them to write words or draw symbols to illustrate their favorite foods, favorite games, favorite sports, and perhaps some things they like to think about.

Ask the Native American children to explain their pictures to the other children in the group. Native American children may prefer to simply look at their pictures, together, as a group. They may look for some similarities in their pictures to identify their group's favorite foods or some things their group likes to think about.

After sharing, the children may combine their pictures to create a "group personality" collage. The purpose of this type of self-disclosing activity for Indian children is twofold: First, they see a type of collective group personality emerge, and second, they begin to think of themselves as a part of the group. They do not compare themselves individually with other members of the group. Instead, they gain a sense of their contribution to the group and of the ways in which they belong and identify, not with individuals in the group but with the group as a whole.

---

## Summing Up

Educators who plan teaching and learning experiences for Native American children and adolescents should:

**1.** Remember that Native American people have a proud history of accomplishments and notable contributions and that these should be part of school curricula.

**2.** Avoid providing curricular and instructional practices that indicate only white, middle-class expectations and that might seem alien to Native American learners.

**3.** Remember that educators who understand Native Americans and the possible cultural basis for educational problems must address achievement levels and school dropout rates.

**4.** Promote positive self-images and cultural images among Native American learners, which may be one of the most effective means for improving academic achievement and school-related problems.

**5.** Adapt teaching styles and other school practices to meet the Native American's learning styles, demonstrating that educators are caring and interested in improving school achievement and overall school success.

**6.** Understand the Native American culture and the learners' cultural characteristics, religious orientations, and socioeconomic backgrounds.

**7.** Provide learning experiences so that learners of other cultures can develop a better understanding of their Native American peers.

**8.** Understand the learner's development, and provide school experiences based on developmental and cultural characteristics.

**9.** Consider Native Americans as individuals who come from different nations, tribes, socioeconomic levels, and levels of educational attainment.

## Suggested Learning Activities

1. Observe a Native American learner and record the cultural mannerisms that might be contrary to the behaviors that schools expect. How might a teacher misinterpret the behavior of Native Americans? How might educators better understand Native American learners and their behaviors?

2. List several stereotypical beliefs about Native Americans. What is the basis of those beliefs? How might those beliefs affect educators' perceptions of these learners? What steps can multicultural educators take to lessen the effect of stereotypical beliefs?

3. Sanders (1987) wrote: "American Indians continue to have the highest dropout rate of any ethnic group at the high-school level, regardless of region or tribal affiliation" (p. 81). In a plan to reduce this dropout rate, address the following points:

   - Extent of the problem
   - Reasons for the problem (be sure to examine cultural factors)
   - Possible solutions or plans to reduce the dropout rate
   - Ways to involve parents, administrators, and special school personnel

## Suggestions for Collaborative Efforts

Form groups of three or four, which, if possible, represent our nation's cultural and gender diversity. Working collaboratively, focus your group's attention toward the following efforts:

1. Study (observe, examine school records, talk with, test) two Native American learners, one who has attended reservation schools and one who has attended white schools. What differences can you list? What has been the effect of acculturation? What differences might you attribute to social class or tribal affiliation? Considering all these differences, how can educators gain an accurate perception of the Native American learner?

2. Talk with several teachers of Native American learners to see what firsthand experiences they have to offer. Specifically, learn their perceptions of cultural characteristics, the influence of families, achievement levels, and language problems. What advice can these teachers offer?

3. Native Americans experience academic problems, including low academic achievement, low reading scores, and high dropout rates. Design a remediation plan to address Native Americans' academic problems. Specifically, look at learning styles, curricular materials, instructional strategies, classroom environments, and motivation (be sure to consider that Native American indicators of motivation might differ from others'). In other words, how does your group believe schools can better address the needs of Native American learners?

## *Expanding Your Horizons: Additional Journal Readings and Books*

Ambler, M. (1997). Without racism: Indian students could be both Indian and students. *Tribal College, 8*(4), 8–11.

*Native American students need a safe and accepting environment to obtain an academic and cultural education.*

Herring, R. D. (1997). The creative arts: An avenue to wellness among Native American Indians. *Journal of Humanistic Education and Development, 36*(2), 105–113.

*Herring, an expert on Native Americans, describes how creative arts are enmeshed in historical and contemporary Native spiritual and humanistic value systems.*

Machamer, A. M., & Gruber, E. (1998). Secondary school, family, and educational risk: Comparing American Indian adolescents and their peers. *The Journal of Educational Research, 91*(6), 357–369.

*Machamer and Gruber examined Native American adolescent self-reports of family connectedness, educational commitment, and educational-related risk taking and concluded that low family connectedness is associated with decreased educational commitment.*

Stachowski, L. L. (1998). Student teachers' efforts to promote self-esteem in Navajo pupils. *The Educational Forum, 62,* 341–346.

*Stachowski maintains that Native American children frequently lack self-esteem and offers ways to promote self-esteem in Navajo students.*

Tan, A., Fujioka, Y., & Lucht, N. (1997). Native American stereotypes, TV portrayals, and personal contact. *Journalism and Mass Communication Quarterly, 74*(2), 265–284.

*This study investigated how white students stereotype Native Americans, often by perceptions learned through television.*

## *Expanding Your Students' Horizons: Appropriate Native American Books for Children and Adolescents*

Bierhorst, John. *The way of the earth: Native America and the environment.* Mulberry, 1995.

Bierhorst, John. *The Mythology of Mexico and Central America.* Mulberry, 1990.

Bierhorst, John. *The white deer and other stories told by the Lenape.* Morrow, 1995.

Bruchac, Joseph (retold by). *Gluskabe and the four wishes.* Cobblehill, 1995.

Carter, Alden R. *The Shoshoni.* Franklin Watts, 1991.

DeFelice, Cynthia. *Weasel.* Macmillan, 1990.

Girion, Barbara. *Indian summer.* Scholastic, 1990.

Goble, Paul. *Adopted by the eagles.* Bradbury, 1994.

Hillerman, Tony. *Coyote waits.* HarperCollins, 1990.

Joosse, Barbara M. *Mama, Do You Love Me?* Chronicle Books, 1991.

Landau, Elaine. *The Sioux.* Franklin Watts, 1991.

Lawlor, Laurie. *Shadow Catcher: The Life and Work of Edward S. Curtis.* Walker, 1994.

Levin, Betty. *Brother moose.* Greenwillow, 1990.

McDermott, Gerald. *Coyote: A trickster tale of the American Southwest.* Harcourt Brace, 1995.

McDermott, Gerald. *Raven: A trickster tale of the Pacific Northwest.* Bradbury, 1993.

Mead, Alice. *Crossing the starlight bridge.* Bradbury, 1994.

Riley, Patricia. *Growing up Native American.* Tupelo, 1993.

Robinson, Margaret. *A woman of her tribe.* Scribner, 1990.

Rodanas, Kristina. *Dance of the sacred circle: A Native American tale.* Little, Brown, 1994.

Stewart, Elisabeth Jane. *On the long trail home.* Clarion, 1994.

Stroud, Virginia A. *Doesn't fall off his horse.* Dial, 1994.

Thomson, Peggy. *Katie Henio: Navajo sheepherder.* Cobblehill, 1995.

Van Lann, Nancy. *In a circle long ago: A treasury of native lore.* Apple Soup Books, 1995.

Walter, Wangerin. *The crying for a vision.* Aladdin, 1994.

Welsch, Roger. *Uncle Smoke stories: Nehawka tales of Coyote the trickster.* Knopf, 1994.

Wisniewski, David. *The wave of the seawolf.* Clarion, 1994.

Wisniewski, David. *Rainplayer.* Clarion, 1994.

## Answers to the Culture Quiz: Native Americans

| | | | | |
|---|---|---|---|---|
| **1.** b | **3.** f | **5.** c | **7.** h | **9.** i |
| **2.** e | **4.** a | **6.** d | **8.** g | **10.** j |

# Teaching and Learning in a Diverse Society

Part III focuses on what educators should consider when planning and implementing programs that teach acceptance and respect for cultural diversity. Chapters 8, 9, 10, 11, and 12 focus on curriculum, instruction, parents and families, and administrators and special school personnel, respectively. The emphasis continues to be on promoting multiculturalism and implementing effective multicultural education programs.

Chapter $8$

# Curricular Efforts

Understanding the material and activities in this chapter will help the reader to:

- Distinguish between the purported changes and the actual progress people from culturally different backgrounds have achieved in U.S. society.

- Prepare a multicultural teaching unit that addresses the needs of learners from culturally different backgrounds and teaches European American learners about diversity.

- State several reasons a school needs a multicultural education program that emphasizes an "across-the-curriculum" approach and encompasses the total school environment.

- List and describe several methods for extending the multicultural education curriculum to the community and having it pervade extracurricular activities.

- Understand the importance of having school administrators, faculty, and staff reflect the cultural diversity of the student body.

## Overview

The tremendous cultural diversity that characterizes U.S. school systems sends a strong message to educators and curriculum developers at both elementary and secondary levels. They must develop a curriculum that addresses the needs of learners and creates a school environment that reflects cultural diversity. To implement such an across-the-curriculum approach, they must carefully select bias-free teaching materials, choose evaluation instruments that take into account cultural differences, encourage appropriate community involvement, and provide extracurricular activities that involve all learners. Just as important as these

---

**THE CULTURE QUIZ: Multicultural Education Curriculum Efforts**

*Directions:* Mark each statement true or false.

_____ 1. Multicultural education should involve a total curricular and instructional approach, because learners might construe less ambitious approaches as less than a serious effort.

_____ 2. The "hidden curriculum" is exemplified by decisions and instructional practices that indicate the school favors middle-class white learners.

_____ 3. Current levels of racism, discrimination, and injustice in the United States indicate that relations between cultures are good and may be at an all-time high.

_____ 4. Even if relations between children and adolescents are positive and without serious incident, multicultural education is nonetheless necessary so that learners acquire knowledge of and respect for cultural diversity.

_____ 5. Homogeneous ability grouping may result in an insidious form of segregation by which children and adolescents are separated by race or socioeconomic class.

_____ 6. Textbooks and other written materials that portray middle-class white characters and values rarely affect culturally diverse children and adolescents, because learners expect instructional materials to reflect the majority culture.

_____ 7. Ethnocentrism is the belief that one person's culture is in some way better than another person's culture.

_____ 8. Multicultural education efforts should avoid adopting an interdisciplinary focus (that includes all subject areas) because individual teachers have their own strengths, weaknesses, and interests.

_____ 9. Multicultural education efforts should focus on extracurricular activities so as to provide equal access and opportunities to all learners, regardless of cultural background.

_____ 10. The curriculum should endorse bilingual education and a multilingual society.

(Answers to the Culture Quiz are located at the end of the chapter.)

---

tangible aspects are those of the "hidden curriculum" and the acts of unconscious (or perhaps even conscious) racism, discrimination, and prejudice that continue to plague our schools.

## Toward Cultural Diversity

Overall school curriculum and teaching and learning situations should reflect the cultural diversity of our nation. Although the *Brown* desegregation case and the civil rights legislation (Ornstein & Levine, 1993) of a number of years ago contributed to better treatment and acceptance of groups from culturally different backgrounds, there is much room for improvement. Educators should place change and progress in proper perspective.

**IMPLEMENTING RESEARCH 8-1   Diversity in the Curriculum**

Wills and Mehan (1996) examine the challenge of including diversity in the school curriculum, particularly the history and social studies curriculum. In their discussion, they consider the debate about whether history is natural, fixed, context-free, and timeless or whether the concept should be (as multiculturalists suggest) expanded to include alternative and competing narratives. Multiculturalism calls for history that is more perspectival, constructed, and relative to time and setting.

Wills and Mehan propose an alternative way to teach history and social studies that maintains a unified historical narrative but also includes previously omitted voices as active participants in significant historical events.

Wills and Mehan explain a number of features in their sociological approach and offer several recommendations:

1.   Teaching from a sociological perspective requires a focus on society. Students should not study individual groups in isolation, but rather groups interacting.
2.   Teaching from a sociological perspective requires teachers and students to recognize that they are constructing a narrative of events about the struggle for rights that constitutes history.
3.   Teaching from a sociological perspective requires a conversational (Why did this event turn out the way it did? What events contributed to a particular event?) and multiperspectival approach, the goal being to understand and explain U.S. history.

Wills and Mehan make a number of interesting points: "The question is no longer whether culture makes a difference, but what difference did culture make in the interactions between Native Americans and white settlers" (p. 10). It is important for students to learn that "history is about explaining and understanding social life, not on evaluating the cultural worth of civilizations" (p. 10). When such a curriculum becomes a reality, "issues concerning social justice, equality, and discrimination are more easily raised" (p. 11).

**Implementing the Research**

1.   Educators undoubtedly need to consider the sociological perspective approach Wills and Mehan suggest—one that focuses on studying groups as interactive, constructing a narrative of events about the struggle for rights, and asking why particular events occurred.
2.   Educators should raise issues concerning social justice, equality, and discrimination in all curricular areas but especially in history and social studies.
3.   Educators should emphasize (as Wills and Mehan suggest) the difference cultural diversity makes in the interactions between cultures.

*Source:* Wills, J., & Mehan, H. (1996). Recognizing diversity with a common historical narrative: The challenges of teaching history and social studies. *Multicultural Education, 4*(1), 4–11.

Implementing Research 8-1 calls for diversity in the curriculum, particularly in history and social studies.

---

**FOLLOW THROUGH 8-1    Determining "Significant" Change**

Undoubtedly, the U.S. education system has made progress toward providing a culturally relevant curriculum—more materials reflect diversity and provide objective portrayals of females, people from culturally different backgrounds, and disabled people. Visit several schools to determine the extent of the changes—how far have we come? What still needs to be done? Are changes superficial or do they show genuine commitment?

---

## The Illusion of Change and Progress

Without doubt, U.S. education is making progress toward better relations between groups of people. The accomplishments of people of differing cultures and of women are recognized; many educators welcome disabled youngsters into their classrooms; most teachers work to reduce racist and sexist behavior in their classrooms; and many work to develop or obtain curricular materials free from bias and prejudice (Sleeter & Grant, 1988).

Consider, however, the racism and nonacceptance that continue to plague society (Pine & Hilliard, 1990)—the growing popularity of "skinheads" and neo-Nazi groups, for instance. In addition, school practices often document either a lack of understanding of learners from culturally different backgrounds or a lack of acceptance and respect for their cultural differences.

### The Continuing Need for Change in Educational Practices

Consider these observations from a number of education researchers:

- African American students suffer academically because their learning styles tend to be oriented toward cooperation, content about people, discussion and hands-on work, and whole-to-part learning (Shade, 1982).
- Young Navajo learners sometimes interpret tests as games (in contrast to Anglo students who approach them with a more serious attitude). This "games" approach is a result of home socialization (Deyhle, 1985).
- Bilingual education teachers often find themselves in conflict with regular classroom teachers over the specific needs of students with limited English proficiency (Sleeter & Grant, 1988).
- Educators interact with, call on, and praise students who are Anglo, male, and middle-class more often than they do other students in the same classroom (Sadker & Sadker, 1982).
- Although curricular materials and textbooks reflect cultural diversity more accurately than they have in the past, Native, Asian, and Hispanic Americans are still barely visible in the curriculum (Sleeter & Grant, 1988).
- Because students are often grouped homogeneously, there is a tendency to segregate learners by culture and by socioeconomic group (Manning & Lucking, 1990).

There continues to be much room for genuine change in teaching and learning situations, compatible treatment of people who are disabled or from culturally diverse backgrounds, improvement of the cultural and ethnic compositions of school faculty and staff, and equitable representation of all people, regardless of culture, in textbooks and other curricular materials. This discussion and the accompanying recommendations do not downplay the significant progress that our society and schools have already made. It is necessary, however, to perceive society and schools objectively and to plan an appropriate agenda for positively reconstructing society and schools during the twenty-first century.

Garcia (1984) contends that schools should accept responsibility for translating illusion into reality and that they can serve as a significant force in countering discrimination and the various "-isms" that affect people from culturally diverse backgrounds, women, and the disabled.

## From Illusion to Reality: Responding to Racism, Discrimination, Ethnocentrism, and Stereotypes

Racism has many damaging and long-lasting effects on the lives of children and adolescents, the character of society, the quality of our civilization, and peoples' prospects for the future. Before an illusion of racial harmony and justice for all can become a reality, schools must take a powerful and pivotal role in teaching about racism and in working toward acceptance and respect for all people, regardless of racial and cultural background. Schools can play a powerful role in combating racism and educational inequities by confronting and challenging racism, hiring teachers from diverse cultures, developing and implementing a genuine multicultural curriculum, improving pedagogical practices that address the needs of all learners, and teaching character development and improvement of self-esteem (Pine & Hilliard, 1990).

Garcia refers to ethnocentrism as the notion some people hold that their group is better than other groups. Ethnocentrism can extend from mild group pride to extreme arrogance. The response to ethnocentrism is complex; some ethnocentrism is good, but too much group pride can result in a negative force—for example, the claims that the Aryan race is superior to all others. A society and its schools must seek to understand the many forms of ethnocentrism and work toward keeping ethnocentrism under control among individuals and student groups (Garcia, 1984).

Schools' responsibilities in our multicultural society extend to countering the dangers of stereotyping, from which even educators are not exempt. What steps can educators take to transform illusions of equality and justice into reality?

First, teachers should be aware of their own biases and stereotypes. Through self-examination or through cultural awareness workshops, educators can gain a better understanding of their attitudes toward people who are culturally different, women, and the disabled. Second, as cultural understandings clarify stereotypical beliefs, educators see the need for expecting as much from learners of differing cultural backgrounds as they do from other students. Too often, teachers tend to "make it easy for the downtrodden" (Garcia, 1984, p. 107). Although educators should recognize the plight of minorities, they must encourage minority students to excel in all areas of academic pursuit. Third, educators should examine curricular materials for evidence of stereotyping. Specifically, does the material present females and minorities in a realistic, nonstereotypical manner? Does the material accurately reflect a holistic view of the past in terms of the contributions of females and people of differing cultural backgrounds in American history (Garcia, 1984)? Fourth, educators should strive to diversify classes of homogeneous ability levels, which have the potential for segregating students by race or socioeconomic group. Heterogeneous classes and cooperative learning activities are very important (Garcia, 1984; Manning & Lucking, 1990).

Because of landmark court decisions, civil rights legislation, and overall improved race relations, U.S. society is not as divided racially and culturally as it was several decades ago. We must not, however, allow illusions of grandeur to overshadow reality. Racism, discrimination, and stereotypes continue to exist and to take a heavy toll on people of differing cultural background, women, and the disabled. Rather than accepting the status quo as the most equitable we can achieve, school curricula should deliberately instill in children and adolescents a sense of respect and acceptance for all people, regardless of their cultural and individual differences.

## Planning and Implementing a Multicultural Education Curriculum

### The Total School Environment

Multiculturalism should extend to and permeate all aspects of the school. In fact, multiculturalism should be such a basic part of the school that it becomes a natural and accepted aspect of the daily routine.

One way that multiculturalism can permeate the curriculum is through an approach that incorporates literature that is culturally appropriate for children and adolescents in teaching the various areas of the curriculum. Norton (1999) recommends a multicultural reading and literature program that crosses curriculum areas. Multicultural literature is essential to all areas of the curriculum to help students grow in understanding themselves and others. Through careful selection and sharing of multicultural reading materials, educators help students learn to identify with the people who created the stories, whether of the past or present. Folk tales, myths, and legends clarify the values and beliefs of people. By reading the great stories on which cultures have been founded, learners can discover the threads that weave the past with the present and the themes and values that interconnect people of all cultures.

**FOLLOW THROUGH 8-2    Researching Cultural Diversity**

Separate into small groups that each selects a different cultural group to research. The following questions may serve as guidelines:

1. Where did the racial, religious, or ethnic group you're studying originate?
2. Why did they leave their homeland?
3. Where in the United States did they originally settle?
4. What kind of work did they do when they first came here?
5. What was their native language?
6. What was their dominant religion?
7. What is a popular myth or legend from their culture?
8. What are three notable themes from their literature?
9. Who are three notable authors from this group?

*Source:* Minderman, L. (1990). Literature and multicultural education. *Instructor, 99*(7), 22–23.

## Reform Efforts

As stated earlier, teaching units are an appropriate and viable means of reaching specific objectives. Serious reform efforts toward a more realistic portrayal of all people, however, will require a major overhaul of elementary and secondary school curricula (Manning, 1991). What steps can educators take to ensure that elementary and secondary school curricula reflect the cultural diversity of U.S. society? The following suggestions represent guidelines for a curriculum that recognizes, reflects, and respects cultural diversity (Sleeter & Grant, 1988).

## Guidelines for Developing Multicultural Curricula*

1. Reform the curriculum in such a way that it regularly presents diverse perspectives, experiences, and contributions. Similarly, present and teach concepts that represent diverse cultural groups and both sexes.

2. Include materials and visual displays that are free of race, gender, and disability stereotypes, and that include members of all cultural groups in a positive manner.

3. Embrace concepts, rather than fragments of information, related to diverse groups.

4. Emphasize contemporary culture as much as historical culture, and represent groups as active and dynamic. The curriculum, for example, should include not

*Source: Sleeter, C. E., & Grant, C. A. (1988). *Making choices for multicultural education: Five approaches to race, class, and gender.* Columbus, OH: Merrill, pp. 153–155.

only the women's suffrage movement but also more contemporary problems confronting women.

**5.** Strive to make the curriculum a "total effort," with multicultural aspects permeating all subject areas and all phases of the school day.

**6.** Make sure the curriculum uses nonsexist language.

**7.** Support a curriculum that endorses bilingual education and the vision of a multilingual society.

**8.** Draw on children's experiential background in teaching and learning. Base community and curricular concepts on children's daily life and experiences.

**9.** Insist on a curriculum that allows equal access for all students. All students, for example, should have the freedom to enroll in college preparatory courses and other special curricular activities.

Diversity comes in many forms, all of which need to be addressed in the curriculum. We maintain that sexual orientation should be included in a definition of multicultural education as well as reflected in curricular efforts. Gay and lesbian adolescents confront many of the same biological, cognitive, and social developmental changes as their heterosexual counterparts. Fear of and misunderstandings about homosexuality can result in negative consequences for adolescents struggling with identity formation that differs from that of the majority of their peers.

By learning about the concerns of gay and lesbian youth, middle and secondary educators can break the barrier of silence that contributes to the difficulties and hurt these teens face. Gay and lesbian adolescents bear a double burden: They experience harassment, violence, and suicidal tendencies because of their age and sexual preference. They sometimes feel fearful, withdrawn, depressed, and full of despair. Curricular efforts should address the needs of gay and lesbian adolescents by including age-appropriate literature to explain sexual orientation as well as others' experiences with being gay or lesbian. Such books help readers develop self-understanding and gain insight into the special developmental needs of gay and lesbian youth (Vare & Norton, 1998).

As Implementing Research 8-2 suggests, the social studies curriculum can be enhanced by a study of Native American governments.

---

**FOLLOW THROUGH 8-3   Identifying Practical Approaches to a Culturally Relevant Curriculum**

Many preservice readers of this book have had field experience in schools; in-service teachers already have teaching experience in schools. Working in groups of three or four, prepare a list of practical approaches that could be used to make the curriculum more representative of diversity in the United States and its schools. Include such tools as curricular materials showing diversity and the provision of bilingual language programs on your list.

**IMPLEMENTING RESEARCH 8-2   Native American Governments in Today's Curriculum**

David Sahr (1997) reports on Native American governments and how they probably influence government today. He looks specifically at the political organization of the Iroquois, the Muscogees (Creeks), the Lakota (Sioux), and the Pueblos. In doing so, he shows how well-ordered, democratic, inclusive, and effective the governments were. Sahr offers several conclusions:

1. A stereotype of Native American chiefs was that they were supreme dictators. In reality, most ruled by consensus, trying to persuade the various factions within their tribes to follow their policies.
2. Attributes of leaders included bravery, good judgment, fairness, charisma, generosity, and skill at important activities. Leaders were usually not chosen by heredity.
3. Articulateness was an essential quality—a leader had to be articulate to reason with his tribe and to convince them to follow his orders.
4. Other features of Native American governments included sharing of power between localities and the whole tribe, including women as well as men in the decision-making process, and forming policy based on the good of the nation as a whole in preference to individual rights.

**Implementing the Research**

1. The social studies curriculum needs to explain how Native American governments were well planned and, in fact, influenced U.S. government today.
2. Students today should recognize how Native American leaders were selected on basis of their bravery, good judgment, fairness, charisma, and generosity—attributes that people and leaders should strive for today.
3. Students can study various aspects of Native American government and trace these aspects to U.S. government today (and possibly to the Constitution).

*Source:* Sahr, D. (1997). Native American governments in today's curriculum. *Social Education, 61*(6), 309–315.

Multicultural aspects must genuinely permeate the entire curriculum and the total school environment. The list Sleeter and Grant (1988) provide goes far toward developing a multicultural curriculum, but Bennett (1986) provides still other perspectives and suggestions for making the curriculum more relevant and responsive to multicultural populations. First, Bennett maintains that the traditional curriculum has contained inaccuracies and omissions concerning the contributions and life conditions of major ethnic groups within U.S. society. Curricular reformers should address this omission for the benefit of learners from culturally different backgrounds as well as majority-culture learners.

**IMPLEMENTING RESEARCH 8-3    Multiculturalism and Mathematics**

Anthony Piccolino (1998) maintains that teachers daily confront the challenge of instilling democratic ideals in students and enculturating moral values within the context of various disciplines. Mathematics is no exception. Students traditionally have perceived mathematics as a static subject that was fully developed several hundred years ago by European mathematicians such as Newton, Pascal, Descartes, Gauss, and others. Piccolino argues in favor of altering this perception of mathematics and recognizing the contributions of various cultures. Similarly, examining the contributions of women to mathematics through the ages, for example, not only helps to promote gender equity, but also offers students the opportunity to appreciate the struggles that many women have had to make to pursue mathematics.

**Implementing the Research**

Piccolino calls for increasing student awareness of various cultures and women's contributions to mathematics. Teach students about:

- Russian-born Sofia Kovalevsky, who left her homeland and migrated to Western Europe and became an outstanding nineteenth-century mathematician.
- Sophie Germain, who in early nineteenth-century France assumed the identity of a man so that she could pursue a career in mathematics.
- Graph theory, which was once commonly believed to have originated in eighteenth-century Western Europe. Recent discoveries indicate that it might also have existed among the African tribes in Zaire.
- Ancient Egyptian sources for solving equations known as the Rule of False Position.
- Ninth-century Arab mathematician al-Khowarizmi who used geometric designs resembling algebra tiles that still appear in contemporary classrooms.
- Edna Lee Paisano, a Native American raised on a reservation, who used her background in statistics to discover that Native Americans were significantly undercounted in the 1980 census.

*Source:* Piccolino, A. V. (1998). Integrating multicultural activities across the mathematics curriculum. *NASSP Bulletin, 82* (597), 84–87.

Some educators think integrating multiculturalism into the mathematics curriculum is difficult. Implementing Research 8-3, however, shows how mathematics can reflect multiculturalism.

## The Hidden Curriculum

Although some aspects of the curriculum are readily discernible to children and adolescents attending a school, other aspects are more subtle and may be equally influential. For example, we have little difficulty determining whether people of differing backgrounds are represented honestly and adequately in textbooks and other curricular materials. We can also ascertain with relative ease whether track-

---

**CASE STUDY 8-1 The "Hidden Curriculum"**

Mrs. Brunson at Calhoun Middle School knows she will have to take a stand at the faculty meeting. No longer can she let injustice prevail. Her only decision is how to make her point in such a way that positive action will result.

"We have a hidden curriculum," she says calmly and matter-of-factly. Although the school's philosophy purports to promote equality and equitable treatment for all, it does not act on that belief. Young adolescents learn from a hidden curriculum that teaches as much as or more than the planned curriculum.

Mrs. Brunson has numerous examples to substantiate her point: school policies that recognize only middle-class European American expectations; the media center that is oriented predominantly toward European Americans; instructional practices and academic expectations that address European American learning styles; and participants in extracurricular activities are mostly European American. What message is the school sending to learners of diverse cultural backgrounds? While the curriculum seeks to show acceptance and respect for diversity, the hidden curriculum conveys an almost totally opposite picture. Learners from different cultural backgrounds often feel unaccepted and perceive that they must adjust to middle-class, white values and customs.

Although the faculty expresses some skepticism, it is apparent that they have not considered the impact of the hidden curriculum. In fact the school is not as multicultural as some believe.

Mrs. Brunson feels better for having expressed herself. Genuine change will be slow, and supporters of the status quo will challenge efforts, but at least the faculty recognizes the problem. This is a first and significant step.

---

ing and ability grouping have resulted in the segregation and relegation to second-class status of all people from different cultural backgrounds and lower-class students. There is, however, another equally important curriculum, one that has a powerful influence on children and adolescents. This very subtle "hidden curriculum" affects learners of all races and cultures. Mrs. Brunson in Case Study 8-1 takes a stand against the hidden curriculum in her school.

What specific aspects might be included in a hidden curriculum? It may comprise any number of events, behavior expectations, and attitudes that might appear relatively unobtrusive to white, middle-class learners, but might appear out of character or context to learners of culturally different backgrounds. Representative examples might include teacher behaviors and expectations conveyed both verbally and nonverbally; textbooks and other curricular materials that portray white, middle-class values and orientations; segregation due to tracking or ability grouping policies; educators' and other students' degrees of acceptance and attitudes toward learners from different cultural backgrounds; and the degree of acceptance of language differences. In other words, middle- or upper-class European American students might expect their teacher to encourage them to compete and excel above others in the class; this same teacher expectation, however, might be anathema to Native American learners. Educators must make a deliberate effort to examine all their behaviors (both conscious and unconscious) to determine what hidden messages they are conveying and to carefully assess every aspect of the

**FOLLOW THROUGH 8-4    Identifying the Hidden Curriculum**

Visit an elementary or secondary school (or consider your own if you already teach) to determine the "hidden curriculum." Try to identify three curricular aspects that might be described as "hidden" and offer possible actions for addressing the problem.

**Problem**

Sports teams are segregated by culture: African Americans play basketball; European Americans play tennis.

**Possible Action**

1. Have orientation sessions for sports teams, making clear that equal access is the policy.
2. Speak with individual students and encourage their participation.
3. Teach during physical education classes that students are not limited to specific sports by cultural background.

curriculum and the total school environment to determine whether learners from different cultural backgrounds are being given a different message from that sent to white students.

## Guidelines for a Multicultural Curriculum

As with all curricular efforts, a multicultural curriculum should be carefully matched with goals and objectives and use established guidelines. Although each program should reflect the needs and goals of the respective school, the following guidelines can serve as a basis for multicultural curricular development (Hernandez, 1989; Banks, 1981).

**1.** Emphasize the interrelationship of multiple groups (i.e., ethnic, religious, regional, socioeconomic, language), rather than treating individual groups separately or in isolation. Such multiple-group emphasis diminishes the likelihood of stereotyping and facilitates integration of multicultural content into the overall curriculum.

**2.** Integrate multicultural perspectives, as appropriate, in all content areas. Although most frequently associated with the social sciences, language, literature, art, and music, multicultural perspectives are valid and applicable in areas such as mathematics, science, home economics, and physical education.

**3.** Use a variety of instructional approaches and materials appropriate to the students' maturity level. In particular, teacher strategies should aim to accommodate differences in learning styles and to maximize academic achievement.

**4.** Focus on the development of cognitive as well as affective skills. Assess learning outcomes in terms of knowledge, attitudes, and skills.

**5.** Emphasize school and area populations, locally oriented activities, and community resources. (Hernandez, 1989, pp. 176–177).

Banks (1988) contends that ethnic pluralism should permeate the total school curriculum and environment. Similarly, school policies and procedures should foster positive cross-cultural interactions and understanding among students, teachers, and staff members. The entire curriculum and school environment should reflect the learning styles of all learners and provide students with continuous opportunities to develop self-esteem and positive cultural identity. Banks provides the following other guidelines for the multicultural curriculum:

1. It should help students understand the totality of the experiences of individual ethnic groups.
2. It should help students understand that there is always a conflict between ideals and realities in human societies.
3. It should explore and clarify ethnic alternatives and options within society.
4. It should promote values, attitudes, and behaviors that support ethnic pluralism.
5. It should help students develop the skills necessary for effective interpersonal and interethnic communication.
6. It should be comprehensive in scope and sequence, should present holistic views of ethnic groups, and should be an integral part of the total school curriculum.
7. It should include interdisciplinary and multidisciplinary approaches.
8. It should use comparative approaches in the study of ethnic groups and ethnicity.
9. It should maximize use of local community resources.
10. It should include assessment procedures that reflect individual ethnic cultures.

## Assessing the Need for Curricular Change

Before planning to adopt a multicultural curriculum, the school must assess its needs to determine the direction and extent of the change. Curricular assessment should also be an ongoing and integral part of curriculum development (Ramsey, 1987). Here are some questions a school should consider in a needs assessment:

1. Do multicultural perspectives permeate the entire school curriculum and environment?
2. Do the attitudes of teachers, administrators, and staff members indicate a willingness to accept and respect cultural diversity?
3. Do textbooks and other curricular materials recognize the value of cultural diversity and gender and social class differences?
4. Do curricular activities and methods provide learners with opportunities to collaborate and cooperate?
5. Do extracurricular activities reflect cultural diversity?
6. Do curricular planning efforts reflect the views and opinions of parents and other community people?
7. Do curricular efforts include bilingual perspectives or provide assistance for students with limited English-speaking skills?

---

**CASE STUDY 8-2    Assessing the Need for Change**

The educators at Lockhaven Elementary knew their school was experiencing demographic changes. Many of the European American families had moved to the suburbs, the African American population had grown to some extent, and there had been an influx of Asian and Hispanic American students. The curriculum and educational practices, however, had stayed basically the same.

The school counselor was the first to mention a need for change, but others had also begun to recognize that the school could no longer meet the needs of the current student population. That the school should assess the need for change became clear, but the questions remained of where to begin and what to assess. Suggestions poured in as the counselor took notes:

• the actual cultural composition of the school and the community

• the cultural composition of the administration, faculty, and staff
• the curriculum and the extent to which it addresses cultural diversity
• the instructional practices and the extent to which they meet the learning styles of learners from differing cultural backgrounds
• the school policies and expectations of students
• the extracurricular program and its accessibility to all learners
• the attitudes (recognition, respect, acceptance) of the educators
• the media center and the extent to which its holdings demonstrate a respect for diversity of all types

The list could go on and on, the counselor thought, but the school had made the initial effort. They had recognized the need for change, and the needs assessment was under way.

---

Case Study 8-2 shows how the educators at Lockhaven Elementary decided to assess the need for change in their school.

## Selecting Bias-Free Curricular and Teaching and Learning Materials

This section on textbooks and other curricular materials shows their significance and influence. It provides examples of omissions, stereotypical images, and the outright racism and sexism often found in teaching and learning materials and suggests guidelines for the selection of objective materials. Although this effort and goal are worthy of all elementary and secondary curricula, it might be of greater importance in a curriculum specifically designed to teach the values of cultural diversity.

Providing bias-free curricular and teaching and learning materials sometimes results in the reinterpretation of history, as is seen in Implementing Research 8-4.

Textbooks, workbooks, worksheets, and virtually all the materials teachers use have a powerful impact on learners' cognitive and affective domains. They provide factual information, but through their words and pictures they also affect students' attitudes toward and beliefs about themselves, other people and cultures, and the world. With their power to influence, texts that have ignored cultural diversity or have dealt with individual cultures erroneously or in stereotypical terms have inflicted damage on children over the decades.

**IMPLEMENTING RESEARCH 8-4    The Interpretation of History**

Asking "who owns history" (p. 76), Miller (1998) argues that what appears in textbooks is always based on someone's vision of the truth—the writer's, the editor's, or the publisher's. What teachers choose to teach is based on their own vision of the truth. The study of history is always about someone's interpretation of events, the process of selecting events, inclusion, exclusion, reorganization, and prioritizing, rather than one of merely unfolding the truth. If we permit textbook publishers to "own history" (p. 76), then we must expect a picture of history that reflects a safe, sell-as-many-copies-as-we-can perspective, one that harks back to the theory of the United States as a melting pot of immigrants eager to discard their cultural traditions. At best, Miller thinks textbooks give a watered-down view of the diverse cultural groups that make up the United States. Textbooks offer a narrow, selective view of the world, a shorthand version of history. They feel the need to condense; they often rely on stereotypes or hold up brief heroic sketches of individual members of cultural minorities to represent the entire group.

**Implementing the Research**

Miller maintains that, faced with this skewed version of history, teachers can take several steps:

1.  Educators must fill in the gaping holes for students so as to allow them to develop a broader, more thorough understanding. Teachers can allow students to study and compare various versions of historical events as portrayed in textbooks, magazines, newspapers, and trade books.
2.  Educators can introduce students to original documents to which their books refer, but rarely place in full context—these sources can include court documents, important pieces of legislation, and historic speeches.
3.  Educators can provide examples of real people telling their own stories—complete with facts, emotions, and outcomes.

*Source:* Miller, H. M. (1998). Teaching and learning about history: Who owns history? *The Reading Teacher, 52*(1), 76–78.

Several factors can affect the influence of textbook characterizations on children and adolescents. First, the amount of time spent interacting with the materials seems to determine, at least in part, the extent to which children internalize and retain attitudes and stereotypes. For example, the longer children are exposed to stereotypical images or omissions, the greater the effect the materials have. Second, children vary in their emotional involvement and identification with the individuals and situations portrayed. In reading, mathematics, and social studies, for example, students' performance is enhanced when they perceive content to be relevant and interesting. On the positive side, culturally relevant materials can facilitate the process of learning to read, making it both easier and faster. On the negative side, the absence of characters and situations with which children are able to identify may contribute to and reinforce feelings of security, inferiority, or superiority depending on an individual's group identity. These nonacademic aspects of textbook content affect variables associated with academic achievement: perseverance, motivation, retention, and skills development, among others (Hernandez, 1989).

Other equally important concerns related to bias in textbooks are omissions and distortions. Omission refers to information left out of a textbook, and a distortion is a lack of balance or systematic omission. Because of omissions, members of some cultural and ethnic groups are virtually unrepresented in textbooks. Hispanic Americans, Asian Americans, Native Americans, and women continue to be underrepresented in educational materials (Hernandez, 1989). The "invisibility" of a group implies that it has less value or significance in U.S. society than others. "Invisibility" applies most often to women, culturally diverse people, disabled individuals, and the elderly (Gollnick & Chinn, 1998).

Distortions result from inaccurate or unbalanced impressions. History and reading materials too often ignore the presence and realities of certain groups in contemporary society, or they confine treatment to negative experiences. In some cases, they provide a single point of view about events that may be technically correct but is nevertheless misleading (Hernandez, 1989).

Sexism and sexist language are other factors to consider when selecting textbooks and other teaching materials. Gollnick and Chinn (1998) have called attention to the sexism that often occurs in children's and adolescents' textbooks, especially at the elementary school level. Children who were asked to draw an early caveman drew only pictures of cavemen. In contrast, when instructed to draw "cave people," the children generate drawings of men, women, and children. In classrooms, teachers can point out sexist language to students. When words appear to exclude women as full participants in society or limit their occupational options, teachers can provide alternatives—for example, mail carrier and police officer as alternatives to mailman and policeman (Gollnick & Chinn, 1998).

The challenge facing multicultural educators is to select textbooks and other materials that objectively represent various groups and people who have been traditionally either ignored or misrepresented. Table 8-1 provides educators with a means of evaluating written material to determine its suitability in our increasingly multicultural schools.

## *Evaluating Curricular Efforts*

Evaluating the multicultural curriculum to determine overall program strengths and weaknesses and to assess how well it meets individual learner needs is as important as the actual content and teaching methods the teacher uses. One basic criterion is to determine whether teaching and learning situations reflect multiculturalism (Sleeter & Grant, 1988).

Other measures of program effectiveness include oral and written tests (teacher-made and standardized), sociograms, questionnaires, surveys, student projects, interviews, anecdotal information, and discussion groups. Indicators such as attendance records, class participation, and incidence of disruptive behavior also provide clues about student acceptance of and interest in the program. Many of these procedures are conducive to staff, parent, and student involvement. Whatever evaluation

## TABLE 8-1   How to Analyze Books for Racism and Sexism

These guidelines are a starting point and are designed to help educators detect racist and sexist bias in children's story books, picture books, primers, and fiction.

1. *Check the illustrations.* Look for stereotypes, oversimplified generalizations about a particular group, race, or sex that generally carry derogatory implications. Look for variations that in any way demean or ridicule characters because of their race or sex.

   *Look for tokenism.* If there are culturally diverse characters, are they just like Anglo Americans, but tinted or colored? Do all culturally diverse faces look stereotypically alike, or are they depicted as genuine individuals?

   *Look at the lifestyles of the people in the book.* Are culturally diverse characters and their settings depicted in such a way that they contrast unfavorably with an unstated norm of Anglo American middle-class suburbia? For example, culturally diverse people are often associated with the ghetto, migrant labor, or "primitive" living. If the story does attempt to depict another culture, does it go beyond oversimplifications of reality to offer genuine insights into another lifestyle?

2. *Check the story line.* Civil rights legislation has led publishers to weed out many insulting passages and illustrations, particularly in stories with black themes, but the attitudes still find expression in less obvious ways. The following checklist suggests some of the various subtle forms of bias to watch for:

   *Relationships:* Do Anglo Americans in the story have the power and make the decisions? Do culturally diverse people function in essentially subservient roles?

   *Standard for success:* What does it take for a character to succeed? To gain acceptance, do culturally diverse characters have to exhibit superior qualities—excel in sports, get A's, and so forth?

   *Viewpoint:* How are "problems" presented, conceived, and resolved in the story? Are culturally diverse people themselves considered to be "the problem"? Do solutions ultimately depend on the benevolence of an Anglo American?

   *Sexism:* Are the achievements of girls and women based on their own initiative and intelligence, or is their success due to their good looks or to their relationships with boys? Are sex roles incidental or paramount to characterization and plot? Could the same story be told if the sex roles were reversed?

3. *Consider the effects of the book on the child's self-image and self-esteem.* Are norms established that limit the child's aspirations and self-esteem? What does it do to African American children to be continuously bombarded with images of white as beautiful, clean, and virtuous, and black as evil, dirty, and menacing? What happens to a girl's aspirations when she reads that boys perform all the brave and important deeds? What about a girl's self-esteem if she is not fair of skin and slim of body?

4. *Consider the author's or illustrator's qualifications.* Read the biographical material on the jacket flap or on the back cover. If a story deals with a culturally diverse theme, what qualifies the author or illustrator to deal with this topic? If they are not members of the culturally diverse group being written about, is there anything in the author's or illustrator's background that would specifically recommend them for this book?

   Similarly, a book that has to do with the feelings and insights of women should be more carefully examined if it is written by a man, unless the book's avowed purpose is to present a male viewpoint.

   These observations do not deny the ability of writers to empathize with experiences other than those of their own sex or race, but the chances of their writing as honestly and as authentically about the experiences of other genders and races are not as good.

5. *Look at the copyright date.* Books on culturally diverse themes—usually hastily conceived—suddenly began appearing in the mid-1960s. There followed a growing number of "culturally diverse experience" books to meet the new market demand, but they were still written by Anglo American authors and reflected an Anglo point of view. Only in the late 1960s and early 1970s did the children's book world begin to even remotely reflect the realities of a multiracial society, and it has only just begun to reflect feminist concerns.

*Adapted from:* Ten quick ways to analyze children's books for racism and sexism. (November 3, 1974). *Interracial Books for Children,* 5(3), 6–7.

is used, the information collected should be well documented, relevant, and useful. The validity of evaluation depends on the questions asked, behaviors observed, and efforts made to sample randomly and to apply common standards.

Gender Perspectives 8-1 examines school girls' relationship to math and science.

---

**FOLLOW THROUGH 8-5   Evaluating the Curriculum**

Evaluating the curriculum for cultural relevance, objectivity, and accuracy should be a major part of any multicultural education program. Suggest eight to ten criteria for evaluating the curriculum to determine whether it recognizes and shows respect for cultural diversity.

---

**GENDER PERSPECTIVES 8-1   Math, Science, and Girls**

Careers in math and science may be the best way for women to reach income parity with men. Women make less than men in nearly all areas, but the wage gap is much less in the math and science fields.

Even in light of this evidence, some educators discourage adolescent girls from enrolling in math and science courses. Reasons include peer pressure, low teacher expectations, and girls' own diminished academic self-esteem. Girls from culturally different backgrounds may feel this discrimination even more. The discrimination against females extends to extracurricular activities as well. While boys learn to repair cars, girls often learn arts and crafts. An international study of computer use revealed that U.S. youngsters learn about computers mostly through home use, but girls are less likely to use their families' computers.

What implications does this article hold for educators who want to address the special needs of girls?

- Teachers should give girls opportunities to enroll in math and science courses (and, in fact, encourage them to do so).

- Teachers should encourage girls to participate in traditional male-oriented extracurricular activities such as math and science clubs.
- Teachers and counselors should give girls objective career advice.
- Teachers should give special attention to teaching boys to understand girls and to be more encouraging of their participation in math and science.

Readers who want more information may write to:

American Association for the Advancement of Science, 1333 H. Street, NW, Washington, D.C. 20005

American Association of University Women, 1111 16th Street, Washington, D.C. 20036

Center for Research on Women, Wellesley College, 106 Central Street, Wellesley, MA 02181

Women's Educational Equity Act Publishing Center, Education Development Center, 55 Chapel Street, Newton, MA 02158

---

*Source:* Math and science path to making things even for girls. (May/June 1994). *High Strides: The Bimonthly Report on Urban Middle Grades,* p. 2.

---

**FOR ADDITIONAL INFORMATION   Internet Addresses**

**Multiculture Nonsexist Education Home Page**
http://www.ops.org/mne/multi.home.html
Provides a look at the Omaha Public Schools'
efforts to address equity issues and to respect
individual differences of all students.

**LSU: Multicultural Resources**
http://lasalle.edu/services/mcis/multi_a.htm
Provides a wealth of multicultural resources for
elementary and secondary schools.

**MilbankWeb: Research Resources:
Pathfinders: Multicultural Education**
http://lweb.tc.columbia.edu/rr/mc/   Provides access to the Milbank Memorial Library
of Teachers College, Columbia University, which

contains the world's largest collection of materials on the educating professions

**Multicultural Literature—Secondary
Classroom**
http://www.indiana.edu/~eric_rec/ieo/
bibs/multisec.html   Provides information on
multicultural literature in secondary classrooms.

**Multicultural Education—Guide**
http://www.lps.org.instruction/guide/
multiguide.html   Provides a description of multicultural education in the Lincoln Public Schools
and the identification, selection, and infusion of
specific knowledge, attitudes, and skills.

---

## A Multicultural Education Unit

Our premise in this book is that multicultural education should be a total school
curriculum and environmental approach rather than an occasional unit. We do,
however, recognize that the situation should not be "either/or," nor should it become a battle of multicultural education curriculum versus the unit approach. We
firmly believe, however, that a once-a-year (or even an every semester) effort in
the form of a multicultural week or perhaps a two- or three-week unit is insufficient to teach knowledge of and respect for cultural diversity. We remind readers,
therefore, to consider units as a part of a total curriculum effort, perhaps as a means
of addressing one or more specific objectives.

### Considerations

Before examining a unit designed to convey knowledge and understanding of
cultural diversity, it is important to define the unit approach and to look briefly
at what units usually include. First, units (sometimes called modules) are designed to teach a specific body of information over a time lasting more than a
class meeting or two. For example, might the unit last one, two, or three days or
weeks or years or longer in some instances? Second, units contain goals, objectives, content, activities, materials, enrichment resources, and evaluational instruments. Although educators may differ about what the unit should include,
generally speaking, it is a comprehensive guide that differs from the one-day lesson plan.

## Example

The next several pages provide an example of an instructional unit. It is important to remember that this unit serves only as an illustration. Educators should assess their students' developmental needs, levels of knowledge, and attitudes and assess the planned instruction accordingly.

## The Unit: Unjust Treatment of People of Culturally Diverse Backgrounds

### Rationale

African Americans were brought to America to be sold into slavery. Native Americans were forced off their lands. Asian Americans, especially Chinese Americans, worked on the railroad linking the Missouri River to the Pacific Coast in 1862. Hispanic Americans work in "sweat factories" or as migrant workers. Japanese Americans were relocated to internment camps after the bombing of Pearl Harbor.

### Objectives and Activities

**1.** Have students define the following terms: *racism, discrimination,* and *injustice* and identify examples of each that have harmed several groups from culturally different backgrounds.

**2.** Have students identify three books or songs that describe the injustices that groups from different cultural backgrounds experienced.

**3.** Have students develop a time line showing culturally diverse people's responses to unjust treatment; for example, African Americans' march on Washington in 1963.

**4.** Have students identify three examples of contemporary racism, discrimination, or injustice and list possible solutions for each.

Individuals, cooperative learning groups, or interest-established pairs or triads may work on these activities.

### Language Arts

- Read *The Drinking Gourd* and *Sing Down the Moon* and have students write a review of each.
- Have students prepare short stories, poems, skits, and plays on the unjust treatment many people received.
- Ask students to write and give a speech that a Native American might have given regarding land being taken away.
- Keep a class scrapbook of unjust practices that currently exist in the United States.
- Help students write a letter to the editor of a newspaper proposing a solution to an injustice people suffer today.

## Mathematics

- Compile a "numbers" list with students: acres of land taken away from Native Americans, numbers of African Americans brought to America to work as slaves, numbers of Asian Americans working on the railroad, and numbers of Hispanic Americans working as migrant workers. Compute estimates of money saved by having workers work in low-paying jobs in poor working conditions.
- On a bar or pie graph, ask students to show numbers of workers from culturally different backgrounds in minimum-wage jobs.
- Have students estimate the value of land taken from Native Americans, and compare the estimate with the amount received (if any money was actually paid).

## Science

- Study terrain as part of your lesson plan—for example, land taken away from Native Americans and farming land on which migrant workers grow produce.
- Have students examine climate conditions necessary for growing various types of produce and determine the effects these conditions have on people.
- Study with students the climatic conditions (e.g., temperature, humidity, heat index) of many "sweat shops" and the effect it has on people.

## Social Studies

- Examine with students the concepts of racism, injustice, and discrimination, and pinpoint historical and contemporary examples.
- Ask students to gather information on immigration patterns by decade or some other time frame.
- Review with students America's resistance to immigrants entering the United States. (For examples of resistance today, see *Newsweek*'s "Immigration backlash" [Thomas & Murr, August 9, 1993], in which a poll indicates that 60 percent of Americans think immigration is bad for the nation, and other news magazines' reports on the Haitian and Cuban refugees seeking to come to America in 1994.)
- Have students prepare an essay explaining the melting pot concept and its limitations and how we currently support the salad bowl concept.
- Ask students to write a position paper for or against the resistance or unjust treatment people received on arrival to the United States.
- Develop a time line with students showing each cultural group's important dates or events—the Emancipation Proclamation, for example.
- Ask students to develop a chart listing injustices and offer possible solutions.

## Art

- Introduce students to works of art depicting injustices people have suffered and struggled to overcome.

- Assign students to create collages, dioramas, and mobiles showing injustices: the bonds of slavery, the plight of Native Americans, and the menial jobs many Asian and Hispanic Americans have been forced to accept.
- Study art of various cultures and ask students to look for common themes and areas. Resources include *Our Hispanic heritage* (1989), Raintree Publishing; Hargrove, J. (1990), *Diego Rivera: Mexican muralist*, Children's Press; and Sills, Leslie (1989), *Inspirations: Stories about women artists*, Albert Whitman.
- Examine Native American art with students and the relationship between the art and the history of Native Americans. Resource: Highwater, Jamake. [1978]. *Many smokes, many moons: A chronology of American Indian history through Indian art.* HarperCollins.

## *Music*

- Listen to songs of various cultures that have helped people to survive, provided a ray of hope, and communicated pain and suffering.
- Ask students to write lyrics for a familiar melody that deal with a contemporary injustice and offer hope.
- Research musical instruments that slaves and other people in bondage used.
- Develop teaching and learning experiences from using such resources as Haskins, James (1987), *Black music in America: A history through its people,* HarperCollins; or Mattox, Cheryl Warren (Ed.) (1990), *Shake it to the one that you love the best: Play songs and lullabies from black musical traditions.* Warren-Mattox Productions.

## *Other Resources*

Selected books appropriate for 10- to 15-year-olds that can complement this unit on unjust treatment of people of culturally diverse backgrounds include:

**African Americans**

Adler, David A. *Jackie Robinson: He was the first.* Holiday House, 1989, 48 pp.

*Nonfiction. This is an accurate and informative account about Jackie Robinson and the time in which he lived.*

Burns, Anthony. *The defeat and triumph of a fugitive slave.* Knopf, 1988, 192 pp.

*Nonfiction. Burns, a runaway slave, was jailed in Boston and lost his legal case under the Fugitive Slave Act of 1850.*

Humphrey, Kathryn Long. *Satchel Paige.* Watts, 1988, 128 pp.

*Nonfiction. The story of the most famous of the African Americans who played on the segregated teams of the Negro Baseball League.*

Katz, William Loren. *Breaking the chains: African American slave resistance.* Atheneum, 1990, 208 pp.

*Nonfiction. This excellent book confutes the often-held belief that many slaves accepted servitude as a way of life.*

Kosof, Anna. *The civil rights movement and its legacy.* Watts, 1989, 112 pp.

*Nonfiction. Kosof recounts her own experiences during the civil rights movement.*

Lester, Julius. *This strange new feeling.* Dutton/ Dial, 1982, 160 pp.

*Fiction. This story tells about Ras and the challenges he faced living in slavery.*

Rummell, Jack. *Langston Hughes.* Chelsea House, 1988, 111 pp.

*Nonfiction. Middle-level students will appreciate Hughes's determination to leave home and pursue his desire to become a poet.*

### Asian Americans

Batancourt, Jeanne. *More than meets the eye.* Bantam, 1990, 166 pp.

*Fiction. This book describes the variety of problems Asian Americans face in today's schools.*

Bode, Janet. *New kids on the block: Oral histories of immigrant teens.* Watts, 1989, 126 pp.

*Nonfiction. Eleven teenagers relate their experiences about leaving their homelands and adjusting to their new life in America.*

Brown, Dee Alexander, and Proctor, Linda. *Lonesome whistle: The story of the first transcontinental railroad.* Holt, Rinehart and Winston, 1980, 144 pp.

*Nonfiction. This book, adapted for young readers, describes the building of the transcontinental railroad and how the railroad selected the Chinese for the work.*

Miklowitz, Gloria D. *The war between the classes.* Delacorte, 1985, 158 pp. Fiction.

*This book focuses on the injustices resulting from social class structures.*

Winter, Frank H. *The Filipinos in America.* Lerner, 1988, 71 pp.

*Nonfiction. This readable and balanced book provides an introduction to the fastest-growing Asian immigrant group in the United States.*

### Native Americans

Ashabranner, Brent. *Morning star, black sun: The northern Cheyenne Indians and America's energy crisis.* Putnam, 1982, 154 pp.

*Nonfiction. Ashabranner examines Native Americans' reverence for the land and how their land was taken away.*

Ashabranner, Brent. *To live in two worlds: American Indian youth today.* Dodd, Mead, 1984, 149 pp.

*Nonfiction. Ashabranner examines the contemporary lives of a number of Native American teenagers and young adults.*

Brown, Dee. *Wounded Knee: An Indian history of the American West.* Dell, 1975, 202 pp.

*Nonfiction. Brown's book corrects the white expansionist view of U.S. history, which Hollywood has reinforced with stereotypes of the Native Americans.*

Cannon, A. E. *The shadow brothers.* Delacorte, 1990, 180 pp.

*Fiction. Cannon shows that Native Americans differ as individuals just as individuals do in all cultures.*

Gregory, Kristiana. *Jenny of the Tetons.* Harcourt Brace Jovanovich, 1989, 119 pp.

*Fiction. A raid has left eleven-year-old Carrie orphaned and wounded and her two younger brothers kidnapped.*

### Hispanic Americans

Beltran Hernandez, Irene. *Across the great river.* Arte Publico, 1989, 136 pp.

*Fiction. Economic hardships force a family to cross the Rio Grande in search of a better life.*

Cullison, Alan. *The South Americans.* Chelsea House, 1991, 112 pp.

*Nonfiction. Recent economic and political problems have driven increasing numbers of South Americans north.*

Meltzer, Milton. *The Hispanic Americans.* HarperCollins, 1982, 149 pp.

*Nonfiction. Meltzer examines the Hispanic population from both a historical and a sociological perspective.*

Mills, Claudia. *Luisa's American Dream.* Four Winds, 1981, 155 pp.

*Fiction. Luisa, a fourteen-year-old girl, hides her Cuban American background and her nationality.*

Pinchot, Jane. *The Mexicans in America.* Lerner, 1989, 94 pp.

*Nonfiction. Pinchot examines issues of importance to Mexican Americans: education, immigration, and civil rights.*

This partial unit could serve as a beginning point or a skeletal outline. Teachers working in interdisciplinary teams can tap their professional expertise in particular content areas and offer many exciting and productive activities and ideas within this topic.

## Other Topics for Multicultural Units

- Contributions of people from culturally different groups (or a specific cultural group)
- Cultural traditions: family and society (in general or for a specific cultural group)
- Books, poems, and short stories (or music or art) by writers from culturally different backgrounds

### Geography and Locations: Pinpointing Locations of Origin*

- Native People of the Southwest (from *A Multicultural Inservice Resource Handbook*, Arizona Department of Education, 1535 W. Jefferson St., Phoenix, AZ 85007)
- *African American Scholars: Leaders, Activists, and Writers* (from NAACP, 4805 Mount Hope Dr., Baltimore, MD 21215)
- *Martin Luther King: A Lifetime of Action* (from Martin Luther King, Jr., Resource Guide, the State Education Department of New York, Long Island Field Services, #1 Regional Field Services, Room 973 EBA, Albany, NY 12234)
- Contemporary contributors from culturally different backgrounds: civil rights activists
- Influential women and their contributions (women in general or women in a specific cultural group)
- Coming to America: immigration in the 1990s. Books we especially suggest for fifth and sixth graders include *If you were there in 1492* (Brenner, Barbara. MacMillan, 1991), *Ajeemah and his son* (Berry, James. HarperCollins, 1992), and *The Chinese American family album* (Hoobler, Dorothy, and Thomas Hoobler. Oxford University Press, 1994) (Fagella, 1994).

## Extending the Multicultural Education Curriculum

### Parental and Community Involvement

Efforts to provide multicultural education curricula and environments must extend beyond the confines of the school. Children and adolescents need to perceive evidence of recognition and respect for cultural diversity in the home and in the community. The home and the community can serve as powerful and positive forces to help reinforce the efforts of the school. Parents and other community members and organizations are valuable resources to help support the school's

*Source: Manning, M. L. (1994) *Celebrating diversity: Multicultural education in middle level schools.* Columbus, OH: National Middle School Association, pp. 98–103.

efforts to promote respect for cultural diversity. They should be made aware of school efforts and should feel that the school seeks and respects their advice and opinions. These two entities can also provide considerable financial and volunteer support for the multicultural education program.

As parents become involved in their children's education and learn more about the school's goals (especially in relation to the goals and materials of the multicultural education curricula), they are more likely to give overall support for school programs. Parents in all likelihood will become more interested in their children's school success and be better able to assist the school in its efforts.

Parents and educators should ask whether the community supports the school and its academic and social tasks. Is the leadership of the community concerned with school effectiveness? Does the community support efforts toward school improvement? Are the achievements of all students and teachers celebrated in the community at public occasions? Are the role models in the community educated people? If the community is not strongly positive, bring the matter to the attention of progressive community leaders with the suggestion that they sponsor a determined effort to improve the community environment (Tyler, 1989).

As Case Study 8-3 suggests that, involving the community can be a task of some magnitude but one that offers many rewards.

---

### CASE STUDY 8-3  Community Involvement

The school personnel at HS 170, an urban secondary school, had reached a basic agreement for their multicultural education program. They established specific objectives for the program, one of which was to involve the community. Extending the program outside the school would show their genuine commitment. Also it would give parents, families, and other community members a chance to provide input and to offer their involvement.

The group decided on several approaches: They sent notices home with the students explaining the basic premises of the program and how parents, families, and the community could respond. They asked radio and television stations to donate brief airtime to inform the community of the effort. They placed posters the students had designed in businesses and other public places.

The group, recognizing the varying work schedules of community members, called meetings at different times and locations. The purposes of the meetings were to:

1. explain the purposes of the program and how it would fit in with the existing academic program;
2. explain the phases of implementation and the rationale and objectives for each phase;
3. explain that all aspects of the program would be subject to evaluation and review for changes and revisions;
4. form a committee to review library and media acquisitions; and
5. explain that the program would be interdisciplinary and would permeate all areas of the school: curriculum, instruction, materials, teaching and learning environment, and teacher attitudes and behaviors.

Perhaps of greatest importance during the meetings, the group demonstrated the objectives of the program itself: recognition, acceptance, appreciation, and respect for all people regardless of differences.

---

**FOLLOW THROUGH 8-6    Involving Parents and Extended Family Members**

Name several ways to involve parents and extended family members of culturally different backgrounds in the curricular efforts of the school. Perhaps it would be best to divide the list into two groups, one for classes and one for the overall school programs. Include ways in which special school personnel (e.g., counselor, communications specialists) can most effectively involve parents and extended family members.

---

## Extracurricular Activities

Perceptive educators readily recognize the need for equitable representation of all races and ethnic groups in extracurricular activities.

**1.** Baker (1983) suggests that athletic programs include minority students and women and that cheerleading teams include both sexes as well as students of culturally different backgrounds.

**2.** Baker (1983) and Gollnick and Chinn (1998) recommend that clubs and organizations not perpetuate racial or gender segregation and that one group not dominate positions of student leadership.

**3.** Baker (1983) also recommends encouraging females to participate in all sports and that there be special arrangements for students who are unable to participate for financial or other reasons.

---

**EXTRACURRICULAR ACTIVITY CHECKLIST**

1. Do all the school's racial and ethnic groups participate in extracurricular activities?
2. Are financial resources equitably distributed among extracurricular activities?
3. Are extracurricular activities segregated along racial lines?
4. Do sponsors or advisers of extracurricular activities encourage learners from culturally different backgrounds to participate in the activities they sponsor?
5. Are arrangements available to support students who lack the financial or other (e.g., travel) resources to participate in extracurricular activities?
6. Are conscious efforts made to include students of differing socioeconomic groups and to involve both boys and girls in the school's extracurricular program?
7. Do the efforts to involve all children and adolescents in extracurricular activities receive the wholehearted support (not just token support) of all administrators, teachers, special service personnel, and staff members?

---

**FOLLOW THROUGH 8-7    Evaluating Extracurricular Activities**

Extracurricular activities can be an important part of the total school day, especially when educators provide culturally relevant curricular activities and involve students from various cultural backgrounds. Evaluate a school's extracurricular activities to determine their cultural relevance and the school's commitment to inclusiveness. What suggestions might you offer the school for improving its extracurricular activities, especially as they relate to students from culturally different backgrounds?

## Summing Up

Multicultural educators planning and implementing culturally responsive curricula should:

**1.** Reflect and recognize that the United States has experienced considerable progress toward acceptance of cultural diversity; that racism, discrimination, and prejudice continue to exist in the United States; and that curricular efforts and overall school environment should demonstrate an emphatic respect for cultural diversity.

**2.** Place reform efforts on an across-the-curriculum approach and on the overall school environment, rather than on a once-a-year or unit approach.

**3.** Have a sound multicultural basis: a careful assessment of overall needs, established guidelines, the selection of bias-free curricular materials, and the provision of evaluative procedures for both learners and curricular efforts.

**4.** Include extensive involvement of community resources, and permeate extracurricular activities as well as the academic curricular aspects.

**5.** Respect and build on, as much as possible, individual learners' native language.

## Suggested Learning Activities

**1.** Visit a school with considerable cultural diversity and evaluate how well cultural diversity is reflected in the textbooks and workbooks. Answer the following questions to determine whether the school includes appropriate cultural perspectives (feel free to include your own questions):

**a.** Does the text portray students from diverse backgrounds in a meaningful, non-stereotypical manner?

**b.** Does the text portray various social classes?

**c.** Does the text portray women and disabled people in meaningful roles?

**d.** Does the text portray Native, Asian, Hispanic, and European Americans as well as African Americans?

**e.** Does the text make provisions for learners with limited English-speaking skills?

**2.** Interview a curriculum coordinator of a large school (or school district) with a large percentage of students from culturally different backgrounds. What approach is the school taking to implement a multicultural education program? What mechanism is in place to ensure that all levels of educators are involved in the program? After the interview, carefully consider your findings, and write a brief paper that summarizes your findings and offers what you think are appropriate suggestions.

**3.** Prepare a multicultural unit (designed for perhaps two or three weeks) that a school could integrate into an overall multicultural education program. In this unit, be sure to include goals, objectives, activities, curricular materials, provisions for evaluation (of both students and the unit itself), and provisions for children and adolescents with limited English-speaking abilities.

## Suggestions for Collaborative Efforts

Form groups of three or four that, if possible, represent our nation's cultural and gender diversity. Working collaboratively, focus your group's attention toward the following efforts:

1. Have each member of your group select a type of curricular material, for example, textbooks, workbooks, worksheets, audiovisuals, and any other curricular materials that elementary or secondary schools commonly use. Prepare an evaluation form (on textbooks as an example here) to answer such questions as: Is the portrayal of children and adolescents of culturally different backgrounds filled with stereotypes and myths? Of the materials on your list, consider the actual numbers of learners of culturally different backgrounds in the school, the accuracy and objectivity of their portrayal, and whether the material addresses differences among people within cultural groups (e.g., Are all Asian Americans alike? Are all Spanish-speaking people alike?).

2. Think about the curriculum when you were in elementary or secondary school. Did you study people of various cultures? Were the roles and contributions of women portrayed? Did you ever wonder why curricular materials failed to include all people? What effects can the omission of groups have on learners? If you did study people from various cultural groups and women, whom did you study? While some progress has been made in portraying the contributions of all people, progress continues to be necessary. What steps do you suggest for ensuring that all people are represented in curricular materials?

3. As a group, visit a school to determine its efforts to help children of limited English-speaking capability. What special considerations are made for these learners? What language programs are in place? What professional staff is available to offer help? What remedial programs are available? Are learners allowed to speak their native languages in schools?

## Expanding Your Horizons: Additional Journal Readings and Books

Ellington, L. (1998). Multicultural theorists and the social studies. *The Social Studies, 89*(2), 57–60.

*Ellington discusses popular conceptions of multicultural education and maintains that too many leading multicultural theorists in social studies advocate separatist multiculturalism.*

Gordon, B. M. (1997). Curriculum, policy, and African American cultural knowledge: Challenges and possibilities for the year 2000 and beyond. *Educational Policy, 11*(2), 227–242.

*Gordon argues that the contemporary challenge for the curriculum field and educational policy is to create pedagogy and implement social action that reflects new visions of humankind.*

Lee, O., & Fradd, S. H. (1998). Science for all, including students from non-English-language backgrounds. *Educational Researcher, 27*(4), 12–20.

*Lee and Fradd call for educational and instruction equity for all students and propose an agenda for research, policy, and practice for all students.*

Leuthold, S. (1997). Crossing the lines: Toward a curriculum of comparative design. *Multicultural Education 5*(2), 16–19.

*Leuthold explores multiculturalism in art and design education.*

Manning, M. L. (1994). *Celebrating diversity: Multicultural education in middle level schools.* Columbus, OH: National Middle School Association.

*Looking especially at middle-level schools, Manning explains how schools' curricula and environment can better reflect our nation's diversity.*

Olmedo, I. M. (1997). Family oral histories for multicultural curriculum perspectives. *Urban Education, 32*(1), 45–62.

*Olmedo describes a rationale and an approach for helping teachers use the life histories of parents and community members to teach social studies and history.*

## Answers to the Culture Quiz: Multicultural Education Curriculum Efforts

| 1. T | 3. F | 5. T | 7. T | 9. T |
|------|------|------|------|------|
| 2. T | 4. T | 6. F | 8. F | 10. T |

$$C \quad h \quad a \quad p \quad t \quad e \quad r \quad \textit{9}$$

# Instructional Practices

Understanding the material and activities in this chapter will help the reader to:

- State the importance of individual and cultural differences among learners, and explain how these differences affect the teaching and learning process.
- Explain the classroom teacher's role in providing teaching and learning situations that are beneficial to culturally diverse learners.
- State how socioeconomic conditions, social class, and parents and families affect culturally diverse learners.
- List the factors educators should consider in evaluating culturally diverse learners.
- List the items educators should consider during self-evaluation to determine teaching effectiveness in multicultural situations.
- Explain special considerations educators should address when planning teaching and learning experiences with Native, African, Hispanic, European, and Asian American children and adolescents.
- List the characteristics of teachers who are effective in multicultural situations.
- Explain the importance and necessity of ensuring that multicultural education permeates the total school environment, provides educational experiences that demonstrate acceptance of culturally diverse learners, and promotes positive self-concepts and cultural identities.

## Overview

Learners at both the elementary and secondary levels deserve the most effective educational experiences possible. In the past, however, educational experiences have all too often emphasized predominantly European American perspectives and neglected or minimized the importance of minority viewpoints and issues. Cultural diversity has been an obstacle for learners to "overcome" or for teachers to "remediate." Either consciously or unconsciously using this philosophy, educators have planned and implemented experiences for European American learners.

Educators have expected all students to learn by using similar cognitive processes, to feel or perceive events similarly, to demonstrate similar patterns of behavior, and to demonstrate achievement using evaluation instruments designed predominantly from a middle-class European American perspective. In essence, teachers have expected culturally diverse learners to shape themselves to fit the European American mold and mode.

Such educational experiences are both unethical and futile. This chapter explores several teaching and learning contexts: learners' individual and cultural differences, characteristics of educators, organization and instruction, the teaching and learning environment, and cultural perspectives that influence the teaching and learning process in multicultural settings.

---

### THE CULTURE QUIZ   Teaching and Learning

*Directions:* Mark the following statements true or false.

_____ 1. The multicultural education program should include efforts that permeate the total school environment—the curriculum, instructional practices, and the promotion of positive self-concepts and cultural identities.

_____ 2. More than four decades after *Brown v. Board of Education of Topeka* segregation of many students by race continues.

_____ 3. Teachers often unknowingly bring to classrooms biases and prejudices toward people different from themselves.

_____ 4. Teacher self-evaluation lacks objectivity and, for all practical purposes, should be avoided.

_____ 5. Research has indicated that ability grouping does not improve academic achievement; the research, however, has not indicated that it hampers intercultural relationships.

_____ 6. Ability-grouping patterns appear to be positively correlated to ethnicity and socioeconomic level, rather than to academic abilities and achievement levels.

_____ 7. Cooperative learning purposes—when students learn cooperatively rather than competitively—increase academic achievement for all students.

_____ 8. A major Native American scholar and author, Lee Little Soldier, wrote that cooperative learning improves academic achievement and matches Native American values and behaviors.

_____ 9. Research has indicated that if the classroom teacher demonstrates appropriate multicultural attitudes, it is less important for the overall faculty and staff composition to represent the cultural diversity of the school.

_____ 10. Governmental efforts such as Headstart, Job Corps, Chapter or Title 1 programs, and other educational programs generally have not helped children and adolescents from culturally diverse families.

(Answers to the Culture Quiz are located at the end of the chapter.)

## Valuing Individual and Cultural Differences

It is important that teachers perceive elementary and secondary learners objectively, regardless of cultural, ethnic, racial, social class, or religious differences. Learners need the psychological security of feeling valued and accepted; therefore, all educational decisions should be based on objective evidence and should be made with the individual's welfare in mind. Because of the tremendous diversity (cultural, racial, ethnic, social class, ability/disability, or combinations thereof) among contemporary learners, educators cannot consider an entire class as a homogeneous group of learners who need the same educational experiences. Just as European American students differ significantly in social class, geographic location, and family background, learners of other cultures also differ in these characteristics and in values, traditions, and customs. It is the school's responsibility to develop an understanding of each learner and to base teaching and learning experiences on reliable and objective information.

Implementing Research 9-1 offers an interesting idea—using storybooks to encourage discussion of human diversity.

### Recognizing and Accepting Diversity

It is an understatement to suggest that teaching and learning situations must demonstrate an emphatic acceptance of learners in all their cultural, ethnic, socioeconomic, and religious diversity. An environment that promotes acceptance of diversity does more than pay lip service to the concept or have goal statements that are merely rhetorical.

For culturally diverse learners to feel genuine acceptance, the teaching and learning process must concretely demonstrate respect for cultural and ethnic differences (Are all cultures and ethnic groups represented in the curriculum?); it must recognize social class (Do children come in contact with children from other socioeconomic levels? Do textbooks portray the various social classes of U.S. society?); and it must accept all religious groups (Do children feel their religious views are accepted?).

---

**FOLLOW THROUGH 9-1    Valuing Differences among Learners**

Learners have many differences—many that educators can see, and others more subtle. Also, as we have repeatedly stated, no one can consider an individual to be like others in his or her culture. Yet, some educators consider all students of one race, for example, to be the same and fail to consider their many differences. Make a list of ways educators can learn about students and their differences (e.g., get to know individual students, meet their immediate parents and extended family members, and study the respective cultures).

**IMPLEMENTING RESEARCH 9-1**   Using Storybooks to Encourage Discussions

Providing accurate, authentic information about the differences among children—such as their beliefs, attitudes, values, and customs—one encounters in the classroom is important to the process of exploring diversity with children. Equally important, children must have ample opportunities to explore and experience information in a variety of ways. Effective teachers continually search for new ways to bridge the gap between what is known by and what is known about children. Children's books serve as one vehicle in that endeavor as teachers open communication and foster an environment of understanding and respect.

Marshall (1998) suggests using books to foster an understanding of and respect for human diversity:

*Talk about human differences.* Through readings, teachers can help children become more aware of situations around them by leading them in exploratory discussions. They can support children whose own lives reflect events in the books and lead all their students to think analytically about themselves and others.

*Talk through human differences.* At times, it is appropriate for children to see others like themselves and to focus on commonalities—a story might not focus on specific issues of diversity, but often portrays people from a variety of diverse cultures. Every child needs to explore and explain feelings and emotions. Numerous children's books can generate discussions about the vast realm of feelings and emotions of all people.

*Talk about topics that relate to issues of diversity.* The themes of many children's books include learning to live appropriately with others. Such books make good launch points for discussion of concerns, friendships, cooperation, caring, and sharing.

### Implementing the Research

1. Educators of children and adolescents need a solid understanding of age-appropriate literature that focuses positively on all forms of diversity, such as culture, gender, socioeconomic status, family structure, and physical and mental ability.

2. Educators should engage in careful selection of books to ensure that they include appropriate topics such as respect, equality, and justice. Educators need to develop instructional techniques that work most effectively with the use of such books to show respect for diversity.

3. Educators should choose only those books that support critical thinking and anti-bias attitudes.

*Source:* Marshall, C. S. (1998). Using children's storybooks to encourage discussions among diverse populations. *Childhood Education, 74*(4), 194–199.

The racism and classism that continue to burden U.S. society make genuine acceptance difficult. Nearly five decades after the *Brown v. Board of Education of Topeka* decision, inequities in education and outright segregation continue in some areas. The goal of school environments that demonstrate genuine acceptance cannot be achieved outright; in fact, it may be a goal for which people will have to strive for years to come.

## Effective Educators in Multicultural Settings

Educators who seek a comprehensive understanding of cultural diversity and expertise in multicultural education should direct attention to both cognitive and affective factors. It will not suffice for educators to have knowledge of culturally diverse learners and yet be unable to recognize learners' individual and cultural needs and the complex relationship between culture and learning. Educators also need to develop appropriate attitudes that show genuine concern and caring, as well as skills to plan and implement instruction that addresses cultural and individual diversity.

The National Council for Accreditation of Teacher Education now requires that all prospective teachers have experience with culturally diverse and exceptional populations. Through such exposure they may gain an understanding of the unique contributions, needs, similarities, differences, and interdependencies of students from varying racial, cultural, religious, and socioeconomic backgrounds (National Council for Accreditation of Teacher Education, 1986).

This section looks briefly at the knowledge, attitudes, and skills teachers need in multicultural settings. It is important to emphasize that these three attributes do not work in isolation. Teachers who work in multicultural situations are responsible for developing expertise in all three areas so they can provide learners with the most effective learning environment.

### Knowledge

Teachers may lack factual information about ethnic, racial, and cultural differences; teacher education programs traditionally have not provided appropriate experiences to prepare teachers to teach in an increasingly multicultural classroom. A teacher's diversity knowledge base should include culture, race, ethnicity, and social class, and the teacher should comprehend the implications for the teaching and learning process. Similarly, teachers must know and understand the ramifications of racism, discrimination, prejudice, and injustice and what it means to be a culturally different learner in a predominantly European American school and world. Teachers need sufficient knowledge to be able to understand culturally different learners and to plan both developmentally and culturally appropriate instruction.

In Case Study 9-1 several educators discuss the importance of knowledge, attitudes, and skills.

### Attitudes

Banks (1981) recommends that preservice and in-service teachers acquire the following characteristics: (1) democratic values and attitudes; (2) a multicultural philosophy; (3) the ability to view events and situations from diverse ethnic perspectives and points of view; (4) an understanding of the complex and multidimensional nature of ethnicity in U.S. society; (5) knowledge of the stages of ethnicity and their implications for curriculum and teaching; and (6) the ability to function at increasingly higher stages of ethnicity (p. 193).

---

**CASE STUDY 9-1   Knowledge, Attitudes, and Skills**

The discussion continues in the teachers' lounge at Ocean View Middle School. When working in multicultural situations, which characteristics does a teacher need the most: knowledge, attitudes, or skills? Although the discussion is professional in nature, it is growing increasingly intense.

"Knowledge is what it takes," says one person. "If we know about diversity and the cultural characteristics of learners, we can plan appropriate teaching and learning activities. Also, we will better understand how others' characteristics differ from our own."

"True," another person responds, "but knowledge is not enough. You need proper attitudes; you need to examine your attitudes toward diversity, and you need to respond to culturally diverse students and their needs. History is full of instances in which people had cultural knowledge yet failed to respond when injustices occurred."

"Your arguments are missing a vital point," states a person from another group. "Even with knowledge and attitudes, you will still fail to provide the most effective educational experiences for culturally diverse learners unless you have skills."

They consider the issue and decide that perhaps, it takes all three—knowledge, attitudes, and skills—to provide an effective multicultural education. Some recognize the shortcomings of their positions. Whereas some had tried to improve their knowledge, others had worked to develop more humane attitudes. One had even taken a "skills course" to improve his ability to work with students of varying cultures.

The effective teacher in multicultural education settings, however, needs knowledge, attitudes, and skills. As the educators file back to their classes, someone says, "Quite a challenge, but just think of the benefits for culturally diverse learners; in fact, for all learners."

---

Teachers, for the most part unknowingly, have long transmitted biased messages to students. Whether lining up students for lunch by sex or allowing ability grouping to result in racial segregation, teachers often send messages to students that one sex or race is entitled to preferential treatment. Most educators do not consciously or intentionally stereotype students or discriminate against them; they usually try to treat all students fairly and equitably. Nevertheless, teachers, like others in U.S. society, have learned attitudes and behaviors that are ageist, disability biased, racist, sexist, and enthnocentric. Some biases are so deeply internalized that individuals do not realize they hold them. Only when teachers can (and are willing to) recognize the subtle and unintentional biases of their behavior can they make positive changes in the classroom (Gollnick & Chinn, 1998).

Changing attitudes is a difficult task at best. What can teachers do to change their attitudes toward other cultures, races, and ethnic groups? Banks (1988) reported that direct contact and involvement with people who differ culturally, ethnically, or racially positively changes racial attitudes. A five-week intergroup education workshop consisting of lectures on racial problems, research projects, and visits to community agencies has had significantly positive effects on racial attitudes. Efforts directed toward change should include a variety of experiences such as seminars, visitations, community involvement, committee work, guest speakers, films, multimedia materials, and workshops (Banks, 1988).

---

**FOLLOW THROUGH 9-2   Gaining Knowledge, Attitudes, and Skills to Work in Multicultural Settings**

Culturally appropriate knowledge, attitudes, and skills are essential for educators who deal with students of culturally differing backgrounds on a daily basis. But how can the knowledge, attitudes, and skills be acquired? List ways (such as reading, in-service workshops, college coursework) you can use to become an effective educator in multicultural situations.

---

## Skills

Daily, teachers must understand many complicated areas: learning styles, the dangers of ability grouping, the benefits of cooperative learning, culturally different perceptions of motivation and competition, learners who may not want to excel at the expense of their peers, and stereotypical beliefs about a culture's ability to learn or not to learn. Generally speaking, teachers need the skills to teach children and adolescents in the various cultural groups and the ability to convey that teachers genuinely want what is best for learners, both as students and as people.

Teachers, working in a position to speak for change, have a responsibility to do whatever is possible to reduce racism, prejudice, and injustice among children and adolescents and to instill attitudes of equality and democratic values, which may continue for life. Teachers, indeed, should be significant influences on the values, hopes, and dreams of their students. The classroom should be an open forum of inquiry, in which teachers and students share and effectively analyze diverse points of view and perspectives. In a democratic classroom, teachers and students who are committed to human freedom should have the liberty to express their views, values, and beliefs with regard to democratic ideals such as human dignity, justice, and equality (Banks, 1988).

## Behaviors Essential in Multicultural Classrooms

**1.** Provide learning experiences that reflect individual cultures' learning styles and perceptions of competition, group welfare, sharing, motivation, and success. For example, some Native American learners may prefer sharing and helping peers to competitive learning activities (Sanders, 1987), and Puerto Ricans may not wish to excel or be set apart from the group as being different or excelling (Christensen, 1989).

**2.** Provide learning experiences that reflect gender differences. To confront gender bias in curricular materials, encourage gender integration through peer tutoring and other small learning groups (Sadker, Sadker, & Long, 1993). Encouraging open dialogue and collaboration (Butler & Manning, 1998).

**3.** Encourage and support the development of bilingual programs (Crawford, 1993).

**4.** Immerse students in a variety of written and oral language activities that are meaningful, relevant, and functional in a pluralistic society (Crawford, 1993).

**5.** Treat all students fairly and establish a democratic classroom wherein all students give and receive equal treatment (Sadker & Sadker, 1982).

**6.** Expect the best from *all* students. Encourage all of them to succeed academically; don't automatically assume minority students will perform less well (Garcia, 1984).

**7.** Group heterogeneously whenever possible to enhance self-esteem and promote ethnic interaction (Gollnick & Chinn, 1998).

**8.** Demonstrate daily the necessity of democratic values and attitudes, a multicultural education philosophy, and an ability to view events and situations from diverse ethnic perspectives and points of view (Banks, 1981).

**9.** Recognize as a myth the belief that culturally diverse parents and families do not care about their children's education. This myth has serious consequences (Chavkin, 1989).

**10.** Encourage cross-cultural friendships and social interaction, cooperation, and socialization among boys and girls in the classroom, on the playground, and in the community.

**11.** Address the special problems that culturally diverse parents and families may face, such as language difficulties and misunderstanding the U.S. school system.

**12.** Acquire factual knowledge about learner differences such as culture, race, ethnicity, social class, and gender and commit to having educational experiences reflect these differences.

**13.** Arrange your classroom so that it reflects cultural diversity in bulletin boards and on the walls, and in selection of artwork and artifacts on display.

## *Educator Self-Evaluation*

Educators of all grade levels and all cultures probably agree that some type of evaluation is necessary periodically to determine whether the school is meeting goals and objectives. Whether of an informal or formal nature, the evaluation instrument should focus on teachers' ability to plan and implement appropriate teaching and learning activities for children and adolescents.

---

**FOLLOW THROUGH 9-3   Determining Other Needed Characteristics and Behaviors**

Work in groups of three or four to identify *other* characteristics or behaviors that educators need to address in multicultural settings. Consider this task from several perspectives: What type of teacher do you want to be? What might parents from a culturally different background want for their child? How might a child or adolescent want his or her teacher to be?

Teachers should also use a self-evaluation instrument designed to measure their ability to provide the environment and learning activities that are responsive to culturally diverse learners. Such a self-evaluation should include several questions designed to provide insight into the teacher's knowledge, attitudes, and skills:

**1.** Have there been efforts to understand and respect cultural diversity among learners, not as a problem to solve but as a challenging opportunity and a rich gift?

**2.** Have there been efforts to provide a classroom in which learners feel free to speak and express diverse opinions? Are students free to express opinions contrary to middle-class European American beliefs? Does the teacher repress them or allow other students to stifle diverse opinion?

**3.** Have there been efforts to have the classroom reflect cultural diversity? Do the walls, bulletin boards, and artwork in the classroom demonstrate respect for cultural diversity, or do the contents of the classroom indicate an appreciation or valuing of only one culture?

**4.** Have there been efforts to provide organizational patterns that do not result in segregation of some learners according to race, culture, ethnicity, or social class?

**5.** Have there been efforts to understand language differences and differing learning styles? Has the school developed organizational patterns and instructional methodologies that might be helpful to culturally diverse learners?

**6.** Have there been efforts to understand culturally different learners' perspectives toward motivation, excelling among one's peers, competition, group welfare, and sharing?

**7.** Have there been efforts to understand culturally diverse parents and extended families and to ensure their participation in learners' academic and social life at school?

**8.** Have there been efforts to treat each learner with respect, to consider each learner as equal to other students, and to treat each learner as a valued and worthwhile member of the class? Are all learners accorded similar academic assistance? Do all learners receive help from the school's special service personnel?

**9.** Have there been efforts to allow (and indeed encourage) all students to work in cross-cultural groups, to carry on conversation and meaningful dialogue, and to feel they are valued members of the group?

**10.** Have there been efforts to instill multiculturalism as a genuine part of the teaching and learning process and overall school environment?

---

**FOLLOW THROUGH 9-4   Evaluating Educators' Efforts**

List ten to twelve criteria by which to evaluate a teacher's (or any school professional's) performance working with students of culturally different backgrounds. Perhaps you will want to separate your list into three categories: knowledge, attitudes, and skills. Or you might just want to write a list of characteristics or behaviors. Consider the perspectives of the educator, the parent, and the learner as you make your list.

---

**CASE STUDY 9-2   Teacher Self-Evaluation**

The faculty at PS High School 93 was accustomed to being evaluated by the principal, a central office evaluational specialist, and occasionally peer teachers. The teachers were beginning to realize, however, that something was missing. Evaluation forms indicated the degree of success, yet a teacher basically knew, better than the instrument could suggest, whether he or she had met the school's expectations and whether he or she was working to maximum potential. There was yet another issue: While the existing instruments evaluated overall performance, they did little to determine the educator's efforts to address the needs of culturally diverse learners.

In keeping with the research on evaluation, the counselor suggested a self-evaluation form for educators. Interested faculty members decided to work as a committee to develop a self-evaluation scale—a measure that each teacher might share with peers or administrators (the decision to share was one they could make at a later date).

While the evaluation committee would study the various possibilities and make final recommendations, broad categories for evaluation might include (with the specifics to be added later):

- The teacher's knowledge, attitudes, and skills
- The teacher's classroom environment
- The teacher's instructional process
- The teacher's curricular materials
- The teacher's management system
- The teacher's evaluation process

The specifics to be added later would provide a base for individual educators to evaluate their efforts and commitment to the multicultural education program.

---

Case Study 9-2 suggests that teacher self-evaluation can be one of the most effective means of evaluating one's performance.

## *Organization and Instruction—Cultural Considerations*

Students are often organized for instructional purposes on the basis of test scores, previous grades, teacher recommendations, and other supposedly objective information. The basic rationale for grouping students is to narrow the abilities range and thus provide teachers with a homogeneous group that is supposedly easier to teach. Two dangers inherent in any grouping process are (1) placing students in the wrong group and (2) having an organization pattern that segregates students by race. Although Manning and Lucking (1990) have adequately documented the dangers of grouping students by ability and achievement, the issue of this section is the danger of practicing exclusivity. Emphatically stated, whether considering race, social class, or gender, organizational patterns should not result in segregation, whereby inferior teachers teach some students or teach in inferior schools, and other students receive preferential treatment. Organizational patterns should result in a student population that is as representative as possible of the entire school population and, if possible, the composition of the community at large.

**IMPLEMENTING RESEARCH 9-2    Community-Centered Approaches**

James Jupp (1998) maintains that the current approach to multicultural instruction is part of a revisionist tradition that promotes the understanding of minority cultures and embraces a world community outlook. At its worst, it is a blind, disorganized, and romanticized misrepresentation of the cultures it pretends to illuminate. At its best, it provides meaningful materials that meet specific community needs. Jupp also maintains that multicultural instruction must serve the local community.

The use of multicultural instruction is often justified as providing an understanding of the diverse cultures in the "world community" (p. 15). The rationalization holds that by understanding other world cultures, we better understand ourselves. The same justification is echoed in many textbooks and manuals.

Jupp maintains that this high-sounding notion of "world community" (p. 15) often boils down to tokenism—a Mexican American short story, a smattering of African and Asian legends, and a few Japanese haiku as part of the curriculum. Such multicultural tokenism provides only a cursory glance at minority cultures and a stereotypical view of the cultures that the material pretends to represent. The problem is further complicated by teachers' lack of knowledge of the broad panorama of world cultures and also by curricular materials that lack quality and depth.

To remedy this situation, Jupp suggests that teachers select multicultural materials that serve the specific communities.

### Implementing the Research

We agree with Jupp that teachers perhaps sometimes take an approach that is too comprehensive. Trying to adopt a world community approach might be the cause of what Jupp describes as a disorganized and romanticized approach.

Educators can examine the diversity of their own communities and design multicultural instruction that reflects local diversity. This approach will likely appeal to students because they will see its relevance to their culture and community.

Teachers working in border communities might focus on Latin American authors such as Isabel Allende or Americo Paredes. Inner-city teachers might focus on Mexican American and African American authors such as Rudolfo Gonzales and Toni Morrison, who deal with urban, ethnic settings.

Teachers in communities with Asian American students might bring in a unit that explores the influence of Eastern religious thought in the United States. Anglo-dominant schools might read Chinua Achebe's *Things Fall Apart* or Peter Abrams' *A Wreath for Udomo,* which deal with problems of colonialism. This community-centered approach is an antidote to the softness of the "world community" approach.

*Source:* Jupp, J. C. (1998). A community-centered approach to multicultural instruction. *English Journal,* *88*(2), 15–16.

One method is for educators to take a community-centered approach as discussed in Implementing Research 9-2.

Perhaps unconsciously some teachers exclude females from learning activities and school experiences. Gender Perspectives 9-1 suggests how females can succeed in school.

---

**GENDER PERSPECTIVES 9-1**   Helping Girls Thrive in School

McDaniel uses Alice from *Alice in Wonderland* and Dorothy in *The Wizard of Oz* to show how schools often fail to help girls identify their special talents and sometimes don't provide the kinds of role models that girls need to develop confidence and competence. McDaniel summarizes the findings of *How Schools Shortchange Girls,* a 1992 report of the American Association of University Women: girls get less attention, less praise, and fewer constructive comments; reports of sexual harassment keep increasing; curricular materials often stereotype girls and women. Parents who want gifted daughters to thrive in school should:

- hold high expectations for girls
- encourage high levels of activity
- promote interests in mathematics outside of school
- monitor television programming for sexist stereotypes
- assign boys and girls household tasks on a nonsexist basis
- introduce girls to a wide variety of professional women
- encourage girls to take mathematics and science courses

---

*Source:* McDaniel, T. R. (1994). The education of Alice and Dorothy: Helping girls thrive in school. *The Clearing House, 68,* 43–45.

## Ability Grouping

Ability grouping may result in a form of segregation. Ability-grouping patterns often parallel students' nonacademic characteristics, such as race or ethnic background, socioeconomic class, or personal appearance. Learners of low socioeconomic status and minority groups often find themselves in lower-ability groups. Such practices may be discriminatory, because the segregation of students is along ethnic and social-class lines (Dawson, 1987). These patterns of grouping appear to be related to ethnicity and socioeconomic standing, rather than purely academic abilities and achievement levels (Riccio, 1985). Case Study 9-3 on page 236 shows how ability grouping can result in a form of segregation.

## Cooperative Learning

People who help one another by joining forces to achieve a common goal generally feel more positively about each other and are willing to interact more positively when performing collective tasks. Rather than treating academic learning

---

**FOLLOW THROUGH 9-5**   Heterogeneous Education

Many teachers complain that teaching heterogeneous groups can be difficult because of the wide array of academic abilities and levels. Name four or five ways educators can teach effectively in heterogenous classrooms (in which students are randomly assigned to classes without consideration of their ability levels).

---

### CASE STUDY 9-3    Culturally Diverse Groups and Ability Grouping

In a meeting with all the fifth-grade teachers, Dr. Mallory, the principal at Southside Elementary School, voiced a concern that some classes consisted almost entirely of culturally diverse students. "How did this happen?" she questioned. While two classes were almost all minority, the other two classes were almost all white.

One teacher explained that the students were in ability groups, based on their achievement test scores, reading grades, and the recommendations of their previous teachers. "The groups just worked out that way," he explained.

The principal pointed out that a form of segregation was occurring and that students did not have adequate opportunities for social interaction. As professional educators they had a responsibility to address the situation. Dr. Mallory explained that evidence shows clearly that ability grouping does not improve student

achievement in the elementary school; ability grouping may seriously impair self-concepts of low-ability learners; teachers interact differently with students from various ability groups; and ability groups too often parallel students' nonacademic characteristics, such as race, ethnicity, and social class. Because they had to change the existing segregation, Dr. Mallory asked for specific suggestions to remediate the situation.

The fifth-grade teachers brainstormed and came up with possibilities: heterogeneous grouping, individualized instruction, mastery learning, and cooperative learning. The teachers decided that because the principal had mandated change (and that she was correct about students being segregated), they would group heterogeneously and then try other means of providing appropriate instruction.

---

and social or intergroup relations as two distinct entities, cooperative learning has contributed positively to overall intergroup relations and particularly to improving relations with multicultural and multiethnic students (Sharan, 1985). Cooperative learning procedures can reinforce the efforts of culturally diverse children to continue their schoolwork successfully. Children who work cooperatively in groups, rather than in isolation, are usually motivated to help each other carry out the assigned or chosen project (Tyler, 1989).

Research on cooperative learning and intergroup relationships has concluded that students in cooperative learning situations had a greater appreciation for cooperative-learning classmates. Specifically, cooperative learning increases contact between students, provides a feeling of group membership, engages learners in pleasant activities, and requires that team members work toward a common goal (Slavin, 1996).

Several research studies have indicated that students' working cooperatively can contribute positively to specific multiethnic populations. Aronson, Blaney, Stephan, Sikes, and Snapp (1978) concluded that both black and white students working in cooperative learning situations liked school better than those of the same ethnic groups working in competitive classrooms. Other research suggests that working cooperatively seems to have particularly strong effects on Hispanic and black students, regardless of achievement levels (Slavin, 1987). One study indicates that European and Asian Americans, in a learning situation similar to the

Jigsaw method, had more positive attitudes toward Mexican Americans than learners in competitive classes. A study of Jigsaw II–related classes that included recent European and West Indian immigrants and white Canadians documented substantially more cross-ethnic friendships than in the control groups (Slavin, 1983).

Concerning specific cooperative learning methods, there have been positive effects with Student Teams–Achievement Divisions (STAD), Teams-Games-Tournament (TGT), Team-Assisted Individualization (TAI), and Jigsaw II (Slavin, 1996). Studies also found that improved student attitudes and behaviors toward classmates of different ethnic backgrounds were extended to classmates of different groups (Sharan & Sharan, 1989/1990). In conclusion, Slavin (1987) summarized by saying that cooperative learning strategies apparently contribute to students' seeing each other in a positive light and forming friendships based on human qualities. Table 9-1 summarizes some cooperative learning methods.

**TABLE 9-1   Overview of Selected Cooperative Learning Methods**

| Method/Proponent | Brief Description/Comments |
| --- | --- |
| *Learning Together* (Johnson & Johnson, 1987, 1989/1990) | Emphasizing cooperative effort, *Learning Together* has five basic elements: positive interdependence (students believe that they are responsible for both their learning and the team's); face-to-face interaction (students explain their learning and help others with assignments); individual accountability (students demonstrate mastery of material); social skills (students communicate effectively, build and maintain trust, and resolve conflicts); group processing (groups periodically assess their progress and ways to improve effectiveness). Uses four- or five-member heterogeneous teams. |
| Student Teams–Achievement Divisions (STAD; Slavin, 1978) | Four-student learning teams (mixed in performance levels, sex, and ethnicity); teacher presents lesson, students work in teams and help others master material. Students take quizzes; cooperative efforts are not allowed on quizzes; teams earn reward. Application to most grades and subjects. |
| Teams-Games-Tournament (TGT; Devries & Slavin, 1978) | Using the same teacher presentation and teamwork as STAD, TGT replaces the quizzes with weekly tournaments in which students compete with members of other teams to contribute points to team scores. Competition occurs at "tournament tables" against others with similar academic records. The winner of each tournament brings six points to her or his team. Low achievers compete with low achievers (a similar arrangement exists for high achievers), a system that provides all students with equal opportunity for success. As with STAD, teams earn rewards. Applicable to most grades and subjects. |
| Jigsaw (Aronson, Blaney, Stephan, Sikes, & Snapp, 1978) | Teachers assign students to six-member teams to work on academic material divided into sections. Each member reads a section; then, members of different teams meet to become experts. Students return to groups and teach other members about the sections. Students must listen to their teammates to learn other sections. |

*Continued*

**TABLE 9-1**   *Continued*

| Method/Proponent | Brief Description/Comments |
|---|---|
| Jigsaw II (Slavin, 1987) | Students work in four- or five-member teams as in TGT or STAD. Rather than being assigned specific parts, students read a common narrative (e.g., a chapter). Students also receive a topic on which to become an expert. Learners with same topics meet together as in Jigsaw, then teach the material to their original group. Students take individual quizzes. |
| Team-Assisted Individualization (TAI) (Slavin, Leavey, & Madden, 1989) | Uses four-member mixed-ability groups (as with STAD and TGT); differs from STAD and TGT in that it combines cooperative learning and individualized instruction and is applicable only to mathematics in grades three through six. Learners take a placement test, then proceed at their own pace. Team members check one another's work and help with problems. Without help, students take unit tests that student monitors score. Each week the teacher evaluates and gives team rewards. |
| Cooperative Integrated Reading and Composition (CIRC, Madden, Slavin, & Stevens, 1986) | Designed to teach reading and writing in the upper elementary grades, CIRC assigns students to different reading teams. Teacher works with one team, while other teams engage in cognitive activities: reading, predicting story endings, summarizing stories, writing responses, practicing decoding, and learning vocabulary. Teams follow sequence of teacher instruction, team practice, team preassessments, and quizzes. A team does not take a quiz until the team feels each student is ready. Teams receive rewards. |
| Group Investigation (Sharan & Sharan, 1989/1990) | Groups form according to common interest in a topic. Students plan research, divide learning assignments among members, synthesize and summarize feelings, and present the findings to the entire class. |

*Source:* Manning, M. L., & Lucking, R. (1991). The what, why, and how of cooperative learning. *The Clearing House, 64,* p. 153. Reprinted by permission.

## *Language Differences*

Language diversity is so great in some parts of the United States that sometimes classroom communication is virtually impossible. In addition, many schools are unable to provide appropriate learning experiences for children whose native language is not English. As a result, language-minority children don't learn the essential lessons of school and do not fully participate in the economic, social, and political life of the United States (Bowman, 1989). As they decide on organizing students for instruction, culturally sensitive educators recognize the dilemma that learners with limited English skills often face.

Maintaining that language differences pose a major stumbling block for Native American students, Little Soldier (1989) offers several precepts for educators:

1. Implement cooperative learning techniques. Native Americans, reared to value cooperation and sharing, are not accustomed culturally to work alone or to compete for grades and teacher approval. Cooperative learning situations in

which warm personal relationships develop have contributed to the language development of Native American pupils.

2. Avoid large-group, formal lessons in the lecture-recitation mode. Native American students tend to withdraw during formal patterns. These learners perceive more opportunity in student-to-student dialogues and group problem-solving efforts.

3. Liberally give encouragement and positive reinforcement. Include language lifting techniques and modeling of correct language patterns. Avoid correcting pupils' oral language errors except during formal language lessons (Little Soldier, 1989).

Bowman (1989) offers several suggestions for educators working with language-minority learners:

1. The use of formal language, teacher leadership and control of verbal exchanges, question-and-answer formats, and references to increasingly abstract ideas often characterize a classroom environment with which many minority children are unfamiliar. Whenever possible, communication is made easier if these ideas overlap with those the learners already know.

2. Language-minority learners should experience familiar communication styles to establish a basis for communication. This basis may include speaking in the child's primary language, using culturally appropriate styles of address, and relying on management patterns that are familiar to and comfortable for children.

3. The meanings of words, gestures, and actions may be quite different from culture to culture. As Little Soldier (1989) suggests, educators should carefully consider language differences and developmental levels for all decisions concerning organizing for instruction.

Educators interested in teaching and learning contexts also need to consider the goals of schooling in a culturally diverse classroom, the topic of Implementing Research 9-3 on page 240.

## The School Environment

The school environment includes all experiences with which learners come in contact: content, instructional methods, the actual teaching and learning process and environment, the professional staff and other staff members, as well as the actions and attitudes of other students. This definition of environment is synonymous with curriculum itself.

### Working toward a Multicultural School Environment

It is important that the multicultural environment demonstrate genuine respect and concern for all learners, regardless of their racial, cultural, or ethnic backgrounds. With a supportive school environment, culturally different children, along with other

---

**IMPLEMENTING RESEARCH 9-3   The Goals of Schooling in Culturally Diverse Classrooms**

Dennis McInerney and Valentina McInerney (1998) maintain that schools often reward learners for achievement behaviors that reflect Western values. These values are often incompatible with some cultures' values and beliefs. For example, in some cultures people have a problem with doing better than others, surpassing norms, and achieving success with little effort, especially at the expense of other people. The authors discuss mastery goals and performance goals, which in Western educational settings have focused on individual achievement of goals. This approach has allowed little attention to be given to group orientations such as working to preserve in-group integrity, interdependence of learners, and harmonious relationships. For example, in some cultures, such as Navajo communities, children and adolescents are motivated by social goals that reflect their need to maintain group allegiance and solidarity. Also, traditional Navajo beliefs hold that too much thinking about the future is taboo.

**Implementing the Research**

1.  Educators need to recognize that Western perceptions of education might conflict with some cultural groups' perceptions of motivation and success. These conflicts might explain their seeming lack of motivation.
2.  Cultural groups that value group orientation (one should not achieve individually at the expense of the group, for example) should be allowed to engage in instructional activities that focus on group projects and cooperative learning.
3.  Students should be given some choice in the selection of learning tasks; that is, they should be allowed to choose instructional activities that reflect their interests and in which they will be intrinsically motivated.

---

*Source:* McInerney, D. M., & McInerney, V. (1998). The goals of schooling in culturally diverse classrooms. *The Clearing House, 71*(6), 363–366.

learners, can learn to take an active role in a democratic society, guided by relevant understanding, and develop skills in communication and computation, social attitudes and interests, and human appreciation. The school environment should support school learning and socialization for all students. A supportive school environment is one in which the morale of both teachers and students is high. Teachers believe in their mission to help guide and stimulate the learning activities of their students and are pleased with their students' responsive behavior (Tyler, 1989).

Although it is impossible to describe in detail all the factors that make a school environment responsive to cultural diversity, briefly discussing several areas illustrates the environment in its broadest sense: the unconditional acceptance of diversity, the promotion of positive self-concepts and cultural identities, and a faculty and staff composition that represents the cultural diversity of the school population. The school environment is by no means limited to these three aspects. These three, however, have a powerful influence on how learners perceive others' opinions of cultural diversity.

**FOLLOW THROUGH 9-6    Addressing Diversity in Its Many Forms**

1. Check district and school policies, procedures, practices, curriculum guides, lesson plans, and instructional materials to be sure they are free of bias toward race, gender, religion, culture, and disabilities.
2. Make newcomers feel welcome through a formal program.
3. Be sure that assignments are not offensive or frustrating to students of cultural minorities. For example, asking students to discuss or write about their Christmas experiences is inappropriate for non-Christian students. Let students discuss their similar holidays.
4. Form a schoolwide planning committee to address the implementation of multicultural education.
5. Contact your district curriculum coordinators for ideas and assistance.
6. Let faculty knowledgeable about multicultural topics provide in-service for others or guest-teach their classes.
7. Take a cultural census of the class or school to find out what cultures are represented; let students be the ethnographers.
8. Form a multicultural club.
9. Select a theme to tie various multicultural activities together; hold school programs with art, music, and dramatic presentations; hold a multicultural fair or festival featuring music, art, dance, dress, and so on; adopt a multicultural theme for existing activities.
10. Hold a school cross-cultural food festival.
11. Have multicultural celebrations and teach-ins with schoolwide activities in all classes.
12. Decorate classrooms, hallways, and the library media center with murals, bulletin boards, posters, artifacts, and other materials representative of the students in the class or school or other cultures the class is studying. Posters and other information are available from foreign government travel bureaus and education agencies, private travel agencies, consulates, the United Nations, and ethnic and cultural organizations.
13. Designate a permanent bulletin board for multicultural news and displays.
14. Help students develop the skills necessary to locate and organize information about cultures from the library media center, the mass media, people, and personal observations.
15. Have students write to foreign consulates, tourist bureaus, minority organizations, and others, for information and decorative materials.
16. Supplement textbooks with authentic materials on different cultures from newspapers, magazines, and other media of the culture. Such materials are available from the Department of Education Foreign Language Documentation Center.
17. Take advantage of community resources. Have representatives of various cultures talk to classes; actors portray characters or events; and musicians and dance groups, such as salsa bands or bagpipe units, perform.
18. Work with the library media center on special bibliographies, collections, displays, and audiovisuals.
19. Hold a mock legislature to debate current or historical issues affecting minorities and cultural groups.
20. Hold oratorical, debate, essay, poster, art, brain brawl, or other competitions with a multicultural focus.

*Continued*

21. Feature stories in the school newspaper on multicultural topics; publish a multicultural newspaper or newsletter.
22. Make reminders during daily announcements about multicultural activities.
23. Use your Newspapers-in-Education program.
24. Develop a radio or television program with a multicultural theme for the educational or local community access channel.
25. Study works in science, art, music, and literature of various cultures, focusing on the contributions of minority individuals.
26. Have students write short stories or essays on multicultural topics.
27. Have student debates, speeches, skits, and so forth on multicultural topics and present them to classes, parent–teacher organizations (PTOs), nursing homes, and other community groups.
28. Study the provisions and freedoms of the Constitution as they relate to minorities.
29. Compare and contrast other cultures with that of U.S. mainstream culture.
30. Discuss the issues and personalities involved in various cultures from historical, political, and literary standpoints.
31. Use skills and information from various disciplines (math, social studies, geography, language arts) to compare population, economy, politics, lifestyle, culture, and other aspects of different culture groups in the United States during different historical periods and as they are today. Discuss the meaning of the differences.
32. Discuss the relevance of the Constitution and government in dealing with today's problems that relate to minorities and cultural diversity.
33. Hold mock campaigns and elections based on multicultural issues.
34. Hold a video film festival dealing with various cultures and multicultural issues.
35. Have children of other cultures and their parents share native songs with classmates; have students share instruments or recordings of their native cultures.
36. Take field trips to local multicultural sites, such as a neighborhood, ethnic recreation or social center, workplace, historical site, museum, restaurant, and grocery.
37. Focus on geography skills and knowledge in geography courses as part of related courses.
38. Establish pen-pal or video exchange programs with students from other cultures.
39. Discuss the importance of international trade and the skills necessary for employment in that area.
40. Focus on the everyday artifacts of cultures that differentiate the way people behave in different cultures, such as greetings, friendly exchanges, farewells, expressions of respect, verbal taboos, ways of using numbers, body language, and gestures. Also consider gender roles, folklore, childhood literature, discipline, festivals, holidays, religious practices, games, music, pets, personal possessions, keeping warm and cool, cosmetics, fashions, and health and hygiene practices. Competitions, dating and courtship, transportation and traffic, sports, radio and television programs, hobbies, foods, family mealtimes, snacking, and cafes and restaurants provide further aspects of culture to compare. Also yards and sidewalks, parks and playgrounds, flowers and gardens, movies and theaters, circuses, museums, vacations and resort areas, careers are rich sources.
41. Discuss what it means to be a member of a minority or different cultural group.
42. Discuss what it means to be a responsible U.S. citizen.

*Source:* Multicultural teaching strategies. (1990). (Technical Assistance. Paper No. 9). Tallahassee: Florida State Department of Education.

---

**FOLLOW THROUGH 9-7    Making Classrooms Reflect Diversity**

Ask your students to suggest ways to make the classroom better reflect the cultural diversity of the students. Consider things like artwork, displays showing contributions of various cultures, and holiday displays, just to name a few. Ask students how school rules, policies, and expectations could better reflect the needs of culturally diverse learners.

---

Recommendations for creating a teaching and learning environment that reflects the cultural diversity of the school include:

- As a part of the daily learning environment, provide and consistently update a variety of multiethnic, multicultural, and self-awareness materials.
- Plan learning experiences that are flexible, unbiased, and inclusive of contributions from diverse cultures.
- Find good people to serve as role models and material resources that focus on problems in a pluralistic society.
- Adopt instructional strategies relevant to the physical, emotional, social, and intellectual development of children of multiethnic heritage.
- Use instructional material that shows individuals from diverse cultural groups working in different occupational and social roles. Make sure all materials are free of bias, omissions, and stereotypes.
- Adopt flexible scheduling that provides ample time and space for children to share their uniqueness through role-play, art, conversation, and games.
- Continuously use ideas and materials that represent cultures throughout the year, not just during special holidays such as Black History Week, Christmas, Thanksgiving, Hanukkah, or Chinese New Year (Southern Association for Children under Six, 1988).

Believing that an educational setting should allow children to feel accepted, encouraged, and respected, Banks (1988) offers several insights into creating appropriate school environments in our culturally pluralistic society:

1. The total school environment should undergo reform, not just the courses and programs. The school's informal "hidden curriculum" is as important as, or perhaps more important than, the formal course of study.
2. Ethnic content should be part of all subject areas from preschool through grade twelve and beyond.
3. Learning centers, libraries, and resource centers should include resources for history, literature, music, folklore, views of life, and the arts of the various groups of people.
4. Ethnic diversity should be reflected in assembly programs; classroom, hallway, and entrance decorations; cafeteria menus; counseling interactions; and, as we previously discussed, extracurricular activities.
5. School-sponsored dances and other such activities should reflect a respect for a culturally pluralistic society.

## Promoting Self-Esteem and Positive Cultural Identities

It is imperative that educators understand the school environment's influence (perhaps an unconscious or unrecognized influence) on a child's self-concept and cultural identity. Without doubt, the school environment affects both the manner in which children perceive themselves and their cultural images.

Self-concept, or self-image, is a complex set of beliefs that an individual holds about himself or herself. A person may have more than one self-image and actually hold positive feelings in some areas and negative images in others. For example, a person might have a positive self-image in intellectual pursuits while harboring negative feelings toward his or her athletic abilities. The actions of others or the way in which learners think others perceive and treat them significantly influences their self-concepts. A person's self-concept affects behavior, school achievement, and social development (Bennett, 1986).

The environment should allow culturally diverse people to feel a sense of being able to cope or to feel that they can control their lives at least to some extent. Youngsters who feel torn between two cultures may have a low self-image because they assume they cannot be successful in either society (Ramsey, 1987).

Luftig (1983) reported a study of Native American adolescents who felt the need to choose between being part of the European American culture or being part of their tribal culture. These adolescents had lower self-esteem than their peers.

Self-concepts of learners relate not only to their race, culture, and social class but also to their feelings of power in the school environment. The task facing educators is to help students build positive perceptions about their reference groups and to develop confidence in actively participating in social discussion and change (Ramsey, 1987).

The educators' goal should be to provide a school environment that either raises or contributes positively to the self-concepts and the racial and cultural pride of all people. Students should not feel like intruders in a school that emphasizes middle-class European American values, expectations, and perspectives.

---

**FOLLOW THROUGH 9-8    Teaching Students to Understand and Appreciate Their Diversity**

Have students clip from magazines and prepare a collage that reveals things about their lives. Talk about the things they might include: birthplace—picture, part of a map; baby pictures; things they like—food, sports; their families—people, pets; or where they have lived or traveled. Have the students write brief biographical descriptions that they can attach to the collage or read to the class.

---

*Source:* Tiedt, P. L., & Tiedt, I. M. (1995). *Multicultural teaching: A handbook of activities, information, and resources.* Boston: Allyn & Bacon, pp. 45–46.

**FOR ADDITIONAL INFORMATION    Internet Addresses**

**Multicultural Resources from James Madison University**
http://falcon.jmu.edu/~ramseyil/
multipub.htm   Provides a wealth of resources for the design and implementation of multicultural education programs.

**Schedule**
http://www.potter.flint.k12.mi.us/
schedule.htm   Provides information on Potter Multicultural Global Elementary School

**A Multicultural Curriculum and Standardized Testing Program**
http://multicultural.mining.co.com/library/
weekly/aa100498.htm   Provides a look at both curriculum and standardized testing from multicultural perspectives.

**KCRPDC Educational Equity**
http://oseda.missouri.edu/rpdc/umkc/
equity.html   Provides a wealth of multicultural education resources such as lesson plans, suggested reading lists, mailing lists, multicultural literature, and instructional activities.

## Diversity among Faculty and Staff

Members of different ethnic groups must be an integral part of the school's instructional, administrative, and supportive staffs. School personnel—teachers, principals, cooks, custodians, secretaries, students, and counselors—make contributions as important to multicultural environments as do the courses of study and instructional materials. Students learn important lessons about culture and cultural diversity by observing interactions among different racial, ethnic, and cultural groups in their school; hearing verbal exchanges between the professional and support staffs; and observing the extent to which the staff is culturally representative of the student population. It is imperative that schools establish and implement policies to recruit and maintain a totally multicultural school staff (Banks, 1988).

## Cultural Perspectives

### Socioeconomic and Class Differences

The student's socioeconomic level and social class deserve consideration as elementary and secondary educators plan teaching and learning experiences. Jarolimek and Foster (1989) aptly illustrated how social stratification in America places some groups at a disadvantage.

If a group of individuals has particular characteristics that are valued by a society, the group so identified will enjoy high status. The reverse is also true. Thus, when speaking of upper and lower classes, we are referring to groups of individuals who either have or do not have qualities in common that are prized by a larger society.

In the United States, upper classes are those groups that have wealth, advanced education, professional occupations, and relative freedom from concern about their material needs. Conversely, lower classes are those groups that live in or on the edge of poverty, have poor education, are irregularly employed or employed in jobs requiring little or no training, often require assistance from government welfare agencies, and are constantly concerned with meeting the basic needs of life (p. 11).

At least two perspectives stand out as being important for educators to consider: (1) some social classes may be able to provide their children with additional experiences that may be conducive to education and academic achievement, and (2) the belief that determination, hard work, and middle-class values pay rich dividends. The problem with the former is that many students do not bring to school experiential backgrounds that contribute to their education. The latter often causes poor people to be perceived as and feel like failures who lack the ambition or determination to pursue long-term goals.

Realistically speaking, culturally diverse students often come from poorer financial backgrounds and homes in which language differences impede communication and upward social mobility. Such obstacles, however, do not mean that these social classes value education and school achievement any less. It is educators' responsibility to provide teaching and learning experiences that build on the strengths and backgrounds of all children and adolescents.

As we suggested in Part I, substantial numbers of Native, African, Asian, Hispanic, and European American children and adolescents experience economic deprivation. Although government efforts and other educational programs (Gollnick & Chinn, 1998) have bettered the lot of many disadvantaged youth, considerable improvement is still necessary as the following list indicates:

1. Native Americans are the poorest economically, the least employed, the unhealthiest. They have the lowest income of all groups in the United States (Dorriss, 1981).
2. Nearly one of every two African American children lives in poverty; almost two-thirds of young African American children live in homes relying on public assistance (Clark-Johnson, 1988).
3. Asian Americans probably have the highest earning power of the culturally diverse populations, but there is a tremendous range in income in this group. The fact that some Asian American families have more than one wage earner raises their income levels (Asian and Pacific Islander data, 1993a,f).
4. Among Hispanic Americans, 38.7 percent of all children live at the poverty level, and 71 percent live in homes in which the head of household is female (Colburn & Melillo, 1987; Valero-Figueira, 1988).

Although these facts are disturbing, it is important to emphasize the economic advances and achievements of culturally diverse learners and their families during the past decade or two. Educators should objectively consider each learner to determine individual strengths and weaknesses. To equate poverty with a particular culture, race, or ethnic group is a serious mistake and can jeopardize a learner's educational future.

What are the implications for educators working with children and adolescents from lower socioeconomic and social classes?

1. Teachers, counselors, and administrators should recognize the dangers of associating negative and harmful expectations with culturally diverse groups and lower classes. In fact, educators should periodically review their beliefs about children and adolescents as well as their behavioral and academic expectations (Gollnick & Chinn, 1998).

2. Educators should examine curricular and instructional efforts to determine whether they reflect only middle-class European American perspectives. Culturally diverse learners and students from low socioeconomic backgrounds need to see a reflection of their values and lifestyles in the educational content and in the instructional methods (Gollnick & Chinn, 1998).

3. Educators should be on a constant lookout for grouping patterns that segregate students along cultural, racial, or ethnic lines. Teachers often place students from lower socioeconomic classes or who are culturally diverse in lower ability groups. Such practices may be discriminatory, because students are segregated along ethnic and social class lines (Dawson, 1987; Manning & Lucking, 1990).

Linton and Foster (1990) suggested that schools need to create "powerful environments" for students they felt to be "underclass youth." Referring specifically to African Americans, Linton and Foster questioned why so many of the poorer classes seem unable to move upward from the horrendous conditions of underclass life. Reasons may include continuing patterns of racism, not enough government assistance, too much government assistance, the large-scale loss of jobs from urban centers, and the abandonment of the ghettos by upwardly mobile African Americans.

To help these underclass youth, Linton and Foster recommend that inner-city schools have powerful environments in which students are "expected to strive and achieve in all dimensions of school life, including curriculum studies and social relationships" (p. 28). The two authors expect the staff to project a success-oriented, winning attitude for students to internalize. Instead of telling the students to meet high expectations, the teachers should tell them how to meet teachers' expectations. Included in this powerful environment would be academic subject matter, personal and interpersonal skills (how to talk, dress, and handle anger), and how to deal with authority figures.

## The Role of Parents and Families

Research (Simich-Dudgeon, 1987) supports the importance of parent involvement and cooperative relationships between parents and schools. First, parental interest and participation in schools and classrooms has a positive influence on academic achievement. Second, parents involved in academic activities with their children gain knowledge that helps them to assess their children's education. They can help their children with areas of education in which they need assistance. Third, the results of parental involvement in tutoring limited English–proficient students are consistent with those for native English–speaking students and their families. To be effective as home tutors, all parents need school support and direct teacher involvement (Simich-Dudgeon, 1987).

Yao (1988) contends that the educators must employ special strategies to accommodate the unique cultural characteristics of Asian immigrant parents. Their agenda should include: (1) educators asking themselves some difficult questions about their prejudices and stereotypical beliefs about Asian Americans, (2) understanding Asian beliefs about education, and (3) providing opportunities for Asian American parents to participate in school activities, to communicate through newsletters, and to serve on advisory committees (Yao, 1988).

Educators working with European Americans usually work only with the mother and the father. Culturally diverse children and adolescents, however, often perceive the roles of grandparents, aunts, and uncles as similar to those of the mother and the father. For this reason, educators should welcome extended families who are interested in the learner's educational progress. Culturally diverse parents and families may not understand the U.S. school system and its emphasis on competition and individual welfare and achievement over group accomplishments. Teachers may offer suggestions and directions to parents and families who are able to assist their children and adolescents. Teachers need a better understanding of culturally diverse families and their values, customs, traditions, and expectations. All too often, teachers view the benefits of parent involvement too narrowly. Not only do children benefit, but parents and teachers as well.

## Learner Evaluation

The evaluation of learners should include a consideration of individual and cultural differences, variations in learning and testing styles, and differences in motivation. Rather than evaluating only what paper and pencil can measure, evaluation efforts should also focus on student behaviors, attitudes, and everyday actions. For example, a student might be able to list examples of racist behavior and offer several valid reasons on paper why racism should be reduced. The evaluation process, however, should also include a consideration of actions. Do students make racist remarks? Do students demonstrate racial harmony? Do students engage in segregationist activities? Generally speaking, have students developed respect and acceptance for, as well as knowledge of, our increasingly culturally diverse world?

## Evaluating Learners' Progress

Sleeter and Grant (1988) offer several recommendations for educators planning and implementing programs that evaluate learners:

1. Evaluation procedures should not include standardized achievement tests that are monocultural in nature and that sort students into different groups that result in different and unequal opportunities.
2. Evaluation procedures should not penalize students by requiring skills that are extraneous to what is being evaluated. For example, a science teacher assessing science concepts should not require students to read and write about their skill level.
3. Evaluation procedures designed to assess students' English proficiency levels should take into account the different contexts in which school communication takes place and the different factors involved.
4. Evaluation procedures should be free of sexist or racist stereotypes.

As we can see, decisions concerning evaluation include both what should be evaluated and a determination of the evaluation methods. As with all curricular efforts, educators should closely match the evaluation with goals and objectives, should measure what was taught, and should measure attitudes and behaviors as well as cognitive knowledge.

## Summing Up

Educators who plan teaching, learning, and classroom environments in multicultural settings should remember to

1. Recognize and respect learner diversity: culture, race, ethnicity, individuality, gender, social class, and religion.
2. Develop the knowledge, attitudes, and skills to teach and relate to culturally diverse children and adolescents.
3. Recognize that some organizational practices contribute to exclusivity and segregation and that, therefore, educators should provide instructional methods to which culturally diverse children and adolescents can most effectively relate.
4. Plan a school curriculum and environment that reflects respect for all cultural, ethnic, social class, and religious differences among people and that promotes learners' self-concepts and cultural identities.
5. Recognize and respond appropriately to cultural perspectives that influence the academic achievement and overall school progress of culturally diverse learners; for example, socioeconomic class and social class, parents and families, and learner evaluation.
6. Implement a teaching and learning environment that affects positively how children and adolescents feel about school, about being culturally different in a

predominantly European American school, and about feeling genuinely accepted and cared about.

7. Provide culturally diverse learners with an administration, faculty, and staff that reflects the cultural diversity of the overall school population.

## Suggested Learning Activities

1. Design a plan for involving culturally diverse parents and immediate families in the teaching and learning process. Explain specifically how you would address the following points: language barriers between culturally diverse parents and you; explaining school expectations to parents and families who might not understand how U.S. schools function; and ways you might involve parents and families.

2. Use a case-study approach to study a culturally diverse learner and to pinpoint cultural differences in the ways the student learns, perceives events, and behaves. In a paper summarizing your observations and reflections, state how the student's behavior and attitudes might affect school achievement and how the school might provide more appropriate teaching and learning experiences for this learner.

3. Observe a teaching demonstration to determine a teacher's "unintended bias." Did the teacher call on more girls than boys or more European Americans than Hispanic Americans, expect Asian Americans to answer more difficult questions, or tend to ignore students from lower socioeconomic groups? How might you help this teacher recognize bias? What items would you include on a teacher self-evaluation scale designed to help teachers recognize unintended bias?

## Suggestions for Collaborative Efforts

Form groups of three or four that, if possible, represent U.S. cultural and gender diversity. Working collaboratively, focus your group's attention toward the following efforts:

1. Have each member of your group survey elementary and secondary school teachers to determine their efforts to include multicultural perspectives in their teaching and learning activities. Look specifically at items such as curriculum content, teacher expectations for achievement and behavior, grouping strategies, testing and evaluation, and involvement of parents and extended family members. How does your group believe teachers could improve their efforts?

2. Devise a checklist to evaluate the degree to which the overall school environment reflects multicultural perspectives. Although your group should include perspectives it feels are important, the basic underlying question should be: Does the overall school environment portray multicultural perspectives? Other questions might be: Is there evidence that cultural, ethnic, social class, and religious diversity is accepted? Are there deliberate attempts to promote positive self-concepts and cultural identities? Is cultural diversity represented among faculty and staff and at all levels of administration?

## Expanding Your Horizons: Additional Journal Readings and Books

Borden, J. F. (1998). The pitfalls and possibilities for organizing quality ESL programs. *Middle School Journal, 29*(3), 25–33.

*Focusing specifically on Asian American students, Borden offers five recommendations for implementing high-quality ESL programs and discusses both pullout programs and immersion programs.*

Gallagher, J. (1998). The language of learning. *Middle Ground, 2*(2), 6–10, 24.

*Gallagher maintains that attacks on bilingual education ignore the varied needs of nonnative speakers and looks at several successful programs.*

Huang, S. L., & Waxman, H. C. (1997). Classroom behaviors of Asian American students in mathematics. (ERIC Document Reproduction Service No: ED 408 166).

*This article examines Asian American classroom behaviors such as classroom activities, classroom settings, and interactions with teachers.*

Manning, M. L., & Lucking, R. (1993). Cooperative learning and multicultural classrooms. *The Clearing House 67,* 12–16.

*This article examines research on cooperative learning's contributions in multicultural classrooms and suggests how educators can use this technique to promote improved interpersonal and multicultural relationships.*

Trentacosta, J., & Kenney, M. J. (Eds.) (1997). *Multicultural and gender equity in the mathematics classroom.* Reston, VA: National Council of Teachers of Mathematics.

*This yearbook presents a vision of how research classroom practices can ensure a mathematics program for all students, regardless of gender, race, ethnicity, and socioeconomic status.*

Tiedt, P. L., & Tiedt, I. M. (1995). *Multicultural teaching: A handbook of activities, information, and resources.* Boston: Allyn & Bacon.

*As the title implies, Tiedt and Tiedt provide a wealth of activities that can be helpful in multicultural education programs.*

## Answers to the Culture Quiz: Teaching and Learning

| | | | | |
|---|---|---|---|---|
| **1.** T | **3.** T | **5.** F | **7.** T | **9.** F |
| **2.** T | **4.** F | **6.** T | **8.** T | **10.** F |

Chapter *10*

# Individual and Cultural Differences

Understanding the material and activities in this chapter will help the reader to:

- List individual and cultural differences and similarities, and explain their influence on learning and achievement.

- Develop positive orientations toward "cultural deficiencies" and "cultural differences" perspectives, and understand the importance of providing educational experiences based on the "differences" perspective.

- List at least six individual differences (e.g., self-esteem, gender, development, motivation, social class, exceptionalities) that affect learning and achievement.

- List several dangers associated with labeling exceptional learners (and, in fact, all children and adolescents), and demonstrate how their exceptionalities affect learning and achievement.

- Describe an educational program (e.g., bilingual education, teaching English as a second language [ESL]) that effectively addresses the needs of language-minority learners.

- Define learning styles, explain the complex relationship between culture and learning styles, and suggest inventories designed to assess learners' styles.

- Recognize the need for a celebration of cultural diversity and how diversity among learners can enrich elementary and secondary school programs.

- Understand the importance of positive cultural identities, and suggest methods to build positive identities among learners.

## Overview

Educator's positive responses to elementary and secondary learners' differences are crucial to celebrating cultural, ethnic, and racial diversity among Native, African,

Asian, Hispanic, and European Americans. Individual and cultural differences can provide an effective framework for teaching and learning experiences and can enrich and contribute to individual teaching and learning situations and to the total school program. This chapter looks at individual and cultural diversities and examines their influence on student learning and overall development.

## The Reality of Individual and Cultural Diversity

All too often classroom teachers, special services personnel, and administrators assume too much homogeneity among learners' abilities, backgrounds, and interests. Some educators still subscribe to the belief that a purpose of the school is to homogenize students (along the lines of the melting pot idea) and to eradicate or "remediate" differences. The reality is that learners' many differences affect their perceptions of learning and achievement, their ways of learning and knowing, and their overall learning and school achievement.

---

**THE CULTURE QUIZ    Individual and Cultural Diversity**

*Directions:* Match the following terms and definitions by placing the correct letter in front of each numbered term.

_____ **1.** Gender

_____ **2.** Learning style

_____ **3.** Bilingual education

_____ **4.** Self-esteem

_____ **5.** Assessment

_____ **6.** Cognitive processes

_____ **7.** Socioeconomic status

_____ **8.** Labeling

_____ **9.** ESL programs

_____ **10.** Exceptionalities

a. develops competence in English and is taught through the subject areas

b. differences of any kind in an educational context (e.g., cultural, social class, disabling conditions, or giftedness)

c. must be applied very cautiously to avoid misplacing learners

d. use of two languages as media of instruction

e. relating to male or female

f. how an individual perceives himself or herself; when present, has immense potential for enhancing a learners' chance of success

g. consistent patterns of behavior–cognitive, affective and physiological

h. may include language development, thinking strategies, hypothesizing, and skills at applying concepts

i. determining learning levels and progress

j. parents' level of wealth; determines learners' experiences

(Answers to the Culture Quiz are located at the end of the chapter.)

---

Educational institutions, regardless of grade or academic level, have the responsibility for recognizing individual and cultural differences and planning appropriate educational experiences for all learners. Differences such as poverty, home and family conditions, and some exceptionalities may appear difficult to overcome; nevertheless, students deserve an affirmative response to their differences and learning needs. It no longer suffices to plan educational experiences only for middle- or upper-class white learners and then expect students of other social classes and cultures to change perspectives on motivation and competition, learning styles, and attitudes and values that their homes and families have instilled in them.

Today, society increasingly considers differences among children and adolescents as entities to be appreciated and on which educational experiences can be built. Teachers should recognize and respect children's and adolescents' attitudes, customs, and sacred values. A positive perspective toward these differences must inform curricular decisions and instructional practices.

Implementing Research 10-1 proposes ways students can deal with cultural differences.

## Differences and Their Influence on Learning

Children's and adolescents' every difference, whether of intellectual, developmental, or gender origin, affects their academic achievement and overall school success. For too many years, educators have planned for the "learner in the middle" (e.g., white, middle-class, nondisabled, male, normally developing) and have expected other learners to conform and to use "middle" cognitive strategies to process information. Schools are challenged to take a more enlightened or multicultural approach and to recognize the multitude of differences among learners.

Perez (1994) maintains that U.S. public schools have never offered an enthusiastic welcome to student differences. In fact, educators sometimes have attempted to remove student differences that they deemed "barriers" to more equal access to opportunities in the larger society.

Perez challenges educators to offer an appropriate response to the increasing diversity in cultures and languages. Schools should reflect the perspective that diversity is not the problem but rather an opportunity for every American to experience other peoples and cultures. Perez offers several ways to seize that opportunity: respect students' names, language, and cultures (Perez, 1994).

### Achievement, Intelligence, and Cognitive Processes

A definition of *learner's achievement level* is previously acquired knowledge that relates to what is being taught. Most educators believe that what students already know affects their present and future achievement. The question the educator should always ask is, "To what extent and how can previous learning contribute to new learning?" The learner who already knows numbers, who is fascinated

**IMPLEMENTING RESEARCH 10-1   Dealing with Cultural Differences**

Students need strategies that help them deal with unfamiliar and disturbing behaviors and beliefs in our schools and communities. When students come in contact with others whose practices and beliefs differ from their own, they often express ridicule, condescension, and disgust; for example, Arabs often stand so close together they can smell each other's breath. Students need to learn that although these practices may differ from theirs, they are neither right nor wrong—they are simply differences. Teachers should be alert to such statements as "They are so primitive!" Another statement calling for the teacher's attention is, "They have their ways, and we have ours," because such a thought implies that the speaker is rejecting any connections between himself or herself and the other persons.

Jane White looks at the amount of interpersonal space people prefer as an example of difference. She defines interpersonal space thus: Intimate space, 0–18 inches; personal zone or personal space, 1.5 feet to 4 feet; social zone, 4 feet to 12 feet; and public zone, 12 feet to 25 feet. White explains all four and provides an example of how the concept of personal space can be taught in the classroom. She discusses space in school, at home, in the community, and around the world.

**Implementing the research**

While White's entire article will prove useful to educators, two points are particularly noteworthy:

1. Educators should allow some time for frank discussion of differences among people. Problems arise when students are making negative evaluative statements or rejecting any aspects of human connections.
2. Educators, especially as schools grow more diverse, should discuss the concept of "personal space," so that students of all cultures will understand that someone from another culture might not be trying to get too close or to avoid getting close to another.

*Source:* White, J. J. (1998). Helping students deal with cultural differences. *The Social Studies, 89*(3), 107–111.

**FOLLOW THROUGH 10-1   Dealing with Unfamiliar Behaviors and Customs**

Name a number of ways in which educators can most effectively deal with unfamiliar behaviors and customs in our schools. For example, using White's (1998) example of "personal space," what activities can you suggest for teaching students that "how far people stand apart" is a cultural mannerism. It is not a matter of right and wrong, and people are not necessarily being rude or overly presumptuous. Name several activities that might engage students that would teach them the concept of and acceptance of "personal space."

with science, or who is interested in geography will have a headstart over learners without special areas of expertise or interests.

A learner's overall intelligence, abilities, or special expertise contribute to the degree to which he or she processes information. Learners organize their perceptions and experiences of the school and physical world into cognitive structures. Much is still to be learned about cognition, but it is known that cognitive development is an active process in which learners assimilate information into cognitive categories and adapt their previous categories to accommodate new information. These functions of assimilation and accommodation cause the change and growth in learners' thinking that constitutes cognitive development. Educators who work with students from differing cultural backgrounds should plan educational experiences that recognize the developmental capabilities of children as well as their cultural perspectives.

The learners' cognitive development is of particular importance in multicultural situations, because teachers cannot assume that all learners process information in the same manner. Norton (1999) argues that children's language, thinking strategies, ability to make comparisons and hypotheses, and skill at applying concepts and information depends on their overall cognitive development, which is grounded in their cultural backgrounds. Rather than assuming too much homogeneity among learners, educators have to consider cultural orientations toward achievement, cultural diversity among learning styles, and the learner's degree of active participation.

## Self-Esteem

We have mentioned repeatedly throughout this text the importance of the learner's self-esteem and its effects on academic achievement. How learners perceive themselves is especially significant for those of differing cultural backgrounds. The learner who feels that others perceive him or her as inferior, deficient in some manner, or in stereotypical terms may begin to feel less than adequate or unable to cope with the U.S. school system. A child's self-esteem and the value he or she places on cultural heritage and background can plummet to a point where success in school and in other areas of life is in jeopardy.

---

**FOLLOW THROUGH 10-2   Promoting Self-Esteem**

Perceptive educators realize the importance of self-esteem and the relationship between learning and students' feelings about themselves. A powerful need exists for all students to have strong self-esteem; however, learners from culturally different backgrounds might experience more challenges developing self-esteem. Name several ways in which educators might promote self-esteem (and cultural identities). For example, your list might include having students make a personal collage that shows "who I am" or the positive contributions of another person of the same cultural background.

## Gender

*Gender* describes masculine and feminine differences—the thoughts, feelings, and behaviors one identifies as being either male or female. Culturally determined masculine and feminine behavior can differ significantly. For example, a boy demonstrating feminine traits might be called a "sissy" in one culture but be accepted in another (Gollnick & Chinn, 1998).

Educational experiences and outcomes differ for males and females:

- Lundeberg, Fox, and Puncochar (1994) reported that as early as the sixth grade girls have less self-confidence than boys, and the differences increase with age. Both boys and girls lose self-esteem as they grow older, but girls show a far greater loss. For example, girls in elementary, middle, and secondary schools experience continuous decreases in self-esteem of 60, 37, and 29 percent, respectively (*Education and gender*, 1994).
- *Everybody Counts: A Report to the Nation on the Future of Mathematics Education* (National Research Council, 1989) indicates that girls and boys progress through the mathematics curriculum and in fact show little difference in ability, effort, or interest until the adolescent years. Then, as social pressures increase, girls' decisions to reduce effort in the study of mathematics progressively limit their future education and eventually their career choices.
- Focusing on risk taking and mathematics achievement, Ramos and Lambating (1996) examined females' reluctance to be risk takers and males' tendency to be greater risk takers. Females' reluctance to guess on multiple-choice tests and their tendency to leave more questions unanswered (true–false, multiple choice, and relationship analysis) contributes to their lower achievement.
- Male and female students in grade 4 and 8 have similar science achievement scores; however, by grade 12, male students have higher scores than females (National Assessment of Educational Progress, 1997).

How can educators address gender differences? How can educators provide females with an education that adopts feminine perspectives? First, women's studies should include consciousness-raising efforts and attempt to create a more enlightened view of women and their unique individual perspectives. Second, education should be as nonsexist as possible. Teachers should scrutinize all instructional materials and seek to eliminate sexist connotations and promote feminine learning styles. Teachers should understand and consider cognitive strategies whenever possible. Third, Title IX of the 1972 Educational Amendment addresses the discriminatory treatment of students based on their sex. Title IX (Gollnick & Chin, 1998) states that "no person shall, on the basis of sex, be excluded from participation in, be denied the benefits of, or be subjected to, discrimination under any education program or activity receiving federal financial assistance."

Examining gender and assessments, Gender Perspectives 10-1 on page 258 looks at a four-year study by the Educational Testing Service.

---

**GENDER PERSPECTIVES 10-1   Gender and Assessments**

Stereotypes hold that girls tend to do better in liberal arts and boys perform better in mathematics and science, but data do not necessarily support the validity of this perception. Latham, reporting on a four-year study by Educational Testing Service (ETS), found that gender gaps in the United States are not nearly as large or as pervasive as the average person might think. Regarding the belief that girls excel in the liberal arts and boys in mathematics and science, some evidence existed in 1960 that such might be the case, but data in 1990 show no male advantage in either subject. The 1990 data, however, did show a slight writing advantage for girls that remained largely unchanged from 1960.

ETS researchers, however, caution against making simplistic assertions across broad subject areas such as mathematics, science, and writing. For example, when math was separated into its component subject areas, they found that females did slightly better on some subskills (such as math computation) and that males did better on others (such as math concepts). Another major finding was that although the gaps across subject areas are minimal at the fourth grade level, gender differences appear to grow by the time students reach the twelfth grade. For example, girls' advantage in writing grows substantially between the fourth and eighth grade, whereas boys' advantage in natural science does not occur until somewhere between eighth and twelfth grades. Differences between the genders probably result from a number of complex factors such as hormonal changes that affect both girls and boys at the onset of puberty. Gender differences that do exist are probably the result of far more than just differential course-taking and culturally defined gender expectations.

*Source:* Latham, A. S. (1998). Gender differences on assessments. *Educational Leadership* 55(4), 88–89.

---

**FOLLOW THROUGH 10-3   Counteracting Gender Bias**

Interview six or eight girls at the middle or secondary school level. In an effort to determine their perceptions of schools' efforts to counteract gender bias, focus your questions around areas such as curricular materials, school environment, interpersonal relationships, and instructional methods. Also ask about overall school philosophy, such as individualism versus group welfare and collaboration and versus competition.

---

## *Developmental Levels and Cognitive Readiness*

The learner's developmental stage is perhaps the most significant individual difference affecting learning. Learners functioning at one developmental level simply cannot comprehend material that requires the thinking and cognitive skills of the next higher developmental level. Rather than assuming that learners can succeed by trying hard or doing more homework, educators should understand that development and readiness, not effort alone, affect what youngsters can learn.

A youngster at the concrete-operations stage cannot master intellectual challenges that demand formal, abstract thinking abilities. Although some memorization might occur, learners will be unable to learn information that is beyond their cognitive ability at any given age. To assume that all learners can perform functions and master content at a level that a few precocious and intellectually advanced students attain ignores individual differences and what is known about cognitive readiness (Toepfer, 1988).

The challenge for educators is to determine developmental and readiness levels and to plan and implement appropriate instruction. Educators might raise some questions about theories that proclaim growth and development as cross-culturally valid. However, development as an individual difference affects learning and crosses cultural boundaries. Regardless of cultural backgrounds and when they reach certain developmental stages, learners cannot master material they are not developmentally ready to learn. The challenge for educators is to diagnose the learner's developmental stage and then provide developmentally appropriate curricular experiences and instructional practices.

## Beliefs, Attitudes, and Values

Understanding children and adolescents from culturally different backgrounds requires knowing their beliefs, attitudes, and values. These idiosyncrasies are based in each learner's culture and influence all aspects of his or her life, whether in motivation, competition, perspectives toward the family, or perceptions of racism and its effects. Numerous illustrations provide evidence of the effects of attitudes: the Asian American student who is taught to revere teachers; the African American child who can listen to someone without looking the speaker in the eye; the Native American learner who values cooperation and sharing as being more worthy than competition; or the Hispanic American adolescent who believes he or she should not stand out among peers.

Perceptive educators recognize the cultural baggage (prejudices, myths, and stereotypes) that children and adolescents bring to school, baggage that affects attitudes toward school, other learners, and learning achievement. The educator's challenge is to understand and to respect these personal aspects and, whenever possible, to provide school experiences that are culturally compatible. Curricular practices and instructional methods that are genuinely multicultural in both theory and practice reflect the values, attitudes, and beliefs of learners of culturally different backgrounds and do not require learners to participate in actions that contradict their cultural beliefs.

---

**FOLLOW THROUGH 10-4   Determining Sources of Motivation**

In a group or individual setting (whichever will prompt students to share personal information), talk with learners to see what motivates them. Does competing with peers motivate them? Do their parents' expectations motivate them? Does the teacher play a significant role in motivation?

**IMPLEMENTING RESEARCH 10-2    Accommodating Differences
and Commonalities**

Addressing diversity in schools today presents a major challenge in our multicultural society. Gallimore and Goldenberg asked, "How can educators be responsive to cultural
differences and avoid stereotypes that mask commonalities shared by all cultural groups?
They maintain that educators should recognize both similarities and commonalities and
provide educational experiences that address cultural differences and similarities.

Cultural features or models of belief and practices and their associated activities are
neither static not rigid. As circumstances change, understanding of how things work and
how to respond are modified and changed to meet new challenges. Some cultural features such as beliefs, practices, and everyday activities mark boundaries and result from
different historical circumstances. Many cultural groups differ sharply among themselves, yet the boundaries between groups (that which differentiates them) such as clothing and food, male and female roles, and religious beliefs.

Gallimore and Goldenberg suggest that teachers may expect to find many commonalities as well as differences among the cultural groups that attend U.S. schools. Educators must be aware of potential discontinuities between home and school (e.g., attitudes
about discipline, beliefs about how children learn, the nature and quality of learning experiences among groups). Cultural groups living in enclaves can be expected to have
many shared cultural beliefs. Schools therefore should also build on commonalities between schools and families, such as their values of formal schooling, school achievement,
good behavior, and parental support and involvement.

**Implementing the Research**

1. Elementary and secondary school educators need to recognize similarities as well
   as differences—both need to be addressed in educational experiences. Also, differences should not be considered as deficiencies—they should be considered strengths
   on which to build.
2. Educators should also carefully avoid basing educational decisions on stereotypes
   of cultures.
3. Educators should understand the discontinuities among home and school expectations for schoolwork, behavior, and attitudes toward school.

*Source:* Gallimore, R., & Goldenberg, C. (1996). Accommodating cultural differences and commonalities in educational practices. *Multicultural Education 4*(1), 16–19.

In Implementing Research 10-2, Gallimore and Goldenberg (1996) examine accommodating differences and commonalities and ask how educators can avoid
stereotypes.

## Motivation

It is important for educators in multicultural situations to understand motivation.
Rather than perceive motivation through middle-class, European American eyes,
educators must understand the complex relationship between motivation and cultural diversity. For example, middle-class European Americans might be motivated

by competition, by an outstanding achievement that sets the individual apart from peers, or by the desire to work independently. Learners from culturally different backgrounds may not hold those same values and might appear unmotivated when they do not want to stand out among their peers or to excel at the expense of others or when they choose to work in cooperative learning situations sharing expertise.

Closely related to learners' motivation and willingness to employ cognitive abilities is their expectation of success or failure. Beliefs related to the likelihood of success, to judgments about their ability, and to emotional reactions of pride and hopelessness all contribute to the extent learners are willing to use cognitive strategies. Over time, learners who believe that lack of ability causes failure are likely to feel a sense of helplessness (Ames, 1990). This theory of the relationship among motivation, feelings of self-worth, and the willingness to use cognitive strategies might be especially useful for educators who work with learners from culturally different backgrounds.

Educators should focus on the particular motivational problems of individual students. School learning requires active effort, and children are not likely to put forth the active effort if they do not see that their schoolwork helps them to achieve their own purposes or to satisfy their own interests. They may respond to their parents' or teachers' pressures, but unless students have a personal reason to complete school assignments, motivation will be difficult to maintain. Educators need to understand motivation from its cultural perspective and then attempt to help learners understand qualities in their assignments that are either interesting or useful (Tyler, 1989).

Case Study 10-1 shows how thirteen-year-old Carl's motivation is misunderstood and suggests that teachers should not view children and adolescents of culturally different backgrounds from middle-class, European American perspectives.

---

## CASE STUDY 10-1   Motivation and Cultural Considerations

Carl, a thirteen-year-old Native American middle-school student, shows a lack of motivation, initiative, and competitive drive. He does not demonstrate any desire to set himself apart from or to rise above others in his class. His teachers see him as "different." Whereas most of the white students in this school strive for success and good grades, Carl does his work but shows no desire to achieve more. The teachers who work together in Carl's unit wonder what to do and how to motivate him.

Although this pattern has been typical of Native Americans in this school, Mrs. Westerly, the special education teacher, recognizes a crucial aspect of this situation that others either have not seen or do not want to admit. Rather than look at Carl from a European American perspective, Mrs. Westerly suggests understanding the Native American perspective. Perhaps, from Carl's cultural perspective, he is motivated. His family has transmitted a cultural heritage that does not emphasize competition or achievement that would set him apart from his peers. He does not value competing with other learners, because it seems far more logical to share ideas and to work cooperatively and in harmony.

The teachers begin to realize that they have evaluated Carl's motivation through a middle-class, European American lens. They had in fact been expecting Carl to conform to behaviors that were completely alien to his cultural heritage and background.

## Socioeconomic Class

The social class differential that exists in the United States includes the family's absolute income, educational background, occupational prestige, place of residence, lifestyle, and relative autonomy and power. It is worth remembering, however, that wealth and material success are relative concepts; one family might consider ownership of a swimming pool a sign of success, whereas another family might perceive the addition of a porch to a mobile home as an indicator of success (Ramsey, 1987). In any event, a family's socioeconomic class and income level determine children's and adolescents' experiences, as do other factors (e.g., conditions of the home, the presence of books and other reading materials and computers, trips with educational significance) that have positive effects on educational progress.

An educator must remember to consider learners and their families individually. It is a serious mistake and an injustice to learners to make assumptions of wealth and social class based on culture, race, or ethnicity. Conversely, a teacher should never predict a learner's educational potential on the basis of socioeconomic level. Just as many higher socioeconomic class learners often fail to respond to their educators' efforts, students from lower-class homes and neighborhoods have achieved extraordinary educational successes.

# Exceptionalities

## The Dangers of Labeling and Erroneous Placement

Labeling learners has such potentially harmful effects that educators who assign labels may be placing children and adolescents at great risk. Although such educators probably have the learner's interest and educational welfare in mind, labeling learners as "slow" or "disabled" can sometimes cause irreparable harm, not only during school programs but throughout their lives. Educators should be cognizant of the disadvantages of labeling and should know when the practice is or is not in the learner's best interest. Disadvantages of labeling children and adolescents (Biehler & Snowman, 1990) include:

**1.** Learners who are identified as disabled or exceptional may be permanently stigmatized, rejected, or denied opportunities for full development.
**2.** Learners labeled as *mentally retarded* (or the equivalent) may be assigned to inferior educational programs in school or illegally placed in institutions.
**3.** Large numbers of learners from culturally diverse backgrounds are inaccurately classified as mentally disabled on the basis of scores they earn on inappropriate tests.

Case Study 10-2 illustrates the dangers of labeling learners and shows how placing learners in categories can affect both students' and teachers' perceptions.

The disadvantages of labeling are sufficient to cause alarm, but another problem may result from labeling: the overt segregation of learners. Sendor (1988) sug-

**CASE STUDY 10-2    The Dangers of Labeling**

Dr. Strobecker, principal of Cedarwood Elementary School, was looking through students' permanent records when several labels caught her eye: "behaviorally maladjusted," "slow learner," "retarded," "below average," "gifted," "troublemaker," "unmotivated," "emotionally disturbed," and other labels that educators can imagine. She realized the dangers of labeling: Teachers sometimes expect too little, sometimes too much; learners are often in the wrong group; and labels assigned to them in the elementary school may affect learners' entire lives. Further, such labeling may be both unprofessional and unethical. She admitted to herself that, although labeling learners had the potential for helping, the practice should be limited to only those cases in which learners will clearly be helped.

Dr. Strobecker knew that, as principal, she had the professional responsibility for addressing the situation. There were several things she might do: first, she should make teachers aware of the dangers of labeling; second, she should encourage teachers to read professional articles that deal with labeling and alternatives; third, she should encourage teachers to diagnose learners by using the most objective and reliable means; and fourth, teachers should assign a label only when the diagnosis is accurate and in the learner's best interest.

**FOLLOW THROUGH 10-5    Avoiding Erroneous Labeling**

Name five or six ways in which educators can avoid the hazards of labeling learners. Your list might include getting to know individuals, talking with parents and extended family members, conversing with others in the culture, and using culturally relevant testing devices for assessment purposes.

gests that grouping and placement practices have segregated learners racially. Using subjective means or teacher recommendations, labeling or placement policies can contribute (either intentionally or unintentionally) to the segregation of students along racial and ethnic lines. Such policies are both unethical and unprofessional and can condemn learners to slow groups or inferior materials and methods. Such situations may occur because educators want learners segregated or because educators erroneously equate race or ethnicity with achievement and ability.

When, if ever, should educators label learners? Teachers should give a learner a label when, and *only* when, it is in the student's best interest and when substantial objective data can document the learner's condition. The label should serve a meaningful purpose and provide a basis for assisting the learner's overall educational progress. Even when this is the case, educators have a moral, ethical, and professional responsibility to assess learners periodically, to diagnose accurately, to follow all due-process procedures, and to ensure that learners are placed in other groups or classes if the disabling or exceptional conditions change.

## Disabling Conditions

Children and adolescents from culturally different backgrounds can experience the same disabling conditions that other children or adolescents experience, such as behavior disorders, mentally disabling conditions, visual impairments, communication disorders, or hearing and visual impairments. It is crucial, however, to ascertain that diagnostic tests accurately reflect the strengths and weaknesses of disabled youngsters from culturally different backgrounds and make decisions accordingly. When working with disabled learners, educators must identify the concept of behavior and its role in determining eligibility for special programs. Most important, professionals who make eligibility decisions should be sensitive to what is educationally best for the student (Patton & Polloway, 1990).

## Gifted and Talented

Some people continue to question the use of *gifted* in the same breath with *cultural diversity*. It has been difficult for some people to understand that a child or adolescent may be verbally gifted (although perhaps in a language other than English), that learners have higher-order cognitive processes in survival techniques (that do not reveal themselves on school assessments), and that the term *culturally different* does not imply that students are lacking in some areas.

Although many papers in the literature urge educators to be sensitive to the special characteristics of culturally diverse populations, most programs for gifted learners continue to use traditional methods of identification, which rely on popular notions of gifted characteristics. Identifying gifted learners from different cultural backgrounds may be difficult. Learners from culturally different backgrounds might be from a home environment that rewards certain types of behavior that are not consonant with conventional notions of giftedness. For example, some Hispanic Americans may provide less reinforcement of highly verbal behavior. Children from such a family, on entering school, may be somewhat reticent and might not stand out in screening for giftedness (Yarborough & Johnson, 1983).

Gifted children are found in every socioeconomic and cultural group. Educators have been less than successful in identifying gifted learners from culturally different backgrounds, perhaps because they are more difficult to recognize and teach. Several factors have contributed to an increased emphasis on identifying gifted learners from culturally different backgrounds: First, broader definitions of giftedness and intellectual ability are contributing to the identification of more learners; and second, there is a new willingness among educators to use a variety of screening and evaluation techniques and instruments (Wolf, 1990).

What instruments and techniques do experts recommend for identifying gifted learners from culturally different backgrounds?

1. Research indicates that gifted students from culturally different backgrounds are likely to score higher on the K-ABC Instrument than on the Stanford-Binet or Wechsler scales, which depend more on verbal skills.

2. A study has attempted to identify and to test for specific types of giftedness using Guilford's Structure of Intellect Model. This is an important step because it relates traditional intelligence measures to the nontraditional structure of the intellect.
3. The subcultural Indices of Academic Potential is a test that requires students to assess their reactions to everyday situations. This test produces a profile of preferences, learning styles, and ways of approaching tasks.
4. The Kranz Talent Identification Instrument is designed to raise awareness of the multiple criteria of giftedness and to assist teachers in screening for talented learners in the classrooms (Wolf, 1990).

After educators have identified gifted learners, they must select programs that match the needs of gifted youngsters from culturally diverse backgrounds. These programs should have a design and method of implementation that considers the learner's psychological, cultural, and linguistic characteristics. Simply integrating learners into an established gifted curriculum may not be successful, because it requires learners to accommodate themselves to the school program, rather than having the program meet the needs of individual learners.

## Language

Language differences continue to challenge educators in the twenty-first century:

1. Significant numbers of groups speak a language other than English at home and do not speak English very well.
2. Linguistic diversity (both limited English proficiency and use of dialects) is controversial, dividing much of the nation.
3. Inseparable relationships exist between language and culture.
4. Effective multicultural education programs place considerable emphasis on accepting linguistic diversity and encouraging learners to be bilingual and bidialectal.
5. Teaching linguistically different students requires effective strategies.

---

**FOLLOW THROUGH 10-6  Determining Giftedness**

Identifying gifted learners from culturally different backgrounds can pose challenges for educators who might be accustomed to looking for particular traits that might relate to a specific culture. Traits suggesting giftedness in learners from differing cultural backgrounds might go undetected. Name several ways educators might determine learners' areas of giftedness, remembering that learners in some cultures might be reluctant to reveal special talents at the expense of other students.

---

Some suggest that linguistically different learners forsake their native languages, and others suggest learning English as a second language. A genuine multicultural education program teaches learners to hold onto their native languages so they can be bilingual and have access to two cultures (Byrnes & Cortez, 1996).

## Dialect Differences

Dialect and the issue of whether to require use of standard American English in the schools are sensitive and controversial subjects. Because there is a close relationship between groups of differing cultural backgrounds and dialects that are often nonstandard, this issue also has civil rights implications. Some consider any requirement that standard English be spoken in schools discriminatory. They think that such a requirement places an additional educational burden on the nonstandard-English-speaking students. Further, the insistence on standard English may hinder the acquisition of other educational skills, making it difficult for these students to succeed. Such a practice may deny nonstandard-English-speaking students the same educational opportunities as others and thus morally, if not legally, denies them their civil rights (Gollnick & Chinn, 1998).

A learner's dialect is closely related to her or his cultural identity and overall self-esteem. School programs that are effective with students of culturally different backgrounds are sufficiently flexible to accommodate the range of dialects learners bring to school. While speaking a nonstandard dialect may have detrimental economic, social, and educational consequences for students, teachers should nonetheless accept, value, and appreciate a student's language (Crawford, 1993).

Dialects also pose a challenging issue for educators, who can address them in several ways: (1) accommodate all dialects, based on the assumption they are all equal, (2) insist on learners speaking only one dialect in school, and (3) accept dialects for certain uses but insist on standard English in other situations. Educators should allow dialects in social and recreational situations (i.e., other than formal classroom discourse) but should encourage students in school settings to use standard English, because it is the primary written and spoken language in the United States. Such a compromise allows students to use dialects as it recognizes the social and economic implications of being able to function in standard English (Gollnick & Chinn, 1998).

---

**FOLLOW THROUGH 10-7    Making Decisions about Dialects**

Decide how you will address dialects and dialectical differences, remembering the close relationship between language (and dialects) and cultural backgrounds. Trying to change a student's dialect can have deleterious effects on his or her self-esteem and cultural identity. Specifically, how do you plan to address dialects?

## Language and Culture: Inseparable Relationships

English as a second language and multicultural education are two closely related concepts. Learners acquire language through socialization, and, in turn, language shapes perception of the physical and social worlds in which they live. It is not possible to effectively address linguistic differences without acknowledging and respecting cultural differences. Likewise, it is not possible to respect cultural differences without acknowledging and respecting the importance of a person's language.

Learners think about and understand the world in their native tongue, which is intricately tied to their identity. Ignoring or devaluing learners' native language denies an important part of the rich past and present cultural experiences learners bring to school. Thus, it is critical for classroom teachers to acknowledge and respect children's home language, whether it is a completely different language or an English dialect (Byrnes & Cortez, 1996).

## Multicultural Programs Emphasizing Language Diversity

Perceptive educators at all school levels understand how respect for language diversity is a prerequisite to effective multicultural programs. They support language diversity by:

1. ensuring that linguistically different learners have teachers trained to work with second-language learners;
2. understanding that a student might have sufficient ability in English to socialize in the hallways, yet may need support to comprehend academic language usage;
3. relating learning to students' life experiences, prior knowledge, and cultural perspectives;
4. validating, respecting, and building, whenever possible, on students' native language abilities; and
5. recognizing, not eliminating, and in fact valuing dialects (Crawford, 1993).

## Effective Strategies for Linguistically Different Learners

O'Malley and Chamot (1990) listed techniques for learning a second language.

*Sound acquisition*—learners can listen carefully to language sounds on a tape or those of a teacher or other native speaker. Then, they can practice the sounds by talking aloud and role-playing verbal situations.

*Grammar*—learners can follow or infer language rules in textbooks, compare native languages with English, and practice grammatical structures, both written and oral.

*Vocabulary*—learners can prepare charts, learn words in context, learn words by association with others, use new words in phrases, and use a dictionary when necessary.

*Listening comprehension*—learners can listen to the radio, records, television, and movies for different accents, dialects, and registers.

*Learning to talk*—learners need to be open to making mistakes, make contact with native speakers, ask for corrections, and learn dialogues.

*Learning to write*—learners can maintain journals and write frequently to pen pals using any of the writing forms commonly accepted in schools.

*Learning to read*—learners can read something in English every day, read things that are familiar, read texts at the beginner's level, and look for meaning from context (O'Malley & Chamot, 1990).

Teachers can help by

1. directing activities (a strategy that research suggests is highly effective in teaching English) during which students listen and respond to effective role models;
2. providing classroom situations in which students follow distinct patterns every day and have the time and environment to concentrate on language and educational content;
3. allowing students to help students—they may be more likely to ask for language clarification from another student than from the teacher, or they may be better able to communicate with another student with similar language skills;
4. asking for volunteers, then asking for group responses, and establishing a pattern of taking turns that requires all students to participate orally;
5. taking special care to speak clearly and to use concrete references, repetitions, rephrasings, gestures, visual aids, and demonstrations;
6. providing curricular materials on an appropriate cognitive level; for example, a teacher should not give a book written for a kindergarten student to a sixth-grader;
7. using whole-language activities whenever possible so students will have opportunities for rich, meaningful interactions with both written and oral language;
8. providing opportunities for recounts (essentially extended versions of known information and answer exchanges), accounts (narratives the teller generates to provide new information), event casts (ongoing narratives interesting to both teller and listener), and stories (the telling of a narrative) in which learners practice second-language skills, both chronologically and thematically (Faltis, 1993);
9. encouraging students to work in cooperative groups so maximum language interaction can occur; primary language speakers can assist second-language learners and provide role models;
10. reading appropriate books aloud (actually an excellent idea for all learners), so linguistically different learners can hear pronunciations and words in context;

11. allowing students to read books and then give oral book reports to small groups; second-language learners can have role models and can practice English skills;

12. allowing learners to write messages, letters, cards, and notes and read them in English;

13. including listening centers with records and tapes so second-language learners can practice listening skills and learn English simultaneously;

14. allowing a panel of reporters or reviewers to interview a person or imaginary author in English and clarifying unclear language points; and

15. allowing students to prepare radio or television broadcasts that include book talks, advertisements for books and other products, or reading sections of books (Crawford, 1993).

## Bilingual Education and English as a Second Language

The language diversity in the United States extends itself into the schools, and in large urban and metropolitan school districts nearly a hundred different languages may be spoken. Whereas some students are bilingual in English and their native language, others either do not speak English at all or have limited English-speaking skills. Indications are that the number of students with limited English-speaking skills will continue to increase (Gollnick & Chinn, 1998).

Some learners are competent in English; others, however, may speak only Spanish, the second most common language in the United States; one of the many Asian languages; or a less common language such as Arabic or Tongian (Haring, 1990). This section looks at efforts such as bilingual education and English as a second language (ESL) programs (or the teaching of English to speakers of other languages), which attempt to address the needs of learners of culturally different backgrounds.

Some confusion exists concerning bilingual education and ESL programs, which many often assume to be synonymous. In the United States, the teaching of English is an integral aspect of bilingual programs, but the teaching of English in and by itself (ESL) does not constitute a bilingual program. Both programs promote English proficiency for student whose English is limited (Hernandez, 1989).

---

**FOLLOW THROUGH 10-8   Supporting Bilingual Education**

Assume that you have been asked by the school board to propose a public service announcement supporting bilingual education programs. What points do you want to address? How will you respond to critics and many communities' feeling that bilingual programs should be eliminated? What other issues need to be addressed in such a controversial program?

*Bilingual education* is generally defined as "the use of two languages as media of instruction" (Baca & Cervantes, 1989, p. 24). Bilingual education has received federal funds as a provision of the Bilingual Education Act of 1968, which Congress reauthorized in 1974, 1978, and 1984 (Gollnick & Chinn, 1998).

Bilingual education reinforces the student's home language and culture, and simultaneously teaches the ability to function in another language. Instruction in both skills and content is usually in the student's home language and in English. The most important legal action related to bilingual education was the 1974 *Lau v. Nichols* decision, which pointed to the need for some type of special instructional program for students with limited English-speaking ability.

ESL programs rely exclusively on English for teaching and learning. Educators use ESL programs extensively in the United States as the primary means of assimilating limited-English-speaking students into the linguistic mainstream as quickly as possible. The main feature of the program is that educators place less emphasis on the maintenance of home language and culture than on English language acquisition (Hernandez, 1989). The emphasis of the ESL program is concentrated in three major areas (TESOL, 1976):

1. *Culture:* Integrating students' cultural experiences and background into meaningful language learning;
2. *Language Development:* Teaching structures and vocabulary relevant to students' learning experiences; and
3. *Content Area Instruction:* Applying techniques from second-language learning to subject learning and to subject matter presented in English.

Table 10-1 provides an overview of ESL programs.

---

**FOR ADDITIONAL INFORMATION   Internet Addresses**

**National Clearinghouse for Bilingual Education (NCBE)**
http://www.ncbe.gwu.edu/   Provides information and resources for educators who design and implement bilingual education programs.

**Bilingual Multicultural Education Classes**
http://www.nau.edu/nauonline/courses/edbme.html   Provides information on English as a second language as well as multicultural education.

**Bilingual/Multicultural Studies Major**
http://www.umfk.maine.edu/registrar/cat94-5.majbilin.htm   Provides information on a college major that addresses the needs of

teachers of children whose home language and culture differ from the language and culture of the classroom.

**Toronto District School Board**
http://www.multi.demon.co.uk/coelho.htm   Provides practical advice and suggestions for educators in schools serving culturally and linguistically diverse communities.

**Bilingual Education Resources**
http:///www.librosdericardo.com/resource.html   Provides a listing of resources for bilingual education.

**TABLE 10-1   Questions and Answers about English as a Second Language**

**What Is English as a Second Language?**

English as a second language (ESL) is intensive English language instruction by teachers trained in recognizing and working with language differences. The ESL program is required by state law in school districts with students who have limited English language skills.

**What Is an ESL Program?**

- An ESL program is structured language instruction designed to teach English to students whose English language skills are limited.
- ESL instruction considers the student's learning experiences and cultural backgrounds.
- ESL is taught through second-language methods that are applied to the teaching of mathematics, science, and social studies.

**What Is the Purpose of an ESL Program?**

- An ESL program develops competence in English.
- English language skills are taught through listening, speaking, reading, writing, and grammar.
- A student's instructional program is modified to make learning English easier.

**Who Should Be Enrolled in an ESL Program?**

- Students in pre-kindergarten through grade 12 who speak or hear a language other than English in their home and who have difficulty in English, are eligible.

**Who Is Responsible for Teaching an ESL Program?**

- Teachers who are specially trained, tested, and certified to teach ESL programs.

*Source: English as a second language program: Benefits for your child.* (1987). Austin, TX: Texas Education Agency.

## Celebrating and Responding to Cultural Diversity

Educators usually do not question the premise that culture plays a major role in a learner's overall achievement and attitudes toward school. The ultimate challenge, however, is to recognize cultural diversity as a strength on which to build a solid education. The first step is to respond to diversity with a sense of positiveness, rather than view it as a hurdle to be overcome.

One example of diversity among groups is the variety of formal and informal rules governing interaction between individuals. When classroom interactional patterns are not consistent or compatible with those that children and adolescents experience in their homes and community, such variations may cause problems. For example, variations in how and when the teacher says something (although perhaps unintentional) as well as what is said may interfere with learning and damage attitudes toward school (Gollnick & Chinn, 1998). Some differences are easily recognized, but educators sometimes overlook the less visible aspects of the culture associated with everyday etiquette and interaction, as well as with the expression of rights, obligations, values, and aspirations.

An excellent example of how cultural backgrounds affect learning is the manner in which teaching and learning environments are structured according to rules that the students and their community do not share. Several differences may surface: how students and teachers interact, how teachers control and monitor behavior, what kinds of behaviors people use to intervene, what kinds of organizational patterns exist, and whether teachers expect learners to participate by interrupting another speaker for a chance to voice an opinion.

Native American learners, for example, might perceive instructional demands as strange or contradictory to cultural expectations. Native American learners who should respond competitively might feel that such instructional expectations violate their desire for cooperation and group efforts (Hernandez, 1990).

Children have many diversities such as family types, ethnicities, cultures, and abilities. The challenge facing educators is to implement educational programs that address differences and create an atmosphere in which harmony and diversity reign. Winter (1994/1995) maintains that each child should be understood as an individual and that individually appropriate learning should be planned. Other directions include creating an atmosphere of acceptance, addressing personal biases, promoting attitudes of acceptance, encouraging open communication, building the competence of children, and incorporating instructional technology.

An equitable response to differences among learners includes:

1. encouraging students to build and maintain self-esteem;
2. using the ethnic backgrounds of students to teach effectively;
3. helping students overcome their prejudices;
4. expanding the knowledge and appreciation of the historical, economic, political, and social experiences of ethnic and national groups; and
5. assisting students in understanding that the world's knowledge and culture have been, and continue to be, created from the contributions of all cultural groups and nations.

A response should also include the provision of environments in which students can learn to participate in the dominant society while maintaining distinct cultural differences. Educators can work toward such responses by demonstrating respect and support for differences, by reflecting diversity in the curriculum, and by using positive differences to teach and interact with learners (Hernandez, 1989).

## Building Cultural Identities

An individual's cultural identity is based on a number of traits and values that are related to national or ethnic origin, family, religion, gender, age, occupation, socioeconomic level, language, geographic region, and exceptionality (Gollnick & Chinn, 1998). The interaction of these factors and the degree to which individuals identify with different subcultures or cultural groups that share political and social institutions and other distinctive cultural elements determines the identity to a large degree (Hernandez, 1989). Rather than allowing "different is wrong" perceptions to prevail and to lower learners' opinions of cultural identities, perceptive educators recognize learners' cultural identities and assist learners in developing positive, healthy, cultural identities.

James P. Comer, a prominent African American psychiatrist and a coauthor of *Black Child Care,* proposes that children of all cultures need to establish a positive racial identity. Comer suggests that children of all racial groups should be able to develop positive feelings about themselves and their cultural group. Negative or ambivalent feelings may result in adverse social and psychological consequences (Comer, 1988).

Case Study 10-3 suggests that affirmative approaches, such as activities that promote the understanding of cultural diversity and assessment of the overall teaching and learning environment, can improve cultural identities.

Educators who celebrate the richness that cultural diversity brings to the classroom readily recognize the need to build or enhance learners' cultural identity. Family and cultural ties are so important to every learner that teachers should give these aspects prime consideration in teaching and learning experiences.

Learners' earliest experiences are of home and family, and language is an important part of this background. Teachers should remember the importance of respecting learners' cultural backgrounds, and at all times they should avoid abusing or dishonoring them. A first step in building a learner's cultural identity is for educators to understand that learner's heritage, values and traditions, and language. While efforts to ensure self-esteem and positive cultural identities should

---

### CASE STUDY 10-3   Enhancing Cultural Identities

Ms. Stepp is a teacher well known for her plans and activities designed to enhance students' self-esteem and cultural identities. Her principal has asked her to do an in-service presentation on working with children and adolescents from culturally diverse backgrounds. The steadily increasing cultural diversity of the school has caused the administrative staff to recognize self-esteem and cultural identity as crucial to the overall success of learners.

Ms. Stepp wonders what ideas, suggestions, activities, and materials she will be able to share. As she plans a rough outline, several broad topics come to mind: student activities (especially designed for each cultural group), informal assessments, the overall teaching and learning climate, and teachers' attitudes and behaviors.

The presentation would include teaching and encouraging respect for home, family, self, traditions, heritages, customs, and anything that accentuates the positive in the learner's culture. The presentation would stress that teachers must have appropriate attitudes and must value and respect cultural diversity, if attempts to improve it are to be successful.

be an ongoing process, educators should also work toward helping learners have positive attitudes toward school (Petty, Petty, & Salzer, 1994).

## Learning Styles

An increasing body of research suggests that equating learning styles with teaching and learning activities contributes to meeting each individual's unique needs (Stewart, 1990). Learning styles have several definitions. First, Cornett (1983) believes that learning styles are consistent patterns of behavior defined in terms of cognitive, affective, and physiological dimensions. To some degree, learning styles are indicators of how individuals process information and respond to the affective, sensory, and environmental dimensions of the instruction process.

A second definition from the National Association of Secondary School Principals (NASSP, 1979) is: Learning styles are characteristic cognitive, affective, and physiological behaviors that serve as relatively stable indicators of how learners perceive, interact with, and respond to the learning environment.

The implications of learning styles, however, extend beyond mere definitions. Style characteristics derive from genetic coding, personality, development, motivation, and cultural and environmental influences. These are relatively persistent qualities in the behavior of individual learners (Keefe, 1990). It is important for educators to know how all students learn, to recognize that students from culturally diverse backgrounds have unique learning styles, and to determine the most appropriate instructional approaches and techniques.

Although the relationship between culture and learning style is not fully understood, it is important to the teaching and learning process. Cultural and cognitive factors and socialization practices influence cognitive and affective preferences and are manifested in incentives and motivation, interpersonal relationships, and patterns of intellectual abilities (Hernandez, 1989). It is important for all educators to know how all students learn. Educators who work in multicultural situations are in a particularly challenging position. They must recognize that all students have unique learning styles, and they must determine the most appropriate instructional approaches and techniques for each.

Individual cultures have distinctive learning style patterns but great variation exists between individuals within groups. Guild (1994) maintains that effective educative experiences and practices must emanate from an understanding of the ways individuals learn.

Guild suggests that researchers agree on several findings: (1) students of any particular age differ in their ways of learning; (2) learning styles are a function of both nature and nurture; and (3) within a group, the variations among individuals are as great as their commonalities (Guild, 1994).

Educators who recognize cultural differences should remember the dangers of generalizing group findings to individuals. The growing numbers and increased recognition of learners from culturally diverse backgrounds have resulted in research that focuses on the intricate relationships between cultural diversity and learning styles. The speculation surrounding the relationship of

**TABLE 10-2    Cultural Diversity and Learning Styles:**
**Representative Examples**

*Mexican Americans.* In Dunn and Dunn's (1978) sample, Mexican Americans were more motivated to learn than were students in the general population. The boys were the most authority-oriented students in the group and were far more parent-motivated than were students in the general population. The students were far more peer-oriented and were more likely to succeed in small-group learning situations.

*African Americans.* Shade (1982) concluded that African Americans have the following tendencies: They view things in their environment in entirety, rather than in isolated parts. They prefer intuitive, rather than deductive or inductive, reasoning. They approximate concepts of space, number, and time, rather than aiming at exactness or accuracy. They rely on both nonverbal and verbal communication.

*Native Americans.* More (1987) reports that many Native Americans show strengths in visual/spatial/perceptual information, and that given a choice, they prefer these modes to verbal modes. They frequently and effectively use coding with imagery to remember concepts and words (mental associations assist in remembering). They are more reflective than impulsive and watch-then-do rather than trial-and-error. They are more likely to participate in global processing for both verbal and nonverbal tasks; for example, students might process using the whole and the relationships between the parts, rather than emphasizing the parts to build the whole.

learning styles and cultural diversity notwithstanding, what does the evidence indicate or suggest? Although reliable research on the learning styles of all cultural groups is not available, Table 10-2 provides a cursory look at several representative findings.

## Summing Up

Educators who base educational experiences on the individual and cultural characteristics of children and adolescents should:

**1.** recognize the various models and orientations of diversity and adopt the culturally different model (Sleeter & Grant, 1988) as the basis for instruction and personal interaction;

**2.** recognize that the learning styles and cognitive processes of learners from different cultural backgrounds may differ from those of the dominant population;

**3.** provide carefully planned experiences for children and adolescents with exceptionalities;

**4.** recognize the importance of self-esteem and positive cultural identities;

**5.** plan activities that teach learners from both culturally different and the majority population the importance of cultural diversity and the many contributions of people from different cultures;

**6.** plan special experiences for learners from language-minority backgrounds, and recognize the differences between bilingual education and ESL programs;

**7.** understand that attitudes, values, and beliefs of culturally different children and adolescents differ from those of the majority culture and not expect minority learners to forsake their cultural identities to achieve school "success"; and

**8.** recognize gender as a variable that affects children and adolescents, and recognize the complex relationship between gender and culture.

## Suggested Learning Activities

1. Visit several schools to determine how or on what basis they group learners or place them in special classes. Does it appear that racial segregation occurs as a result of grouping or placement? To what extent are students "labeled"? What efforts are being made to reduce the negative effects of labeling?

2. List several ways to improve learners' self-esteem and cultural identities. What factors might educators consider to improve self-esteem? How might teachers determine the level of a learner's self-esteem and cultural identity?

3. Respond to the language dilemma many learners face: Many cannot speak English well enough to understand educators or to cope in a predominantly English-speaking society. What are the roles of administrators, classroom teachers, speech correctionists, and language specialists? What suggestions can you offer for helping learners with limited English-speaking skills?

## Suggestions for Collaborative Efforts

Form groups of three or four that, if possible, represent U.S. cultural and gender diversity. Working collaboratively, focus your group's attention toward the following efforts.

1. Survey several programs designed to address the needs of gifted learners from different cultural backgrounds. What instruments or techniques determine eligibility? To what extent do the instruments measure the unique abilities and talents of learners from different backgrounds? Do the programs expect learners to change to meet the demands of the program, or do programs reflect knowledge of cultural diversity?

2. Make a list of commonly held stereotypical beliefs about boys and girls (e.g., boys should not cry, girls have a tendency to giggle a lot). Observe the girls and boys in your class to test the validity of your list. Next, have the boys and girls make a list, and have a discussion of the differences between girls and boys. How might an educator's expectation of girls or boys affect teaching situations? How do members of your group feel these stereotypical beliefs affected them when they were in elementary or secondary school?

3. As a group activity, draw five columns on a sheet. Label them Native, African, Asian, Hispanic, and European American, and list your group's beliefs, attitudes, and values about each culture. Seek your students' input. Next, list school policies, practices, and expectations that the students might want to reconsider for the sake of cultural implications.

## *Expanding Your Horizons: Additional Journal Readings and Books*

Carr, C. L. (1998). Tomboy resistance and conformity: Agency in social psychological gender theory. *Gender & Society, 12*(5), 528–553.

*Carr studied gender as an individual difference among fourteen women who described themselves as tomboys to determine when they rejected femininity and accepted masculinity.*

Dilworth, M. E. (Ed.). (1998). *Being responsive to cultural differences: How teachers learn.* Thousand Oaks, CA: Corwin.

*This book offers suggestions for teachers to expand their skills and techniques for culturally relevant teaching.*

Manning, M. L. (1993). Cultural and gender differences in young adolescents. *Middle School Journal, 25*(1), 13–17.

*Manning offers a review of the research on cultural and gender differences and offers suggestions for responding to these differences.*

Manning, M. L. (1998). Gender differences in young adolescents' mathematics and science achievement. *Childhood Education, 74,* 168–171.

*This article looks at gender differences in middle-school-age mathematics and science achievement and offers specific recommendations.*

Martinez, R. O., & Dukes, R. L. (1997). The effects of ethnic identity, ethnicity, and gender on adolescent well-being. *Journal of Youth and Adolescence, 26*(5), 503–516.

*Martinez and Duke concluded that whites and Native Americans have lower ethnic identity, and African Americans and Hispanic Americans have higher ethnic identity.*

McInerney, D. M., Roche, L. A., McInerney, V., & Marsh, H. W. (1997). Cultural perspectives on school motivation: The relevance and application of goal theory. *American Education Research Journal, 34*(1), 207–236.

*These researchers studied goals and achievement in students from diverse cultural backgrounds.*

Valdes, G. (1998). The world outside and inside schools: Language and immigrant children. *Educational Researcher, 27*(6), 4–18.

*Valdes maintains that immigrant children and schools face serious challenges as our nation grows more diverse.*

## *Answers to the Culture Quiz: Individual and Cultural Diversity*

| | | | | |
|---|---|---|---|---|
| **1.** e | **3.** d | **5.** i | **7.** j | **9.** a |
| **2.** g | **4.** f | **6.** h | **8.** c | **10.** b |

Chapter *11*

# *Parents and Families of Culturally Diverse Backgrounds*

Understanding the material and activities in this chapter will help the reader to:

- State several reasons for including parents and families of culturally diverse backgrounds in parent involvement programs in elementary and secondary schools.

- Understand that both immediate and extended families should be included in schools, especially because African, Asian, European, Hispanic, and Native Americans place considerable value on the extended-family concept.

- State at lease five reasons that parents and families of culturally different backgrounds resist teachers' efforts.

- Understand that considerable diversity (including intracultural, generational, and socioeconomic differences) results in difficulty as teachers plan for "typical" or "prototype" families.

- List the essential elements of effective parent involvement programs.

- Explain procedures and factors that parents and teachers should consider during conferences.

- Explain the essential aspects and considerations of forming a parent advisory committee designed to address the needs and concerns of families from culturally different backgrounds.

- Understand the importance of parent and family education, and explain how such programs can assist families from culturally diverse backgrounds.

# Overview

For years, educators have recognized the importance of involving parents in children's education. Whether through involving, conferring, or educating, efforts to include parents in the educational process have paid rich dividends. Until the past decade or so, however, educators mainly worked with middle- and upper-class European Americans and ignored other races, cultures, and ethnic groups, probably because educators lacked knowledge of unique backgrounds and special needs

---

**THE CULTURE QUIZ   Diversity among Parents and Family**

*Directions:* Mark the following statements true or false.

_____ **1.** The tremendous diversity (i.e., cultural, ethnic, social class, and generational) among families prohibits educators from describing or assuming a typical or prototype family.

_____ **2.** Educators who work with large numbers of culturally diverse students face a serious challenge because, realistically speaking, many minority families either do not have time for, or do not care about, their children's education.

_____ **3.** Educators must recognize the extended family concept, and understand the importance of including both immediate and extended-family members in school experiences.

_____ **4.** Evidence has suggested that the Asian student's great respect for teachers can actually pose a barrier, because parents might be reluctant to communicate with teachers.

_____ **5.** The parents' social class plays little role in the learner's academic achievement and should receive only token consideration as the teacher plans learning experiences.

_____ **6.** Firsthand contact with families from culturally diverse backgrounds is probably the least effective means of learning about student's home backgrounds, because it is time-consuming and because most families of differing cultural backgrounds maintain secrecy.

_____ **7.** In some cases, learners who have attended U.S. schools might speak better English than their parents or families, and this might result in the family being embarrassed or feeling unable to cope or deal with educators.

_____ **8.** It is best to address parents from differing cultural backgrounds by their first names to communicate a sense of familiarity and personal understanding.

_____ **9.** Parent education programs for parents and families should include efforts to transmit childrearing values, skills, and techniques.

_____ **10.** Teachers should not expect parents and families of different cultural backgrounds to serve on committees and advisory councils because they might not understand expectations of U.S. school systems.

(Answers to the Culture Quiz are located at the end of the chapter.)

of culturally diverse parents and families. As schools increasingly reflect the cultural diversity that characterizes the nation, educators will be challenged to involve, educate, and confer with all parents and families. This chapter focuses attention on parent involvement and conferences and suggests that educators should implement parent education programs designed to acquaint families of culturally different backgrounds with U.S. school systems.

## Involving and Educating Parents and Families

That parent involvement has a positive effect on student achievement and overall school progress is undeniable. An even more compelling reason to seek the involvement and participation of parents is to have them understand the U.S. school system, its expectations, and its predominantly middle-class white educators. Families from diverse cultures may feel uncomfortable conversing with educators and participating in school-sponsored events. The educator's challenge is to involve parents of all cultural, ethnic, racial, and social class groups, rather than only middle- and upper-class European American parents.

The issue for educators, however, is more complex than simply convincing parents to visit the school. It includes making conscientious efforts in several areas: explaining the school's function, making parents feel welcome and valued, educating parents about their children and adolescents, and involving parents in their children's and adolescents' education whenever possible. Only with the involvement and participation of all parents can schools genuinely reflect multiculturalism and address the needs and concerns of learners and parents from culturally different backgrounds.

### The Advantages of Parent Involvement and Education

The reasons for, and advantages of, parents and teachers working as partners and for teachers providing appropriate educational experiences for parents have been well documented. A strong positive correlation exists between parent involvement and pupil school achievement, increased student attendance, positive parent-child communication, improved student attitudes and behavior, and more parent-community support of the schools (Chavkin 1989; Hoover-Dempsey, Bassler, & Brissie, 1987).

Children of all backgrounds deserve the full consideration of teachers and parents; for children and parents of culturally different backgrounds the need may be even greater. Many parents and families of culturally different backgrounds do not understand school expectations. Some expect high achievement in all areas from their children and adolescents. Many have difficulties communicating with the school (Yao, 1988). Much can be gained, in terms of improved overall school achievement and improved cultural and interpersonal relationships between parents, teachers, and students, when educators actively seek parent and family involvement.

## Understanding Both Immediate and Extended Families

Another important reason for educators to promote parent involvement is to recognize the differences between European American and other families' beliefs toward the family. Whereas European Americans focus more on the immediate family, families of most other cultures include extended-family members, such as grandparents, aunts, uncles, and cousins.

The implications of extended families are readily apparent for educators. Rather than conferring with, educating, or involving only the mother and father, educators should make conscientious attempts to recognize immediate and extended families.

Implementing Research 11-1 looks at parenting styles and focuses on urban adolescents.

---

### IMPLEMENTING RESEARCH 11-1   Parenting Styles

Boveja (1998) examines parenting styles and urban adolescents' learning and studying strategies. She concludes that urban adolescents who perceive too much or too little support and control from their parents are likely to be at risk in their intellectual development, thus reducing their school achievement abilities.

Based on the premise that parents play a critical role in their children's education, she calls for a working alliance between parents and the school. Boveja also concludes that adolescents who perceived their parents as being authoritarian tend to engage in more effective learning and study strategies. They are more social and have high educational expectations.

The children of permissive or undemanding parents often have lower educational aspirations and achievement as well as below-average use of learning and study strategies. Boveja suggests three reasons for this finding: (1) the relationship between school systems and parents might not result in effective working alliances, (2) the significant number of low learning strategies among urban adolescents could be caused by adolescents having learning disabilities, and (3) many urban adolescents have additional life responsibilities and personal and emotional challenges that compete with academic competency as a priority.

#### Implementing the Research

1. Parents should be made aware during conferences and parent education efforts of the importance in being authoritarian and having high expectations for adolescents' behavior and academic achievement.
2. Educators need to strive for a close working alliance between parents and the school through conferences, involvement activities, and parent education programs.
3. Counselors should understand urban adolescents' life responsibilities and personal challenges that can interfere with learning and academic achievement and should provide, whenever possible, age-appropriate and culturally relevant counseling intervention.

---

*Source:* Boveja, M. E. (1998). Parenting styles and adolescents' learning strategies in the urban community. *Journal of Multicultural Counseling and Development, 26*(2), 110–119.

## *Reasons Parents Might Resist Teachers' Efforts*

Some parents resist teachers' efforts to involve them in the educational process, whether these efforts include conferences, involvement activities, or serving on committees. Why might parents and extended family members from minority cultures resist teachers' efforts? First, some cultures may harbor distrust and negative feelings toward professionals of other cultural backgrounds. Parents and children who harbor such attitudes have difficulty believing that professionals of differing cultural backgrounds understand them and want what is best for them. Parents with such powerful feelings of distrust will, in all likelihood, shun a teacher's efforts to build a working relationship between school and family.

Second, family members often fear disclosing personal problems or familial matters that might reflect negatively on themselves, the family, or the father's ability to manage home affairs. To reveal difficulties in the family may arouse feelings of shame in some cultures and the perception of having failed the family (Hartman & Askounis, 1989).

Third, some groups view a child's failure in school achievement or behavior to be a negative reflection on them and their parenting skills. West (1983) tells the story of a teacher who felt that she was not "reaching" a Vietnamese student. Although he was not disruptive, he was not participating fully in class. When she requested a parent-teacher conference, the father came to school full of dismay and feeling his son had done something terrible. The teacher repeatedly explained that she liked the student and was only trying to improve communication.

Fourth, home and school language differences can contribute to parents' resistance. Olsen (1988) reports several instances: immigrant children who had to translate and explain school events and bulletins sent home to parents; a Mexican mother in San Francisco who did not understand repeated notices, written in English, that her daughter was failing to attend school; and one Chinese father who understood that the grading system began with *A* and progressed downward. When the daughter received *S* for *satisfactory,* the father became confused and beat his daughter for her bad grades. To further complicate the situation, when he called the school, he could not understand the secretary and repeatedly hung up the telephone (Olsen, 1988).

Case Study 11-1 discusses how teachers might misunderstand parents and families of differing cultural backgrounds.

---

**FOLLOW THROUGH 11-1   Addressing Language Barriers**

Consult with the communication disorders specialist or ESL specialist in a school and the social service agencies in the community to learn how to work with and assist parents and family members whose language poses a barrier to effective communication. Make a list of publications, resource people, and special programs that help parents and families from culturally diverse backgrounds.

---

**CASE STUDY 11-1   Differing Expectations**

The teachers at Park Street Elementary School, an urban school with a significant Asian American population, did not understand what had happened. The Asian American parents and families who had come to the PTA meeting the previous night were quiet, even subdued, and offered very few comments or suggestions during the discussion times. "Why did they even come?" one teacher asked. "During individual conferences, they just sat there and listened. They were not any help."

A teacher who had more enlightened knowledge and more firsthand contact with Asian Americans overheard the conversation and recognized the need to clarify several points.

First, she explained, Asian Americans often place teachers on a pedestal and, generally speaking, consider teachers as worthy of honor and respect. Giving advice or suggestions to teachers is often considered as speaking against an authority figure. In their culture, teachers know what is best, and to question a teacher's decision can be construed as a personal attack.

Second, she explained that the Asian American concept of family causes individuals to be reluctant to reveal information; admitting problems might be considered a negative reflection on the family. Educators must remember to take care in trying to understand the source of a problem. Their efforts must not be construed as prying or as a personal criticism of the family.

Third, she explained that the extended-family concept resulted in other family members coming to the PTA meeting. Not only do the parents feel a responsibility for a learner's progress, but other relatives feel a sense of duty and take pride or shame in the learner's behavior.

---

In effect, the teachers in Case Study 11-1 understood neither Asian American parent and family members nor their expectations of schools and teachers. A more enlightened perspective would allow those teachers to understand that all the visitors were interested, even if reticent. Such understanding might lead to more productive parent conferences in the future.

Parents often do not understand the U.S. school system and its expectations. For example, major differences exist between American teachers and Indochinese teachers: Indochinese teachers are accorded higher levels of respect than are teachers in the United States; they are often awarded honorific titles; they expect students to bow, avoid eye contact, and not ask questions. Because Indochinese parents in their native land do not take active roles in schools, they have difficulty understanding PTA and other parent involvement programs. They view the teacher as the expert and feel that making suggestions to teachers about the education of children is inappropriate. Likewise, immigrant parents are often baffled by group activities, independent projects, and library research, because in their cultures, the lecture method is considered the most effective means of teaching (West, 1983).

Parents from multicultural backgrounds have indicated that the staff and institutional structure of the school intimidate them. They may feel awkward about approaching school personnel, particularly if they have had previous negative contacts with the school (Chavkin, 1989).

Speaking only of Asian American immigrant parents, Yao (1988) maintains that Asians' great respect for teachers and the learning process can actually pose a potential barrier. These parents are often reluctant to challenge the teacher's authority, and they sometimes feel that communicating with teachers may be perceived as disrespectful. Although these parents are usually attentive listeners, they seldom initiate contact with teachers and administrators, rarely ask questions, and seldom offer comments.

Cultural conflicts over childrearing expectations and differing value systems also disturb many Asian families. As they arrive at the need to make childrearing decisions on such issues as diet preference, sex education, dating patterns, and obedience to parents, these families are often torn between Eastern and Western manners, expectations, moral standards, and traditions (Yao, 1988).

## Understanding Cultural Diversity

Educators can readily see the reasons for understanding cultural diversity among families. However, they might have more difficulty reducing the myths, stereotypes, and other baggage that educators (and other professionals in U.S. society) have about parents and families from differing cultural backgrounds. Follow Through 11-2 provides a checklist by which educators can examine their beliefs and attitudes toward families from culturally different backgrounds.

---

**FOLLOW THROUGH 11-2    Examining Perceptions**

Ask yourself these questions:

1. Are my opinions of parents and families based on myths and stereotypes or on accurate and objective perceptions?
2. Have my experiences included positive firsthand contact with people from culturally different backgrounds?
3. What means have I employed to learn about the customs, traditions, values, and beliefs of all people?
4. Do I understand the extended-family concept, or do I only think "too many people live in the same house because of poverty conditions"?
5. Am I prejudiced, or do I have genuine feelings of acceptance for all people regardless of culture, ethnicity, race, and socioeconomic background?
6. Do I hold the perceptions that Native Americans are alcoholics, that African American families are headed by single females, that Asian Americans are the model minority and have achieved what represents the American Dream, or that Hispanic Americans have large families and live on welfare?
7. Can I perceive that aunts, uncles, and grandparents are as important as more immediate family members (that is, the mother and father)?
8. Do I understand the rich cultural backgrounds of families, and am I willing to base educational experiences on this diversity?
9. Do I know appropriate sources of information to learn more about parents and families from culturally diverse backgrounds?
10. Do I have the motivation, skills, and attitudes to develop close interrelationships with parents and families from culturally different backgrounds?

---

When reaching decisions about families, we cannot overemphasize the need for objectivity. Educators cannot objectively reach decisions concerning whether, and to what extent, to involve parents and families when they believe such statements as, "These parents just don't care," "The father is an alcoholic," "The father never lets his wife speak," or "Neither the mother nor the father has any ambition; they are satisfied to live off welfare." Educators who stereotype parents will probably do little to get to know and involve parents and families in their individual classrooms and certainly not in the overall school program.

An educator should not think he or she knows the prototypical "Native American family," "African American family," or any other "family." For example, African American families are so diverse that some believe that there is no such thing as a "typical" African American family (Ho, 1987).

Ho (1987) suggests that the educator should regard the family as a social system interacting with a number of other systems and that he or she must understand the historical significance of the family. Just as educators recognize that European American families differ in many ways, they must make conscientious attempts to understand the differences among families of all cultures.

Social class differences play a significant role in determining how a person acts, lives, thinks, and relates to others. Low wages; unemployment or underemployment; lack of property, savings, and food reserves; and having to meet the most basic needs on a day-to-day basis easily lead to feelings of helplessness, dependence, and inferiority. Differences in values, attitudes, behaviors, and beliefs among the various socioeconomic groups warrant the professional's consideration, especially because some minority groups' members come from the lower socioeconomic classes (Atkinson, Morten, & Sue, 1993).

Educators should understand that parents of differing cultural backgrounds view parenting differently, as Implementing Research 11-2 on page 286 shows.

Regrettably, a person's social class is sometimes thought to indicate his or her ambitions or motivation to achieve. It is a serious mistake to stereotype people according to social class, to assume, for example, that the lower classes lack ambition, do not want to work, or do not want to improve their education status. It is not unreasonable to suggest that people of the lower socioeconomic classes, whether Native, African, Asian, Hispanic, or European American, want to improve their social status in life, but that they meet with considerable frustration when faced with low education, high unemployment, conditions associated with poverty, and the racism and discrimination still prevalent in U.S. society.

Generational differences are another reason that an educator must not assume homogeneity within a culture. Older generations may be more prone to retain old-world values and traditions, because they tend to live in close proximity to people of similar language, traditions, and customs, whereas young people are likely to move anywhere in the United States.

One generational difference involves facility with the English language. While older generations may have lived in cultural enclaves with others who speak their native languages or who speak English at similar levels of fluency, younger generations who can communicate effectively in English are better able to cope in a predominantly English-speaking society. Another example includes elderly Asian

---

**IMPLEMENTING RESEARCH 11-2    Parenting: A Multiethnic Perspective**

Lynn Okagaki and Peter Frensch examine relations between parenting and school performance of fourth- and fifth-grade children in 75 Asian, 109 Latino, and 91 European American families. Aspects studied included parental expectations for children's educational attainment and grades, basic childrearing beliefs, self-reported behaviors, and the researchers' perceptions of parental efficacy.

They conclude that parents' beliefs and behaviors differ across ethnic groups. For example, Asian American parents hold high educational expectations for their children—they want their children to have more education than other parents do; they set higher standards for the minimum amount of education that they will accept from their children, they want their children to complete more years of schooling than they did, and they set higher standards for their children's grades. Other ethnic differences include European American families' parental beliefs and behaviors positively relate to children's school performance and that expectations of educational achievement positively relate to children's school achievement for Asian American parents but not for Latino parents.

**Implementing the Research**

1. Educators need to recognize that ethnic groups differ in their educational expectations of students and that these expectations can affect students' achievement and attitudes toward school.
2. Educators during parent-teacher conferences need to understand the mindsets that parents might bring to educational situations.
3. Educators should understand the research on multiethnic perspectives toward parenting, yet diligently work to avoid stereotyping of parents.
4. Efforts to educate parents (i.e., parent education programs) should include ethnically relevant perspectives rather than only middle-class, European American perspectives.

---

*Source:* Okagaki, L., & Frensch, P. A. (1998). Parenting and children's school achievement: A multi-ethnic perspective. *American Educational Research Journal, 35*(1), 123–144.

American people, who are often concerned about the acculturation of younger-generation Asian Americans. If they become too acculturated to U.S. society, how will the younger generations regard visiting and caring for older generations (Osako & Liu, 1986)?

## *Effective Parent Involvement Programs*

The Southwest Educational Development Laboratory (SEDL) has identified and described characteristics of promising parent involvement programs. Some of the selected programs are affiliated with resources such as the National Educational

---

**FOR ADDITIONAL INFORMATION   Internet Addresses**

**Parents Involvement in Middle-School Life**
http://familyeducation.com/experts/advice/ 0,1183,1-1144,00.html Focuses on communication and lack thereof between parents and teachers.

**Involved Dads Get an "A"**
http://familyeducation.com/article/0,1120, 3–220,00.html  Provides information supporting father involvement in children's education.

**Working with Families**
http://www.speakeasy.org/~moonshyn/ family.html  Provides information on learning to work with families.

**How to Define Parent Involvement**
http://list.pta.org:8001/GMDocs/GMHtml/ EMOCJABD.html Provides information on various definitions of parent involvement.

**Annotated Bibliography Reference #20**
http://scov.csos.jhu.edu/p2000/bibref20.htm Provides information from the Center on Families, Communities, Schools, and Children's Learning.

---

Association or the National School Volunteer Program, and others are the result of the efforts of local schools. The programs share seven essential elements:

1. Written policies, which legitimize the importance of parent involvement and help frame the context for program activities
2. Administrative support, including a main budget for implementing programs, material and product resources, and people with designated responsibilities
3. Promising training programs for both staff and parents
4. Programs that make the partnership approach their essence
5. Two-way communication between home and school that occurs frequently and regularly
6. Use of networking to identify additional resources and encourage people to share information, resources, and technique expertise
7. Regular evaluation, during key stages and at the end of the cycle or phase of the program, that provides indicators of progress and outcomes (Williams & Chavkin, 1989).

Most programs designed to work with families have mainly served English-speaking families who know how to benefit from parent–teacher programs. Educators need to consider cross-cultural perspectives when working with families. To lessen the problems associated with communication, both written and oral, the educators in the parent involvement program at Emerson School in Rosemead, California, sent letters in four languages to parents and conducted meetings in six languages. The program encourages parents to offer, in their native languages, their input and opinions about school services. The school then translates their responses and reports back in the parents' native languages (Davis, 1989).

## Parents and Families of Culturally Different Backgrounds

A prerequisite to understanding culturally diverse parents and families is gaining accurate and objective knowledge about expectations, needs, and challenges facing people with differing cultural backgrounds. Without doubt, educators can improve their understanding by reading books and journals, taking courses, and attending professional conferences. Although these means can provide considerable insight into cultural diversity and should be an integral part of the educator's learning agenda, firsthand contact with individuals continues to be one of the most effective means of gaining an accurate perspective of cultural diversity.

Firsthand contact has an advantage that other means cannot always provide: directly learning about "people" and their individual attitudes, values, and beliefs. With understanding and knowledge, the potential exists for genuine feelings of caring and empathy to develop between people of differing races, cultures, and ethnic backgrounds.

Case Study 11-2 encourages teachers to have firsthand contact with people from culturally different backgrounds.

Although there is probably no adequate substitute for firsthand contact with parents and families, it is possible to gain information through a parent survey. Without doubt, the most effective means would be to use a parent survey in addition to firsthand contact. It is important for the educators who design the survey to remember that some questions may be culturally sensitive; for example, questions that might not be offensive to European American populations might be construed as an invasion of privacy by many parents and families from culturally different backgrounds. Examples of culturally sensitive questions are those on childrearing techniques, sex education, dating patterns, and parental authority.

---

### CASE STUDY 11-2    Firsthand Contact

Mr. Johnson, principal at Central Middle School, encourages teachers in his school to have firsthand contact with people from various cultures. He praises teachers who take courses focusing on cultural diversity, attend seminars and conferences, and read professional books and journals. These are all excellent sources, he thinks, but he still wants teachers to have firsthand contact, which is imperative if genuine knowledge and respect are to develop.

Mr. Johnson encourages firsthand contact in several ways: First, he expects and encourages teachers to be integral members of the community and to participate in as many social and cultural activities as possible. Second, he encourages parents and families from culturally different backgrounds to visit the school any time, not just for parent conferences. During these impromptu visits, Mr. Johnson urges teachers to meet parents and families and to discuss items of interest. Third, he encourages home visits, which are scheduled at times convenient for the parents. These visits provide a means for teachers to get to know family members on a more personal basis. Although the principal requires the teachers to record their observations and perceptions, the purpose of the visits is neither to judge nor to condemn. He believes that knowledge of cultural diversity contributes to improving attitudes toward people with differences, regardless of degree or type.

---

**FOLLOW THROUGH 11-3    Selecting Parent Survey Questions**

1. Do you feel educators in your child's or adolescent's school understand and meet the overall needs and concerns of learners from different cultural backgrounds?
2. Do you feel school policies recognize that children and adolescents of culturally different backgrounds differ from the European American population?
3. Does the media center (children's and adolescents' books, films, other visual material) reflect the cultural diversity of the school?
4. How well has the school succeeded in employing a faculty and staff (administrators, teachers, library media specialists, special personnel, speech therapists, guidance counselors, psychologies, school nurses) that reflects the cultural diversity of the student body?
5. Do you feel school expectations (competition, motivation, achievements, aspirations) reflect the values and expectations of learners of culturally diverse backgrounds?
6. Do you feel extracurricular activities in the school reflect the needs and interests of children and adolescents of culturally diverse backgrounds?
7. Do teaching methods and strategies (lecture format, small group, cooperative learning, ability grouping) reflect a concern for the educational well-being of all learners?
8. Has the school provided opportunities to offer opinions, input, advice, and suggestions concerning improvement of the school program or changing an aspect you would like to see changed?
9. Is your child progressing toward or succeeding at goals that you feel are important?
10. Do you feel the school provides information and assistance concerning social service organizations?
11. What comments or suggestions do you want to offer concerning your child or adolescent in school?

---

Although the questions in Follow Through 11-3 might be included on a parent survey, any final determination should depend on the degree of cultural diversity and the specific information sought.

Educators may decide to develop the survey in the parents' native language, rather than risk that the survey will not be completed or that problems will result from poor communication. Generally speaking, parent surveys should be clear and short, require only a brief amount of time to complete, and avoid conveying middle-class European American perspectives.

We remind readers that the questions in Follow Through 11-3 are sample questions; they are neither intended to be all-inclusive nor designed for a specific culturally diverse group. Educators with a large percentage of one culturally diverse population might want specific questions designed to pinpoint certain areas.

## Visiting Parents and Families in the Home

Home visits may be one of the most effective ways for teachers to get to know learners, their immediate and extended families, and their home environment and culture. Families from different cultural backgrounds often perceive family roles

---

**FOLLOW THROUGH 11-4    Visiting in the Home**

Visiting in the homes of children and adolescents can raise sensitive issues, especially with parents and families of culturally different backgrounds. Perceiving family life and parenting practices from different cultural perspectives can result in misunderstanding. For example, a middle-class African American educator might fail to understand a Hispanic or Asian American family. Make a list of "do's and don'ts"—those behaviors you should demonstrate and should not demonstrate in an effort to show understanding and respect for the parents' cultural heritage.

---

differently, have differing expectations of the schools, and expect older family members to play significantly greater childrearing roles than European Americans might expect. The only way to understand such differences is to get to know the families personally.

Home visits can provide valuable information about learners and their homes, but perhaps an even greater benefit is that learners and their families see that educators care and are interested in all children and adolescents. Parents from culturally different backgrounds may also feel more at ease in their own surroundings than they would in the (perhaps) strange and sterile school environment.

Before the home visit, educators should call or send a note to the parents and establish a time that is convenient for both the teacher and the parent. At the beginning of the visit, the teacher should talk informally with the parents and the child for a few minutes to establish a friendly tone and to reduce the parents' anxiety. At all times, teachers should remember that they are visitors and should avoid judging situations and conditions in the home. Parents will have greater confidence in the teacher if they think the discussion will be held in confidence (Shea & Bauer, 1985).

## Communication

Educators should be careful about how they speak to parents, especially parents and families from non-native-English backgrounds. Misunderstandings might also result not only from language differences, but also if the parent or the teacher (or both) misunderstand each others' eye contact or body posture (Studer, 1993/1994).

Believing that educators should speak so parents can and will listen, Studer (1993/1994) offers several suggestions:

1. Listen actively rather than passively.
2. Pose questions in such a way that parents and families do not feel their privacy is being invaded.
3. Listening includes attending skills, such as use of particular body postures. Other listening behaviors include squaring shoulders and looking directly at the speaker, using a posture of uncrossed arms and legs, leaning toward the speaker, and maintaining eye contact (Studer, 1993/1994).

Educators in multicultural situations must recognize that these behaviors are to be understood rather than expected. Listening behaviors that are typical and expected of middle-class white parents might be far different from those people of other cultural backgrounds exhibit. For example, maintaining eye contact might be considered rude in some cultures. Likewise, body postures are also culturally based. Educators should not assess parents' and families' interest and commitment to children's education by using middle-class European American standards and expectations.

Humans communicate at several levels simultaneously: through verbal expression, or what they say; through body language or nonverbal expression, or how they behave; and through emotional responses, or how they show what they feel. The more congruent these levels of expression are, the more meaningful or understanding the communication becomes to others (Shea & Bauer, 1985). One can easily recognize the importance of understanding the various types of communication with families of differing cultural backgrounds.

Whether communicating through speaking directly, telephoning, or writing to parents, educators are responsible for not allowing language or communication differences, verbal or nonverbal, to interfere with overall communication. Several factors warrant consideration: First, as we mentioned previously, the parents' English skills might not allow effective communication. Second, nonverbal communication might pose a problem; for example, the European American who looks the Native American directly in the eye while communicating might be considered rude, and the educator might think a Native American's glancing away to indicate disinterest or irritation.

Another example of problems that can result from nonverbal communication is Asian American parents and families, who are especially sensitive to nonverbal messages and who may construe a teacher's folded arms or other casual gestures as indicative of an indifferent attitude (Chavkin, 1989). Third, educators should avoid jargon with which parents might be unfamiliar: *PET, assertive discipline, critical thinking, cooperative learning, mastery learning, percentiles,* or terms associated with computers or technology, for example.

Telephoning represents another means of communicating with parents and demonstrates the teacher's personal interest in both the learner and the parents. Positive telephone contacts can significantly affect a child's school performance; conversely, negative calls can have a negative effect. As with other forms of communication, teachers must exercise caution when using the telephone to communicate with parents.

Telephoning is a great way to encourage parents to attend meetings, conferences, and other school events (Shea & Bauer, 1985). It can be extremely threatening, however, to parents and families of culturally different backgrounds, because they have come to expect bad news whenever a representative of the school calls. Writing specifically about telephoning parents from culturally different backgrounds, Marion (1979) proposed guidelines for minimizing parent and teacher misunderstanding:

1. Address parents as Mr. or Mrs., because parents from different backgrounds often do not receive the same respect and courtesy as other people.

2. Use a tone of voice that expresses respect and courtesy, because a call from school often raises anxiety levels.
3. Discuss the child's or adolescent's positive points before discussing the problem to be solved.
4. Use language the parent understands and a tone that does not sound condescending.
5. Respond with empathy if the parent has difficulty understanding unfamiliar educational concepts.

Educators can also write notes and letters to keep parents informed of children's progress and of administrative and record-keeping problems and concerns, schedule changes, special events, holidays, workshops, field trips, and other items of interest. Effective notes are clear, concise, and positive and may speak to parents and family members in their primary language. Unless used systematically, however, notes and letters have limited value in reinforcing the child's academic performance or social and emotional behavior and are best used as one component of the overall parent and teacher communication (Shea & Bauer, 1985).

## Involving Parents and Families as Volunteers

Parent volunteers can contribute significantly to the quality of the services offered to learners in the school (Shea & Bauer, 1985). The National School Volunteer Program cites four reasons for using volunteers in the classroom and school:

1. relieving the professional staff of nonteaching duties,
2. providing needed services to individual children to supplement the work of the classroom teacher,
3. enriching the experiences of children beyond those normally available in school, and
4. building a better understanding among citizens of school problems, and stimulating widespread citizen support for public education.

Although parents are the most frequent volunteers, siblings, relatives, older elementary and secondary students, college students, senior citizens, business and professional groups, and other members of the community can volunteer to participate in school activities (Shea & Bauer, 1985).

Although Shea and Bauer (1985) were referring to volunteers working with children who have disabilities, many of their recommendations and suggestions also apply to parents and family members of different cultural backgrounds. Volunteers should participate in a brief preservice training program and an on-the-job training program. Preservice training programs should introduce volunteers to school procedures and expectations and spell out their roles and functions. This training should emphasize the importance of confidentiality and attendance. It should offer an opportunity for parents to discuss the program with experienced volunteers and to visit with the teacher in the classroom setting. On-the-job training is a continuous process in which volunteers learn their specific activities (Shea & Bauer, 1985).

Parents and extended family members from all cultures have numerous talents and skills to share with children and adolescents. People from differing cultural backgrounds, however, often consider educators and schools as both authoritarian and worthy of honor and praise. Therefore, some people might be hesitant to "interfere" with school routines or may feel that their talents are not worthy to be shared with the school. The administrator's and teacher's role in this situation is to encourage and convince people that schools are open to new ideas and that their talents are worth sharing. To accomplish such a goal, educators should send home, at the beginning of the school year, a parent involvement questionnaire designed to determine skills, talents, and areas of interest.

Serving on committees is another way parents and extended family members can become involved in classrooms and school. Through committee work, parents contribute to the classroom and school and learn about program development, operation, staffing, and evaluation. Parents also develop an appreciation for staffing concerns, curriculum development, fiscal exigencies, materials and equipment needs, and other demands of the instructional program (Shea & Bauer, 1985).

Gender Perspectives 11-1 looks at parents' perceptions of goals of Project SPLASH!, especially with regard to gender issues, self-esteem, and motivation.

As with other forms of involvement, these parents and families might not understand the purpose of committees and how they function. Educators must work toward making the composition of the committee representative of the diversity of the student body. Guidelines for parents working on school committees include:

1. Remember the committee's purpose and objectives.
2. Be confident of the committee's ability to accomplish the assigned task.
3. Begin small, and take one step at a time.
4. Function within the school, and become an integral part of the classroom or school.
5. Seek financial, administrative, informational, and other assistance when necessary.

---

**GENDER PERSPECTIVES 11-1   Parents' Perceptions: Gender Issues, Self-Esteem, and Motivation**

Murphy and Sullivan described Project SPLASH!, a program for minority adolescent girls with high potential in mathematics and science. Specifically, they looked at characteristics of program interventions that have the potential for increasing the numbers of women and minorities in the fields of science and mathematics. Murphy and Sullivan also looked at parent perceptions of the program, specifically its goals as well as gender issues, causal attribution, self-esteem, and motivation. Goals evolve as practicing scientists mentor the girls. Students revealed preferences for coeducational programs, active learning, outdoor education, and informal grading. Murphy and Sullivan found higher self-esteem among African American girls than among Hispanic American girls.

---

*Source:* Murphy, D. S., & Sullivan, K. (1997). Connecting adolescent girls of color and math/science interventions. (ERIC Document Reproduction Service No: ED 410 106)

---

**FOLLOW THROUGH 11-5    Involving Parents and Families in Schools**

Design a program to involve parents and families from culturally different backgrounds. Plan how you will invite and obtain their participation, help them understand that elementary and secondary schools need their participation, and teach them appropriate activities or utilize their individual expertise. Name several points that educators should consider (and propose an appropriate response) such as parents' language difficulties, lack of understanding of U.S. schools, and the immense respect that many parents and families have for educators.

---

Parents of different cultural backgrounds should not serve only on committees that deal with multicultural concerns; these parents may serve on any committee in which they have an interest. Committees might include curriculum, discipline and related problems, teacher evaluation, student–teacher relations, home study and work habits, extracurricular activities, student assessment and test results, career education, school dropouts, or any other aspect of the school (Shea & Bauer, 1985).

## Parent-Teacher Conferences

The parent-teacher conference presents an opportunity for parents and teachers to exchange information about the child's school and home activities. It also provides an occasion to involve parents in planning and implementing their child's educational program. When teachers contact parents to schedule progress report conferences, they should explain the purpose of the conference.

To lessen the parent's anxiety about the conference, teachers might provide parents with a written agenda. Educators should also remember that the purpose of the conference is the child and school progress, not the teacher's or parent's personal, social, emotional, or marital problems. Although these issues may affect the learner's overall school progress, educators should direct the focus of the conference toward areas of school function (Shea & Bauer, 1985).

The agenda for the parent-teacher conference might include discussion of the learner's test scores or assessment results. Although most parents, regardless of cultural background, might benefit from an explanation of the terms normally associated with measurement and evaluation, parents might need even more detailed information. Test results are often a concern for parents and children, and parents may react strongly to results that indicate their child or adolescent is functioning at a lower level than most learners. Educators should ask parents from differing cultural backgrounds to state their understanding of the information and make sure parents understand the results and conclusions. Teachers should make a sincere effort to alleviate any anxiety that parents express over possible misuse of test results (Shea & Bauer, 1985).

---

**FOLLOW THROUGH 11-6     Determining Concerns during Parent–**
**Teacher Conferences**

Make a list of possible concerns and barriers that might interfere with the success of the parent-teacher conference. How will you motivate parents and families (who might feel that speaking forthrightly to the teacher is disrespectful) to speak, voice concerns, and make suggestions?

---

Spaulding (1994) offers four suggestions for effective parent conferences. These might be even more important for educators meeting with parents and families from different cultural backgrounds:

1. Begin to work toward positive relationships with parents and families before school begins.
2. Talk regularly with students' parents; tell them of accomplishments and concerns, and ask for their advice and suggestions. Extra efforts might be necessary to convince parents to become active participants, especially because some cultures hold teachers in high regard and are reluctant to question or offer advice.
3. Ask students to join in parent conferences and to offer their opinions. Culturally diverse parents and their children might have difficulty with this suggestion, because some cultures place value on children being "seen and not heard."
4. Make the conference as comfortable as possible; reinforce students' accomplishments, avoid using confusing jargon, show parents how they can help, and end the conference on a positive note.

## Parent Advisory Councils

A parent advisory council can be an excellent means of providing parents and families of culturally diverse backgrounds opportunities to voice opinions and generally influence the overall operation of the school. By having a council composition that reflects the cultural diversity of the student body, council representatives (or parents who make suggestions and comments through selected representatives) can offer specific suggestions for devising the school curriculum and making the teaching and learning environment more multicultural in nature. Council members might want to discuss the cultural diversity of the administrative and teaching staff, how the curriculum and teaching and learning process reflect diversity, policies that groups of differing cultural backgrounds might not understand, methods of making the school more multicultural in nature, or any topic that might seem relevant at the time.

---

### CASE STUDY 11-3   Parent Advisory Councils

Dr. Suarez, principal at Westview High School, carefully planned his parent advisory council. The composition was all-important this academic year. The state department of education had mandated increasingly stringent academic rules that would threaten the academic standards of slower students; the number of students of diverse cultural backgrounds was increasing; several acts of racism had plagued the previous school year; and his faculty was almost all white and middle-class. He thought parents could play a significant role this year, especially if he could convince leaders of the various diverse communities to participate.

He wondered what issues he might raise as the council progressed with its work. His list grew: grades, racism, evaluation, his district's inability (or lack of initiative, he thought) to employ faculty and staff members from culturally diverse backgrounds, language programs, school policies, curricular materials, instructional practices—the list seemed endless. "This will certainly be a challenging year," he thought. He wanted a council with cultural diversity proportional to that of the student body.

What problems might this diversity on the council bring? Again, his list grew: differing expectations of schools and teachers, misunderstandings about U.S. school systems, language and communication problems, reluctance to take an active role, and not understanding the role of the council. For the members with different cultural backgrounds, he planned an additional meeting to provide opportunities to answer questions, resolve concerns, and become better acquainted. Even with the pressing issues and the challenges of involving all members, regardless of culture, on the council, Dr. Suarez perceived this as a positive time—a time when his school's role in helping learners from different backgrounds could be defined more accurately and a time of enhanced acceptance and understanding.

---

Case Study 11-3 examines how Dr. Suarez carefully planned for cultural diversity on the parent advisory council.

An advisory council can serve as a liaison between school and classroom and between home and community, and it can function as a permanent parent-to-parent communications committee to announce meetings, special events, personnel changes, and other notices of interest. The advisory committee can also assume responsibility for organizing and directing ad hoc or temporary committees (Shea & Bauer, 1985).

Orientation sessions might be in order, especially for parents and families who may not understand the purpose of the council, may feel that parents would be meddling in schools' business, or may not understand procedures by which meetings work. An orientation meeting can help council members feel better prepared and feel more comfortable about future meetings. Suggested topics for an orientation session include: council role and authority, purpose, district organization, value and functions of committees, decision-making procedures (perhaps including a brief session on Robert's Rules of Order), how to disagree and the value of expressing a different view, and expectations of members (Jennings, 1989).

## *Parent and Family Education*

The concept of parent education dates back to the 1800s and carries differing definitions and perceptions that have resulted in a variety of forms and emphases. A wide array of activities continues to be appropriate for parent education programs. These range from family and cultural transmission of childrearing values, skills, and techniques to more specific parenting behaviors. Specifically, however, we define the term *parent education* as planned activities that are designed to educate parents about their children and adolescents, goals of U.S. school systems, and ways they can help their child or adolescent experience success, both academically and behaviorally, in school.

Although schools should develop parent education programs specifically for individual learners and their parents, some programs help parents with special needs, enhance knowledge of family life, teach techniques for changing attitudes and behaviors, help parents change their own negative behaviors, provide health and sex education information, and teach parents how to help with the education process.

The need for parent education has been documented: Parents become more involved and develop more positive attitudes toward school activities; parents often dread the changes in their child's or adolescent's development; parents sometimes absolve themselves of responsibility; and parents often need assistance in understanding curricular areas. The need results from the heightened concern about pressures related to more working mothers, the effects of geographic mobility, divorce rates, and economic uncertainties as well as from parents needing relevant information for children's social, physical, emotional, and intellectual development.

The realities, however, pose a dilemma that demands educators' understanding. Although parent education programs have become routine aspects of many early childhood programs, evidence indicates that many middle- and secondary-school educators have not developed parent education programs. Early childhood education appears to have made substantial progress in planning and implementing parent education programs and has provided the framework in both theory and practice for schools or other levels.

Implementing Research 11-3 on page 298 tells about a parent education program designed for Hispanic parents.

### *Rationale for Parent Education Programs*

Two reasons speak to the importance of parent education: understanding the various developmental periods and responding appropriately to children's and adolescents' behavior. Although we address each reason separately, close and intricate relationships between the two areas warrant parental recognition and understanding.

Effective parent education programs provide experiences that show a developmental basis for children's and adolescents' behavior. Rather than allowing parents to assume that they have failed in parenting roles or to absolve themselves of

**IMPLEMENTING RESEARCH 11-3    Hispanic Parent Education Program**

Murray and colleagues describe the Padres Trabajando por la Paz (PTP), a violence intervention program for Hispanic parents to increase parental monitoring. The program focuses on violent behaviors such as homicide, assault, delinquency, and victimization.

The authors explain the need for a parent education intervention program designed to prevent school violence. They maintain that violence contributes to a significant proportion of the mortality and morbidity among adolescents. While all causes of death among adolescents have decreased over the past three decades, mortality by homicide has increased. For children aged 1–14 years, homicide is a significant cause of death.

In 1991, 12-year-old children were at greater risk for violent victimization than people aged 24 years or older. In addition, children who are the victims or witnesses of violence are at increased risk of depression, anger, anxiety, and stress disorders. To reduce the effects of violence on children, the American Psychological Association recommends a comprehensive approach to violence prevention, including interventions for parents. Padres Trabajando por la Paz (PTP) is a parent education intervention designed specifically for Hispanic parents.

The PTP program uses an innovative program planning process called intervention mapping. Intervention mapping provides an explicit step-by-step guide to integrating theory, empirical findings from the literature, and data collected from parents and families. The process includes intervention, needs assessment, and program evaluation. During each step of the process, educators revisit theory, literature, and parents' and families' needs and interests to tailor the intervention.

The intervention planning process is conducted in five steps: Step 1 includes designing program objectives that address the parents and their children; health-promoting behaviors; theory, literature, and practice; and a matrix of learning and change objectives. Step 2 involves matching intervention models from theory, literature, and information collected from the parents. Step 3 involves translating methods into practical strategies. Step 4 includes program adoption and strategies. Step 5 includes planning for monitoring and evaluation.

### Implementing the Research

We think that Hispanic parents (and probably all parents) should:

1. ask middle-school students about their plans when they leave the house, such as where they are going, who they will be with, and when they plan to return;
2. obtain a list of telephone numbers of their children's friends, so contact, if necessary, can be made;
3. call parents of their child's friends to show concern and interest and to make parental expectations known; and
4. visit the school to participate in parent education programs and to learn of efforts to reduce violence.

*Source:* Murray, N., Kelder, S., Parcel, G., & Orphinas, P. (1998). Development of an intervention map for a parent education intervention violence to prevent violence among Hispanic middle school students. *Journal of School Health, 68*(2), 46–52.

responsibility for behavior, programs can help parents understand the developmental changes and the contemporary world of children and adolescents.

Specifically, parents need to understand the cause-and-effect relationship between development and behavior. The cause of certain behavior may result from children's and adolescents' quest for independence and from peer pressure to experiment with alcohol, drugs, sex, and other challenges to authority.

Basically, educators should provide programs that convince parents that their children are not necessarily "going bad" or "turning into hoodlums" and that, although understanding changes in behavioral patterns may be difficult for parents, children and adolescents need to feel accepted and understood. Parents need to understand that feeling guilty or absolving themselves of responsibility may result in even worse attention-getting, or even delinquent, behaviors. Parents need to understand the effects of one-parent homes on development and behavior. At the same time, educators should emphasize that not all behavior results from family disruption.

Parent education programs should also be culturally sensitive as Implementing Research 11-4 on page 300 suggests.

## Special Needs of Parents and Families

Planning parent education programs for parents and families from differing cultural backgrounds requires that educators look at issues, topics, and formats from the perspective of these parents and families. Prepackaged programs, or programs that European Americans in middle- or upper-class suburban schools use might not be adequate for culturally diverse parents and families, whatever their social class.

Although special needs vary with culture, social class, and geographic area, what specific needs might parents and families have? Educators, after an objective and accurate needs assessment, might find that parents of diverse cultural backgrounds require educational assistance in understanding such areas as: school expectations, parent's roles in the school, tests and assessment scores, children's and adolescents' development, appropriate social services agencies and organizations that can provide assistance, homework and how to get help, school committees and parent advisory councils, and other involvement activities. This list provides only a few examples, but it suffices to show that parent education programs should be designed for a specific cultural group and not rely on a program that parents may not understand or feel is not culturally relevant.

Methods and activities selected for the parent education program determine the success of the effort. Programs for minority parents should not rely too heavily on reading material (unless participants are clearly proficient in English), should not expect parents to take active vocal roles in the beginning stages, and should not expect or require parents to reveal situations or information that may be personal or a negative reflection on the family or the home.

**IMPLEMENTING RESEARCH 11-4    Culturally Sensitive Parent Education**

Gorman and Balter (1997) maintain that the recent growth of culturally sensitive parent education programs necessitates an evaluative look at their effectiveness. First, they contend, the need for parent education is clear; malnutrition, poverty, risk of living in neighborhoods with high rates of crime and drug dependency are some of the problems. Intervention with parents has included material supports, emotional encouragement, information presentation, therapeutic guidance, and skills development.

Parent education offers a wide array of programs with purposes that vary in both content and format. For example, parent education programs can be seen as strengthening parents' informal support systems to empower them to raise their children successfully; other programs claim to primarily prevent child maltreatment through skill building, as well as to promote child welfare through encouraging parent child communication.

They discuss Parent Effectiveness Training (PET) and Systematic Training for Effective Parenting (STEP), which have been criticized for being irrelevant to nonwhite, non–middle-class parents and for being culturally insensitive. For example, the families described in the programs are two-parent units with adequate financial resources and parents who have at least a high-school education. These two researchers call for culturally sensitive parent education such as the Effective Black Parenting Program (EBPP) for African American parents, the Los Niños Bien Educados Program for Latino American parents, and the Parent-Child Development Center for Mexican American parents. After a detailed discussion of these three programs, Gorman and Balter note that the move to include multiculturalism in parent education programs is an encouraging sign. If parent education programs are to be effective, they must be made available to all populations as well as be acceptable and relevant.

**Implementing the Research**

1. Educators planning and implementing parent education programs need to provide educative experiences that reflect the unique needs of parents from culturally different backgrounds.
2. Parent education programs need to be genuinely culturally relevant. "Add-on" sessions that might have little relevance to the content of the primary program are not adequate.
3. Differences among parents and families should not be considered "deficits" in need of improvement or elimination; instead, differences in parents and parenting behavior should be seen as strengths on which to build positive family interactions.

*Source:* Gorman, J. C., & Balter, L. (1997). Culturally sensitive parent education: A critical review of quantitative research. *Review of Educational Research, 67*(3), 339–369.

In Implementing Research 11-5, Rivera and Rogers-Adkinson (1997) explain the need for appropriate social skills training programs for children in need and their parents.

## Formats of Parent Education Programs

Teachers must reach a decision about whether to employ a prepackaged parenting program that may lead to a loosely organized discussion group or to develop

---

**IMPLEMENTING RESEARCH 11-5** *Culturally Sensitive Interventions with Parents*

Rivera and Rogers-Adkinson provide an overview of cultural influence on social behaviors of children from diverse backgrounds and suggest practical applications for developing and implementing social skills training programs for these children and their parents. They explain that the culture in which children grow up has an impact on the social behaviors they exhibit in various situations. Such culturally based behaviors can be misinterpreted by mainstream peers and adults who may also conclude they are functioning unsuccessfully in the mainstream school environment.

The challenge for educators is to distinguish between social skills differences and deficiencies. In explaining their point, they provide a detailed and comprehensive table showing cultural influences on social behaviors of Hispanic, African, Asian, and Native American children and adolescents.

**Implementing the Research**

The authors provide several guidelines for working with parents:

1. Be familiar with parents' views of their children's social behaviors and their children's social difficulties. A child's apparent social deficiencies in the mainstream environment may be deemed appropriate at home.
2. Respect parents' and families' cultural differences and respond in culturally appropriate ways.
3. Consider parents' family structures. Proposing a democratic family structure might seem inappropriate for families who believe (by tradition) in more autocratic or patriarchical structures.
4. Consider conflicts with cultural beliefs and values. Parent training programs that emphasize empowering the child to make choices and ultimately accept responsibility for consequences may not seem appropriate for Hispanic or Asian parents.

*Source:* Rivera, B. D., & Rogers-Adkinson, D. (1997). Culturally sensitive interventions: Social skills training with children and parents from culturally and linguistically diverse backgrounds. *Intervention in School and Clinic, 33*(2), 75–80.

a program that addresses parental needs for a particular school. Prepackaged programs have several advantages (e.g., they require less preparatory time and little revision), but they may not be applicable to a diverse range of cultures.

Developing a parent education program based on specific family and community needs might prove effective, and parents might receive it more enthusiastically. The format of the program can take several directions and should reflect the needs and interests of individual schools and parents.

Before scheduling planning sessions, educators should conduct an assessment or needs inventory to determine preferred methods and content. Parent education modes may include lectures, discussion groups, CD-ROMs, computer programs, videotapes, cassettes, and PowerPoint presentations. Parents may schedule appointments with available parent educators to discuss confidential and personal

---

**FOLLOW THROUGH 11-7   Designing Parent Education Programs**

In all likelihood, it will be difficult to purchase a prepackaged parent education program that meets the needs of parents from a number of cultural backgrounds. For example, African American parents might not experience the same challenges as Native Americans. Likewise, first-generation Asian Americans probably do not experience the same problems as third-generation Asian Americans. We think it might be more feasible to design programs with individual cultural groups in mind. Name a number of methods (such as firsthand contact and surveys, perhaps written in native languages) that will provide information on directions the parent education program should take.

---

matters concerning their children and adolescents that they do not want revealed in large group settings.

Parent education sessions will undoubtedly stimulate questions, comments, and other discussion. Rather than relying on a lecture format with a large group, the leader of the session should allow time for parents to speak or meet in small groups. Sometimes, one of the leader's most effective approaches may be to let parents know that other parents experience similar problems.

## Helping Parents Understand Their Roles and School Expectations

A major role of parent education programs should be to help parents of differing cultural groups understand the school's expectations and the parent's role in the teaching and learning process. Designing such a program requires educators to assess the needs and concerns of the specific culture. For example, although Native and Asian American parents might have similarities, they have substantial differences that necessitate culture-specific programs.

First, educators need to recognize that some parents and families, especially of more recent generations, might not understand U.S. school expectations and perspectives, which place emphasis on individual achievement, competition, and responsibility for one's own possessions. Parents and families of differing cultural backgrounds should not encourage their children and adolescents to adopt middle- or upper-class white perspectives.

---

**FOLLOW THROUGH 11-8   Discussing School Expectations**

Discuss with a group of parents from differing cultural backgrounds their expectations of the U.S. school systems. After listening, begin thinking about expectations that need clarification and of ways to respond to the needs of children, adolescents, and their parents. How do their expectations differ from those of European Americans? How can educators convey school expectations to parents and families?

---

Instead, educators can explain to parents the differing cultural expectations (e.g., group versus individual achievement, competition versus working together, sharing versus ownership) of various cultural groups. Educators should also explain the school's expectations in other areas, such as curricular matters, instructional strategies, classroom management and discipline, homework and extracurricular activities, and other aspects of the school that parents and families may need assistance in understanding.

Second, educators should make clear the parents' role and responsibilities in their children's or adolescents' education. Sometimes, people from different cultural backgrounds may think they do not know enough about U.S. school systems to make a contribution, or they may perceive the school as an authoritarian institution that does not appreciate input and suggestions. The educator's role is to change misconceptions of the schools and to show that learners' academic achievement and overall school progress can be enhanced when parents take an active role in the school. In meeting this goal, educators need to show all parents and families that:

1. They are responsible for encouraging and helping their children and adolescents in all phases of the teaching and learning process.
2. They are encouraged to visit the school and voice their input, recommendations, and suggestions.
3. They are encouraged to participate in conferences, involvement activities, parent education sessions, and parent advisory councils.

## Summing Up

Educators who want to involve parents and families from culturally different backgrounds should:

1. Understand the extended family concept, and plan educational experiences for both immediate and extended-family members.
2. Understand that parents and families may resist teachers' efforts to involve them in school activities.
3. Understand parents as individuals with intracultural, socioeconomic, and generational differences.
4. Learn as much as possible about parents and families through firsthand contact, parent surveys, and any other means that provide accurate and objective information.
5. Visit the homes of students to gain a better understanding of family backgrounds, values, customs, and traditions.
6. Ensure that communication between the school and family reflects a genuine understanding of the problems that might result from language and communication differences, both verbal and nonverbal.
7. Plan and conduct parent-teacher conferences so that parents will understand the purposes and procedures of the conference process.

8. Ensure that parent advisory councils have a composition that represents the cultural, ethnic, and racial composition of the student body, and ensure that the councils address the specific needs and concerns of parents and families from differing cultural backgrounds.

9. Understand that parent education programs are especially important for parents who might not understand the school's roles and expectations and who may need assistance with their child or adolescent in a predominantly European American school and society.

## Suggested Learning Activities

1. Prepare a parent survey designed to obtain information from parents and families of different cultural backgrounds. List questions that will provide specific information about what parents and families expect from schools, how teachers can help children and adolescents, and how parents and families can contribute to the educational process. In preparing this survey, what are some precautions you might want to consider?

2. Design procedures for an effective parent advisory committee, with the purpose of involving parents and families. Your design should consider what means you will use to engage participants of all cultural backgrounds, the overall goals of the committee, how the committee will report to the general school population, a sample agenda (for an individual meeting and for the school year), how you will accommodate participants who are not proficient in English, and any special factors that educators should consider when dealing with minority populations.

3. Design a parent involvement program that builds on the strengths of cultural diversity. How might you capitalize on the knowledge and experiences of parents and extended-family members? Specifically, how could you determine their strengths and convince them to participate and share areas of expertise in parent involvement programs? How might you deal with problems resulting from language difficulties?

## Suggestions for Collaborative Efforts

Form groups of three or four that, if possible, represent our nation's cultural and gender diversity. Working collaboratively, focus your group's attention toward the following efforts:

1. With the help of your group, prepare a survey to determine the reasons that parents might resist educators' efforts. Using the results, write a plan in which your goal is to obtain the family's participation and involvement.

2. Arrange an opportunity for each member of your group to meet with a parent or extended family member to learn what problems they experience with U.S. schools. Have as many cultural groups represented as possible. As a group, decide on a list of questions that might provide the information you want. Then, as a group, share your responses to determine whether you can establish a plan or agenda for addressing par-

ents' and families' concerns. Caution: Remember that some cultures hold schools and educators in high regard and, therefore, might not want to share concerns and problems. In such cases, you should respect their privacy.

3. Prepare a list of booklets or pamphlets designed to educate parents and families from culturally different backgrounds about children and adolescents or the U.S. school system and its goals. Whenever possible, offer suggestions written in the parents' native language (unless the parent is proficient in English). Examples include: Sida o AIDs (available from Network Publications, P.O. Box 1830, Santa Cruz, CA 95061-1830) and the many fine publications in Cantonese, Korean, Spanish, and Vietnamese (catalog available) from the California State Department of Education, 721 Capitol Mall, P.O. Box 944272, Sacramento, CA 94244-2720.

## *Expanding Your Horizons: Additional Journal Readings and Books*

Little, M. (1997). Teacher-parent cooperation: A Navajo perspective. *Journal of Navajo Education, 14*(1–2), 26–31.

*Little discusses Navajo acculturation and loss and maintains that parents need to understand the importance of their involvement in the bilingual classroom.*

Manning, M. L. (1995). Understanding culturally diverse parents and families. *Equity and Excellence in Education, 28*(1), 52–57.

*Manning looks at the need to understand parents and families from the various cultural backgrounds and other topics such as familial characteristics, the extended family concept, and the need for parents and families to understand U.S. school systems.*

Rapoport, R. N. (1997) Families as educators for global citizenship: Five conundrums of intentional socialization. *International Journal of Early Years Education, 5*(1), 67–77.

*Rapoport examines changes in global culture and values and their impact on families.*

Uno, D., Florsheim, P., & Uchino, B. N. (1998). Psychosocial mechanisms underlying quality of parenting among Mexican American and white adolescent mothers. *Journal of Youth and Adolescence, 27*(5), 585–605.

*These researchers studied adolescent mothers; looked specifically at financial stress, parenting stress, global stress, social support, and parenting behaviors.*

## *Answers to the Culture Quiz: Diversity among Parents and Family*

| | | | | |
|---|---|---|---|---|
| **1.** T | **3.** T | **5.** F | **7.** T | **9.** T |
| **2.** F | **4.** T | **6.** F | **8.** F | **10.** F |

Chapter *12*

# *Administrators and Special School Personnel*

Understanding the material and activities in this chapter will help the reader:

- Explain why the cultural diversity of administrators, faculty, and staff should reflect that of the student population.

- List several roles of administrators, special educators, library media specialists, counselors, and communication disorders specialists in a school that promotes multiculturalism at all levels.

- List several ways administrators can lead school personnel in efforts to promote multiculturalism.

- Explain the unique challenges that face special-education teachers in diagnosing and remediating learners from culturally different backgrounds.

- Explain how the library media specialist can select appropriate print and nonprint materials that accurately portray children and adolescents from all cultural backgrounds.

- Explain how the school counselor can understand culturally different children and adolescents and select culturally appropriate counseling techniques and testing instruments.

- Explain how the communication disorders specialist can accurately distinguish between communications disorders and communications variations.

- Explain, from the teacher's perspective, how the various professionals can work together and how the teacher can most effectively utilize the various areas of expertise for the benefit of learners of all cultural backgrounds.

## *Overview*

Genuine multicultural education efforts include more than lofty goals and school philosophies. The school's effort to recognize and celebrate cultural diversity should demonstrate total school involvement by including the efforts of all school personnel. A commitment to multicultural education also includes an administration, faculty, and staff that reflects the cultural diversity of the student body. Employing school personnel of all cultural backgrounds at all levels shows respect for diversity; however, educators still need to work together, within their individual areas of expertise, to provide learners with educational experiences that address both individual and cultural needs. This chapter shows, from the classroom teacher's perspective, how administrators and special school personnel can contribute to the overall multicultural education program.

---

### THE CULTURE QUIZ   Administrators and Special School Personnel

*Directions:* Mark the following statements true or false.

_____ 1. The multicultural education program should include the efforts of all professional faculty and staff members, rather than only the isolated efforts of classroom educators.

_____ 2. Current levels of teacher education result in teachers qualified to deal with multiculturalism; therefore, staff development programs within schools are not necessary.

_____ 3. Perhaps the best measure of a school's commitment to cultural diversity is the actual cultural, ethnic, and racial composition of the administration, faculty, and staff.

_____ 4. Community members sometimes view the multicultural education program as a frill or a program that takes away from academic programs.

_____ 5. Special educators often use the Black Test of Bicultural Homogeneity to determine the intelligence of individuals, because the instrument is based on the African American culture.

_____ 6. PL 94-142 was designed primarily to ensure that learners had instruction in their native languages.

_____ 7. In the past, classes for special-needs learners were overpopulated by children who were poor, bilingual, culturally different, or severely frustrated with school.

_____ 8. Sociolinguistics refers to the study of how language varies with social situation and culture, for example, differences between home and school language.

_____ 9. The library media specialist should ensure that print and nonprint media reflect diversity and should work with classroom educators to provide appropriate multicultural experiences to all learners.

_____ 10. A major role of the communication disorders specialist is to work with learners from culturally diverse backgrounds and to eradicate dialectical differences whenever possible.

(Answers to the Culture Quiz are located at the end of the chapter.)

## Administrators, Faculty, and Staff: Toward Total School Efforts

While multicultural education programs and curricula may have lofty goal statements, perhaps the best measure of a school's commitment to cultural diversity is the actual cultural, ethnic, and racial composition of the administration, faculty, and staff. Specifically, do school personnel reflect the cultural diversity of the student population? If school personnel are predominantly from one background, one might justifiably ask whether the school administration is striving for the goals of the multicultural education program. Learners of various cultural backgrounds who hear the rhetoric of multiculturalism but see members of their cultural group represented only in custodial positions might question the school's commitment to equal opportunity.

Defending the goal of employing school personnel of varying cultural backgrounds is not difficult. First, having diverse school personnel shows students a commitment to include all people, regardless of cultural, ethnic, and racial backgrounds; second, such a policy shows a respect for the legal mandates that ensure equal opportunity for people of all cultures. Having the school staff reflect the diversity of the student body is undoubtedly a fundamental goal and a prerequisite to showing respect for cultural diversity and for equal opportunity under the law. Deliberate recruitment programs aimed at professionals of differing cultural backgrounds can contribute to employing faculty and staff more representative of our nation's diversity.

Responsive multicultural education programs include a commitment by professionals at all levels to multiculturalism and an acceptance of all learners regardless of diversity. While classroom teachers might have the most influence because of their proximity to many learners, administrators have a major responsibility for ensuring the implementation of multicultural procedures. Similarly, special educators and communication disorders specialists must project equal dedication, enthusiasm, and commitment to the overall school goals of acceptance and respect. The following sections examine the roles of administrators and special school personnel, show how classroom educators can most effectively work with these professionals for the benefit of learners, and suggest a means of evaluating professional efforts.

## The Roles of Administrators in Multicultural Education

The administrator's primary responsibilities include ensuring that multicultural education programs are carefully and methodically planned and that procedures are implemented to meet specific goals and objectives. Administrators require the ability and motivation to challenge and to lead school personnel toward responsive efforts. Although their participation might not include extensive firsthand efforts with youngsters of differing cultural backgrounds, their commitment and leadership remain crucial to the success of the overall school program and to generating other professionals' enthusiasm toward multicultural efforts. Administrators' efforts and the zeal they bring to this task undoubtedly determine the degree of success of the multicultural education program.

A major role of administrators is to provide learners with faculty and staff that reflect the cultural diversity of the student body and the community. The recent push for increased teacher certification standards might challenge principals who seek teachers from as many cultural backgrounds as possible. Most states have initiated minimum competency tests for all beginning teachers. Some claim that these tests measure teaching effectiveness, but an unintended result is that the number of minority teachers is rapidly declining.

The principal's job grows even more complicated considering that at the present rate of decline, African Americans will make up less than 5 percent of the U.S. public school teaching force by the year 2000 (McKenna, 1988; Lomotey, 1989). Through affirmative action programs and deliberate recruitment attempts designed to attract qualified applicants of differing cultural backgrounds, administrators can locate faculty and staff members with whom learners can identify. Administrators above the principal's level have significant responsibilities in these recruitment and employment areas; school administrators, however, are in a prime position to employ personnel of different cultural backgrounds and must accept responsibility for the degree of diversity among their schools' faculty and staff.

Implementing Research 12-1 on page 310 looks at the Clarks' proposal that principals need to be transformational and visionary leaders, especially in leading educators toward responsive learning environments.

A second challenge to administrators is to provide appropriate leadership efforts for an all-school approach to multicultural education. Teachers often base their dedication or enthusiasm for educational programs on the administrator's apparent commitment. Administrators should demonstrate leadership toward specific objectives, convey a genuine respect for cultural diversity, and demonstrate a willingness to be involved. These efforts may be among the most important, because the administrator is a major influence in the overall effectiveness of the programs and can lead faculty and staff members toward excellence in all professional endeavors.

A third challenge for principals is to deal affirmatively with the racial attitudes of their staffs. For many teachers and other staff members, joining the school ranks is their first sustained contact with members of another culture, and they may enter the situations not only lacking knowledge but fearful of confronting the issue of race. Such feelings can lead to an uneasiness that not only hurts work performance but can also do further harm to racial relations.

Principals, teachers, and other staff members in this situation should confront their own fears and learn to discuss race and racial issues openly. They also need to acquire information and perspectives that have not been a part of their education. They must plan and implement strategies that will reduce both racism and discrimination (Sleeter, 1990).

Another role in which administrators can offer significant contributions is communicating with, and involving, parents and community leaders. The administrator

---

**IMPLEMENTING RESEARCH 12-1    Developmentally Responsive
Learning Environments**

Donald Clark and Sally Clark, two noted and respected writers, call for principals to be transformational leaders, informed leaders, visionary leaders, instructional leaders, and collaborative leaders. Transformational leaders are those who elevate others to higher levels of motivation and morality. They inspire others to follow a higher purpose even as they take specific steps to promote the process. Such leadership brings about a supportive framework for making meaningful change.

Informed leaders, as the term implies, are those principals whose knowledge about every aspect of the school enables them to convince teachers, parents, and community members that they can achieve goals. Visionary leaders can see what programs and efforts will be like on implementation; they have a comprehensive knowledge base that allows them to offer concrete proposals for turning visions into reality.

Principals as instructional leaders encourage teachers to examine their belief systems, to consider new ideas, become current in the latest research, and share personal expertise. Collaborative leaders model and encourage collegiality and collaboration—they know collaboration enhances the ability of the school to respond to problems and opportunities as well as increasing effectiveness, efficiency, and productivity.

**Implementing the Research**

While Clark and Clark do not focus on culture per se, the leaders they describe will be effective with teachers and students and also have the potential for contributing to the effort to make schools more culturally relevant. For example, principals can:

1. transform schools into places where cultural, gender, and other forms of diversity are respected;
2. serve as leaders who are informed about cultural diversity (i.e., its richness as well as its challenges) and about ways to make schools more culturally relevant and culturally responsive; and
3. act as visionary leaders who can see how to reduce racism, discrimination, prejudice, and injustice (unfortunately, elimination is probably unlikely).

---

*Source:* Clark, D. C., & Clark, S. N. (1998). Creating developmentally responsive learning environments. *Schools in the Middle, 8* (2), 12–15.

is in a position to assume the role of communicating the purposes of the multicultural education program to all parents.

Parents and other community members may erroneously view the multicultural education program as a "frill" or as a program that takes much-needed resources away from the curriculum or other school activities. Parents may be skeptical of programs that were not integral parts of their own educational experience and of which they might have little knowledge. Programs that are misunderstood will likely receive little support from the general public. Such a situation requires a skilled and competent administrator who is able to garner the support of parents and other community members.

Referring specifically to African Americans, Lomotey (1989) suggested that principals who work in effective schools demonstrate confidence in students' ability to learn, a commitment to ensure students' success, and an understanding of students and their communities. Lomotey's research in school climate, principal leadership, school culture, and effective schools indicates that principals should:

1. believe that all their students can learn and reflect this belief in their goals;
2. be concerned with the least successful students in their schools, rather than being satisfied that some students are doing above-average work;
3. broaden the base of recognized achievement by acknowledging nontraditional accomplishments, particularly with minority students; and
4. acknowledge students who have exceptionally good attendance or punctuality records.

Principals must believe that all students can learn, have confidence in their students, involve parents in their children's education, reflect on the impact of the reform movement, and push for appropriate role models for all learners (Lomotey, 1989).

## From the Perspective of Classroom Educators: Working with Administrators

Classroom educators need administrators' attention and support. Teachers and administrators must not work in isolation and risk the possibility that they will move toward different goals. Administrative support of teachers is imperative.

What, then, can educators do as they work with, and seek assistance from, administrators? Classroom educators who have direct contact with learners of various cultural backgrounds are in the best position to determine learner needs and convey these needs to administrators.

Educators, keeping in mind the many demands placed on administrators, must make their concerns known and insist on changes. Presenting the problem or concern is the first step. Working with the principal (suggesting, providing input, and offering recommendations) is the second step. Classroom educators, who have a better perspective on problems than administrators, must take responsibility for explaining the problems in accurate and objective terms. Once a

---

**FOLLOW THROUGH 12-1   Seeking Information from Principals**

Ask one or more principals or assistant principals to describe their multicultural education programs and their specific roles in the program. Specifically, seek information on how they have led school efforts to ensure that their school effectively reflects U.S. diversity. Ask also about school philosophy, library materials, efforts to celebrate cultural diversity, programs for students whose English proficiency is limited, and cultural diversity among their faculty and staffs.

---

### CASE STUDY 12-1   Culturally Relevant Educational Experiences

Mrs. Miller, a seventh-grade teacher at Evergreen Middle School, had twenty-eight students in her class: twelve European Americans, eleven African Americans, two Hispanic Americans, and two Asian Americans. Mrs. Miller recognized that the school, its policies, and its teaching and learning practices were predominantly white and middle-class in perspective. Many students had to obey rules they did not understand, work toward meeting expectations and levels of motivation compatible with white perspectives, and learn to use cognitive styles similar to those of middle-class white learners. Mrs. Miller recognized the need for change but also realized she had limited time, resources, and expertise. For her students' welfare, she decided to seek the principal's assistance.

Mrs. Johnson, the principal, listened attentively to Mrs. Miller's concerns. She agreed not only that the sixteen students of culturally different backgrounds needed culturally relevant educational experiences, but also that the twelve European American students needed to acquire a better understanding of the other learners (and vice versa). Mrs. Johnson and Mrs. Miller decided to form a committee to address the learners' needs. The committee consisted of Mrs. Johnson, Mrs. Miller, another seventh-grade teacher, one European American parent who had expressed interest, and three parents from other cultural groups (one from each group represented). Mrs. Johnson made a list of her and the committee's recommendations:

1. The task called for commitment of administrators, faculty, and parents; it was not something Mrs. Miller should tackle alone.
2. All parents—majority culture and minority cultures—should be notified (and their advice sought) of the effort to meet learners' needs and to provide multicultural experiences for all learners.
3. Textbooks and other curricular materials should be examined for bias, stereotypes, and cultural relevance.
4. Teaching and learning practices and the school environment should be examined from an administrative perspective.

Mrs. Johnson thought these steps served as a good starting point and that, from an administrative perspective, it was a manageable agenda. Viewing this agenda as only a first phase, Mrs. Johnson started to consider how the efforts could become a total school effort.

---

problem has been explained and classified, the classroom educator's responsibility is to follow through on appropriate plans and strategies.

Case Study 12-1 looks at a teacher who seeks an administrator's support on behalf of seventh-grade students.

Implementing Research 12-2 discusses the relationships between race, gender, and educational leadership.

## *Evaluation of Administrators' Efforts and Commitment*

Administrators' effort and commitment to multicultural education should be evaluated, just as educators' teaching effectiveness and learners' academic achievement are evaluated. The Evaluation Checklist provides examples of items to assess in determining administrators' effectiveness.

**IMPLEMENTING RESEARCH 12-2     Race, Gender, and Educational Leadership**

Diane Pollard interviewed African American elementary school principals (twelve women and eight men) in an urban school district about the impact of their race and gender on their views of themselves in their administrative role. She examined the findings within the historical framework of roles African American principals have played and the contemporary social conditions under which they work. Pollard drew several conclusions: (1) race and gender were considered integrated rather than separate or oppositional statuses—the respondents did not refer to themselves as African American females or African American males; they demonstrated a "both/and" perspective toward race and gender; (2) these educators discussed their race/gender and, in some cases, socioeconomic status as important not only in terms of their views of themselves as principals but also as integral to their mission as educational leaders—in other words, they felt their race/gender brought unique perspectives to their roles as principals; (3) although they realized they faced a variety of challenges, they did not limit themselves to a defensive perspective. In fact, some tried to use their race/gender status to their advantage in several ways, for example, by trying to play a special role for their students, especially their African American students.

## Implementing the Research

1. Elementary and secondary schools need more African American (as well as Asian, Hispanic, and Native American) principals as schools continue to increase in cultural diversity.
2. Principals from differing cultural backgrounds should realize that their race might prove to be an obstacle, especially when working with racist or unaccepting families. This challenge and reality needs to be confronted head-on on an individual basis. Defensive policies are no solution.
3. Principals of all cultures and both genders who have struggled to attain their goals need to play special roles with students—sharing their experiences, motivating students who are facing challenges, providing effective advising and mentoring, and offering encouragement when appropriate.

*Source:* Pollard, D. S. (1997). Race, gender and educational leadership: Perspectives from African American principals. *Educational Policy, 11*(3), 353–374.

### Evaluation Checklist

**1.** The principal demonstrates and models respect for all forms of diversity among students and their parents and families.

**2.** The principal seeks to employ faculty and staff of as many different cultures as possible.

**3.** The principal seeks to provide financial resources and other less tangible forms of support for the multicultural education program.

**4.** The principal works cooperatively with the school faculty and staff to provide effective multicultural educational experiences.

**5.** The principal supports a total school program (curriculum, instruction, and environment), rather than the occasional teaching-unit approach.

**6.** The principal accepts responsibility for acting as a catalyst and for providing significant leadership for the multicultural education program.

**7.** The principal arranges for convenient sessions for parents and families of differing cultural backgrounds to voice concerns and suggestions.

**8.** The principal recognizes cultural differences among people as traits to be valued rather than to be eliminated or remediated.

**9.** The principal evaluates the efforts of faculty and staff and offers constructive criticism and positive suggestions in areas needing improvement.

**10.** The principal coordinates efforts of faculty and staff members toward a common goal of recognizing and building on cultural differences.

## The Role of Special Education in the Multicultural Education Program

Special-education personnel can play significant roles in the multicultural education program. Tasks confronting them include the cultural considerations surrounding testing and assessment, the legal aspects of educating children with disabilities, the psychosocial variables affecting the teaching and learning process, and the effective coordination of efforts between special-education and regular classroom teachers.

Students of culturally different backgrounds are overrepresented in special-education classes. In the past, children who came from poor families or from homes where English was the second language or not spoken at all often ended up in special-needs classes. The role of special-education teachers includes responding to the increasing cultural diversity among learners by using culturally appropriate assessment devices and making placement decisions that reflect an understanding of cultural differences.

Implementing Research 12-3 explains how special-education teachers can take a role in mentoring programs.

---

**FOR ADDITONAL INFORMATION**   **Websites for Administrators**

**Ohio Association of Secondary School Administrators**
http://www.oassa.org/   Provides information on variety of topics for middle-level and secondary administrators and others.

**American Association of School Administrators (AASA)**
http://www.aasa.org/   Provides information for both elementary and secondary-school administrators about effective leadership.

**Principal Magazine: November 1998**
http://www.naesp.org/comm/p1198.htm
*Principal* magazine provides elementary school principals with a wealth of information on various administrative topics.

---

**FOLLOW THROUGH 12-2    Speaking with Special Education Personnel**

Talk with several special-education teachers to learn how they objectively assess learners from culturally different backgrounds who have disabilities. Specifically, try to determine how they deal with the influence of culture during assessment, how they distinguish between differences and disabling conditions, and how they determine whether characteristics result from an actual disability or limited language proficiency.

---

**IMPLEMENTING RESEARCH 12-3    Mentoring Programs and Special Education**

Kim Townsel (1997) maintains that mentoring programs provide many at-risk youths with viable opportunities for ongoing contacts with positive adult role models. Mentors offer learners their support, concern, and structured time as well as internal assets such as educational commitment, positive values, and social competence. Townsel's article focuses specifically on African American children with emotional and behavioral disorders, but it has implications for special-education teachers developing mentoring programs for youth of all cultural backgrounds. Specifically, Townsel suggests components of a mentoring program that can help facilitate successful and positive experiences.

Elements of successful mentoring include: (1) using existing support systems and family systems, (2) enhancing and supporting cultural dynamics and professional relationships, (3) identifying the qualities of resiliency, (4) illustrating the cycles children move through as they develop, and (5) developing a program philosophy.

**Implementing the Research**

Townsel's article provides several directions for special-education teachers implementing mentoring programs such as:

1. Involve parents, families, and community members in mentoring programs because children in some cultures, especially African Americans, benefit from these networks of support.
2. Include parents in the referral process of children with emotional and behavioral disorders, not just seeking their permission and approval but also making them full partners in the process.
3. Provide mentors with appropriate training in mental health issues, so they can better deal with the challenges children face.

*Source:* Townsel, K. T. (1997). Mentoring African American youth. *Preventing School Failure, 41*(3), 125–127.

## Testing and Assessment

Special-education teachers, like all educators, should exercise extreme caution when labeling learners of different cultural backgrounds. They must carefully distinguish between disability and difference. They must not make placement decisions based on faulty evidence or culturally biased assessment instruments.

Teachers should not consider learners intellectually inferior because of poor performance on standardized tests. Scores on standardized tests too often influence teachers' expectations of learners' academic performance in the classroom. Teachers must maintain high expectations for all learners, regardless of cultural background. A standardized test score can provide an indication of a student's degree of assimilation but provide little evidence of an individual's intelligence (Gollnick & Chinn, 1998).

In developing tests, and in using the results of standardized tests, special-education teachers, as well as all educators, should recognize the inherent cultural bias that favors students of the majority culture. In fact, few tests have been developed from the perspective of a culturally diverse group. One such test is the Black Test of Bicultural Homogeneity (BITCH), which is based on urban African American culture and includes language and terms familiar to this culture. Although African Americans consistently score higher on this test than do members of the majority culture, it is rarely used to determine intelligence of individuals or groups (Gollnick & Chinn, 1998).

Special-education teachers should be constantly aware of the cultural biases among tests and remind themselves not to rely on test scores as the only indication of students' intelligence. Like all educators, special-education teachers should employ a number of culturally appropriate assessments and other sources of information to avoid basing placement decisions and judgments of intelligence on faulty data.

## Legal Perspectives

Special-education teachers must understand the increasingly prominent role of the federal government in special education. The government has done more in recent years to promote the education rights of learners with disabilities than in the entire previous history of the nation. During this period, legislation has been notable for an affirmation of the education rights of students with disabilities. It addresses the problems of students who have disabilities as well as those who have limited proficiency in English. It also has provisions for nondiscriminatory assessment, parental involvement, and expanded instructional services (Hernandez, 1989).

From the teacher's perspective, the Education for All Handicapped Students Act of 1975 (PL 94-142) was a landmark law for students with disabilities in general and for culturally and linguistically different populations in particular. Among the most important provisions of PL 94-142 are those addressing the right to due process, protection against discriminatory testing during assessment, placement in the least restrictive education environment, and individualized education programs (Hernandez, 1989). In essence, PL 94-142 addresses the basic rights and equal protection issues with respect to the evaluation, identification, and placement of learners with disabilities. Under this law, assessment should serve to identify learners with disabilities and to guide instructional planning based on established educational goals (Hernandez, 1989).

Litigation, as well as PL 94-142, has also dramatically affected the educational system. Court cases have examined the legality of assessment, classification, and placement of low-achieving children (*Diana v. State Board of Education*, 1970; *Larry P. v. Wilson Riles*, 1972) and the right of learners who are severely disabled to a free and public education (*Pennsylvania Association for Retarded Children v. the Commonwealth of Pennsylvania*). These cases and other, similar litigation have led to the establishment of the following legal standards:

1. Assessment of intellectual capabilities using measures in English is inappropriate for students with limited English proficiency.
2. Identification of children as mildly mentally retarded requires consideration of factors such as adaptive behavior, sociocultural group, and motivational systems, in addition to measures of intelligence.
3. The degree to which culturally different groups have been overrepresented in special-education classes for the EMR is sufficient to constitute bias. Causes of the overrepresentation have included: (a) failure to consider linguistic and cultural factors, (b) failure to identify appropriately and to determine the eligibility of disabled students, and failure to provide proper procedures and special services, and (c) excessive reliance on IQ test results as placement criteria.
4. Factors such as item bias on measure of IQ and discriminatory instruments alone does not suffice to account for misplacements and disproportionate representation of learners from culturally different groups in special-education classes (Hernandez, 1989).

In summary, from a classroom educator's perspective, the placement procedures that special-education teachers employ must be in accordance with PL 94-142 and the litigation addressing the rights of the disabled. Classroom teachers are responsible for helping special educators understand all learners and the role of psychocultural factors in learning and assessment.

## From the Perspective of Classroom Educators: Working with Special-Education Teachers

From the perspective of the classroom educator, the special-education teacher should be considered a major instructional resource. Although teacher accreditation requirements mandate that all teachers have at least a basic knowledge of disabilities, most regular classroom teachers lack expertise in the techniques of working with children who have disabilities, especially those from culturally diverse backgrounds. When student needs can be addressed in the regular classroom, classroom educators should seek help from special-education teachers. Similarly, regular educators should rely on qualified special-education teachers to handle students who, by law, cannot benefit from education in a regular classroom setting.

Special-education teachers must respond to the classroom educator's request to assess students in need and provide culturally appropriate testing and assessment. They work with regular classroom teachers to provide appropriate educational experiences for all students with disabilities (regardless of cultural background). They must understand the effects of cultural factors on the teaching and learning process. The classroom teacher should perceive special-education personnel as valuable resources whose training and expertise can contribute to the education of nearly any exceptional (or so-called normal) learner.

Classroom educators must follow appropriate procedures for referring students to special-education teachers. They must help special-education teachers understand learners' cultural diversity and provide follow-up as the special-education teacher recommends. It is important that regular classroom teachers view special-education teachers as partners and not as people on whom to "dump" unwanted students. Special-education teachers can provide educational assistance to learners who have disabilities as well as those who do not. In many cases, the organization of the school and the legalities of the referral process require regular classroom teachers to take the initial steps.

Case Study 12-2 shows how a secondary social studies teacher sought the professional assistance of the special-education teacher.

---

**CASE STUDY 12-2    Seeking the Special Educator's Help**

Mrs. Heath, a tenth-grade social studies teacher, noticed that four or five of her Native American students seemed uninterested. She wondered whether the students were really unmotivated, whether they had reading problems and attention deficits, or whether the curricula topics simply were uninteresting to them. Fully realizing the consequences of making judgments based on erroneous beliefs, Mrs. Heath took her concern to the special-education teacher in the school.

Mrs. Blackmon listened carefully to Mrs. Heath's concerns. Mrs. Blackmon first decided to test the students' reading abilities to determine their reading vocabulary and comprehension skills. Second, she explained to Mrs. Heath that the Native Americans could listen without looking a person in the eye, and that "looking interested" might be more of a "white perspective," one that might not cross cultural boundaries.

Mrs. Blackmon felt that, although the students' reading abilities were below grade level, they basically could read. She offered several suggestions to help Mrs. Heath and the students. First, she would work with the students two or three times a week to improve their reading comprehension. Second, she would help Mrs. Heath to provide some culturally relevant materials. Third, she would help Mrs. Heath to develop a better understanding of Native American learners.

Without labeling or making unjustified placements, both teachers realized the importance of working as a team to help the Native American learners. Each recognized that working separately would not result in the most effective educational experiences for the learners. A coordinated effort, with each teacher reinforcing and building on the effects of the other, would best address the needs of the Native American learners.

**FOLLOW THROUGH 12-3    Devising a Plan to Help Learners Who Have Disabilities**

Work with special-education teachers to devise a plan to make learners with disabilities from culturally different backgrounds feel more a part of the whole school. List at least four or five specific ways to involve these learners in the mainstream of the school.

*A Self-Evaluation Checklist for Special-Education Teachers*

The following checklist provides special educators with a means of self-evaluation to determine strengths, weaknesses, and overall commitment to promoting cultural diversity. Ask yourself each question and answer it in terms of your responsibilities as a special-education teacher.

1. Do I value and respect cultural diversity in all forms and degrees?
2. Do I recognize differences between disabilities and cultural diversity, or do I perceive differences as liabilities or deficiencies in need of remediation?
3. Do I coordinate the efforts of administrators, faculty, and staff to provide the least restrictive environment for all disabled learners?
4. Do I support a racially and culturally diverse faculty and staff for all youngsters with disabilities?
5. Do I insist that screening and placement procedures recognize cultural diversity and that such procedures follow legal mandates and guidelines for special education?
6. Do I work with parents and families on a regular basis, help them understand programs for learners with disabilities, and make referrals to appropriate social service agencies?
7. Do I use testing and assessment instruments with the least racial, cultural, and social-class bias?
8. Do I provide opportunities for youngsters with disabilities to be mainstreamed or integrated with nondisabled learners of all cultural backgrounds whenever possible?
9. Do I plan learning experiences that recognize differences in language and dialect?
10. Do I support community recognition and efforts to provide appropriate educational experiences for learners with disabilities from both majority and minority cultural backgrounds?

## *Library Media Specialists*

The library media specialist in a multicultural setting must understand the cultural diversity of his or her school and build a library and media collection that shows positive portrayals of all cultural groups. Library or media specialists also work

---

**FOLLOW THROUGH 12-4**   **Determining Culturally Appropriate Reading Materials**

Work with a library media specialist as he or she engages in the book selection process. What selection criteria are used? Is a particular assessment device used? What "red flags" (e.g., stereotyped images, lack of diverse characters, insensitive use of dialects) indicate to library media specialists that reading materials might be inappropriate? Is selection done by one person or by a committee consisting of educators and parents from a number of different cultural groups?

---

with classroom educators in positive, constructive ways that demonstrate a respect for and commitment to providing appropriate multicultural education experiences.

## Selecting Culturally Appropriate Print and Nonprint Media

School library media specialists, like all educators, are challenged to meet the needs of an increasingly diverse student population. Chapter 8 emphasized the importance of positive portrayals of children and adolescents from varying cultural backgrounds and the necessity of addressing problems of sexism, racism, stereotyping, and outright omissions. Libraries are responsible for ensuring that books, magazines, audiovisual materials, computer software, and all library and media materials positively and realistically represent characters of many cultural backgrounds with whom learners can relate.

One of the better and more pragmatic solutions to library media specialists' and teachers' problems has been offered by the Council on Interracial Books for Children, which regularly evaluates children's materials, trade books, textbooks, and other educational resources (Nauman, 1987). This text (especially Using Children's Literature and the Suggested Children's Books in Chapters 3, 4, 5, 6, and 7) provides examples of accurate literary descriptions of children and adolescents from various cultural backgrounds.

Library media specialists can refer to Table 8-1 (a checklist for determining racism and sexism in children's books) and to the following guidelines Nauman (1987) suggests for professionals. Books and other library materials should:

1. Reflect authentic cultural and ethnic perspectives
2. Reflect differences in lifestyle, socioeconomic levels, interests, and abilities
3. Portray characters who represent positions in society apart from, and uninfluenced by, their ethnic heritage
4. Reflect a variety of geographic locations of culturally diverse groups
5. Use language that shows the richness of the culture portrayed, with dialect used only as a positive, differentiating mechanism
6. Accurately depict history and include opportunities to see differing viewpoints
7. Provide accurate illustrations that show truthfully the ethnic qualities of the characters and avoid stereotypes, tokenism, and demeaning implications.

---

**FOLLOW THROUGH 12-5**   Coordinating Efforts of Educators and Library
Media Specialists

How might educators and library media specialists coordinate efforts to most effectively
serve children and adolescents of various cultural backgrounds? Consider books, poems,
speakers, films, plays, skits, computer software, and occasions to celebrate diversity.

---

## Coordinating Efforts with Classroom Educators

Like other professionals working in elementary and secondary schools, library
media specialists and classroom educators must work together for the welfare of
children and adolescents. Library media specialists can be a valuable resource for
regular classroom teachers. They can supplement learning experiences or provide
a children's literature–based approach to instruction. Some classroom teachers
received their education training before accrediting associations required experiences in multicultural education. For these teachers especially library media specialists can suggest culturally appropriate books for all children.

## From the Perspective of Classroom Educators:
## Working with Library Media Specialists

The professional paths of classroom educators and school library media specialists
should probably cross more than they do. Teachers bring or allow learners to visit the
library during a specified time, during which the library media specialist might or
might not have an activity planned. Teachers sometimes remain with students during the library period and make suggestions or encourage students' interest in books
and reading. In other situations, teachers leave the students and work elsewhere.

From the perspective of classroom educators, the library media specialist
should be considered a prime resource professional. He or she can teach learners
about the library and about books and magazines that provide positive cultural
images. Teachers and library media specialists must work together.

Library media specialists' roles in supporting the multicultural education program include stocking the library and media center with books, magazines, and other
materials that accurately portray children and adolescents from various cultural
groups; assisting classroom educators to choose and use these books; ensuring that
library collections have works by nonwhite authors and illustrators; ensuring that
library holdings and materials are accessible to all students, regardless of social class
and cultural background; and assisting students as they search for reading materials.

The classroom educator's responsibilities include working with the library
media specialist (suggesting acquisitions and completing book request forms) to
secure a multicultural library; encouraging students of all cultures to read books
that provide accurate portrayals of learners from different cultural backgrounds;
encouraging learners to read books by qualified authors; and working with the library media specialist to plan activities that feature well-written reading materials.

---

**CASE STUDY 12-3    Improving Knowledge of Multicultural Books**

Mrs. D'Micio, the sixth-grade teacher, and Mrs. Benton, the library media specialist, discussed with some intensity cultural diversity and children's books.

"Children's literature just has not kept pace with the cultural diversity in our society," Mrs. D'Micio said.

"Perhaps not to the extent it should have, but there are some very good children's and adolescents' books that do include people from many different backgrounds," Mrs. Benton responded.

Mrs. D'Micio looked at her class rolls and thought, "Well, it has been about ten years since I took a children's literature course. Maybe there are some good books around now." She asked Mrs. Benton, "Can you help me find some books for my students? They are sixth-graders, you know."

Mrs. Benton responded in the affirmative and began thinking of the sources she could consult: *Books in Print*, Charlotte Huck's *Children's Literature in the Elementary School*, Donna Norton's *Through the Eyes of a Child*, the *Hornbook Magazine*, and trade book publishers that specialize in multicultural books, such as Children's Book Press (1461 Ninth Avenue, San Francisco, CA 94122).

Mrs. Benton gave Mrs. D'Micio a great list and began collecting books that provided accurate portrayals of children and adolescents in various cultural groups. She also wondered whether other teachers in the school would like such books to supplement their instruction or to suggest to their students and decided to begin a program designed to increase the library's holdings of multicultural books. She also decided to make all teachers in the school aware of the books and appropriate uses.

---

Case Study 12-3 shows how one teacher improved her knowledge of multicultural books by seeking help from the school library media specialist.

### *Self-Evaluation for Library Media Specialists*

The following checklist provides self-evaluation questions library media specialists can use to rate their own effectiveness.

**1.** Do I acquire a collection of print and nonprint media that provides positive and accurate examples of children and adolescents from various cultural groups?

**2.** Do I have an overall library program that contributes to the school's multicultural education program?

**3.** Do I work with teachers and other educators to plan appropriate multicultural experiences for all learners?

**4.** Do I have a system that makes library materials accessible to all learners, regardless of cultural or socioeconomic background?

**5.** Do I plan developmentally and culturally appropriate teaching and learning activities for learners of all cultural groups?

**6.** Does the library have multicultural materials that are appropriate for varying reading, interest, and developmental levels?

**7.** Have I established and approved criteria for evaluating the appropriateness (cultural, gender, socioeconomic, etc.) of print and nonprint media?

**8.** Do I seek input and suggestions for library purchases from teachers, organizations promoting cultural diversity, and interested parents?

**9.** Have I acquired a professional library of print and nonprint materials for educators who want to improve their professional knowledge of cultural diversity?

## Counselors' Roles in Multicultural Education

The role of school counselors includes understanding culturally different children and adolescents, providing culturally responsive counseling, understanding testing and assessment issues, and working with classroom teachers for the welfare of all learners.

Jean Mavrelis (1997) in Implementing Research 12-4 on page 324 examines language and communicational styles. While she refers specifically to school administrators, her ideas pertain to counselors as well.

### Understanding and Counseling

Cultural, intracultural, ethnic, and racial differences are important considerations in the counseling of children and adolescents in multicultural situations. Learners are not a homogeneous population. They differ widely as individuals and particularly as pertains to culture, gender, generation, and socioeconomic status.

Children are basically now oriented and view their world, their cultures, their peers, their language, and their morality from a child's perspective. Adolescents function developmentally in a stage between childhood and adulthood and are developing self-concepts and cultural identities that will affect their entire adult lives.

### Native Americans

Herring (1989) describes the dismal situations of many Native American children and suggests that guidance and counseling are the best vehicles for helping these children. Herring's suggestions include:

**1.** Counseling intervention should be highly individualized.
**2.** Assessment should have minimal socioeconomic or cultural bias.
**3.** Counselors should recognize learning styles and life purposes.
**4.** The child's culture must not be devalued.
**5.** Methodologies should place high value on self-worth.
**6.** The school counselor should help the school staff become sensitive to the needs of Native Americans.

### African Americans

School counselors should consider African American learners' individual heritages and special needs, rather than assuming too much cultural homogeneity or

**IMPLEMENTING RESEARCH 12-4   Language and Communicational Styles**

Jean Mavrelis (1997) suggests that to show genuine respect for multiculturalism and students' diversity, differences in communicational styles need to be understood. Educators and counselors need to integrate these styles into educational philosophies, communication with parents, and other aspects of teaching-learning-counseling experiences. Mavrelis explains that understanding different communication styles requires addressing those differences effectively rather than dismissing or ignoring them.

Early in our lives we learn a system of communication that develops from a set of cultural values, attitudes, and beliefs common to the particular cultural context in which we have been socialized. The cultural context for many people in the United States is a combination of Anglo mainstream values and those of a particular ethnic group such as African, Mexican, Irish, or Greek. Native Americans, Asian Americans, and Hispanic Americans have also been socialized with a set of unique cultural communicational styles. Individual communication styles should not be considered right or wrong. Instead, they need to be perceived as differences to be respected and understood.

Mavrelis provides several examples: a Korean American girl who was placed in a remedial English class because she was shy and quiet during her language interview at school; African American educators in one school who thought European Americans rude for not speaking; and differing cultural expectations for friendship and loyalty among administrators and educators.

**Implementing the Research**

Counselors can take a number of steps to address differences in communication styles:

1. perceive communicational styles as *differences*—people of all cultures communicate differently and should not consider others' styles right or wrong;
2. provide training to teachers and other staff members, so that they will understand differing communication styles. They will understand that people who might appear rude or disrespectful may have been socialized to communicate in different ways;
3. insist that educators teach students about differences in communicational styles in an effort to avoid confrontations that result from students' misunderstanding one another; and
4. remind educators that gender differences also exist in communication styles— female students are more likely to develop identity in connection and relationship with others, and male students through separation and competition.

*Source:* Mavrelis, J. (1997). Understanding differences in multicultural communication styles. *The High School Magazine, 5*(2), 30–37.

approaching counseling situations from a white perspective. Specifically, school counselors can organize self-awareness groups that emphasize self-appreciation through cultural heritage; explore the nature and importance of positive interpersonal relationships; conduct social behavior guidance groups; and offer motivation sessions and guidance workshops in areas such as academic planning, study skills, and time management.

## Asian Americans

Reminding counselors of the tremendous cultural and individual diversity among Asian Americans, Hartman and Askounis (1989) suggest:

**1.** Determining individual strengths and weaknesses, and assessing cultural backgrounds.
**2.** Understanding each learner's degree of acculturation.
**3.** Understanding Asian Americans' difficulty in exhibiting openness. In a culture that regards restraint as a sign of emotional maturity, admitting problems is thought to reflect badly on the entire family.
**4.** Understanding that overly confrontational, emotionally and tense approaches may cause additional problems and turmoil for Asian American learners.
**5.** Learning about individuals and their respective cultures; asking about the culture, accepting the learner's world, developing cultural and ethnic sensitivity and consciousness, and avoiding stereotyping.

## Hispanic Americans

For the most effective, multicultural intervention, Nieves and Valle (1982) offer several counseling suggestions:

**1.** Use active counseling approaches that are concrete, specific, and focus on the student's behalf.
**2.** Develop an awareness of the Puerto Rican culture.
**3.** Use approaches that take the client's frame of reference as a vehicle for growth.
**4.** Examine prejudices and attitudes toward Puerto Ricans.
**5.** Make home visits if possible, and make reference to the family during sessions.
**6.** Call students by their correct names. In Puerto Rico and elsewhere, people have two last names: The first is that of the family, and the second is from the mother. Using the wrong name is an insult and may raise identity questions.
**7.** Accept the role of expert, but work to relinquish the role of authority. Clients must accept responsibility for their own lives.

## European Americans

Counselors working with European Americans should consider the tremendous diversity among individuals as well as individual cultures. European Americans come from many different geographical regions and cultural backgrounds. For example, children and adolescents with Hungarian backgrounds differ significantly from those with Greek backgrounds. Likewise, Polish people differ from Italians.

---

**FOLLOW THROUGH 12-6   Providing Culturally Appropriate
Counseling Intervention**

Ask several school counselors about the special challenges of counseling children and
adolescents from African, Asian, European, Hispanic, and Native American backgrounds
(as well as other cultures). Ask about differences in counseling intervention, differing
worldviews, and different perspectives toward life and school. How do counselors adjust their strategies to reflect children's and adolescents' cultural backgrounds?

---

Counselors should use extreme caution when forming decisions about cultural
backgrounds, religious beliefs, and other personal characteristics. Suggestions for
counseling European Americans include:

**1.** Understanding some cultures' (such as that of Italians) allegiance and commitment to family members and to the overall welfare of the family

**2.** Understanding the language problems of some children and adolescents and
how these problems affect schoolwork, interpersonal relationships, and willingness to become active participants in U.S. society

**3.** Understanding cultural traditions that, in some cases, have been taught and
emphasized for many generations, and understanding how these cultural traditions might conflict with U.S. values and expectations.

**4.** Understanding that considerable effort might be necessary to build trust in the
counseling relationship.

**5.** Understanding such differences as social class and generational status (e.g.,
the differences in perspectives of a first- and a third-generation child or adolescent) and the effects of these differences on counseling sessions.

## Testing and Assessment

The counselor's goal in assessment is to minimize ethnocentrism and to maximize
culturally appropriate information. Assessment in counseling and psychotherapy
includes interviewing, observing, and testing, as well as analyzing documents. To
what extent does cultural diversity affect assessment? Will a characteristic indigenous to a specific culture be mistakenly perceived and assessed using European
American middle-class standards?

Two important issues in multicultural assessment include whether psychological constructs or concepts are universally valid and how to counter the effects
of diagnosing and placing false labels. Other questions related to multicultural assessment are:

**1.** What level and type of assessment is indicated?
**2.** Which tests are most useful and why?
**3.** What are the ethical and legal responsibilities associated with multicultural
assessment?

Are multicultural groups being assessed with instruments actually designed for middle-class white clients? Lonner and Ibrahim (1989) maintain that without appropriate assessment strategies, counseling professionals are unable to diagnose problems, to develop appropriate goals, and to assess the outcomes of intervention. Specific assessment issues include initial client assessment, clinical judgment, standardized and nonstandardized assessment, and the outcome of counseling evaluation (Lonner & Ibrahim, 1989).

## From the Perspective of Classroom Educators: Working with Counselors

Counselors may work with individuals, small groups, and large classes. The classroom educator may initiate the first contact between a school counselor and a troubled student.

Classroom teachers, who have daily contact with learners, may be the first professionals to detect a potential problem. Individual teachers are in a prime position either to ask the counselor for direct assistance or to refer students with problems to the counselor. It is wise for teachers and counselors to determine the best means of referring students, of coordinating and scheduling large group counseling, and of determining the correct needs of learners from diverse cultural backgrounds.

Counselors may provide several forms of assistance to classroom teachers and their students. Considering the many demands on the counselor's time and expertise, however, the teacher may have to initiate contact or inform the counselor of special areas of concern. Generally speaking, counselors can:

**1.** Determine and facilitate joint efforts of administrators and other educators to improve an adolescent's self-concepts and cultural identity

**2.** Provide assistance in suggesting culturally appropriate instruments and in interpreting test scores of learners of culturally different backgrounds

**3.** Work with families of all cultural backgrounds (both immediate and extended) in parent education endeavors

**4.** Offer parents meaningful roles in school governance, and offer families opportunities to support the teaching and learning process at home and at school

**5.** Provide individual and small-group counseling in areas of concern to all learners, such as peer acceptance and approval

**6.** Provide large-group counseling sessions in areas such as involvement meetings, rules meetings, and values-clarification meetings

**7.** Suggest culturally relevant materials to help all children and adolescents better understand each other's cultures

**8.** Work with older students in career planning, and suggest appropriate subjects needed to pursue career plans

**9.** Help learners deal with concern over body development, the desire for social acceptance, and the conflicts between adult expectations and peer expectations of culturally appropriate behaviors

**10.** Design special programs for at-risk learners who are from culturally different backgrounds

---

**FOLLOW THROUGH 12-7    Addressing Concerns of Children and Adolescents
of Different Cultures**

Through "thinking sessions" with a counselor, plan several large-group topics that address subjects of concern to children and adolescents of different cultures. Make two lists, because topics vary according to students' developmental differences.

*Children*

1. Making friends across cultures
2. Feeling accepted regardless of cultural diversity

*Adolescents*

1. Friends' versus family expectations
2. Expanding socialization in a predominantly white world

---

Classroom educators should view their roles and those of counselors as complementary. Because classroom educators have the most daily contact with learners from various cultural backgrounds, they are usually in the best position to detect learners with problems, make referrals, and to follow up on counselors' efforts. Likewise, the classroom teacher and the counselor should always know each other's purposes and strategies and, whenever possible, provide joint efforts for the benefit of the learners.

Case Study 12-4 looks at how a third-grade teacher sought the counselor's assistance.

---

**CASE STUDY 12-4    The Importance of Friendships**

Mr. Scott, a third-grade teacher, recognized that several of his Hispanic American students appeared bothered that the white children did not ask them to play. He was unsure whether the Hispanic American children lacked the social or linguistic skills to participate or whether they felt unwanted. Mr. Scott decided to seek the counselor's help with the situation.

Mr. Scott and the counselor, Ms. Wilkie, discussed the options and decided on a joint effort with three main purposes: (1) to help the Hispanic American students to feel better about themselves and their cultural heritages; (2) to help the European American students to gain a better understanding of the Hispanic cultures; and (3) to develop situations in which both cultures could play or learn together.

Ms. Wilkie decided on several small-group sessions with the Hispanics and several large-group counseling sessions with the entire class. In the small-group sessions, she tried to help the Hispanic American children better understand themselves and, overall, experience feelings of acceptance about themselves and their culture. The large-group sessions with the entire class focused on accepting cultural diversity and understanding and accepting peers.

Working as an integral part of the team, Mr. Scott planned play and learning activities that required learners of both cultures to work together. With the suggestions and materials that Ms. Wilkie provided, Mr. Scott continued the effort to improve the Hispanic American learners' self-concepts and cultural identities. He also provided follow-up efforts that stressed the importance of friendships and of making all people feel comfortable and accepted in both learning and play situations.

### Self-Evaluation for Counselors

As with all professionals, the counselor's efforts and commitment to promoting cultural diversity and to working with classroom educators should be evaluated periodically. The following checklist can serve as a means of self-evaluation.

Counselors should ask themselves the following questions.

**1.** Do I recognize that all children and adolescents differ in their cultural background, perspectives, traditions, and worldviews?

**2.** Do I plan culturally appropriate counseling strategies that reflect learners' cultural backgrounds?

**3.** Do I recognize that traditional tests and assessment devices may not measure the abilities and talents of all learners because of their differing cultural backgrounds?

**4.** Do I recognize that families differ according to cultural backgrounds (e.g., in sex roles, expectations, and childrearing techniques)?

**5.** Do I work with classroom educators for the overall welfare of learners from all cultural backgrounds?

**6.** Do I suggest special service agencies and resources that respond to the needs of learners and their families in all cultures?

**7.** Do I recognize the dangers of racial bias and cultural stereotypes and work to overcome these limitations?

**8.** Do I recognize the richness that cultural diversity adds to both elementary and secondary schools?

**9.** Do I recognize the need for all students to experience appropriate multicultural education experiences?

**10.** Do I recognize the need to use resources (e.g., films and other materials) that portray positive images of children's and adolescents' cultural backgrounds?

## Communications Disorder Specialists

Whereas several titles designate the professional working with speech-disabled learners, *speech-language clinician, speech correctionist, speech clinician,* and *speech therapist,* we prefer *communications disorder specialist* because the term is sufficiently broad in nature to include communication problems of children and adolescents from various cultural groups. The communications disorder specialist who works in multicultural settings has a broad knowledge of communication and understands unique communication situations, such as dialects, bilingualism, and teaching of English as a second language (TOESL), as well as the various assessment challenges and the differences between home and school language.

### Roles in Multicultural Education

Because communication is such a vital human aspect to learners of all cultural and ethnic backgrounds, communications disorder specialists play an important role in helping educators distinguish between disorders and differences. They can also help learners who are experiencing differences with communication for any reason. All communications disorder specialists need to become sensitive to cultural diversity and to develop cross-cultural communication competencies as they work with children classified as non-English-proficient (NEP) and as having limited English proficiency (LEP) (Cheng, 1987).

A primary role of the communications disorder specialist is to distinguish between communication disorders and communication variations and to convey to classroom educators the differences between the two. Communication disorders include speech disorders (impairment of voice, articulation, or fluency) and language disorders (the impairment or deviant development of comprehension of a spoken or written symbol system).

Communication variations include communication differences or use of dialects (a variation of a symbol system that a group of individuals uses, which reflects and is determined by shared regional, social, cultural, and ethnic factors) and argumentative communication (systems used to supplement communication skills, such as prosthetic devices [McCormick, 1990a]).

Communications disorder specialists in multicultural situations must distinguish between disorders and variations. Learners who use a particular dialect or regional accent should not be labeled as having a disorder in need of elimination.

A second, closely related role of the communications disorder specialist is to understand and to help classroom educators to understand the difference between school language and home language. A learner may appear so quiet and withdrawn that the educator wonders if the child or adolescent has physical or emotional problems. The same child or adolescent at home and in the community shows considerable verbal proficiency.

When substantial differences exist between conversational language use in the home and official use in the classroom, children and adolescents often appear to have low verbal ability. Despite being verbal in nonschool settings, these learners may talk very little in the classroom and, even then, use only simple words and sentences (McCormick, 1990b). In such a situation, the communications disorder specialist might have to convince the classroom educator that the child or adolescent is not speech-disabled and is not in need of remediation or therapy.

Another goal of the communications disorder specialist is to understand dialect differences—among learners from differing cultural backgrounds as well as learners of the majority culture. Understanding and responding appropriately to the dialect of the learner within a classroom can be a complex and sensitive issue.

First, the specialist and teacher should recognize that dialects are not communicative disorders and should not treat them as such. The American Speech and Hearing Association (1983) has taken a strong position that dialect varieties do not constitute speech or language disorders. The teacher should note, however, that a dialect and a communications disorder can coexist. If, for example, a learner with a Spanish or African American dialect also has defective articulation or stutters, the classroom educator should refer the learner to the communications disorder specialist.

**FOLLOW THROUGH 12-8  Distinguishing between Communication Disorders and Variations**

How can educators and communications disorder specialists best distinguish between communication disorders and variations? List several ways to address disorders and variations under the following headings. *Articulation* and *Dialects* serve as examples:

| *Disorder* | *Response* | *Variation* | *Response* |
|---|---|---|---|
| Articulation | Specific work on pronunciation of letters and patterns of letters | Dialects | To what extent does the dialect interfere with communication? |
| | | | Accept as part of cultural heritage. |

Teachers and communications disorder specialists should learn to distinguish accurately between linguistic diversity and disorders. Dialects should not be considered less than but merely different from that which is recognized as standard English. A teacher is in a strategic position to promote understanding and acceptance of a child who has a dialectal difference (Oyer, Crowe, & Haas, 1987).

## *From the Perspective of Classroom Educators: Working with the Communications Disorder Specialist*

The classroom educator should view the communications disorder specialist as a valuable resource person with a wide range of expertise. Working in a complementary fashion for the welfare of learners, the communications disorder specialist and the classroom educator can determine whether communication problems exist that need to be remediated or whether students are simply manifesting variations that should be accepted and appreciated.

Considerable interaction should occur between classroom educators and communications disorder specialists. First, the communications disorder specialist and the teacher need to consult with each other about their goals for a learner and how they expect to accomplish these goals. They should evaluate what success they achieve. Such interaction can be formal or informal, or the communications disorder specialist can provide the teacher with copies of written therapy progress reports sent home to parents.

Second, the classroom teacher has more contact with parents and spends more school hours with learners, who may talk about their feelings, wants, and life at home. Some information that a teacher receives from learners or their parents may be important to the communications disorder specialist, and the teacher should pass it on.

Third, the teacher is in an ideal position to provide the communications disorder specialist with information about a learner's speech and language function in the classroom and in informal situations, such as in the hallway or lunchroom or on the playground. The teacher may also be able to provide reminders to the child during the habit-forming stages of therapy, when the child can best produce the targeted speech behaviors but still must make them a habit in all communicative situations. Fourth, the communications disorder specialist requires the teacher's input on referrals and in establishing whether there is an adverse effect on education because of a communicative problem (Oyer, Crowe, & Haas, 1987).

The communications disorder specialist's responsibilities include appropriate assessment, therapy, scheduling, and consultation with teachers and parents (Oyer, Crowe, & Haas, 1987). Other responsibilities in multicultural situations include understanding the communication problems of children and adolescents, conveying to teachers an assessment of disorders and variations, and providing a climate of understanding and acceptance for all learners.

The classroom teacher plays a major role in the lives of learners by serving as an important role model and a major force in shaping ideas and has an influence on emotional development (McFarlane, Fujiki, & Britton, 1984). The classroom educator's responsibilities include being a good speech model; creating a classroom atmosphere conducive to communication; accepting learners, and encouraging classmates to accept learners with communications problems; consulting with the communications disorder specialist; detecting possible communications disorders and making referrals; reinforcing the goals of the communications disorder specialist; and helping the learner catch up on what he or she missed while at therapy (Oyer, Crowe, & Haas, 1987). Another responsibility is fully participating when a decision has been made to place the child in a limited- or non-English-proficient program.

Case Study 12-5 shows how disorders and variations can be confused and how the communications disorder specialist can work with classroom teachers.

### Self-Evaluation Checklist for Communications Disorder Specialists

This self-evaluation checklist enables communications disorder specialists to evaluate their efforts and commitment to multicultural education.

Ask yourself these questions.

**1.** Do I recognize and accept all learners, regardless of cultural, ethnic, or social class backgrounds?

**2.** Do I recognize how the increasing cultural diversity in U.S. school systems affects the roles and responsibilities of the speech professional?

**3.** Do I distinguish between communicative disorders and communicative variations?

**4.** Do I understand dialects as "differences" and not as "disorders"?

**5.** Do I plan appropriate communication for NEP or LEP students and seek the appropriate professionals to help these students?

---

**CASE STUDY 12-5  Responding to Communication Differences**

Ms. Tyler, a ninth-grade reading teacher in an inner-city school, felt somewhat overwhelmed as she took her concerns to the communications disorder specialist, Mrs. Clyburn. She said, "I have four, perhaps five, African American students whom I have difficulty understanding, two Hispanic American students who have tremendous difficulty with English and intersperse Spanish with English, and one bilingual Japanese American. What do I do, Mrs. Clyburn? There is such a wide variety of communication disorders in my class."

Mrs. Clyburn said, "Let's talk about your situation first; then, I will meet with the students individually to decide whether the apparent problems really are disorders."

About a week later, after Mrs. Clyburn met with the students, she met with Ms. Tyler concerning the students. First, Mrs. Clyburn found that the African American students had dialectal differences or variations instead of outright disorders. Second, she recommended the Hispanic American students for the LEP program so they could receive individual or small-group instruction. Third, she determined that the Japanese American student could speak both Japanese and English as long as speaking two languages did not interfere with communication.

Ms. Tyler and Mrs. Clyburn agreed to meet again later in the month to see whether the classroom teacher could better understand African American dialects and to discuss the Hispanic Americans' progress in the LEP program. Ms. Tyler felt better. She understood her students better, and she knew what should be accepted and what should be remediated. I will continue working with Mrs. Clyburn, she thought.

---

**6.** Do I work with professionals responsible for bilingual students and assist as needed?

**7.** Do I work with classroom teachers and other school personnel in joint efforts to help children and adolescents of differing cultural backgrounds with communications disorders?

**8.** Do I understand the various speech and language disorders, and am I able to assist learners from differing cultural backgrounds who are having communications problems?

## Summing Up

Educators who are working toward the involvement of the entire school professional staff in the multicultural education program should:

**1.** Encourage all administrators and special school personnel to offer wholehearted commitment and support to the multicultural education program. They should not perceive the effort as someone else's responsibility.

**2.** Convey to administrators, special education teachers, counselors, library media specialists, and the communications disorder specialist the importance of a total school effort in the multicultural education program.

**3.** Emphasize the necessity for cultural diversity among the administration, faculty, and special school personnel that reflects the composition of the school and community.

**4.** Encourage administrators, special-education teachers, library media specialists, counselors, and communications disorder specialists to recognize and respond appropriately to their unique roles in the multicultural education program.

**5.** Encourage administrators and special school personnel to work with regular classroom educators.

**6.** Convey the importance of evaluating all professionals (by self, peer, or administrator) for the purpose of learning ways to contribute to the overall multicultural program.

## Suggested Learning Activities

1. Visit an elementary or secondary school to learn how administrators and special school personnel contribute to the multicultural education program. Are roles clearly defined, or are they assumed, whereby professionals simply do whatever appears to benefit the learner? How might administrators and special school personnel better address the needs of learners of differing cultural backgrounds?

2. Some professionals and the general public feel that learners of minority cultures are overrepresented in special-education classes. Meet with a special-education teacher to discuss the concern of overrepresentation. What legal mandates and placement procedures protect minorities from being placed in special-education classes simply for being different from mainstream learners?

3. Visit an elementary or secondary school counselor in a multicultural setting to determine such factors as:

   a. Differences in assessing and counseling children or adolescents from culturally different backgrounds
   b. Best methods of working and coordinating efforts with classroom teachers
   c. Interaction settings; that is, individual, small group, and large group, and which mode appears most effective with learners from culturally different backgrounds
   d. Ways counselors can best help classroom educators who work daily with learners from differing cultural backgrounds

## Suggestions for Collaborative Efforts

Form groups of three or four that, if possible, represent our nation's cultural and gender diversity. Working collaboratively, focus your group's attention toward the following efforts:

1. Prepare an evaluation scale that determines how print and nonprint media portray culturally different children and adolescents. Pinpoint such factors as objectivity, accuracy, stereotyping, gender values, and actual people from the various cultural groups (and

what they are doing) and their contributions to an increasingly multicultural world. With the help of a library specialist, prepare a list of print and nonprint materials that provide an honest portrayal of all people, regardless of cultural background.

2. Brainstorm in your group to list special ways that administrators and special school personnel can contribute to multicultural education programs. How does your group think these professionals can contribute to or complement classroom teachers' efforts? What books or other materials can your group suggest to help each of these professionals?

3. Have your group members think about when they were in school or about a school they have visited during a practicum or other field experience. What evidence did they find that special school personnel and classroom educators work as a team? Considering the recent journal articles and books on teaming efforts, do you think these professionals will work in a more collaborative manner in the future? For years, professionals basically worked alone, doing their own job with little knowledge of each other's jobs. What efforts do you suggest for all educators working in collaborative teams?

## *Expanding Your Horizons: Additional Journal Readings and Books*

Bay, M., & Lopez-Reyna, N. (1997). Preparing future bilingual special educators: The lessons we've learned. *Teacher Education and Special Education, 20*(1), 1–10.

*These authors describe the goals and curriculum of a teacher education program designed to prepare educators to work with children with disabilities who also have limited English proficiency.*

Calderon, M. (1997). Staff development in multilingual multicultural schools. (ERIC Document Reproduction Service No. 410 368).

*Calderon presents recommendations for a staff development program that focus on learning theory, pedagogy, curriculum, technology, and assessment.*

Lewis, J. B., deMarrais, K. B., & Prater, G. (1998). Teaching Navajo bilingual student special education students: Challenges and strategies. (ERIC Document Reproduction Service No. 417 895).

*The authors contend that Native American students are often placed in special-education programs because they have poor language skills and are unprepared for an unfamiliar environment and*

*because traditional classrooms do not meet their needs.*

McIntyre, A. (1997). Constructing an image of a white teacher. *Teachers College Record, 98*(4), 653–681.

*McIntyre maintains that white teachers need to reflect on their identities and their understanding of multiculturalism to improve culturally relevant teaching practices.*

Ovando, M. N., & Traxwell, D. (1997). Superintendents' multicultural competence. *Journal of School Leadership, 7*(4), 409–431.

*Ovando and Traxwell interview multicultural experts and superintendents to determine competencies needed to promote multiculturalism.*

Winzer, M. A., & Mazurek, K. (1998). *Special education in multicultural contexts.* Columbus, OH: Prentice-Hall.

*This book examines the impact of cultural and linguistic diversity on the learning of children with disabilities and giftedness.*

## *Answers to the Culture Quiz: Administrators and Special School Personnel*

| | | | | |
|---|---|---|---|---|
| 1. T | 3. T | 5. F | 7. T | 9. T |
| 2. F | 4. T | 6. F | 8. T | 10. F |

# The Future of
# Multicultural Education

Part IV examines issues that educators face, such as multicultural education as a concept; racism, discrimination, and injustice; blaming the victim; testing and assessment; language and communication; accepting professional responsibilities; and involving parents and families. They will continue to challenge educators for years to come, but deliberate action must be taken to address them now.

# Chapter 13

# *Issues for the Twenty-First Century*

Understanding the material and activities in this chapter will help the reader to:

- Describe multicultural education as an issue challenging educators, its differing definitions, and the difference between ideal and practice

- Explain how racism continues to affect the United States, although conditions are better than they used to be

- Explain why people often blame victims for the conditions affecting their lives, instead of seeking more plausible causes

- List the arguments, pro and con, of standardized testing, and explain how culture affects testing

- Describe how the issue of language and communication affects individuals and social institutions

- List the responsibilities of professional educators in multicultural education programs

- Describe how various contemporary issues affect the progress and success of multicultural education programs

## Overview

Multicultural education has progressed considerably as a means of explaining diversity and teaching acceptance of all people, but several issues remain unresolved. Educators should do whatever they can to at least reduce the impact of each issue, they cannot, however, solve them all. A societal response is necessary to combat racism and discrimination, the tendency to blame victims for their plights, and the issue of testing and assessing learners of culturally different

---

**THE CULTURE QUIZ**    **Issues in Multicultural Education**

*Directions:* Mark each statement as true or false.

_____ 1. All too often, people blame victims for their conditions, instead of seeking more plausible causes.

_____ 2. Realistically speaking, multicultural education has never been totally accepted in the education community.

_____ 3. Multicultural education should address cultural differences only. Other programs should focus on ethnic, racial, gender, and disability conditions.

_____ 4. Although racism has been (and still is) evident in U.S. schools, another form, institutional racism, is less blatant and just as dangerous.

_____ 5. Research indicates that IQ and other tests of mental ability have been replaced in an attempt to define abilities of learners with respect to their individual cultures.

_____ 6. English is the primary language of the United States, but many dialects are spoken throughout the country.

_____ 7. The gap between stated ideals and actual practice in multicultural education programs has, surprisingly, been closed.

_____ 8. Progress toward equal treatment of all people has been made, but, there is still room for tremendous improvement in reducing racism and discrimination and in providing a just and equal society for all people.

_____ 9. Multicultural education efforts began during the early years of the twentieth century and have met most goals and objectives.

_____ 10. Examples of nonverbal communication include inattentive appearance and the tendency to avoid looking the speaker in the eye.

(Answers to the Culture Quiz are located at the end of the chapter.)

---

backgrounds. This chapter examines some of the issues, not to make educators feel guilty or negligent, but to describe obstacles to the progress of multicultural education and to show where present and future challenges lie.

## Issue: Multicultural Education as a Concept

As it progresses in its third decade, multicultural education has changed in definition and has not been wholehearted endorsed in all circles. In multicultural education, as in U.S. society as a whole, disturbing gaps exist between stated ideals and actual practice. In addition, while multicultural education appears to be the most effective means of teaching acceptance of cultural diversity, several other approaches serve to address racial, gender, and socioeconomic class differences.

### Scope of Multicultural Education

Questions that linger include: Does multicultural education include only ethnic, cultural, and racial differences? Should multicultural education address gender and class differences? Should multicultural education include sexual orientation? Should multicultural educators use unit approaches or adopt total-school approaches?

As stated previously, we support a broad definition that includes all types of cultures, including ethnic, cultural, racial, gender, sexual orientation, and social class. Also, in line with our thinking, we support including European Americans in multicultural education for the effort to be truly multicultural.

## Differences between Stated Ideals and Practice

Concerned educators do not have to look far for disturbing gaps between ideal and actual practice: children's language differences are not taken seriously, the only language used is English; segregation is practiced; and learners of culturally different backgrounds are labeled as inferior or culturally disadvantaged.

Case Study 13-1 looks at a situation in which a high-school principal recognizes that her school is not really meeting its goals and stated philosophy.

---

**CASE STUDY 13-1     Differences between Goals and Practice**

Dr. MacDonald, a high-school principal, looked objectively at her school's lofty goals, objectives, and philosophical statements, which spoke eloquently of valuing, recognizing, accepting, and respecting all people, regardless of differences. She compared these statements with what was actually happening in the school. Couldn't the students see that much of what was occurring was only rhetoric with no substance? Without being overly pessimistic or cynical, Dr. MacDonald asked herself several questions concerning the extent to which educators respect and address diversity:

- Do school policies reflect an understanding of cultural diversity?
- Do instructional practices recognize the differing learning styles of learners from various cultures?
- Is there an understanding of motivation and competition in relation to learners from diverse cultural heritages?

- Are efforts made to promote social interaction between learners of all cultures?
- Is there genuine respect for all people?
- Do educators recognize and address testing and assessment differences among cultures?
- Do language programs assist students of limited English proficiency?
- Are the teachers and other school personnel professionally trained and competent to deal with and teach children and adolescents from culturally different backgrounds?

Dr. MacDonald decided that an affirmative action plan was necessary to address these and other issues and concerns. Such an effort would take a large-scale approach and would include discussion groups, committees, in-service programs and activities, speakers, and an improved professional library.

---

**FOLLOW THROUGH 13-1     Narrowing the Gap between Ideals and Practice**

What specific directions can educators take to make multicultural education more concrete? What could we do to turn "ideals" into "practice"? In other words, what could we do to make multicultural education programs effective?

**FOR ADDITIONAL INFORMATION**   Internet Addresses

**Multicultural Issues Committee**
http://www.vcn.bc.ca/scd/culture.htm   Promotes awareness and appreciation of the multicultural nature of the community.

**Ten Things Men Can Do to End Sexism and Male Violence against Women.**
http://www.cs.utk.edu/~bartley/other/10Things.html   Provides articles, essays, and books about masculinity and gender inequality to give a better understanding of individual men and women.

**Sexism/Sex and Gender Discrimination**
http://www.nau.edu/wst/access/sxism/sxismsub.html   Studies of women, gender, and sexism, such as general discussions of job discrimination.

**FairTest: Introduction**
http://fairtest.org/   Information from the nation's only nonprofit advocacy group (National Center for Fair & Open Testing) that works to prevent unfair use of standardized tests.

**Racism**
http://www.avalon.net/~foshe.racism.htm   Provides information on racism, specifically the most blatant forms centering on the actions of hate groups.

## Approaches to Race, Class, and Gender

Educators may address diversity with approaches other than multicultural education: teaching the exceptional and the culturally different, human relations, single-group studies, and education that is multicultural and social versus reconstructionist. Rather than outlining the advantages and disadvantages of each approach, we state that each has expressed purposes, goals, and directions. From an issues perspective, however, each in some ways takes away from or competes for resources for other programs. While we do not in any way discredit other approaches, it does appear that multicultural education is a broad and comprehensive approach to addressing diversity of all kinds and degrees.

## Issue: Racism, Discrimination, and Injustice

Without doubt, people today are more aware of racism, discrimination, and injustices. Even during times of racist acts, evidence suggests that there has been notable progress: more people from diverse cultures are joining the workforce in positions that require more than manual labor or custodianship. Opportunities in housing (although admittedly not equal) have improved, doors to higher education are open to the culturally diverse, and federal legislation guarantees equal rights for all people.

Examples of progress and the improved relationships between majority cultures and people of culturally diverse backgrounds can be looked on with pride, but educators must be careful not to assume that "all is well." There is room for improvement in reducing racism and discrimination and in providing a just and equal society for all people.

## Lingering Racism and Discrimination

Nearly forty years after *Brown v. Board of Education* and almost thirty years after the Civil Rights Act of 1964, racism and discrimination continue to impede the progress of many people. Acts of violence are perpetuated toward people of all races and cultures; increasing racial violence is occurring on college campuses; and the number of "skinheads" or Neo-Nazi groups is on the rise.

Blatant, crude, and overt racism has come out of the closet again and has surfaced in our schools. Public slurs, threats, racist slogans, physical assaults, and racial conflicts occur in schools in every part of the country. Schools, which should be a civilizing influence in our society, instead appear to be incubators of racial intolerance (Pine & Hilliard, 1990).

While *Brown v. Board of Education* made segregation illegal, de facto segregation (or segregation by fact, when for example, no African Americans living near a predominantly white school attend that school) continues to exist. Similarly, even with the Civil Rights Act, notable gaps in income and job level continue to exist among racial groups, and, in some cases, differences are becoming more acute.

Institutional racism affects many children in the United States. Although people have given voice to such issues as equal opportunity, desegregation, and inequities in educational achievement in recent years, very few schools have developed deliberate and systematic programs to reduce prejudice. Society has done away with racism through legislative and special programs, but overt racism and institutional racism continue to occur. Whereas many educators are on guard against racism of all forms, institutional racism, which is less blatant and therefore more dangerous, continues to hurt the aspirations and talents of learners of culturally diverse backgrounds (Pine & Hilliard, 1990).

Victims of the more subtle and covert forms of racism suffer a form of social prejudice. This includes being neglected as potential friends and being "overlooked" in employment promotions and in special employment recognition.

## Goals for U.S. Society

People of all cultures, both majority and minority, should work independently and in concert toward achieving several broad goals for U.S. society:

1. Unconditional acceptance of all people regardless of cultural, ethnic, racial, gender, or socioeconomic background;
2. Equal social, economic, and educational opportunities for all people; and
3. Awareness of the need to acquire objective information about all individuals and groups in an attempt to dispel or reduce stereotypes, myths, and misconceptions.

These goals may appear to be broad, lofty, and perhaps idealistic, but we must strive to meet them to make the United States a more humane, caring, and respecting nation.

---

**FOLLOW THROUGH 13-2   Keeping a Constant Vigil against Racism**

As stated previously, it is unlikely that racism will ever be completely eliminated. Still, racism affects and hurts all cultures and deserves to be addressed. Concerned educators and others should keep a constant lookout for racism—racist remarks, racist jokes, and racist actions. Name four or five specific steps educators can take to address racism.

---

## Issue: *Blaming the Victim*

An issue facing some learners and their educators is where to place the blame for the minority person's plight. In essence, should the victim or the society be held accountable? For example, should lower-class African Americans blame themselves for their high unemployment rates and poverty, or should they blame a racist society that allows discrimination? Must Native Americans blame themselves for their high school dropout rates and high levels of alcoholism? Should Hispanic and Asian learners get the blame for their poor English skills? Responsive educators recognize that such questions are examples of the "blaming-the-victim" issue. They realize that children and adolescents are often victims of racism and discrimination and that all too often they cannot change the conditions surrounding their lives.

As Case Study 13-2 shows, it is possible to adopt the blaming-the-victim attitude and perhaps fail to realize its dangers.

There are two orientations toward victims. First, people who hold a person-centered orientation emphasize the individual's motivation, values, feelings, and goals. A person's success or failure is attributed to individual skills or inadequa-

---

**CASE STUDY 13-2   Blaming the Victim**

Mrs. Smith said despairingly, "I don't know what to do! Why don't they try to better understand themselves, improve their grades? They just sit there all day and do nothing. They didn't know today what I taught yesterday. How do they expect to make something of their lives? I will never understand those people."

The assistant principal, Mr. Allen, overheard this classic blaming-the-victim statement and thought that this tendency failed to recognize the real problem. All too often, victims, especially people from culturally diverse groups, are blamed for being uneducated, slow learners, poor, and unable to find employment.

Mr. Allen thought of the consequences of such thinking and of considering all people from a middle-class, white perspective. He thought a serious effort must be made to look for more valid social, economic, or educational causes. The implications of blaming the victim can be widespread and can influence educational decisions such as grouping, questioning, curricular issues, and teaching and learning activities. Yet the problem extends even further: students are being blamed for not wanting to learn when they really do want to learn and are considered too unmotivated to change when, actually, significant change is extremely difficult.

---

**FOLLOW THROUGH 13-3   Avoiding Blaming the Victim**

People sometimes find it convenient to blame the victim for such factors as language difficulties, being poor or homeless, and even for being culturally different. Working in groups of three or four, name several examples of "blaming the victim." Think of an exercise that will show middle- and secondary-school students the problems associated with blaming the victim.

---

cies, and many people correlate ability and effort with success in society. Second, the system-blame view holds that success or failure is generally dependent on the social and economic system rather than on personal attributes.

It is easier for some people to blame victims for their condition than to look for more specific societal and economic causes. The consequences of blaming the victim, however, often extend further than just thinking that people deserve blame for their shortcomings. Blaming learners for their conditions is a practice that excuses or justifies many unjust actions: poor-quality educational programs in areas with "victims," outdated and worn-out textbooks and curricular materials; teachers who give "victims" less wait time during questioning sessions, belief that poor or minority students cannot learn, and a plethora of other reactions.

## More Humanistic Perspectives

Educators should offer a personal and professional commitment to victims of discrimination. Teachers must understand how children and adolescents become victims and the difficulty victims have in changing their lives. On a larger scale, educators should do their part in working to reduce the racism, poverty, despair, injustice, and discrimination that contribute to the victimization of people.

## Issue: Testing and Assessment

Standardized testing dates back to the mid-1800s, and in fact, the problems associated with standardized testing have been similar over the years. The first documented use of standardized tests dates back to the period 1840–1875, when American educators changed their focus from educating the elite to educating the masses. The earliest tests were intended for individual evaluation, but test results were inappropriately used to compare students and schools.

As millions of immigrants came to the United States in the nineteenth century, the standardized test became a way to ensure that all children were receiving the same standard of education. At the turn of the century, the focus of testing shifted from achievement testing to ability testing for the purpose of classifying students. Schools wanted to weed out students who were not going to succeed academically. Consequently, many ethnic groups faced new discrimination.

Criticism about standardized testing grew during the first half of the 1900s, but standardized ability testing quickly took hold. Educators used both ability and achievement tests to classify students, reflecting schools' lingering elitism and teachers' failure to address the needs of low-achieving learners and those from diverse cultures. During the latter half of the twentieth century, three factors affected standardized testing: (1) changing demographics caused by immigration, (2) technological challenges introduced during the Cold War and exacerbated by the computer age, and (3) racial inequality.

Educators have the professional responsibility to recognize the relationship between culture and testing and the arguments for and against standardized testing. They must remember the danger of labeling and placing learners in lower groups based on scores that might not be valid.

### Arguments Supporting Standardized Tests

Arguments that support standardized testing include their widespread public and professional acceptance, their relative cost-efficiency in administration and reporting, their usefulness in accountability, their usefulness in placing students in special programs and ability groupings, and their role in making curricular decisions (Miller-Jones, 1989). Implementing Research 13-1 looks at the continuing tensions over standardized testing.

### Arguments Critical of Standardized Tests

Arguments critical of standardized testing include how well tests address the following questions:

1. Is the knowledge domain understood well enough to be adequately represented in a sample of items?
2. Are test items biased, or can they be written in a manner that does not favor a particular social or cultural experience?
3. Are test items, especially for achievement devices, fair? That is, do the test items reflect the kind of subject matter that most students are likely to encounter (Miller-Jones, 1989)?

Educators have known for several decades that standardized testing instruments are prepared from white, middle-class perspectives, but they continue to

---

**FOLLOW THROUGH 13-4   Reducing the Harmful Effects of Testing**

How do you or how does your group think educators might address cultural bias in assessment instruments? Suggest how a test item might be culturally biased. Testing is not likely to "go away," especially since the move toward testing appears to be growing stronger. How can educators reduce some of the more harmful effects of testing?

---

**IMPLEMENTING RESEARCH 13-1   The Standardized Testing Controversy**

Thomas Haladyna, Nancy Haas, and Jeanette Allison (1998) provide a brief history of standardized testing and ask, How do we measure achievement in today's students? For what purposes should standardized tests be used? Do standardized achievement tests adequately measure school achievement, or are performance tests and portfolios more appropriate? Tensions mount as both educators and parents seek to answer these questions.

A valid use of test scores is to provide a national ranking. Standardized tests also predict future achievement, provide a means of curriculum evaluation, assist with policy decisions, and serve as a device to identify weak areas of the curriculum. An invalid use of test scores is to offer financial incentives to teachers with high student test scores. It is also not valid to use them for graduation or certification testing, as a means of evaluating teaching, or as a method of evaluating and comparing schools and school districts.

**Implementing the Research**

Haladyna, Haas, and Allison (1998) offer several recommendations:

1. Test score interpretation must be valid—test scores measure only a sample of a large domain of knowledge—they should not be considered a means of evaluating the school curriculum or instructional emphasis.
2. Test score uses must be valid—ask about the validity of test scores before using them for purposes other than stated (e.g., evaluating teachers).
3. Keep standardized tests standardized—for example, do not teach the test, do not change the test times or conditions, and do not exclude certain students in an effort to raise test scores.
4. Examine and evaluate the consequences of standardized testing—for example, reporting test scores by racial or ethnic categories rarely serves useful purposes.

---

*Source:* Haladyna, T., Haas, N., & Allison, J. (1998). Continuing tensions in standardized testing. *Childhood Education, 74*(5), 262–273.

test children and adolescents from culturally diverse backgrounds using these instruments, which do not satisfactorily measure intelligence. Why do educators and testing specialists administer these assessment devices, especially when they have concluded that learning styles and cognitive strategies differ from culture to culture (Haladyna, Haas, & Allison, 1998)?

## *Issue: Language and Communication*

Language and communication have been sensitive and controversial issues with far-reaching implications for learners and educators. Whereas some argue that English should be the primary language for all, others feel that a person's native language is a personal and precious aspect of his or her cultural heritage. The issue extends further, however. Should students be allowed to learn in their native language? What should educators do about dialects? Should learners actually become bilingual? This section focuses on dialects, bilingual education, English as a second language, and nonverbal communication.

Implementing Research 13-2 examines language and immigrant children.

---

**IMPLEMENTING RESEARCH 13-2   Language and Immigrant Children**

Guadalupe Valdes (1998) discusses the education of immigrant children—a topic that needs to be a part of the national conversation as educators seek to deal with the challenges facing educational institutions. She also gives readers some notion of the (figurative) distance between homes and schools and what it is like for immigrant children to arrive in U.S. schools without knowing English.

The dilemma concerning language is a difficult one for the educational system. On the one hand, immigrant students must learn English; they cannot be truly accommodated by the schools until they are able to profit from instruction conducted in English. On the other hand, considerable confusion exists in educational circles and the public mind about how students can best acquire the academic English necessary to succeed in school.

Valdes states that children worldwide who do not speak the societal language face many difficulties in schools. It does not matter whether these youngsters are indigenous minorities or whether they are the children of newly arrived and often unwelcome immigrants. Since the times of increased immigration from southern and eastern Europe at the turn of the century, there has been a concern in the United States about immigrants' ability to understand and embrace the principles of democracy. Language was seen as a part of the nationalization process.

In recent years, English has become a central topic surrounding the education of immigrant students. Part of the difficulty is that most policy makers and the public have little information about what actually happens in schools. Nevertheless, far-reaching decisions are often made about immigrant children and how they should be taught English.

**Implementing the Research**

1. Educators in all curricular areas need to develop an understanding of students learning English as a second language (ESL)—their problems, strengths, challenges, and individual characteristics.
2. Educators need to gain an understanding of the language dilemma—immigrant students must learn English, but what is the best way to teach them so that they will succeed in school?
3. Policy makers need to understand the challenges that immigrant students face—they need to realize the far-reaching consequences of their decisions.
4. Children and adolescents need instruction in English for social, personal, and economic success. It might also be necessary to provide educational experiences in their own native language, at least until students develop proficiency in English.

---

*Source:* Valdes, G. (1998). The world outside and inside schools: Language and immigrant children. *Educational Researcher, 27*(6), 4–18.

## Dialects

Although English is the primary language of the United States, numerous English dialects are spoken throughout the country. Dialects are variations of a language that groups of speakers share. The language variation typically corresponds to other differences among groups, such as ethnicity, religion, culture, geographic location, and social class (Gollnick & Chinn, 1998). It is important to emphasize that all people speak in a dialect of their native language.

*Dialect* is a popular term that carries a negative connotation. It sometimes refers to a particular variety of English that may have a social or geographic basis and that differs from what is usually considered "standard" English. Dialects may include such variations as black English, Hawaiian Pidgin English, and rural Appalachian English (Gollnick & Chinn, 1998).

What should multicultural educators do about dialects? One group has suggested that students be allowed to learn in their own dialects and that to do otherwise only further disables learners. Others have argued that schools have the responsibility for teaching each student standard English to better cope with the demands of society. There is little doubt that the inability to speak standard English can be a decided disadvantage to an individual in certain situations, such as seeking employment (Gollnick & Chinn, 1998).

There are several alternatives for handling dialect in the educational setting: The first is the accommodation of all dialects, based on the assumption that they are all equal. The second is the insistence that only a standard dialect be allowed in the schools; this alternative allows for the position that functional ability in such a dialect is necessary for success in personal as well as vocational pursuits. A third alternative is a position between the two extremes, and it is the alternative educators most often choose. They accept native dialects for certain uses but encourage and insist on standard English in other circumstances. Students in such a school setting may read and write in standard English, because this is the primary written language they will encounter in this nation. They are not required to eliminate their natural dialect. Such a compromise allows the student to use two or more dialects in the school. This compromise acknowledges the legitimacy of all dialects, while it recognizes the social and vocational implications of being able to function using standard English (Gollnick & Chinn, 1998).

## Bilingual Education

Today, there are nearly 3 million limited-English-proficient (LEP) students in U.S. schools. According to the National Center for Education Statistics, 58 percent of all LEP students were born in the United States and 74 percent are Spanish speakers. The next largest language group is the Vietnamese with 3.9 percent. Although "bilingual" programs for non-Spanish languages groups can be found, few actually teach children to read and write in their native languages before teaching them these skills in English. These programs are bilingual only in the sense that they contain some measure of native-language support (Chavez & Amselle, 1997).

The theory behind bilingual education is that children must first fully develop their native language before they can achieve academic proficiency in a second language—a process that takes five to seven years, according to its proponents. In practical terms, children must be taught to read and write in their native language before they are taught those skills in English (Chavez & Amselle, 1997).

In her review of the research on bilingual education programs, Rosalie Porter (1997) summarizes the findings of a General Accounting Office report that looked at five school districts. She thinks these findings are representative of all public schools with LEP students:

- Immigrant students are almost 100 percent non-English-speaking on arriving in the United States.
- LEP students arrive at different times of the school year, which causes upheavals in classrooms and educational programs.
- Some high school students have not been schooled in their native lands and lack literacy in any language.
- There is a high level of family poverty and transiency and a low level of parental involvement in students' education.
- There is an acute shortage of bilingual teachers and of textbooks and assessment devices in the native languages. (Porter, 1997)

According to Rosalie Porter (1997), the efforts being made and the money being invested in special programs to help immigrant, migrant, and refugee schoolchildren who do not speak English when they enter schools is largely misguided. The politically righteous assumption is that these groups cannot learn English quickly and must be taught all their subjects in their native languages for three to seven years while having English introduced gradually.

Porter does not think such policy is most beneficial for LEP students. In fact, her experience and a growing body of research show no benefits from native-language teaching either in better learning English or better learning school subjects. Further explaining the issue, Porter also discusses the difficulty of voicing criticism of bilingual education programs "without being pilloried as a hater of foreigners and foreign languages and of contributing to the anti-immigrant climate" (p. 31).

Implementing Research 13-3 takes a closer look at Porter's perspectives.

Proponents of bilingual education have recommended aggressive development of the native language before the introduction of English. This argument is based on the belief that competencies in the native language provide important cognitive foundations for second-language acquisition and for academic learning in general. The ease of transferring skills acquired in the native language to English is an important component of this belief (Hakuta & Garcia, 1989).

The other side of the debate recommends introduction of the English curriculum from the very beginning of the student's schooling experience, with only minimal use of the native language. This approach is typically combined with an English as a second language (ESL) component. One appeal of the English-only method is its consistency with on-task arguments. Being exposed to English for longer periods of time should aid students in their acquisition of English (Hakuta & Garcia, 1989).

**IMPLEMENTING RESEARCH 13-3   The Politics of Bilingual Education**

Rosalie Porter (1997) maintains that several questions exist—with no more consensus now than five years ago: Are there measurable benefits for limited-English-speaking students when they are taught in their native language for a period of time; would benefits extend to their learning of the English language for academic achievement and their mastery of school subjects? Has a clear advantage emerged for a particular pedagogy among the best-known models—transitional bilingual education, English as a second language, structured immersion, dual immersion, and developmental bilingual programs? While clear-cut answers do not exist, growing evidence shows an almost total lack of accountability in some states that have heavily invested in bilingual programs during the last fifteen to twenty years.

Porter looks at the research from the General Accounting Office, the American Legislative Council (ALEC), the El Paso Bilingual Immersion Project, the New York study, and the California Study. Selected findings include:

- The El Paso Bilingual Immersion Project found that the Iowa Test of Basic Skills (in English) results for grades 4 and 5 show superior performance in all academic areas for students in the immersion program over students in the transitional program.
- The New York study found that students at all grade levels in ESL-only programs exited programs faster than those served in bilingual programs.

**Implementing the Research**

Educators of LEP children and adolescents need to:

1. understand the difficulty of voicing criticism of bilingual education programs (i.e., being considered opposed to foreigners and foreign languages and anti-immigrant) and still be willing to take an assertive stand for what is best for LEP learners.
2. take a planned approach to learning about the various LEP programs—transitional bilingual education, English as a second language, structured immersion, dual immersion, and developmental bilingual programs—and the advantages and disadvantages of (as well as the research on) each.
3. make a conscientious attempt to help LEP learners: being sure they have the most effective language program, involving parents and families, and addressing language-related issues such as self-esteem and cultural identity.

*Source:* Porter, R. O. (1997). The politics of bilingual education. *Society, 34*(6), 31–39.

## English as a Second Language

English as a second language programs are often confused with bilingual education. In the United States, the learning of English is an integral part of bilingual programs. However, the teaching of ESL, in and by itself, does not constitute a bilingual program. Both bilingual education and ESL programs promote English proficiency for limited-English-proficiency (LEP) students.

The approach to instruction distinguishes the the two programs. Bilingual education accepts and develops native language and culture in the instructional

---

**FOLLOW THROUGH 13-5**    Understanding Nonverbal Communication

Working in groups of three or four, have each person consider his or her own culture to determine nonverbal communication. Name several types of nonverbal communication from each culture, and explain how these forms of communication might be misunderstood.

---

process. Bilingual education may use both the native language and English as the medium of instruction. ESL instruction, however, relies exclusively on English as the medium to assimilate LEP children into the linguistic mainstream as quickly as possible. Hence, some educators place less emphasis on the maintenance of home language and culture than on English-language acquisition, and they view ESL programs as viable means of achieving these goals (Gollnick & Chinn, 1998).

## Nonverbal Communication

The issue of nonverbal differences and misunderstandings can be frustrating for both students and educators. To reduce the difficulty often associated with this form of communication, educators must analyze particular nonverbal behaviors when students do not respond as educators expect. Miscommunication may result from several nonverbal behaviors: a student may appear inattentive even when he or she is listening, a student may look away from the teacher when called on or addressed, or a student may interrupt at times that appear inappropriate to educators.

It is easy to jump to the conclusion that a student is not showing respect, when actually she or he is simply not following the unwritten rules of the classroom. In most school settings, educators expect learners from culturally different backgrounds to become bicultural and to adopt the nonverbal communication of the majority culture of the school. The ill effects of the issue lessen when educators also learn to operate biculturally in the classroom (Gollnick & Chinn, 1998).

## Issue: Accepting the Responsibility to Be Professionally Qualified and Committed

First and foremost, educators must accept responsibility for being trained to work with students of differing cultural backgrounds. Regardless of the multicultural education program and its goals, efforts will succeed only when educators are trained in cultural diversity, understand the effects of culture on learning, and are able to convey genuine feelings of acceptance and respect for all people. Professional education for all teachers, not just those planning to teach in multicultural areas, should include content methodologies courses that show the relationship between culture and learning and how to address this relationship in teaching situations; firsthand practica and clinical experiences in working with learners from diverse cultural backgrounds and socioeconomic classes; and appropriate experiences in interpersonal skills.

We reemphasize that professional responsibilities include broad expertise in content, instructional techniques, and the ability to work with learners from differing cultural backgrounds. Responsibilities extend even further, however. Having knowledge of people, but holding on to racist attitudes and the belief that "different is wrong," will not provide responsive multicultural education. Knowing that a relationship exists between cultures and education is a prerequisite to effective teaching, but continuing to teach with styles and strategies appropriate only for one culture fails to meet the needs of children and adolescents of other cultures.

Case Study 13-3 examines Dr. Thomas's thoughts concerning professional competencies of teachers who work in multicultural situations.

---

**CASE STUDY 13-3    Professional Competence**

As Dr. Thomas, a staff development specialist, looked at his district's guidelines for determining professional competence, he wondered what specific attributes or characteristics teachers should have, especially regarding cultural diversity. Although he considered his initial efforts to be only brainstorming, he placed items into several categories:

**A.** Overall Competencies

1. Knowledge
2. Attitudes
3. Skills

**B.** Educational Competencies

4. Curricular practices
5. Instructional techniques

6. Classroom rules and policies
7. Language considerations
8. Testing and assessment

Dr. Thomas knew his thoughts represented only a beginning point, but he did realize that teachers working with learners of different cultures need an understanding of how culture affects learning and achievement. He also realized that in all likelihood the teachers in his district needed appropriate in-service training and activities to make them more effective with learners from different cultures.

---

**FOLLOW THROUGH 13-6    Developing Individual Professional Improvement Plans**

Educators often develop their own individual professional plans to develop competencies as a means to better understanding of cultural diversity and the effects of culture on learning and of providing culturally appropriate educational experiences for all students. Suggest a development plan such as college coursework, reading of professional journals, and in-service training.

---

**FOLLOW THROUGH 13-7   Deciding What Curricular Materials Should Reflect**

What should contemporary curricular materials portray to reflect our nation's diversity? We know we need to move away from an overreliance on two-parent homes and European American middle-class people, but who and what should curricular materials reflect?

---

## Ensuring Cultural Diversity in All Curricular Materials

A major responsibility, and one that educators must accept, is the commitment to ensure cultural diversity in all curricular materials. Educators play a significant role as they scrutinize all print and nonprint materials for bias and racism. This issue includes omissions as well as distortions. Educators are responsible for being on the lookout for material that shows people's culture in a derogatory light or in demeaning situations or that shows minorities in stereotypical images. Only two decades ago, families were portrayed as two-parent, white, and living in white houses with picket fences. Educators in most situations can readily perceive that most learners would be unable to understand or relate to such images in stories. While there has been considerable progress, educators continue to be responsible for insisting on materials and adopting textbooks that include culturally diverse characters and their families only in positive, fulfilling roles.

## Ensuring That Multicultural Emphasis Permeates All Curricular Areas and the School Environment

Another major responsibility of educators is working toward multiculturalism in all areas of the curriculum and school environment. A basic assumption of this text is that multicultural education should be a broad-based effort that has the full cooperation and support of all school personnel, rather than a half-hearted effort.

Because they are representative of our culturally pluralistic society, schools must plan appropriate learning experiences for different children: Native, African, Asian, Hispanic, and European American, as well as children and adolescents from differing economic, social, and religious backgrounds. Educators must answer many questions. Which (or perhaps whose) religious holidays will be observed? How will cultural differences affect testing and assessment? What special problems will learners from diverse cultures bring to school? How will learning styles differ?

These and other questions raise the overall question of what, specifically, should educators do? A one-time multicultural week or single unit featuring African American history, tacos, and oriental dresses and customs will not suffice. Such approaches have not worked and will not work, because mere awareness of diversity does not necessarily result in acceptance and respect of individuals within the cultural group. The curriculum, learning environment, and the mind-set of learners and faculty and staff must become multicultural in nature and must reflect the cultural diversity of the school.

Well-meaning multicultural education programs may serve only cosmetic purposes if students and school personnel harbor long-held cultural biases and stereotypes. Schools must not presuppose learners' abilities and behaviors based on stereotypes and myth: the school curriculum must genuinely respect cultural diversity and regard all learners objectively.

### Involving Parents, Families, and the Community

Educators' recognition of the role of parents, the family, and the community in the multicultural education effort is an absolute prerequisite to the multicultural education program's success. Actually, two aspects are at stake, and both play a significant role in determining the success of the multicultural education program. First, including both immediate and extended families and community members demonstrates concretely that educators are serious about accepting and promoting multiculturalism outside the school boundaries. When educators show that their efforts do not stop at the schoolhouse gate, such a commitment adds credence to the multicultural education program's efforts.

Second, parents, families, and community members can play significant roles when they come to visit schools and offer their participation. Educators may have to deal with parents' language differences, misunderstandings associated with U.S. school systems, and the reluctance of some parents to share strengths. Although overcoming these challenges requires both time and energy, the benefits outweigh the efforts expended.

Our devoting an entire chapter (Chapter 11) to including parents and families from differing cultural backgrounds shows how important we believe the role of parents and families in education to be. The main issue is the extent to which educators genuinely want to effect multiculturalism. Children and adolescents who see only white parents in schools could easily conclude that cultural diversity is not as valuable as educators suggest. Although educators usually find it is easier to gain the attention of middle- and upper-class white parents, perceptive educators recognize the need to involve parents and families of many different cultures.

## Summing Up

Educators who understand the issues facing multicultural education and the challenges that such programs will face in the future should:

**1.** Understand that several issues affect the social and educational progress of children and adolescents from different cultural backgrounds and contribute to the degree of support the multicultural education receives.

**2.** Remember that although *multicultural education* may have several definitions, its overall rationale is to assist all learners to gain a better understanding and acceptance of others' cultural, ethnic, racial, and socioeconomic backgrounds.

**3.** Understand the futility of blaming the victim for life conditions, develop more enlightened perspectives of the reasons people become victims, and recognize the difficulty in overcoming victim status.

**4.** Understand that a relationship exists between culture and testing and that learners' cultural backgrounds can significantly affect standardized test scores.

**5.** Remember that the language issue includes dialectal differences, bilingual education, and teaching of English as a second language and that all educators need to address learners' language differences and needs.

**6.** Accept that educators have professional responsibilities that are prerequisite for responsive multicultural education programs to become a reality.

**7.** Remember that the ultimate success of any multicultural education program depends on every teacher's commitment to the program and to the acceptance of and respect for all people, regardless of differences or backgrounds.

## Suggested Learning Activities

1. In a study of racism, look at specific examples of racist acts during the latter half of the twentieth century. Begin with the integration of America's schools during the 1950s and 1960s and the accompanying racial violence. Then, examine the more current acts of racism occurring in the United States. What programs do schools have that teach the dangers of racism and that reduce racism and its effects on children and adolescents?

2. Discuss with several educators ways in which teachers may, knowingly or unknowingly, blame the victim for learning problems, socioeconomic conditions, or language problems. List several consequences of blaming the victim. Rather than blaming victims for particular conditions, how can educators gain a better, or more objective, perspective of learners' conditions?

3. Write *your* definition of *multicultural education*. In your opinion, what differences should multicultural education include? Should it be only cultural, or should it include social class, gender, and religion? For example, do you think there is a culture of religion or a culture of social class? Does your definition include only knowledge of differences, or is appreciation of differences acknowledged or implied? Why are individual definitions of multicultural education important?

## Suggestions for Collaborative Efforts

Form groups of three or four that, if possible, represent U.S. cultural and gender diversity. Working collaboratively, focus your group's attention toward the following efforts:

1. In an honest and frank discussion of racism, has any member of your group felt like a victim of racism? Remember, racism can affect all cultures, and, regrettably, there are

racists in all cultures. How did the act of racism make that person feel? How do you believe racism affects teaching and learning situations? Why do you think racist acts are increasing? How can schools address racism?

2. Make a list of assessment instruments (and the addresses of publishers) that claim to reduce cultural bias in their test items. Provide two or three examples of culturally biased test items. How might educators determine cultural bias in assessment instruments?

3. Survey a number of schools in an urban area with a significant percentage of students from culturally different backgrounds. What programs do these schools have to address language differences? Do language-minority youngsters receive equal opportunities, or are learners sometimes expected to learn and deal with language problems simultaneously? Looking at your survey, what language programs or approaches appear more likely to meet the needs of language-minority learners?

## *Expanding Your Horizons: Additional Journal Readings and Books*

Chavez, L., & Amselle, J. (1997). Bilingual education theory and practice: Its effectiveness and parental opinions. *NASSP Bulletin, 81*(586), 101–106.

*Chavez and Amselle pinpoint the problems of bilingual education and maintain that bilingual education has failed to live up to its promises.*

Epstein, D. (1997). Boyz' own stories: Masculinities and sexualities in schools. *Gender and Education, 9*(1), 105–115.

*Epstein argues that struggles around gender, homophobia, and implicit heterosexism derive from macho versions of masculinity.*

Grant, N. (1997). Some problems of identity and education: A comparative examination of multicultural education. *Comparative Education, 33*(1), 9–28.

*Grant considers issues concerning the education of minorities in Europe and elsewhere.*

Haladyna, T., Haas, N., & Allison, J. (1998). Continuing tensions in standardized testing. *Childhood Education, 74*(5), 262–273.

*These authors look at the history of standardized testing, the role of professional associations, use of test results, and effects on teachers and students.*

Porter, R. O. (1997). The politics of bilingual education. *Society, 34*(6), 31–39.

*Porter, in a somewhat controversial article, argues that educational research does not support the effects of transitional bilingual education programs.*

Williams, R. L. (1997). The Ebonics controversy. *Journal of Black Psychology, 23*(3), 208–214.

*Williams provides two schools of thought about the Ebonics controversy, especially the possible use of Ebonics as a bridge to standard English.*

## *Answers to the Culture Quiz: Issues in Multicultural Education*

| 1. T | 3. F | 5. F | 7. F | 9. F |
| 2. T | 4. T | 6. T | 8. T | 10. T |

# References

Abrams, R. D. (1993). Meeting the educational and cultural needs of Soviet newcomers. *Religious Education, 88*(2), 315–323.

Alba, R. D. (1985). *Italian Americans into the twilight of ethnicity.* Englewood Cliffs, NJ: Prentice-Hall.

Alexander, C. (1989). Gender differences in adolescent health concerns and self-assessed health. *Journal of Early Adolescence, 9,* 467–479.

Ambler, M. (1997). Without racism: Indian students could be both Indian and students. *Tribal College, 8*(4), 8–11.

American Association of University Women. (1992). *How schools shortchange girls.* Annapolis Junction, MD: AAUW.

Ames, C. A. (1990). Motivation: What teachers need to know. *Teachers College Record, 91,* 409–421.

Anokye, A. D. (1997). A case for orality in the classroom. *The Clearing House, 70*(5), 229–231.

Aronson, E., Blaney, N., Stephan, C., Sikes, J., & Snapp, M. (1978). *The jigsaw classroom.* Beverly Hills, CA: Sage.

Asakawa, K., & Csikszentmihalyi, M. (1998). The quality of experiences of Asian American adolescents related to future goals. *Journal of Youth and Adolescence, 27*(2), 141–163.

American Speech and Hearing Association. (1983). Social dialects. *ASHA, 25*(9), 23–24.

Atkinson, D. R., Morten, G., & Sue, D. W. (1993). *Counseling American minorities: A cross-cultural perspective* (4th ed.). Dubuque, IA: Wm. C. Brown.

Axelson, J. A. (1985). *Counseling and development in a multicultural society.* Monterey, CA: Brooks/Cole.

Baca, L. M., & Amato, C. (1989). Bilingual special education: Training issues. *Exceptional Children, 56,* 168–173.

Baca, L. M., & Cervantes, H. T. (1989). *The bilingual special education interface.* Columbus, OH: Merrill.

Backes, J. S. (1994). Bridging the gender gap: Self-concept in the middle grades. *Schools in the Middle, 3*(3), 19–23.

Bailey, N. J., & Phariss, T. (1996). Breaking the wall of silence: Gay, lesbian, and bisexual issues for middle level educators. *Middle School Journal, 27*(3), 38–46.

Baker, G. C. (1994). Teaching children to respect diversity. *Childhood Education, 71,* 33–35.

Banks, C. A., & Banks, J. A. (1997). Reforming schools in a democratic pluralistic society. *Educational Policy, 11*(2), 183–193.

Banks, J. A. (1981). Education in the 80's: Multiethnic education. Washington, D.C.: National Education Association.

Banks, J. A. (1987). *Teaching strategies for ethnic studies.* Boston: Allyn & Bacon.

Banks, J. A. (1988). Multiethnic education: Theory and practice. Boston: Allyn & Bacon.

Banks, J. A. (1993). Multicultural education: Progress and prospects. *Phi Delta Kappan, 75,* 21.

Banks, J. A. (1998). The lives and values of researchers: Implications for educating citizens in a multicultural society. *Educational Researcher, 27*(7), 4–17.

Banks, J. A., & Banks, C. A. M. (1993). *Multicultural education: Issues and perspectives* (2nd ed.). Boston: Allyn & Bacon.

Barry, A. L. (1998). Hispanic representation in literature for young adults. *Journal of Adolescent and Adult Literacy, 41*(8), 630–637.

Basen-Engquist, K., Tortolero, S., & Parcel, G. S. (1997). HIV risk behavior and theory-based psychosocial determinants in Hispanic and non-Hispanic white adolescents. *Journal of Health Education, 28*(4), S-44-S-50.

Bay, M., & Lopez-Reyna, N. (1997). Preparing bilingual special educators: The lessons we've learned. *Teacher Education and Special Education, 20*(1), 1–10.

Bell-Scott, P., & McKenry, P. C. (1986). Black adolescents and their families. In G. K. Leigh & G. W. Peterson (Eds.), *Adolescents in families* (pp. 410–432). Cincinnati, OH: Southwestern.

Benenson, J. F. (1990). Gender differences in social networks. *Journal of Early Adolescence, 10,* 472–495.

Bennett, C. I. (1986). *Comprehensive multicultural education: Theory and practice.* Boston: Allyn & Bacon.

Biehler, R., & Snowman, J. (1990). *Psychology as applied to teaching* (6th ed.). Boston: Houghton Mifflin.

Blacks are slipping through the health gap. (November 27, 1998). *The Virginia-Pilot,* pp. A1, A14.

Boddie, J. L. (1997). Making the grade in high school: African American urban males. *The High School Magazine, 5*(2), 50–55.

Bond, M. H., & Shiraishi, N. (1974). The effect of body lean and status of an interviewer on the nonverbal behavior of Japanese interviewees. *International Journal of Psychology, 9*(2), 117–128.

Borden, J. F. (1998). The pitfalls and possibilities for organizing quality ESL programs. *Middle School Journal, 29*(3), 25–33.

Boveja, M. E. (1998). Parenting styles and adolescents' learning strategies in the urban community. *Journal of Multicultural Counseling and Development, 26*(2), 110–119.

Bowman, B. T. (1989). Educating language-minority children: Challenges and opportunities. *Phi Delta Kappan, 71,* 118–120.

Boyd, B. F. (1998). Issues in education: A guide to multicultural education. *Childhood Education, 75*(1), 33.

Butler, D. A., & Manning, M. L. (1998). *Gender differences in young adolescents.* Olney, MD: Association for Childhood Education International.

Butler, D. A., & Sperry, S. (1991). Gender issues and the middle school curriculum. *Middle School Journal, 23*(2), 18–23.

Byrnes, D. A., & Cortez, D. (1996). Language diversity in the classroom. In D. A. Byrnes & G. Kiger (Eds.), *Common bonds: Anti-bias teaching in a diverse society* (pp. 65–78). Olney, MD: Association for Childhood Education International.

Byrnes, D. A., & Kiger, G. (1996). *Common bonds: Anti-bias teaching in a diverse society* (2nd. ed). Olney, MD: Association for Childhood Education International.

Calderon, M. (1997). Staff development in multilingual multicultural schools. (ERIC Document Reproduction Service No: 410 368).

Carr, C. L. (1998). Tomboy resistance and conformity: Agency in social psychological gender theory. *Gender & Society, 12*(5), 528–553.

Casteel, C. A. (1997). Attitudes of African American and Caucasian eighth-grade students about praises, rewards, and punishments. *Elementary School Guidance and Counseling, 31,* 262–272.

Chang, J. I. (1997). Contexts of adolescent worries: Impacts of ethnicity, gender, family structure, and socioeconomic status. (ERIC Document Reproduction Service No: ED 417 003).

Chapman, A. (1997). A great balancing act: Equitable education for girls and boys. Washington, D.C.: National Association of Independent Schools.

Chavez, L., & Amselle, J. (1997). Bilingual education theory and practice: Its effectiveness and parental opinions. *NASSP Bulletin, 81*(586), 101–106.

Chavkin, N. F. (1989). Debunking the myth about minority parents. *Educational Horizons, 67*(4), 119–123.

Chen, S. (1987, April 6). Suicide and depression identified as serious problems for Asian youth. *East-West News, 9,* 3–4.

Cheng, L. L. (1987). Cross-cultural and linguistic considerations in working with Asian populations. *American Speech and Hearing Association, 29*(6), 33–36.

Christensen, E. W. (1989). Counseling Puerto Ricans: Some cultural considerations. In D. R. Atkinson, G. Morten, & D. W. Sue (Eds.), *Counseling American minorities: A Cross-cultural perspective* (3rd ed.) (pp. 205–212). Dubuque, IA: W. C. Brown.

Clark, D. C., & Clark, S. N. (1998). Creating developmentally responsive learning environments. *Schools in the Middle, 8*(2), 12–15.

Clark-Johnson, G. (1988). Black children. *Teaching Exceptional Children, 20,* 46–47.

Closing the educational gap for Hispanics: State aims to forestall a divided society. (1987,

September 16). *The Chronicle of Higher Education*, p. 1.

Coballes-Vega, C. (1992, January). Considerations for teaching culturally diverse children. *ERIC Digest*, 1–2.

Cohen, E. G., & Lotan, R. A. (Eds.) (1997). *Working for equity in heterogeneous classrooms: Sociological theory in practice.* New York: Teachers College Press.

Coladarci, T. (1983). High-school dropout among Native Americans. *Journal of American Indian Education, 23,* 15–21.

Colburn, D., & Melillo, W. (1987, June 16). Hispanics: A forgotten help population. *Washington Post*, p. 16.

Collier, C., & Hoover, J. J., (1987). *Cognitive strategies for minority handicapped students.* Lindale, TX: Hamilton Publications.

Comer, J. P. (1988). Establishing a positive racial identity. *Parents, 63*(3), 167.

Cornett, C. E. (1983). *What should you know about teaching and learning styles* (Fastback 191). Bloomington, IN: Phi Delta Kappa.

Crawford, L. W. (1993). *Language and literacy learning in multicultural classrooms.* Boston: Allyn & Bacon.

Darling-Hammond, L. (1998). New standards, old inequalities: The current challenge for African American education. In L. A. Daniels, D. McSween, & R. Jefferson-Franzier (Eds.), *The state of black America 1998* (pp. 109–171). New York: National Urban League.

Davis, B. C. (1989). A successful parent involvement program. *Educational Leadership, 47*(2), 21–23.

Davison, D. M., & Miller, K. W. (1998). An ethnoscience approach to curriculum issues for American Indian students. *School Science and Mathematics, 95*(5), 260–264.

Dawson, M. M. (1987). Beyond ability grouping: A review of the effectiveness of ability grouping and its alternatives. *School Psychology Review, 16,* 348–369.

Derman-Sparks, L. (1993/1994). Empowering children to create a caring culture in a world of differences. *Childhood Education, 70,* 66–71.

Deyhle, D. (1985). Testing among Navajo and Anglo students: Another consideration of cultural bias. *Journal of Educational Equity and Leadership, 5,* 119–131.

Dilworth, M. E. (Ed.). (1998). *Being responsive to cultural differences: How teachers learn.* Thousand Oaks, CA: Corwin.

Dirda, M. A. (November 9, 1997). Classrooms and their discontents. *Washington Post* 19: 2.

Divoky, D. (1988). The model minority goes to school. *Phi Delta Kappan, 70,* 219–222.

Dorriss, M. A. (1981). The grass still grow, the rivers still flow: Contemporary Native Americans. *Daedalus, 110*(2), 43–69.

Draguns, J. G. (1989). Dilemmas and choices in cross-cultural counseling: The universal versus the culturally distinctive. In P. D. Pedersen, J. G. Draguns, J. Lonner, & J. E. Trimble (Eds.), *Counseling across cultures* (3rd ed.) (pp. 1–21). Honolulu: University of Hawaii Press.

Duncan, G. (1993). Racism as a developmental mediator. *The Educational Forum, 57,* 360–369.

Dunn, R., Gemake, J., Jalali, F., Zenhausern, R., Quinn, P., & Spiridakis, J. (1990). Cross-cultural differences in learning styles of elementary-age children from four ethnic backgrounds. *Journal of Multicultural Counseling and Development, 18,* 68–93.

Dunn, R. S., Beaudry, J. S., & Klavas, A. (1989). Survey of research on learning styles. *Educational Leadership, 46,* 50–58.

Dunn, R. S., & Dunn, K. J. (1978). *Teaching students through their individual learning styles: A practical approach.* Reston, VA: Reston Publishing.

Dunn, R. S., & Dunn, K. J. (1979). Learning styles/teaching styles: Should they . . . can they . . . be matched? *Educational Leadership, 36,* 238–244.

Eaton, M. J., & Dembo, M. H. (1997). Differences in the motivational beliefs of Asian American and non-Asian students. *Journal of Educational Psychology, 89*(3), 433–440.

Edelman, M. W. (1989). Black children in America. In J. Dewart (Ed.), *The state of black America* (pp. 63–76). New York: National Urban League.

Education and gender (1994, June 3). *Congressional Quarterly Researcher, 4*(21), 482–503.

Elkind, D. (1984). Erik Erikson's eight stages of man. In H. E. Fitzgerald & M. G. Walveren (Eds.), *Human development* (pp. 11–18). Guilford, CT: Dushkin Publishing Group.

Ellington, L. (1998). Multicultural theorists and the social studies. *The Social Studies, 89*(2), 57–60.

*English as a second language program: Benefits for your child.* (1987). Austin, TX: Texas Education Agency.

Epstein, D. (1997). Boyz' own stories: Masculinities and sexualities in schools. *Gender and Education, 9*(1), 105–115.

Espiritu, Y. L. (1997). Race, gender, and class in the lives of Asian Americans. *Race, Gender, and Class, 4*(3), 12–19.

Evans, K. M. (1997). Multicultural training needs for counselors of gifted African American children. *Multicultural Education, 5*(1), 16–19.

Fagella, K. (1994). Coming to America. *Instructor, 103,*(6), 42–43.

Faltis, C. J. (1993). *Joinfostering: Adapting teaching strategies for the multilingual classroom.* Columbus, OH: Merrill.

Feng, J. (1994, June). Asian-American children: What teachers should know. *ERIC Digest,* 1–2.

Fitzpatrick, J. P. (1987). *Puerto Rican Americans* (2nd ed.). Englewood Cliffs, NJ: Prentice-Hall.

Foner, N. (1997). The immigrant family: Cultural legacies and cultural changes. *International Migration Review, 31*(4), 961–974.

Frisby, C. L. (1993). One giant step backward: Myths of black cultural learning styles. *School Psychology Review, 22,* 535–557.

Fuchs, D., & Fuchs, L. S. (1998). Competing visions for educating students with disabilities: Inclusion versus full inclusion. *Childhood Education 74*(5), 309–316.

Fuligni, A. J. (1997). The academic achievement of adolescents from immigrant families: The roles of family background, attitudes, and behavior. *Child Development, 68*(2), 351–363.

Gade, E., Hurlburt, G., & Fuqua, D. (1986). Study habits and attitudes of American Indian students: Implications for counselors. *The School Counselor, 34,* 135–139.

Gallagher, J. (1998). The language of learning. *Middle Ground, 2*(2), 6–10, 24.

Gallagher, J. (1998). Multiculturalism at a crossroads: Can the push for pluralism in education survive the pull of America's melting pot? *Middle Ground, 1*(3), 10–14, 42.

Gallimore, R., & Goldenberg, C. (1996). Accommodating cultural differences and commonalities in educational practices. *Multicultural Education 4*(1),16–19.

Garcia, R. L. (1984). Countering classroom discrimination. *Theory into Practice, 22,* 104–109.

Gillespie, C. S., Powell, J. L., Clements, N. E., Swearingen, R. A. (1994). A look at the Newbery medal books from a multicultural perspective. *Language Arts, 48*(1), 40–50.

Gillette, M. D., & Chinn, P. C. (1997). Multicultural education: Responding to a mandate for equitable educational outcomes. *Teacher Education and Practice, 13*(1), 1–13.

Goldenberg, C. N. (1987). Low-income Hispanic parents' contributions to their first-grade children's word-recognition skills. *Anthropology & Education Quarterly, 18,* 149–179.

Gollnick, D. M., & Chinn, P. C. (1998). *Multicultural education in a pluralistic society* (5th ed.). Columbus, OH: Merrill.

Gollnick, D. M., Sadker, M. P., & Sadker, D. M. (1982). Beyond the Dick and Jane syndrome: Confronting sex bias in instructional materials. In M. P. Sadker & D. M. Sadker (Eds.), *Sex equity handbook for schools.* New York: Longman.

Gonzalez, E. (1989). Hispanics bring *corazon* and *sensibilidad. Momentum, 20*(1), 10–13.

Gordon, B. M. (1997). Curriculum, policy, and African American cultural knowledge: Challenges and possibilities for the year 2000 and beyond. *Educational Policy, 11*(2), 227–242.

Gorman, J. C., & Balter, L. (1997). Culturally sensitive parent education: A critical review of quantitative research. *Review of Educational Research, 67*(3), 339–369.

Grant, C. A., & Sleeter, C. E. (1986, April). *Race, class, and gender in educational research: An argument for integrative analysis.* Paper presented at the meeting of the American Educational Research Association, San Francisco, CA.

Grant, N. (1997). Some problems of identity and education: A comparative examination of multicultural education. *Comparative Education, 33*(1), 9–28.

Graybill, S. W. (1997). Questions of race and culture: How they relate to the classroom for African American students. *The Clearing House, 70*(6), 311–318.

Grossman, H., & Grossman, S. H. (1994). *Gender issues in education.* Boston: Allyn & Bacon.

Guild, P. (1994). The culture/learning style connection. *Educational Leadership, 51*(8), 16–21.

Guinn, B. (1997). Health locus of control and HIV / AIDS knowledge among Mexican American young adolescents. *Journal of Health Education, 28*(4), S-13–S-16.

Hakuta, K., & Garcia, E. E. (1989). Bilingualism and education. *American Psychologist, 44,* 374–379.

Haladyna, T., Haas, N., & Allison, J. (1998). Continuing tensions in standardized testing. *Childhood Education, 74*(5), 262–273.

Hale-Benson, J. E. (1986). *Black children: Their roots and their culture* (rev. ed.). Baltimore, MD: Johns Hopkins University.

Hall, E. T. (1981). *Beyond culture.* Garden City, NH: Anchor.

Halle, T. G., Kurtz-Costes, B., Mahoney, J. L. (1997). Family influences on school achievement in low-income, African American children. *Journal of Educational Psychology, 89*(3), 527–537.

Haring, N. G. (1990). Overview of special education. In N. G. Haring & L. McCormick (Eds.), *Exceptional children and youth* (pp. 1–45). Columbus, OH: Merrill.

Hartman, J. S., & Askounis, A. C. (1989). Asian American students: Are they really a 'model minority'? *The School Counselor, 37,* 109–111.

Hernandez, H. (1989). *Multicultural education: A teacher's guide to content and process.* Columbus, OH: Merrill.

Herring, R. D. (1989). Counseling Native American children: Implications for elementary school counselors. *Elementary School Guidance and Counseling, 23,* 272–281.

Herring, R. D. (1997). The creative arts: An avenue to wellness among Native American Indians. *Journal of Humanistics Education and Development, 36*(2), 105–113.

Hispanic youth edging past blacks in number, (1998). *Census and You, 33*(9), 3.

Ho, M. K. (1987). *Family therapy with ethnic minorities.* Newbury Park: Sage.

Hodgkinson, H. (1998). The demographics of diversity. *Principal 78*(1), 26–32.

Hoover-Dempsey, K. V., Bassler, O.C., & Brissie, J. S. (1987). Parent involvement: Contributions of teacher efficacy, school socioeconomic status, and other school characteristics. *American Education Research Journal, 24,* 417–435.

House, D. J. (1997). The relationship between self-beliefs, academic background, and achievement of adolescent Asian American students. *Child Study Journal, 27*(2), 95–110.

Huang, S. L., & Waxman, H. C. (1997). Classroom behaviors of Asian American students in mathematics. (ERIC Document Reproduction Service No: ED 408 166).

Hubbard, L. (1997). A gendered look at the academic achievement of low income African American high school students: Strategies of success. (ERIC Document Reproduction Service No: ED 414 287).

Hudley, C. A. (1997). Teacher practices and student motivation in a middle school program for African American males. *Urban Education, 32*(2), 304–319.

Indian tribes, incorporated. (1988, December 5). *Newsweek,* pp. 40–41.

Isen, H. G. (1983). Assessing the black child. *Journal of Non-White Concerns, 11,* 47–58.

Isom, B. A., & Casteel, C. P. (1997/1998). Hispanic literature: A fiesta for literacy instruction. *Childhood Education, 74*(2), 83–89.

James, C. S. D. (1997). Coping with a new society: The unique psychosocial problems of immigrant youth. *Journal of School Health, 67*(3), 98–102.

Janzen, R. (1994). Melting pot or mosaic? *Educational Leadership, 51*(8), 9–11.

Jarolimek, J., & Foster, C. D. (1989). *Teaching and learning in the elementary school* (4th ed.). New York: Macmillan.

Jaynes, G. D., & Williams, R. M. (1989). *A common destiny: Blacks and American society.* Washington, D.C.: National Academy Press.

Jennings, W. B. (1989). How to organize successful parent involvement advisory committees. *Educational Leadership, 47*(2), 42–45.

Jensen, J. V. (1985). Perspective on nonverbal intercultural communication. In L. A. Samovar, & R. E. Porter (Eds.), *Intercultural communication: A reader* (4th ed.) (pp. 256–272). Belmont, CA: Wadsworth.

Jupp, J. C. (1998). A community-centered approach to multicultural education. *English Journal, 88*(2), 15–16.

Kang, H., & Dutton, B. (1997). Becoming multicultural: Focusing on the process. *Multicultural Education, 4*(4), 19–22.

Kao, G., & Tienda, M. (1998). Educational aspirations of minority youth. *American Journal of Education, 106*(3), 349–384.

Keefe, J. W. (1987). *Learning style: Theory and practice.* Reston, VA: NASSP.

Keefe, J. W. (1990). Learning style: Where are we going? *Momentum, 21*(1), 44–48.

Kim, H., Rendon, L., & Valadez, J. (1998). Student characteristics, school characteristics, and educational aspirations of six Asian American groups. *Journal of Multicultural Counseling and Development, 26*(3), 166–178.

Kitano, H. H. L. (1989). A model for counseling Asian Americans. In P. B. Pedersen, J. G. Draguns, W. J. Lonner, & J. E. Trimble (Eds.), *Counseling across cultures* (pp. 139–151). Honolulu: University of Hawaii Press.

Koff, E., Rierdan, J., & Stubbs, M. L. (1990). Gender, body image, and self-concept in early adolescence. *Journal of Early Adolescence, 10*, 56–68.

Kostelnik, M. J., Stein, L. C., Whiren, A. P., & Soderman, A. K. (1988). *Guiding children's social development.* Cincinnati, OH: Brooks/Cole.

Kreidler, W. J. (1995). Say good-bye to bias. *Instructor, 104*(5), 28.

Latham, A. S. (1998). Gender differences on assessments. *Educational Leadership, 55*(4), 88–89.

Lawrence, V. J. (1997). Multiculturalism, diversity, cultural pluralism . . . "Tell the whole truth, and nothing but the truth." *Journal of Black Studies, 27*(3), 318–333.

Lee, E. S., & Rong, X. (1988). The educational economic achievement of Asian-Americans. *The Elementary School Journal, 88*, 545–560.

Lee, E., Menkart, D., & Okazawa-Rey, M. (1998). *Beyond heroes and holidays: A practical guide to k-12 anti-racist, multicultural education and staff development.* Washington, D.C.: Network of Educators on the Americas.

Lee, O., & Fradd, S. H. (1998). Science for all, including students from non-English-language backgrounds. *Educational Researcher, 27*(4), 12–20.

Lee, O. (1997). Diversity and equity for Asian American students in science education. *Science Education, 81*(1), 107–122.

Lee, W. M. L. (1996). New directions in multicultural counseling. *Counseling and Human Development, 29*(2), 1–11.

Leuthold, S. (1997). Crossing the lines: Toward a curriculum of comparative design. *Multicultural Education 5*(2), 16–19.

Lewis, B. (1998). The historical roots of racism. *The American Scholar, 67*(1), 17–25.

Lewis, J. B., deMarrais, K. B., & Prater, G. (1998). Teaching Navajo bilingual student special education students: Challenges and strategies. (ERIC Document Reproduction Service No: 417 895).

Lewis, R. G., & Ho, M. K. (1989). Social work with Native-Americans. In D. R. Atkinson, G. Morten, & D. W. Sue (Eds.), *Counseling American minorities* (3rd ed.) (pp. 65–72). Dubuque, IA: Wm. C. Brown.

Lind, M. (1998, August 16). The beige and the black. *The New York Times Magazine*, 38–39.

Linton, T. E., & Foster, M. (1990). Powerful environments for underclass youth. *The Education Digest, 55*(7), 27–31.

Little, M. (1997). Teacher-parent cooperation: A Navajo perspective. *Journal of Navajo Education, 14*(1–2), 26–31.

Little Soldier, L. (1985). To soar with the eagles: Enculturation and acculturation of Indian children. *Childhood Education, 61*, 185–191.

Little Soldier, L. (1989). Cooperative learning and the Native American student. *Phi Delta Kappan, 71*, 161–163.

Locke, D. C. (1989). Fostering the self-esteem of African American children. *Elementary School Guidance and Counseling, 23*, 254–259.

Lomotey, K. (1989). Cultural diversity in the school: Implications for principals. *National Association of Secondary School Principals Bulletin, 73*, 81–88.

Lonner, W. J., & Ibrahim, F. A. (1989). Assessment in cross-cultural counseling. In P. B. Pedersen, J. G. Draguns, J. Lonner, & J. E. Trimble (Eds.), *Counseling across cultures* (3rd ed.) (pp. 299–333). Honolulu: University of Hawaii Press.

Lopata, H. Z. (1994). *Polish Americans.* New Brunswick: Transaction.

Low, J. M., & Wong, P. L. (1998). Effects of a Hmong intern on Hmong students. *Multicultural Education 5*(4), 12–16.

Lucero, E. L. (1997). Promoting multiculturalism in the early grades. *Principal, 76*(5), 5–6, 8, 10–11.

Luftig, R. L. (1983). The effect of schooling on the self-concept of Native American students. *The School Counselor, 30*, 251–260.

Lum, D. (1986). *Social work practice and people of color: A process-stage approach.* Monterey, CA: Brooks/Cole.

Lundeberg, M. A., Fox, P. W., & Puncochar, J. (1994). Highly confident but wrong: Gender differences and similarities in confidence judgments. *Journal of Educational Psychology, 86*, 114–121.

Lundy, B., Field, T., McBride, C., Field, T., Largie, S. (1998). Same-sex and opposite-sex best friend interactions among high school juniors and seniors. *Adolescence, 33*(130), 279–289.

Machamer, A. M., & Gruber, E. (1998). Secondary school, family, and educational risk: Comparing American Indian adolescents and their peers. *Journal of Educational Research, 91*(6), 357–369.

Mahiri, J. (1998). Streets to schools: African American youth culture and the classroom. *The Clearing House, 71*(6), 335–338.

Manning, M. L. (1989). Multicultural education. *Middle School Journal, 21*(1), 14–16.

Manning, M. L. (1991). More than lipservice to multicultural education. *The Clearing House, 64*, 218.

Manning, M. L. (1993). Cultural and gender differences in young adolescents. *Middle School Journal, 25*(1), 13–17.

Manning, M. L. (1994). *Celebrating diversity: Multicultural education in middle level schools.* Columbus, OH: National Middle School Association.

Manning, M. L. (1995). Understanding culturally diverse parents and families. *Equity and Excellence in Education, 28*(1), 52–57.

Manning, M. L. (1996). Addressing the fears of diversity. *Kappa Delta Pi Record 33*, 4–7.

Manning, M. L. (1998). Gender differences in young adolescents' mathematics and science achievement. *Childhood Education 74*, 168–171.

Manning, M. L., & Baruth, L. G. (1991). Appreciating cultural diversity in the classroom. *Kappa Delta Pi Record, 27*(4), 104–107.

Manning, M. L., & Lucking, R. (1990). Ability grouping: Realities and alternatives. *Childhood Education, 66,* 254–258.

Manning, M. L., & Lucking, R. (1991). The what, why, and how of cooperative learning. *The Clearing House, 64*, 152–165.

Manning, M. L., & Lucking, R. (1993). Cooperative learning and multicultural classrooms. *The Clearing House, 67*, 12–16.

Marcell, A. V. (1994). Understanding ethnicity, identity formation, and risk behavior among adolescents of Mexican descent. *Journal of School Health, 64*, 323–327.

Marinoble, R. M. (1998). Counseling and supporting our gay students. *The Education Digest, 64*(3), 54–59.

Marion, R. (1981). *Educators, parents and exceptional children.* Rockville, MD: Aspen Systems.

"Married with children": More likely to describe Hispanic households. (1998). *Census and You, 33*(4), 3.

Marshall, C. S. (1998). Using children's storybooks to encourage discussions among diverse populations. *Childhood Education, 74*(4), 194–199.

Martinez, R. O., & Dukes, R. L. (1997). The effects of ethnic identity, ethnicity, and gender on adolescent well-being. *Journal of Youth and Adolescence, 26*(5), 503–516.

Martz, C. (1993). Educating European immigrants before World War I. *Educational Horizons, 71*(3), 139–141.

Math and science path to making things even for girls. (May/June 1994). *High Strides: The Bimonthly Report on Urban Middle Grades*, 2.

Mavrelis, J. (1997). Understanding differences in multicultural communication styles. *The High School Magazine, 5*(2), 30–37.

McCollum, V. J. C. (1997) Evolution of African American family personality: Considerations for family therapy. *Journal of Multicultural Counseling and Development, 25*, 219–229.

McCormick, L. (1990a). Cultural diversity and exceptionality. In N. G. Haring & L. McCormick (Eds.), *Exceptional children and youth* (pp. 47–75). Columbus, OH: Merrill.

McCormick, L. (1990b). Communication disorders. In N. G. Haring & L. McCormick (Eds.), *Exceptional children and youth* (pp. 327–363). Columbus, OH: Merrill.

McDaniel, T. R. (1994). The education of Alice and Dorothy: Helping girls thrive in school. *The Clearing House, 68*, 43–45.

McFarlane, S. C., Fujiki, M., & Britton, B. (1984). *Coping with communicative handicaps.* San Diego: College-Hill Press.

McGoldrick, M. (1982). Irish families. In M. McGoldrick, J. K. Pearce, & J. Giordano (Eds.), *Ethnicity and family therapy* (pp. 310–339). New York: Guilford Press.

McInerney, D. M., & McInerney, V. (1998). The goals of schooling in culturally diverse classrooms. *The Clearing House, 71*(6), 363–366.

McInerney, D. M., Roche, L. A., McInerney, V., & Marsh, H. W. (1997). Cultural perspectives on school motivation: The relevance and application of goal theory. *American Education Research Journal, 34*(1), 207–236.

McIntyre, A. (1997). Constructing an image of a white teacher. *Teachers College Record, 98*(4), 653–681.

Miller, H. M. (1998). Teaching and learning about history: Who owns history? *The Reading Teacher, 52*(1), 76–78.

Miller-Jones, D. (1989). Culture and testing. *American Psychologist, 44*, 360–366.

Miller-Lachmann, L. (1992). *Our family, our friends, our world: An annotated guide to significant multicultural books for children and teenagers.* Providence, NJ: R. R. Bowker.

Mindel, H. C., & Habenstein, R. W. (1981). Family lifestyles of America's ethnic minorities: An introduction. In C. H. Mindel & R. W. Habenstein (Eds.), *Ethnic families in America: Patterns and variations* (pp. 1–13). New York: Elsevier.

Minderman, L. (1990). Literature and multicultural education. *Instructor, 99*(7), 22–23.

Mirande, A. (1986). Adolescence and Chicano families. In G. K. Leigh, & G. W. Peterson (Eds.), *Adolescents in families* (pp. 433–455). Cincinnati, OH: Southwestern.

Mitchum, N. T. (1989). Increasing self-esteem in Native American children. *Elementary School Guidance and Counseling, 23*, 266–271.

Moitoza, E. (1982). Portuguese families. In M. McGoldrick, J. K. Pearce, & J. Giordano (Eds.), *Ethnicity and family therapy* (pp. 412–437). New York: Guilford Press.

Mondykowski, S. M. (1982). Polish families. In M. McGoldrick, J. K. Pearce, & J. Giordano (Eds.), *Ethnicity and family therapy* (pp. 393–411). New York: Guilford Press.

More, A. J. (1987). Native American learning styles: A review for researchers and teachers. *Journal of American Indian Education, 27*(1), 17–29.

Morganthau, T. (1993, August 9). America: Still a melting pot? *Newsweek,* 16–25.

*Multicultural teaching strategies.* (1990). (Technical Assistance Paper No. 9). Tallahassee, FL: State Department of Education.

Murphy, D. S., & Sullivan, K. (1997). Connecting adolescent girls of color and math/science interventions. (ERIC Document Reproduction Service No: ED 410 106).

Murray, C. B., & Clark, R. M. (1990). Targets of racism. *The American School Board Journal, 177*(6), 22–24.

Murray, N., Kelder, S., Parcel, G., & Orphinas, P. (1998). Development of an intervention map for a parent education intervention violence to prevent violence among Hispanic middle school students. *Journal of School Health, 68*(2), 46–52.

Nation's black families number 8 million. (1997). *Census and You, 32*(7), 3.

National Assessment of Educational Progress. (1997). *NAEP 1996 science report card for the nation and the states.*

National Association of Secondary School Principals. (1979). *Student learning styles—diagnosing and prescribing programs.* Reston, VA: Author.

National Council for Accreditation of Teacher Education. (1986). *Standards, procedures and policies for accreditation of professional teacher education units.* Washington, D.C.: Author.

National Research Council. (1989). *Everybody counts: A report on the future of mathematics education.* Washington, D.C.: National Academy Press.

National Urban League. (1998). *The state of black America 1998.* New York: Author.

Nauman, A. K. (1987). School librarians and cultural pluralism. *The Reading Teacher, 41*(2), 201–205.

Nel, J. (1994). Preventing school failure: The Native American child. *The Clearing House, 67,* 169–174.

Nelson, C., & Keith, J. (1990). Comparisons of female and male early adolescent sex role attitude and behavior development. *Adolescence, 25,* 183–204.

Nieves, W., & Valle, M. (1982). The Puerto Rican family: Conflicting roles for the Puerto Rican college student. *Journal of Non-White Concerns in Personnel and Guidance, 4,* 154–160.

Norton, D. E. (1990). Teaching multicultural literature in the reading curriculum. *The Reading Teacher, 44*(1), 28–40.

Norton, D. E. (1999). *Through the eyes of a child.* (4th ed). Columbus, OH: Merrill.

Ogbu, J. (1988). Class stratification, racial stratification, and schooling. In L. Weiss (Ed.), *Class, race, and gender in American education.* Albany: State University of New York Press.

Okagaki, L., & Frensch, P. A. (1998). Parenting and children's school achievement: A multiethnic perspective. *American Educational Research Journal, 35*(1), 123–144.

Oliver, M. L., & Shapiro, T. M. (1998). The racial asset gap. In L. A. Daniels, D. McSween, & R. Jefferson-Franzier (Eds.), *The State of Black America 1998* (pp. 15–36). New York: The National Urban League.

Olmedo, I. M. (1997). Family oral histories for multicultural curriculum perspectives. *Urban Education, 32*(1), 45–62.

Olsen, L. (1988). Crossing the schoolhouse border: Immigrant children in California. *Phi Delta Kappan, 70,* 211–218.

O'Malley, J. M., & Chamot, A. U. (1990). *Learning strategies in second language acquisition.* Cambridge: Cambridge University Press.

Ornstein, A. C., & Levine, D. U. (1989). Social class, race, and school achievement: Problems and prospects. *Journal of Teacher Education, 40*(5), 17–23.

Ovando, M. N., & Traxwell, D. (1997). Superintendents' multicultural competence. *Journal of School Leadership, 7*(4), 409–431.

Oyer, H. J., Crowe, B., & Haas, W. H. (1987). *Speech, language, and hearing disorders.* Boston: Little, Brown.

Padilla, A. M. (1981). Pluralistic counseling and psychotherapy for Hispanic-Americans. In A. J. Marsella, & P. B. Pedersen (Eds.), *Cross-Cultural Counseling and Psychotherapy* (pp. 195–227). New York: Pergamon.

Park, C. (1997). Learning style preference of Asian American (Chinese, Filipino, Korean, and Vietnamese) students in secondary schools. *Equity and Excellence in Education, 30*(2), 68–77.

Patton, J. R., & Polloway, E. A. (1990). Mild mental retardation. In N. G. Haring & L. McCormick (Eds.), *Exceptional children and youth* (pp. 195–237). Columbus, OH: Merrill.

Payne, C. (1984). Multicultural education and racism in American schools. *Theory into Practice, 22,* 124–131.

Pedersen, P. (1988). *A handbook for developing multicultural awareness.* Alexandria, VA: American Association of Counseling and Development.

Perez, S. A. (1979). How to effectively teach Spanish-speaking children, even if you're not bilingual. *Language Arts, 56,* 159–162.

Perez, S. A. (1994). Responding differently to diversity. *Childhood Education, 70,* 151–153.

Petty, W. T., Petty, D.C., & Salzer, R. T. (1994). *Experiences in language: Tools and techniques for language arts methods.* Boston: Allyn & Bacon.

Piccolino, A. V. (1998). Integrating multicultural activities across the mathematics curriculum. *NASSP Bulletin, 82*(597), 84–87.

Pine, G. J., & Hilliard, A. G. (1990). Rx for racism: Imperatives for America's schools. *Phi Delta Kappan, 71,* 593–600.

Pollard, D. S. (1997). Race, gender and educational leadership: Perspectives from African American principals. *Educational Policy, 11*(3), 353–374.

Pope, M. (1995). The "salad bowl" is big enough for us all: An argument for the inclusion of lesbians and gays in any definition of multiculturalism. *Journal of Counseling and Development, 73,* 301–304.

Porter, R. O. (1997). The politics of bilingual education. *Society, 34*(6), 31–39.

Purkey, W. W., & Novak, J. M. (1984). *Inviting school success: A self concept approach to teaching and learning.* Belmont, CA: Wadsworth.

Ramos, I., & Lambating, J. (1996). Risk taking: Gender differences and educational opportunity. *School Science and Mathematics, 96*(2), 94–98.

Ramsey, P. G. (1987). *Teaching and learning in a diverse world.* New York: Teacher's College Press.

Rapoport, R. N. (1997). Families as educators for global citizenship: Five conundrums of intentional socialization. *International Journal of Early Years Education, 5*(1), 67–77.

Riccio, L. L. (1985). Facts and issues about ability grouping. *Contemporary Education, 57,* 26–30.

Richardson, E. H. (1981). Cultural and historical perspectives in counseling Indians. In D. W. Sue (Ed.), *Counseling the culturally different* (pp. 216–255). New York: John Wiley.

Rivera, B. D., & Rogers-Adkinson, D. (1997). Culturally sensitive interventions: Social skills training with children and parents from culturally and linguistically diverse backgrounds. *Intervention in School and Clinic, 33*(2), 75–80.

Rosario, M., Rotheram-Borus, M. J., & Reid, H. (1996). Gay-related stress and its correlates among gay and bisexual male adolescents of predominantly black and Hispanic backgrounds. *Journal of Community Psychology, 24,* 136–157.

Rotenberg, K. J., & Cranwell, F. R. (1989). Self-concepts in American Indian and white children. *Journal of Cross-Cultural Psychology, 20*(1), 39–53.

Rotheram-Borus, M. J., & Phinney, J. S. (1990). Patterns of social expectations among black and Mexican American children. *Child Development, 61*, 542–556.

Rotunno, M., & McGoldrick, M. (1982). Italian families. In M. McGoldrick, J. K. Pearce, & J. Giordano (Eds.), *Ethnicity and family therapy* (pp. 340–363). New York: Guilford Press.

Rumberger, R. W., & Larson, K. A. (1998). Toward differences in educational achievement among Mexican American language-minority students. *Sociology of Education, 71*, 69–93.

Sadker, M. P., & Sadker, D. M. (1982). Between teacher and student: Overcoming sex bias in classroom interaction. In M. P. Sadker & D. M. Sadker (Eds.), *Sex equity handbook for schools* (pp. 96–132). New York: Longman.

Sadker, M. P., Sadker, D. M., & Long, L. (1993). Gender and educational equity. In J. A. Banks & C. A. M. Banks (Eds.), *Multicultural education: Issues and perspectives* (2nd ed.) (pp. 111–128). Boston: Allyn & Bacon.

Sahr, D. (1997). Native American governments in today's curriculum. *Social Education, 61*(6), 309–315.

Sanders, D. (1987). Cultural conflicts: An important factor in the academic failures of American Indian students. *Journal of Multicultural Counseling and Development, 15*, 81–90.

Santiestevan, H. (1986). Hispanics and education. *Social Education, 50*, 396.

Schmuck, P. A., & Schmuck, R. A. (1994). Gender equity: A critical democratic component of America's high schools. *NASSP Bulletin, 78*, 22–31.

Schorr, L. (1998). Building community. In L. A. Daniels, D. McSween, & R. Jefferson-Franzier (Eds.), *The state of black America 1998* (pp. 37–51). New York: The National Urban League.

Scourby, A. (1984). *The Greek Americans*. Boston: Twayne.

Sendor, B. (1989). Root out racial bias in student placement. *American School Board Journal, 176*(3), 24–25.

Shade, B. (1982). Afro-American cognitive style: A variable in school success? *Review of Educational Research, 52*, 219–244.

Sharan, S. (1985). Cooperative learning and the multiethnic classroom. In R. Slavin, S. Sharan, S. Kagan, R. Lazarowitz, C. Webb, & R. Schmuck (Eds.), *Learning to cooperate, cooperating to learn* (pp. 255–276). New York: Plenum.

Shea, T. M., & Bauer, A. M. (1985). *Parents and teachers of exceptional children: A handbook for involvement*. Boston: Allyn & Bacon.

Silva, C., & Patton, M. M. (1997). Multicultural education: Theory to practice. *Teacher Education and Practice, 13*(1), 22–38.

Simich-Dudgeon, C. (1987). Involving limited-English-proficient parents as tutors in their children's education. *ERIC/CLL News Bulletin, 10*(2), 3–4, 7.

Slavin, R. E. (1983). *An introduction to cooperative learning*. New York: Longman.

Slavin, R. E. (1987). *Cooperative learning* (2nd ed.). Washington, D.C.: National Education Association.

Slavin, R. E. (1996). Cooperative learning and middle and secondary schools. *The Clearing House, 69*(4), 200–204.

Sleeter, C. E., & Grant, C. A. (1988). *Making choices for multicultural education: Five approaches to race, class and gender*. Columbus, OH: Merrill.

So, A. Y. (1987). Hispanic teachers and the labeling of Hispanic students. *The High School Journal, 71*, 5–8.

Southern Association for Children Under Six. (1988). *Multicultural education: A position statement*. Little Rock, AR: Author.

Spaulding, S. (1994). 4 Steps to effective parent conferences. *Learning, 23*(2), 36.

Stachowski, L. L. (1998). Student teachers' efforts to promote self-esteem in Navajo pupils. *The Educational Forum, 62*, 341–346.

Stanford, B. H. (1996). Gender equity in the classroom. In D. A. Byrnes, & Kiger, G. (Eds.), *Common bonds: Anti-bias teaching in a diverse society* (2nd ed.) (pp. 79–94). Olney, MD: Association for Childhood Education International.

Steinberg, L., Blinde, P., & Chan, K. (1984). Dropping out among language minority youth. *Review of Educational Research, 54*, 113–132.

Stewart, W. J. (1990). Learning-style-appropriate instruction: Planning, implementing, evaluating. *The Clearing House, 63*, 371–374.

Struchen, W., & Porta, M. (1997). From role-modeling to mentoring for African American youth:

Ingredients for successful relationships. *Preventing School Failure, 41*(3), 119–123.

Studer, J. R. (1993/1994). Listen so that parents will speak. *Childhood Education, 70,* 74–76.

Sue, D. W. (1981). *Counseling the culturally different.* New York: John Wiley.

Sue, D. W. (1989). Ethnic identity: The impact of two cultures on the psychological development of Asians in America. In D. R. Atkinson, G. Morten, & D. W. Sue (Eds.), *Counseling American minorities: A cross-cultural perspective* (3rd ed.), (pp. 103–115). Dubuque, IA: Wm. C. Brown.

Sue, D. W., & Sue, S. (1983). Counseling Chinese Americans. In D. R. Atkinson, G. Morten, & D. W. Sue (Eds.), *Counseling American minorities: A cross-cultural perspective* (2nd ed.) (pp. 97–106). Dubuque, IA: Wm. C. Brown.

Swisher, K., & Deyhle, D. (1989, August). The styles of learning are different, but the teaching is just the same: Suggestions for teachers of American Indian youth. *Journal of American Indian Education, Special Issue,* 1–11.

Tan, A., Fujioka, Y., & Lucht, N. (1997). Native American stereotypes, TV portrayals, and personal contact. *Journalism and Mass Communication Quarterly, 74*(2), 265–284.

Tellez, K., & Estep, M. (1997). Latino youth gangs and the meaning of school. *The High School Journal, 81*(2), 69–81.

Ten quick ways to analyze children's books for racism and sexism. (1974, November 3). *Interracial Books for Children, 5*(3), 6–7.

TESOL (Teachers of English to Speakers of Other Languages). (1976). Position paper on the role of English as a second language in bilingual education. Washington, D.C.: Author.

The Hispanic Policy Development Project. (1997). The challenges of change. New York: Author.

Tiedt, P. L., & Tiedt, I. M. (1995). *Multicultural teaching: A handbook of activities, information, and resources.* Boston: Allyn & Bacon.

Toepfer, C. F. (1988). What to know about young adolescents. *Social Education, 52,* 110–112.

Townsel, K. T. (1997). Mentoring African American youth. *Preventing School Failure, 41*(3), 125–127.

Trentacosta, J., & Kenney, M. J. (Eds.) (1997). *Multicultural and gender equity in the mathematics classroom.* Reston, VA: National Council of Teachers of Mathematics.

Tyler, R. W. (1989). Educating children from minority families. *Educational Horizons, 67*(4), 114–118.

Uno, D., Florsheim, P., & Uchino, B. N. (1998). Psychosocial mechanisms underlying quality of parenting among Mexican American and white adolescent mothers. *Journal of Youth and Adolescence, 27*(5), 585–605.

U.S. Bureau of the Census. (1990). *Persons of Hispanic origin in the United States.* C 3.223.10: 1990. CP-3–3. Washington, D.C.: Author.

U.S. Bureau of the Census. (1992). *Statistical abstracts of the United States* (112th ed.). Washington, D.C.: Author.

U.S. Bureau of the Census. (1993a, September). *We the American . . . Asians.* Washington, D.C.: Author.

U.S. Bureau of the Census. (1993b, September). *We the American . . . Blacks.* Washington, D.C.: Author.

U.S. Bureau of the Census. (1993c, September). *We the . . . first Americans.* Washington, D.C.: Author.

U.S. Bureau of the Census. (1993d, September). *We the American . . . Foreign born.* Washington, D.C.: Author.

U.S. Bureau of the Census. (1993e, November). *We the American . . . Hispanics.* Washington, D.C.: Author.

U.S. Bureau of the Census. (1993f, September). *We the American . . . Pacific Islanders.* Washington, D.C.: Author.

U.S. Bureau of the Census. (1996, September). Almost half of the nation's chronic poor are children. *Census and You, 31*(9), 7.

U.S. Bureau of the Census. (1997a). *Statistical abstracts of the United States* (117th ed.). Washington, D.C.: Author.

U.S. Bureau of the Census. (1997b). More recent immigrants are generally younger. *Census and You, 32*(6), 1.

U.S. Commission on Civil Rights. (1975). *A better chance to learn: Bilingual-bicultural education.* Washington, D.C.: Author.

Valero-Figueria, E. (1988). Hispanic children. *Teaching Exceptional Children, 20,* 47–49.

Vander Zanden, J. W. (1989). *Human development* (4th ed.). New York: Knopf.

Valdes, G. (1998). The world outside and inside schools: Language and immigrant children. *Educational Researcher, 27*(6), 4–18.

Vare, J. W., & Norton, T. L. (1998). Understanding gay and lesbian youth: Sticks, stones, and silence. *The Clearing House, 71*(6), 327–331.

Vogl, B. D., & Jaros, G. G. (1998). Can we achieve a celebration of diversity. *The Educational Forum, 62,* 334–340.

Vontress, C. E. (1976). Counseling the racial and ethnic minorities. In G. S. Belkin (Ed.), *Counseling: Directions in theory and practice* (pp. 277–290). Belmont, CA: Wadsworth.

Walker, J. L. (1988). Young American Indian children. *Teaching Exceptional Children, 20,* 50–51.

Waller, J. (1997). The foundations of teaching racial tolerance: Three myths about racism in America. *The High School Magazine, 5*(2), 38–43.

Warren, J. W., & Twine, F. W. (1997). White Americans: The new minority? Non-blacks and the ever-expanding boundaries of whiteness. *Journal of Black Studies 28*(2), 200–218.

Weaver, H. N. (1998). Indigenous people in a multicultural society: Unique issues for human services. *Social Work, 43*(3), 203–211.

Welts, E. P. (1982). Greek families. In M. McGoldrick, J. K. Pearce, & J. Giordano (Eds.), *Ethnicity and family therapy* (pp. 269–288). New York: Guilford Press.

West, B. E. (1983). The new arrivals from Southeast Asia. *Childhood Education, 60,* 84–89.

White, J. J. (1998). Helping students deal with cultural differences. *The Social Studies, 89*(3), 107–111.

Williams, D. L., & Chavkin, N. F. (1989). Essential elements of strong parent involvement programs. *Educational Leadership, 47*(2), 18–20.

Williams, R. L. (1997). The Ebonics controversy. *Journal of Black Psychology, 23*(3), 208–214.

Willis, S. (1994). Teaching language-minority students. *ASCD Update, 36*(5), 1–5.

Wills, J., & Mehan, H. (1996). Recognizing diversity with a common historical narrative: The challenges of teaching history and social studies. *Multicultural Education, 4*(1), 4–11.

Wilson, R. (1989). Black higher education: Crisis and promise. In J. Dewart (Ed.), *The state of Black America 1989* (pp. 121–135). New York: National Urban League.

Winawer-Steiner, H., & Wetzel, N. A. (1996). German families. In M. McGoldrick, J. K. Pearce, & J. Giordano (Eds.), *Ethnicity and family therapy* (2nd ed.) (pp. 496–516). New York: Guilford Press.

Winter, S. M. (1994/1995). Diversity: A program for all children. *Childhood Education, 71*(2), 91–95.

Winzer, M. A., & Mazurek, K. (1998). *Special education in multicultural contexts.* Columbus, OH: Prentice-Hall.

Wolf, J. S. (1990). The gifted and talented. In N. G. Haring & L. McCormick (Eds.), *Exceptional children and youth* (pp. 447–489). Columbus, OH: Merrill.

Wrigley, T. (1997). Raising achievement for Asian pupils. *Multicultural Teaching 16*(1), 21–25.

Yao, E. L. (1985). Adjustment needs of Asian immigrant children. *Elementary School Guidance and Counseling, 19,* 222–227.

Yao, E. L. (1988). Working effectively with Asian immigrant parents. *Phi Delta Kappan, 70,* 223–225.

Yarborough, B. H., & Johnson, R. A. (1983). Identifying the gifted: A theory-practice gap. *Gifted Child Quarterly, 27,* 125–138.

Yee, L. Y. (1988). Asian children. *Teaching Exceptional Children, 20*(4), 49–50.

Yetman, N. R., & Steele, C. H. (Eds.). (1975). *Majority and minority: The dynamics of racial and ethnic relations* (2nd ed.). Boston: Allyn & Bacon.

Young, J. L. (1994). Sapphires-in-transition: Enhancing personal development among black female adolescents. *Journal of Multicultural Counseling and Development, 22,* 86–95.

Youngman, G., & Sandongei, M. (1983). Counseling the American Indian child. In D. R. Atkinson, G. Morten, & D. W. Sue (Eds.), *Counseling American minorities: A cross-cultural perspective* (pp. 73–76). Dubuque, IA: Wm. C. Brown.

Zentella, A. C. (1997). Latino youth at home, in their communities, and in school. *Education and Urban Society, 30*(1), 122–130.

Zychowicz, M. J. (1975). American Indian teachings as a philosophical base for counseling and psychotherapy. Unpublished doctoral dissertation. Northern Illinois University, De Kalb.

# Author Index

# Subject Index

**Note:** A *t* or *f* following a page number indicates a table or a figure, respectively.